SOCIOLOGY
The Search for Social Patterns

Ira Peck
Larry S. Krieger

Academic Consultants:

John Lofland, Ph.D.
Lyn Lofland, Ph.D.
Department of Sociology
The University of California at Davis

SCHOLASTIC INC.

Teaching Consultants

Janice Aragon
Cypress-Fairbanks High School
Houston, Texas

William Hatcher
Shafter High School
Shafter, California

Ronald Helms
Fairmont East High School
Kettering, Ohio

Mary Syms
Jesse H. Jones Senior High School
Houston, Texas

Leslie Engstom
Roosevelt High School
Minneapolis, Minnesota

Margaret Wiener
Hume-Fogg High School
Nashville, Tennessee

Larry S. Krieger has taught sociology since 1971, first in Siler City, North Carolina, and then in Holmdel, New Jersey. He is now Social Studies Supervisor for Edison, New Jersey. Much of the material in this program is a product of this experience. Krieger has a bachelor's degree in history and a Master of Arts degree in teaching from the University of North Carolina at Chapel Hill, as well as a master's degree in sociology from Wake Forest University.

Ira Peck is a professional writer. Born in New York City, he attended public schools there and Harvard College, where he majored in history. As a journalist, he worked as a newspaper reporter and a magazine editor. More recently, he has been the author of numerous books including *The Life and Words of Martin Luther King* and *Patton*. He is also the principal author of the AMERICAN ADVENTURES Program.

Andy Levin is the featured photographer in this edition. One of the world's leading photojournalists, he specializes in taking pictures of people as they go about their everyday lives. Levin's photographs have appeared in *Life. Discover/National Geographic. A Day in the Life of America. A Day in the Life of the Soviet Union*, and numerous other magazines and books.

Scholastic Inc. ISBN 0-590-35410-8

Copyright © 1989, 1988, 1980 by Scholastic Inc. All rights reserved. Printed in the U.S.A.

12 11 10 9 8 7 6 5 4 3 2 1   4   8 9/8 0/9 1
23

Staff:

Publisher: Eleanor Angeles
Editorial Director: Carolyn Jackson
Revision and Production Editor: Jonah Bornstein
Editorial Assistant: Lynn Meyers
Art and Design: Irmgard Lochner, Murray Belsky, Hal Aber
Photo Researchers: Linda Sykes, Larry Krieger

Grateful acknowledgment is made to the following authors and publishers for the use of copyrighted material. Every effort has been made to obtain permission to use previously published material. Any errors or omissions are unintentional.

American Anthropological Association for the excerpts from "The Body Ritual Among the Nacirema" by Horace Miner from *The American Anthropologist*, Volume 50, Number 3, copyright © 1956 by American Anthropological Association.

The Associated Press for the article about Sandra Laing, copyright © 1967 by The Associated Press.

Atheneum Press for the excerpts from MISS MANNERS GUIDE TO REARING PERFECT CHILDREN, copyright © 1984 by Atheneum Press.

Basic Books and George Allen & Unwin, Ltd., for the excerpt from TWO WORLDS OF CHILDHOOD: U.S. AND U.S.S.R. by Urie Bronfenbrenner, copyright © 1970 by the Russell Sage Foundation, New York.

Bobbs Merrill Company, Inc., for the excerpts from THE TERRORIST MIND by Gerald McKnight, copyright © 1974 by Gerald McKnight.

The Courier News for the excerpt from "Self-Help: Finding Strength in Numbers," by John McDonnell, copyright © January 5, 1988 by The Courier News.

Lester David for the excerpts from his article, "A Case of Teen Divorce," copyright © 1976 by Triangle Communications, Inc.

Doubleday and Company, Inc., for the excerpt from THE SILENT LANGUAGE by Edward T. Hall, copyright © 1959 by Edward T. Hall.

Doubleday and Company, Inc., and A.P. Watt for the excerpt from LOOKING BACK by Joyce Maynard, copyright © 1972, 1973 by Joyce Maynard.

Grove Press, Inc., and Hutchinson Publishing Group, Ltd., for the excerpt from THE AUTOBIOGRAPHY OF MALCOLM X by Malcolm X and Alex Haley, copyright © 1965 by Alex Haley and Malcolm X, copyright © 1965 by Alex Haley and Betty Shabazz.

Houghton Mifflin Company for the adaptation from FAREWELL TO MANZANAR by Jeane Wakatsuki Houston and James D. Houston, copyright, © 1973 by James D. Houston.

Alfred A. Knopf and International Creative Management for the excerpt from DOWN THESE MEAN STREETS by Piri Thomas, copyright © 1967 by Piri Thomas.

Little, Brown & Company, Inc., and Harold Matson Company, Inc., for the adaptation from THE GLORY AND THE DREAM by William Manchester, copyright © 1973, 1974 by William Manchester.

Macmillan Publishing Company, Inc., for the adaptation from AN INTRODUCTION TO SOCIOLOGY by R. Serge Denisoff and Ralph Wahrman, copyright 1975 by Macmillan Publishing Company, Inc.; the excerpt from "Learning the Student Role: Kindergarten as Academic Boot Camp" by Harry L. Gracey from READINGS IN INTRODUCTORY SOCIOLOGY by Dennis H. Wrong and Harry L. Gracey, copyright © 1972 by Harry L. Gracey.

Eula A. Morrison for the adaptation of her article, "The Day I Learned About Prejudice" from *Mademoiselle*, copyright © 1966 by The Conde Nast Publications, Inc.

National Geographic Society for the excerpt from the Special Publication, VANISHING PEOPLES OF THE EARTH, copyright © 1968 by the National Geographic Society; "The 'Long Walk' to Navajo Nationhood" by Wine Deloria from THE WORLD OF THE AMERICAN INDIAN, copyright © 1979 by the National Geographic Society.

The New York Times for the excerpt from "Factors That Affect Social Mobility" by Bernard Weintraub, copyright © 1973 by The New York Times Company.

Pantheon Books, a Division of Random House, Inc., and Wildwood House, Ltd., for excerpts from WORKING: PEOPLE TALK ABOUT WHAT THEY DO ALL DAY AND HOW THEY FEEL ABOUT WHAT THEY DO by Studs Terkel, copyright © 1972, 1974 by Studs Terkel.

Prentice-Hall, Inc., and The Bodley Head for the excerpt from FUTURE SHOCK by Alvin Toffler, copyright © 1970 by Alvin Toffler.

The San Francisco Chronicle for the excerpt from "Symbolic Clash of Two Cultures" by Lisa Hobbs, copyright Chronicle Publishing Company.

Scholastic Update for the excerpts from "Future Bound: Glimpses of Life in the 21st Century" by Lee Kravitz, copyright © 1986 by Scholastic Update.

Science Digest for the excerpt from "I Became a Bum" by Steven Bacon, copyright © 1971 by the Hearst Corporation.

Social Policy Corporation, New York, for "The Dirty Work Movement" by Herbert J. Gans from *Social Policy*, copyright © 1971 by Social Policy Corporation.

Times Books, a Division of Quadrangle/New York Times Book Company, Inc., for the excerpt from THE RUSSIANS by Hedrick Smith, copyright © 1976 by Hedrick Smith.

U.S. News & World Report for the excerpt from "Jam Sessions," copyright © 1987 by U.S. News and World Report.

John Wiley & Sons for the excerpt from SOCIOLOGY: A CRITICAL APPROACH TO POWER, CONFLICT AND CHANGE by J. Victor Baldridge.

contents

part one: the sociological perspective   1

part two: social problems   323

Charts, Graphs, and Map

to the student:

If you have decided to study sociology because you're interested in people, you're in the right place. Although we are rarely conscious of it, human beings frequently act together in repeated and predictable ways. These behavior patterns occur in groups, which are the focus of sociology. In this book, we present many patterns which sociologists have found. In each case, these patterns are illustrated with real life examples such as:

• People all across the nation start to call each other "good buddy," in imitation of a new American hero — the long-haul truck driver.

• A young couple falls madly in love, gets married, has a baby, and finds their life together radically changed.

• A former high school student tells how she tried to talk, walk, dress, and even eat her lunch in the same way that popular leaders did in her school.

Studying the program will not make you a sociologist, but we hope you will gain from it a new understanding of human behavior that you can use in your life every day. Each chapter ends with an Application in which you are asked to apply some of the principles described in the chapter to a situation or reading we supply.

Although sociologists find patterns in almost every kind of human group behavior, they frequently disagree about what causes these patterns they detect. For this reason, sociology is a lively discipline.

The second part of this book examines five social problems of our time — crime, aging, cities and suburbs, environment, and terrorism. We study these problems much as a sociologist would by first identifying the problem and then trying to find some of its causes. At the end of each chapter, we learn about some of the solutions that have been suggested to solve these problems and ask what you think should be done about them.

Looking at the world through the sociologist's point of view can be an exciting adventure. In the first chapter, we join a high school football game already in progress.

PART ONE

the
sociological
perspective

High school cheers could give a sociologist many clues to social patterns.

chapter 1

basic concepts

It is a beautiful fall day in Edison, New Jersey. About 3,500 students and local residents are arriving at the football field near J.P. Stevens High School. They have come to watch a Thanksgiving Day game between the J.P. Stevens Hawks and their cross-town rivals, the Edison High School Eagles.

The players, coaches, and students on both sides look forward all year to this traditional "Big Game." The Eagle supporters, many of them dressed in the school colors of red and gold, take seats on the visitors' side of the field. The green and gold clad fans of J.P. Stevens file into their stands on the home side. As the crowd waits for the game to begin, the award winning Eagle Marching Band entertains them with precision drills and spirited songs.

A glance at the scoreboard clock tells the excited crowd that the game will begin in a few minutes. The cheerleaders from

both schools now form a double line at opposite ends of the field. The fans burst into cheers as the two teams run past their cheerleaders and charge onto the field.

Before the game begins, the referees escort the captains from both teams to the center of the field. The head referee introduces the captains, explains a few rules, and encourages them to play a good, clean game. The referee then tosses a coin to determine which team will receive the ball first. The captains shake hands and return to their sidelines.

After the coin-tossing ceremony, a color guard from J.P. Stevens marches onto the field. Fans on both sides rise as the Stevens band plays "The Star-Spangled Banner." Most people place their right hands across their chests while singing. As the national anthem ends, the crowd cheers and the referees signal for the game to begin.

The game begins and the cheerleaders on both sidelines encourage enthusiastic fan support. When the Eagle cheerleaders shout, "Who's the best?" the students shout, "The Eagles!" Across the playing field the Hawk cheerleaders ask their supporters, "Who will win?" and receive a loud cheer, "The Hawks!"

The two teams play as hard as they can. Early in the game, the Hawks thrill their supporters by scoring the game's first touchdown. The Hawk players congratulate each other by slapping "high fives." Their cheerleaders jump up and down while the band plays the school fight song. Across the field, the Eagle fans silently look on, hoping their team can get back into the game.

As the game progresses, the Hawks continue to increase their lead. By half-time, the scoreboard reads J.P. Stevens 16, Edison High 0. During halftime the two teams gather in separate locker rooms. The coaches encourage their players and adjust the game plans.

Twenty minutes later, the two teams return to the field and the game resumes. The fired-up Hawks score again, thus building their lead to 23 to 0. Despite the score, the Eagles refuse to give up. In the game's closing minutes they score two touchdowns. However, it is not enough. The Hawks win 23 to 12.

After the game, players from both schools shake hands. At an awards ceremony, a local fire company presents a handsome trophy to the winning team. The Edison Elks club awards a trophy to the most valuable player on each team. The victorious Hawk supporters celebrate while the disappointed Eagle fans promise that next year will be different.

The Sociological Point of View

Whether any sociologists were present at the game is not known. But let's suppose for a moment that you are a sociologist—rather than a student—analyzing the event. Rather than judge the cheerleaders' spirit or the football team's skill, a sociologist would attempt to find and understand patterns of social behavior in the game. The search for social patterns is the main interest of sociologists. *Social patterns* occur whenever groups of people act and interact in repeated and predictable ways.

As a sociologist, you might begin your search for social patterns by studying the *social characteristics* of the groups at the game. Social characteristics are aspects of people's social backgrounds (age, race, ethnicity, and sex, for example) that influence the way they act.

As a sociologist, you might begin by identifying those groups which included high school students to those which did not. For example, only high school students participated in the marching bands, cheerleading squads, and football teams. The coaching staffs and referees were comprised entirely of adults. The crowd included people of all ages.

As an observant sociologist you would also notice the sexual composition of each group. The cheerleaders, for example, are all females. In contrast, the football teams, coaching staffs, and referees are all males. Both males and females played in the bands and sat in the crowd.

The roles which age and sex played at

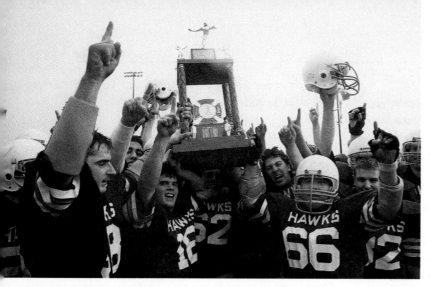

Social Patterns shaped the behavior of everyone at the Big Game— what they wore, where they sat, and when they cheered, for example. Sociologists use special terms to describe social patterns.

the game suggest a number of social patterns. As a sociologist studying the game, you might also want to find out if it took place in a predictable pattern. You would carefully note the exact sequence of events—the opening performance by the visiting band, the arrival of the teams onto the field, the coin-toss, the playing of the national anthem by the home band, the first half of play, the halftime entertainment, the second half of play, and, finally, the awards ceremony.

You might want to watch several football games in Edison to see if these events were repeated in sequence. If so, these are predictable social patterns.

But suppose you wanted to find out if the football games in Edison were part of a larger social pattern. To do this, you would have to visit other schools. You might find that certain social characteristics changed from school to school, but you would probably find that all of the games promoted school spirit, winning, good sportsmanship, and having a good time.

᪣ What social patterns occur at your high school's football games? How do they compare with the social patterns in Edison?

Social interaction. All social patterns stem from social interaction. Sociologists study this interaction with the same diligence (although not the same methods) as astronomers study the stars. *Social interaction* is a basic form of human behavior; it occurs whenever two or more people act toward, or respond to, one another. Fre-

quently, people interact with words. When the cheerleaders shout, "All for Edison, stand up and holler," and the students respond by shouting, they are interacting.

But interaction can also be silent. For example, when the band leader raises his baton, the musicians know that they are going to begin a tune, and they react by getting ready to play it.

Social patterns help give order to our daily lives. Whether we are aware of them or not, they influence our behavior at pep rallies, in classrooms, at sports events, at home, and in many other situations. They determine how we talk to teachers, salesclerks, neighbors, parents, brothers, and sisters. They tell us what to expect in school, on the job, or in marriage. Without social patterns, we would all be confused. You expect your teacher, for example, to talk about the subject you are studying. This is patterned behavior. If your algebra teacher were to talk constantly about his or her favorite recipes, you would probably be baffled.

Whom do sociologists study? Sociologists look for the ordered, recurring patterns of social life. They focus their search on groups because this is where social interaction takes place. Sociologists define a *group* as two or more people who interact with each other and engage in a common activity. The groups that sociologists study may be as small as a couple on a date or as large as a society containing millions of people. The number and variety of groups they observe is almost endless. They include groups among rich people and poor people, college professors and students, police and criminals, white-collar workers and migrant workers, suburbanites and city-dwellers, and many, many more.

As you can see from our observations of a football game, the search for social patterns can be an adventure which leads to a new understanding of the groups that surround and influence us. In this chapter, we'll be dealing with some of the basic terms and concepts which sociologists have developed to describe and explain social patterns. The vocabulary you develop in this chapter is important because it gives us insight into the social patterns in the world around us.

The social patterns that sociologists look for are not always apparent. Sometimes sociologists have to dig deep to find them. In their studies of groups, sociologists use much the same approach employed by biologists, physicists, psychologists, and other scientists. Called the *scientific method,* this approach strives toward an objective, orderly procedure for arriving at accurate conclusions. (The scientific method will be discussed in detail in Chapter 2.)

Sociology, then, may be defined as the scientific study of the patterns of human group life.

Astronomers look for patterns in the universe, while sociologists look for patterns among people.

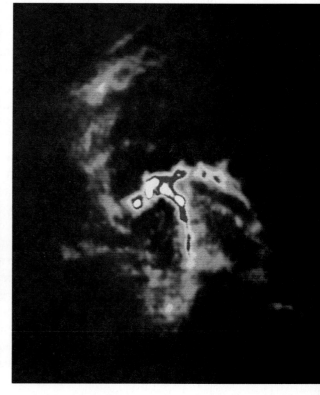

The Elements of Groups

In their studies of human groups, sociologists recognize five common patterns — norms, values, status, social ranking, and roles. In this section, we will define and illustrate each of these basic elements.

Norms. *Norms* are rules, or standards, of behavior that have been developed by a group and that its members are expected to follow. In effect, norms tell people how they should act, or what they should say, in specific social situations. The Edison cheerleaders, for example, wear short costumes, step high, and carry batons when they appear with the school band. But in class, these girls are expected to wear school clothing, to walk conventionally, and to leave their batons at home. All this behavior is governed by norms.

Frequently, norms are collected as a formal guide to behavior. A student handbook is such a collection of norms. So are drivers' manuals, sports rule books, and even the 10 Commandments. Norms not only guide our behavior, they also tell us what behavior we can expect from others.

Social norms even shape our conversations. The writer Mark Twain once criticized people for engaging in so much aimless talk about the weather. Certainly the weather does seem to inspire a great deal of trivial conversation, but Eric Berne, a keen observer of social behavior, suggested that it is not aimless. In *Games People Play,* he described and translated a typical greeting:

"Hi!" (Hello, or good morning.)
"Hi!" (Hello, or good morning.)
"Warm enough forya?" (How are you?)
"Sure is. Looks like rain, though." (Fine, how are you?)
"Well, take cara yourself." (OK.)
"I'll be seeing you." (OK.)
"So long." (Good-bye.)
"So long." (Good-bye.)

What first appears to be an empty exchange, Berne said, demonstrates carefully calculated social norms. It is the customary way that two people who are only casual acquaintances will briefly and impersonally pay their respects to each other. Neither is interested in probing into the other's feelings, yet a certain amount of recognition is called for when they meet. What could be more convenient than a passing comment about the weather? Good friends might also engage in the same conversation if they were in a hurry but wanted to signal they were still good friends.

🖎 Describe a conversation you might have at school which would be governed by norms.

Acceptance of norms. Norms vary considerably in the extent to which they are followed. Some norms apply to every member of a society while others apply to small groups. For example, in the United States, transportation by private automobile is a norm. Among the Amish in Lancaster County, Pennsylvania, however, horse-drawn vehicles are the norm.

Norms may also vary from one situation to another. For example, the norms

Norms determine how people mourn in a society whether in New Guinea or the United States.

that guide student behavior at a football game from the norms that students are expected to follow in the classroom.

    ⋙ Look at this list of activities:
      kissing;
      applauding;
      crying;
      praying;
      telling jokes;
      staring at someone;
      giving flowers.
Describe a social situation in which each would be normal. Describe a situation in which each would be unusual.

What is proper behavior? When the proper rules of behavior are unclear, people sometimes turn to others for advice. The following letters were sent to the nationally syndicated columnist, "Miss Manners."

Dear Miss Manners:
    I sometimes invite children from my four-year-old's nursery school over to play with her in the afternoon. These children are literally addicted to television. They demand that I turn on the cartoons at three o'clock, which, as you may not know, is when two hours of cartoon fun starts. When I refuse, they mope and ask

to be taken home.

I was brought up to believe it is bad manners to watch TV when company is present. Furthermore, I see no value in preschool children's sitting like lumps for half the afternoon. I invite other children over so that my daughter will play. If I wanted her to sit watching sugar commercials, I wouldn't bother inviting other children; she could do that alone. In my position, would Miss Manners stick to her guns, or would Miss Manners graciously give her guests what they want?

Dear Miss Manners:

I would like to know if it's necessary to write a thank you note for presents my son receives at his birthday party. He will be four. It seems ridiculous to me, but some of my friends do this.

Dear Miss Manners:

I am just starting out on a teaching career, somewhat intimidated by what experienced teachers tell me of today's discipline problems . . . My first class will be second-graders . . . My hope is that if I get them young enough, and show enough authority, I will set the proper tone and they will pick it up. Can you suggest some rules for classroom decorum? I want to be fair. But if there is trouble, how do I find out who is really responsible, without turning the children into tattletales, and getting them into deeper trouble with their peers?

Dear Miss Manners:

HELP! Please help me explain to my teenage son why manners are important, especially table manners. Sometimes I can hardly sit through a meal with him, and he feels all my explanations of why table manners are

important are ridiculous. His younger sister and brother watch him very carefully, and are now beginning to pick up his poor table habits.

Dear Miss Manners:

Recently, at my high school, there has been a slight disagreement concerning the definition of casual, semiformal, and formal dress. Would you please give the final word on what these three terms refer to?

☙ How would you answer each of these letters?

Three types of norms. By regulating almost every phase of our behavior, norms order and simplify our daily lives. Sociologists have identified at least three types of norms — folkways, mores, and taboos.

Folkways are norms that are a matter of custom or tradition. They are generally considered "the right thing to do," but there usually is no legal punishment if you violate them. The normal penalty for flaunting a folkway is usually no worse than a mild expression of disapproval or, perhaps, ridicule.

Many folkways are associated with rules of etiquette. Emily Post, a leading authority on etiquette, describes "the guest whom no one invites a second time" as someone who "leaves a borrowed tennis racket out in the rain . . . stands a wet glass on polished wood . . . tracks muddy shoes into the house . . . [or] brings a pet dog that was not house-trained." The author would doubtless stare at such an offender with disapproval, but she could not have him or her arrested.

Russian folkways: people drink from a common cup at vending machines and get weighed in public.

Some norms are considered very important by the group. Norms which are considered morally significant and whose violation is considered a serious matter are called *mores*. Unlike folkways, which should be obeyed, mores must be obeyed because they are considered important to the group's survival. In our society, there are mores condemning murder, rape, and theft. People convicted of violating these mores may be punished by long imprisonment, or, possibly, by death.

When a society considers breaking one of its mores utterly loathsome, this offense is called a *taboo*. Because taboos are considered "unthinkable," prohibitions against them may not even be written into law. Cannibalism is a taboo in our society.

To break this taboo would probably bring social ostracism.

When large societies want to enforce norms, however, they usually fashion formal controls to enforce them. *Laws* are formally written rules of conduct that are enforced by governments. The more complex a society becomes, the more its norms are written into laws. Our society has a bewildering number of laws covering offenses from jay-walking to treason.

Values. The rules that guide our behavior in specific situations do not develop at random. They stem from widely held group beliefs about what is right, or good, or important. These conceptions of desirable behavior are called *values*. Let's see how a particular value can generate a variety of norms. A great majority of Americans would agree, for example, that cleanliness is very important. We have

In 1922 there were laws against scanty beach attire in Chicago. The French woman below broke a taboo in 1944, by having a German man's baby.

been taught to believe, in fact, that it is "next to godliness." It is one of our values. Now think of all the things we do because we value cleanliness. Here are just a few of them:

• We bathe or shower frequently; brush our teeth; shampoo our hair; clean our nails; and use a host of creams, deodorants, and mouthwashes.

• We wash our dishes, scrub our pots and pans, mop our floors, dust our furniture, vacuum our rugs, wash our windows, and disinfect our bathrooms.

• We get rid of bugs, smells, stains, grease, household germs, and even "ring-around-the-collar."

The things that we do to keep clean are norms. We do them because we believe in cleanliness, which is a value.

Like norms, values vary from one group to another. In our society, for example, we believe that winning is very important. "Winning isn't everything; it's the only thing," said Vince Lombardi, the late football coach. Yet among some groups, winning isn't as important as "how you play the game." Still other groups think that winning is inappropriate in certain situations. In New Guinea, for example, the Tangu tribe believes that winning creates hard feelings among the losers in a game. The Tangu solution is quite simple: The object of all games is to play to a tie, no matter how long it may take.

⇜ List three norms that follow from each of these values:
  privacy;
  keeping "cool."

Within any society, values and norms may change over a period of time. Look at the photographs of turn-of-the-century and contempory beach scenes on this page. They present a striking contrast in standards of behavior. In the early 1900's, people were determined to shield their skin from the sun. Almost all wore street clothes and

shoes as they strolled along the beach. The dresses worn by the women came down to their feet. Men's bathing suits covered most of their bodies. Except for these suits, attire would have been just as appropriate for strolling along Main Street. In the 1970's and 1980's, many people were determined to expose as much of themselves as possible to the sun and to each other.

⊷ What values do you think are behind the norms shown in these pictures? For example, modesty was an important value at the turn of the century.

Values and norms in conflict. Although norms stem from values, there are times when the two can conflict. In October 1972, for example, an airliner crashed high in the Andes Mountains. More than two months later, 16 survivors of the crash were rescued. Investigators were curious about how they were able to last so long without food. Finally the survivors, members of a rugby team and some of their fans, admitted that they had cannibalized their dead companions. All the survivors tried to justify what they had done. Some compared it to a transplant operation — they were using part of a dead person to save another person's life. Others said that if they hadn't eaten the dead, it would have been the same as committing suicide. Suicide, of course, was against their religion. These explanations reveal the conflict that tormented the survivors. Cannibalism was a violation of one of their basic taboos. Yet they resorted to it in response to a very basic value — survival.

Status. Social behavior is patterned not only by the norms and values of one's group; it is also patterned by the position that each person occupies within that group. Sociologists call this position *status.* In school, your status is that of a student. At home, you have another status, that of a son or a daughter. In the community, you and your friends have still another status, that of teenagers. Sociologists distinguish between two basic kinds of statuses, ascribed and achieved.

An *ascribed status* is a social position that is assigned to a person at birth or at later stages of life. This kind of status would include the person's gender, race, or age. An *achieved status* is a position that people usually acquire through their own efforts. Teachers, doctors, lawyers, and journalists, among others, have all put forth effort in acquiring their status.

⊷ Now look at the "Peanuts" cartoon. Who would say that Lucy's status as a "fussbudget" is achieved? Who would say it is ascribed?

Social ranking. In every group, statuses are ranked. The term *social ranking* refers to the evaluation — high or low — of a status according to criteria that a group's members consider important. For example, the position of general in the Army will be evaluated more highly than that of private because of its power and the level of training required to fill it. Similarly, in our society, doctors have a higher status ranking than short-order cooks. A doctor must have considerably more education and receives a much higher income.

From one society to another, there may be differences in the way that statuses are ranked. In France, for example, artists generally rank higher than they do in the U.S.; and in Sweden, public school teachers enjoy a much higher rank than those in the U.S. The differences will probably be even greater between societies that are industrialized and those that are not. A fortune-teller, for example, will probably have a much higher rank in a developing country than in one in which science and technology are valued highly.

Determining the order in which groups rank their statuses is a difficult and challenging task. Status symbols provide sociologists with an observable means of evaluating the rank of various positions. A *status symbol* is any material object or privilege that is associated with a social position and indicates its rank. A general's uniform, a doctor's white coat, and a construction worker's hard hat are all status symbols.

Status symbols can sometimes be misleading, however. People who don't have much money may buy expensive cars in order to appear affluent. And children of upper- and middle-class families may wear tattered jeans and sneakers in order to sig-

© 1953 United Feature Syndicate, Inc.

The role of the classroom teacher has changed drastically since the turn of the century.

nify they don't want to be associated too closely with their own social group.

🖙 The following are statuses within most schools — vice-principal, custodian, student, teacher, principal, guidance counselor, and cafeteria worker.How do the following objects and privileges show the rank of each position? Desks? Telephones? Offices? Restrooms? Times and places for smoking?

Roles. The status that a person occupies within a group involves certain obligations. As a student, for example, you are expected to do homework, study for examinations, and get at least passing grades. Parents are expected to provide for and protect their children. The specific pattern of behavior that we expect of a person because of his or her status is called a *role.*

School teachers today have a wide variety of life-styles, but this has not always been so. Once the life of female teachers in the United States was accompanied by strict role expectations. The following provisions were part of a contract for Georgia public school teachers in 1927:

I promise to take a vital interest in all phases of Sunday-school work, donating of my time, service, and money without stint for the uplift and benefit of the community.

I promise to abstain from all dancing, immodest dressing, and any other conduct unbecoming a teacher and a lady.

I promise not to go out with any young men except in so far as it may be necessary to stimulate Sunday-school work.

I promise not to fall in love, to become engaged or secretly married.

I promise not to encourage or tolerate the least familiarity on the part of any of my boy pupils.

I promise to sleep at least eight hours a night, to eat carefully, and to take every precaution to keep in the best of health and spirits, in order that I may be better able to render efficient service to my pupils.

I promise to remember that I owe a duty to the townspeople who are paying me my wages, that I owe respect to the school board and the superintendent that hired me, and that I shall consider myself at all times the willing servant of the school board and the townspeople.

~§ What role expectations do you think are a part of the status of the teacher today?

Role conflict. Just as people have a number of statuses, so they play a number of roles.

We are able to play a wide variety of roles because as a rule they are not played at the same time or place. Sometimes, however, two or more roles cannot be separated neatly, and then conflicts arise that create serious personal problems. Many parents are torn between the need to earn money and their wish to spend more time at home with their children. Student athletes are often caught between the demands of the sports arena and the classroom. When there are opposing demands within a role or between two roles played by the same person, sociologists call this *role conflict.*

During World War II, for example, General George S. Patton's Third Army

was bogged down in Europe by heavy rains. Patton asked his military chaplain, Colonel James H. O'Neill, to compose a prayer for good weather. The following conversation took place:

Patton: Chaplain, I want you to publish a prayer for good weather. I'm sick and tired of these soldiers having to fight mud and floods as well as Germans. See if you can get God to work on our side.

O'Neill: Sir, it's going to take a pretty thick rug for that kind of praying.

Patton: I don't care if it takes the flying carpet. I want the praying done.

O'Neill: May I say, General, that it isn't a customary thing among men of my profession to pray for clear weather to kill fellow men?

Patton: Chaplain, are you teaching me theology or are you the Chaplain of the Third Army? I want a prayer.

O'Neill: Yes, sir.

O'Neill's status as an Army chaplain had placed him in conflicting roles. It was contrary to his religious calling to pray for "clear weather to kill fellow men." As an Army chaplain, however, he could not disobey a direct order from his commanding officer.

Roles are determined by the presence of other people playing other roles. A doctor, for example, must interact with patients, a teacher with students, and a merchant with customers. If the interaction continues over a period of time, each will know what kind of social behavior to expect from the other, and a formalized role relationship will develop.

Role change. What happens when a person makes a dramatic change in the role that he or she usually plays? For Steve Bacon, a writer and editor for a research company, it proved to be a nightmare. Bacon wanted to find out what it is like to be very poor. He volunteered to take part in an experiment conducted by the Trenton, New Jersey, Department of Community Affairs. For two days, he would play the role of a homeless man — a "bum." Bacon let his beard grow, put on very shabby clothes, and then reported to a Community Affairs social worker in a nearby town. He was given a "welfare allowance" of two dollars, all he would have for food and shelter in the next 48 hours. He was also given a list of welfare agencies and charity organizations that might offer him further help. He was to pose as a taxi driver from Chicago who was stranded in New Jersey without money to return home. Bacon wrote about his experience for *Science Digest.* His story, entitled "I Became a Bum," follows:

> It all seemed like a lark setting out . . . about 9:30 P.M. without a wallet or identification. I headed for the local Salvation Army with two dollars in change in my pocket. They'd put me up for the night, I was sure, and I'd find work [the next] morning. The temperature was below freezing as I walked the mile to the mission, but the way was brightened by Christmas lights twinkling overhead. Only after arriving at the dingy, three-story brick building did I lose my false sense of security. It was closed, locked tight and shuttered. . . .
>
> Well, I've really let myself in for it, I thought, heading back up the thoroughfare through

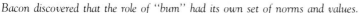

Bacon discovered that the role of "bum" had its own set of norms and values.

the center of town. The local YMCA was close by, and I thought of asking if they had an inexpensive room or even a cot they could put up in the hallway. A bit self-conscious, I walked into the building and set my bag on the floor in front of the desk while the guy behind it eyed me suspiciously.

"Do you have a room?" I asked.

"Sure," he said, turning to the card file. Then he turned back and gave me a good going over. "Nope, I'm wrong. We're all filled up."

"Do you know where I can stay for the night?" . . . I told him I didn't have much money.

"Well, there are some hotels and boarding houses down on Front Street," he said. "It's kind of dangerous down there, but that's all there is."

A long walk the length of Front Street confirmed my worst fears. There were cheap, shabby hotels, but the least I could get a room for was five dollars — some three dollars more than I had to live on for the next two days.

A thin, gray-haired derelict stood in a doorway, and I asked him if he knew where I could find a bed for the night. After he told me what I had already discovered — that there wasn't an open mission in town — I asked him about the railroad station which was close by.

"I just got chased out," he said. "They have some new detectives over there." He told me about the local police and that I should avoid them if at all possible. Grateful for his advice, I suddenly felt ashamed at the number of times I had ignored others like him who are often in situations even more desperate than mine.

I had no choice now. It would have to be the railroad station, at least until the police or railroad detectives caught up with me. I walked into the dirty waiting room and sat down. A few minutes later, tired from walking in the cold for the last two hours, I was lying down. A sharp rap on the sole of one shoe interrupted my dozing. It was coupled with an admonition from the cop on the beat to "sit up." [Later] a railroad detective got his crack in. "The last train leaves at 1 A.M.," he

said. "You can't spend the night here." . . .

"Where can I stay?" I protested when he asked me to leave. "I don't have any money."

"There's an all-night restaurant over there," he said, pointing across the street. "You can sit over there."

A cup of coffee was the price of my refuge from the cold. I ordered it, spreading out in a booth and trying to get as comfortable as possible. Pouring plenty of sugar into it, I sipped it slowly to make it last. This game went on for an hour until the restaurant owner began to lose his patience.

He growled to the cook, shook his head, and slammed a tray on the counter. "No," I didn't want anything more, I answered to his repeated inquiries. "You stay here all night?" he finally asked. "That isn't nice." Mumbling something about waiting for a friend, I got up and paid 16 cents for the coffee. I now had $1.84 and three hours to go until daylight.

The streets of the town were deserted as I walked through them. I again tried the railroad station, and the railroad employee took a sort of sadistic pity on me. "OK," he grinned. "You can come back in, but you stand on your feet until morning." Anything was better than the cold, and I stood next to a steam radiator, letting the warmth sink in.

The first order of business would be a place to stay and then a job, and I resolved to get working on that as soon as I could get something to eat. Six o'clock found a greasy spoon opening down the street, and for 68 cents the waitress delivered fried potatoes, two pieces of toast, scrambled eggs, and coffee. I felt warm and well fed as I strode out — without leaving a tip — with $1.16 in my pocket.

A little later, I staked out the city welfare office and hung around the door waiting for the 9 A.M. opening. Poverty was having an effect. I found myself becoming deferential as the arriving workers glanced at me, then quickly turned away. . . . When the welfare office opened for business, I found myself telling my story in a quavering voice to a brusque, stout, discourteous woman employee.

Yes, city welfare could offer some help, but I had to have an address within the city. "But I need help to find a place to stay," I almost shouted. Yes, it was too bad, but those were the rules. I should come back when I had a place to stay.

After this setback, I made a mile trek to a store-front agency in a predominantly black and Puerto Rican neighborhood. A sympathetic social worker listened to my story, made a phone call, and then handed me a slip of paper with an address. Reverend Baker, minister of the local Baptist church, would help me find a place to stay.

I found Baker's church and wandered in, hat in hand. He greeted me warmly, and a short time later I was installed in the windowless "pink" room on dangerous Front Street. Despite the roaches, the dripping water, and the bed that sagged into a back-breaking "U," I was asleep 10 minutes later.

It was dark outside when I awoke to the thuds of furniture being thrown against the wall by the delirious drug addict next door. That didn't bother me but I was hungry again, and I put on my coat and sleepily started to cross the street, being narrowly missed by a car which came rushing through. "Too bad he didn't run him over," I heard a bystander say to the woman next to him. "I wish they'd run the drifters out of town."

Picking myself up, I went into a pizza parlor where 66 cents bought two slices of pizza and a cup of coffee. Fifty cents left and one day to go. I would have to find a job tomorrow if I wanted to eat. [The social worker] told me to go to the manpower pool and get there early. . . . There was already a line by 7 A.M. the next morning.

"You want a job loading trucks?" the heavy, gray-haired counselor asked me when my turn came.

"Sure. But I need money right now to eat. When do they pay?" I asked him.

"You don't get paid till Friday," the man told me. "We don't give advances." My heart sank, and I stared at him, making him a bit nervous. "Sorry," he said, "those are the rules."

I wandered back into the cold. Thirty cents bought me coffee and a roll, and I decided to try an employment agency. They were no help either. When I told them there was no place they could call for references, the girl practically pushed me out the door.

I had to have money, and the only way left to get it was to panhandle. Cautiously I approached a well-dressed citizen, asking if he could spare a little change. No luck. He walked on by and so did the next five people I asked, their eyes turning away from me to the street, a store window or — in a few cases — staring at me with disgust. A sudden inspiration took me down the street to a bus stop. Two women were waiting for the bus. Keeping an eye out for cops, I told them I needed just enough change to get home. It worked. One dug out a dime, and the other gave me 15 cents.

Embarrassed to let them see I was panhandling, I waited until they boarded the bus, then tried another tired commuter. He refused and so did the next, but I kept at it for over an hour until I had 65 cents — the hardest money I have ever earned. What stopped me was the waspish little man who screamed, "Get out of here! Get going before I call the police!"

I returned home shaken, silent, thoughtful. A panhandler stopped me as I got off the bus and made his pitch. I reached into my pocket and gave him the contents.

❧ What new norms and values did Steve Bacon acquire by playing the role of a "bum"? What other norms, values, and role relationships do you think he might have acquired had he played this role even longer?

Society and Institutions

The largest group to which a person belongs is a society. A *society* refers to all the people who live within a certain geographic area, share a common way of life, and have a feeling of solidarity that binds them together as a unit. The most familiar societies are nations with formal governments. When we speak of American society, for example, we usually mean all the people who live in the United States. However, not all societies are nations. Many tribes with fewer than a thousand members comprise complete societies. They have their own languages and unique life-styles that they pass on from generation to generation.

Every society, whether large or small, has certain basic needs that must be fulfilled if it is to endure. Among these needs are: to create new members so as to replace old members as they die; to train the young and instill in them the norms and values of the society; to explain the meaning of existence and reinforce moral values; to provide food and shelter; to maintain order and security.

In simple societies, these needs may be met by the group without any formal organization. For example, the young may be trained without schools. But as societies become more complex, they form patterns to meet their basic needs. The distinctive and stable pattern of norms, values, statuses, and roles that develops around a basic need of a society is called an *institution*. Five major social institutions are:

1. *The family.* The institution that is responsible for replenishing the members of a society, regulating sexual behavior, and providing for the rearing of children.

2. *Education.* The institution that is responsible for teaching children the values, norms, roles, and the accumulated knowledge of a society.

3. *Religion.* The institution that is concerned with explaining the meaning and purpose of life, offering hope for the future, and providing moral guidance.

4. *The economic system.* The institution that is concerned with the production, distribution, and consumption of goods and services in a society.

5. *Government.* The institution that is responsible for maintaining order within a society, enforcing its norms, and protecting it from outside enemies.

The five major institutions usually complement each other, and often their functions overlap. In our society, the family, school, and church or synagogue all teach moral values to children. Cooperation between two or more institutions is often essential if they are to succeed in their goals. The educational system depends on parents to prepare their children for school work. Parents depend on the schools to educate their children and prepare them to take their places in society. The public schools depend on government for their funding.

Institutions may also be in conflict with each other within a society. For example, the government's desire for environmental protection may conflict with the economic system's desire for maximum profits and productivity.

Social Control

Every group seeks to encourage conformity to its norms. Any process that helps
to achieve this end is a form of *social control*. Without social control, social patterns would fall apart. Probably the most
effective process of social control is something that we usually call our *conscience*.
Most of us do not steal, for example, because we have been taught — and believe
— that stealing is wrong. "I wouldn't be
able to live with myself," we might say
when we are tempted to do something
wrong. When we conform to rules because
our sense of self-respect demands it, the
process of social control is internal.

Because internal social control
doesn't always work, groups also apply
external pressures to persuade or compel
members to conform to their rules. Thus,
teachers may assign detention hall, parents may deny car and dating privileges,
students may gossip about each other, and
employers may withhold raises. The most
visible form of external social control is
exercised by people and organizations
specifically empowered to enforce conformity to society's laws. Policemen,
judges, and prison guards are the most obvious agents of external social control.
When social control takes the form of
punishment, sociologists call it *negative
sanction*.

The following article from the *New
York Post* shows how a group may use
social control to enforce its standards:

*Birmingham, England — When 58-year-old
Arthur Steele retires from the Birmingham main
post office in two years, he will have gone three
years without a single workmate having spoken to
him. It is an almost monastic ordeal by silence for
postal driver Steele, who made the mistake of
working for four-and-a-half hours on the day the
national postmen's strike started in January 1971.
Since then, for a whole year, he has been ignored
officially at work and there is unlikely to be any
letup. Mike Edwards, secretary of the Birmingham
postmen, made this clear. He said, "We are not
prepared to forgive and forget."*

Group norms aren't always enforced
by imposing negative sanctions. Conformity to norms is often gained by offering
rewards. A soldier who shows courage in
battle may be awarded a medal or promotion. A student who shows outstanding
abilities may be elected class president.
All such rewards are meant to encourage
behavior that groups believe is desirable.
We call these rewards *positive sanctions*.

⌇ Describe the form of social control
and the type of sanctions which would
probably occur in the following situations:
   • A student turns in another student
for cheating.
   • A student turns in a lost wallet containing $20.
   • A student answers a teacher's question with a wisecrack.
   • A student gives very good answers
to a teacher's questions.

In this chapter we have seen how our
behavior, far from being haphazard, occurs
in patterns. In the next chapter, we will
study some of the research methods
sociologists use in their search for these
social patterns.

Ethnomethodology

Imagine that you are a clerk working in a large department store. A customer brings a sweater with a $40 price tag to your counter and declares: "I'll give you $20 for this sweater." How would you respond to the offer? Would you be surprised and confused? What norms of behavior did the customer break?

The interaction between a customer and a clerk usually involves a well-known pattern of norms which we take for granted. Yet, when this pattern is deliberately challenged, it can reveal the norms and values underlying our daily lives. Thus, department store clerks assume that they are operating in a fixed-price system. They do not have norms to tell them how to react if a customer tries to bargain over the price of a product.

A group of sociologists known as ethnomethodologists believe that commonplace patterns of daily life should not be overlooked. "Ethnos" is a Greek word meaning "people" or "folk." *Ethnomethodology* is thus a method for studying society's unwritten rules for social behavior.

Harold Garfinkel, a leader in the field of ethnomethodology, has developed a number of techniques for uncovering hidden social patterns. Garfinkel asked his students to expose rules of every day life by breaking them. He instructed them to act like strangers in their own homes. They addressed their parents as "Mr." and "Mrs.," and politely asked if they could use the phone or have a snack. Below, Garfinkel reports the vivid results produced by this simple experiment.

Family members were stupefied. They vigorously sought to make the strange actions intelligible and to restore the situation to normal. Reports were filled with accounts of astonishment, shock, anxiety, embarassment, and anger with charges by various family members that the student was mean, inconsiderate, selfish, nasty, impolite. Family members demanded explanations: What's the matter? Did you get fired? Are you sick? What are you being so superior about? Are you mad? Are you out of your mind? One student acutely embarassed his mother in front of her friends by asking if she minded if he had a snack from the refrigerator. "Mind if you have a little snack? You've been eating little snacks around here for years without asking me. What's gotten into you?"

In other experiments, Garfinkel's students disrupted casual conversations. For example, when asked, "How are you?" one student unexpectedly replied: "How am I in regard to what? My health, my finances, my school work, my peace of mind, my . . ." The surprised acquaintance angrily responded: "Look! I was just trying to be polite. Frankly, I don't care how you are."

Garfinkel's experiments help us understand the rules that regulate social interaction. They illustrate how the search for social patterns can be a rewarding, surprising, and even a painful learning experience.

Thinking Critically

1. What is ethnomethodology? What techniques do ethnomethodologists use to uncover social patterns?

2. What strategies do you think an ethnomethodologist would use to study social patterns in your sociology class?

application

In this chapter you learned a number of important concepts which will help focus your search for social patterns. As a beginning sociologist you might have already noticed that the patterns in your life are also linked to broader social patterns. The American sociologist C. Wright Mills called this ability to see the link between our personal experiences and the wider society, *sociological imagination.*

As you practice your sociological imagination you will begin to see social life in a different way. Common sense will sometimes prove to be inaccurate. New information may occasionally challenge widely accepted theories. The following true-false statements express a number of widely held views. Read each statement and determine if is true or false. Your answers will serve as an interesting point of reference as you study the different chapters in this text. Your teacher can provide you with the answers and with additional information about each statement.

1. The accuracy of a survey depends upon interviewing as many people as possible. (**T/F**)

2. A sociologist would agree that modern industrial societies are more cultured than traditional agricultural societies. (**T/F**)

3. A sociologist would be interested in the way people space themselves on a park bench. (**T/F**)

4. Learning begins at birth and continues throughout all of life. (**T/F**)

5. By age 16, the average American has spent more time watching television than attending classes in school. (**T/F**)

6. Sociologists agree that "nature," or our genetic history, has little influence in shaping our personalities. (**T/F**)

7. A person's performance of a task can be affected by his or her status in a group. (**T/F**)

8. As communication between two groups increases, the likelihood of cooperation always increases. (**T/F**)

9. There are no examples of modern industrial societies which permit arranged marriages. (**T/F**)

10. The divorce rate in the United States has begun to decline. (**T/F**)

11. The average American family earns $51,200. (**T/F**)

12. Most poor Americans are unemployed and live in cities. (**T/F**)

13. Immigration into the United States is currently at a historic low. (**T/F**)

14. Blacks are the largest minority group in the United States. (**T/F**)

15. Native Americans are the nation's poorest minority group. (**T/F**)

16. Sociologists do not study fads, fashions, and crazes. (**T/F**)

17. The average age of the U.S. population is slowly decreasing. (**T/F**)

18. Robbery is the most common violent crime in the United States. (**T/F**)

19. Motor-vehicle theft is the most common property crime in the United States. (**T/F**)

20. More doctors specialize in treating the elderly than any other branch of medicine. (**T/F**)

21. The majority of elderly Americans live in nursing homes. **(T/F)**

22. The United States pours 200 million tons of poisonous gases and dust particles into the air each year. **(T/F)**

23. More Americans live in the suburbs than in the central cities. **(T/F)**

24. More terrorist acts occur in Latin America than in any other region of the world. **(T/F)**

summary

Sociologists seek to find underlying patterns of human behavior by studying the regular, ordered details of life that derive from our membership in groups. Sociologists define a **group** as two or more people who are **interacting,** or communicating, in order to influence each other's thoughts and actions. Social groups pattern our daily lives through **norms,** which tell us how to act or what to say in particular situations; **values,** which are group beliefs about what is right or important; **status,** which is the position that each person occupies within a group; **ranking,** which is a measure of the relative prestige of each status; and **role,** which is the behavior that is expected of each status. Norms, values, status, ranking, and role are the elements common to social groups.

Our earliest associations are with small groups — the family, the school clique, gangs, clubs, and teams. The largest group to which anyone can belong is a **society,** which consists of all those people in a specific geographic area who share a common culture and have a sense of solidarity as a social unit. Every society has certain needs which must be satisfied if it is to endure. In simple societies, the group may meet these needs informally. But in complex societies, the most fundamental needs are fulfilled through the **institutions** of the family, religion, education, the economy, and government.

In all groups, whether large or small, **interaction** creates recurring social patterns. Groups encourage conformity to these patterns and discourage deviance, through processes of **social control.** These may vary from an individual's conscience (internal control) to controls exercised by law enforcement authorities (external control). When social control is maintained by punishment or the threat of punishment, it is called **negative sanction.** When social control is maintained by reward, it is called **positive sanction.**

Sociology is the scientific study of the patterns of human group life.

more questions and activities

1. Give the sociological definitions of norms and values, and list two examples of each from the description of the football game in Edison.

2. Explain what sociologists mean by *interaction,* and where and how it occurs.

3. List the five major institutions common to every society and tell the function each performs.

4. From the time you wake up in the morning until you go to bed, keep a list of everything you do that is governed by norms. Keep a separate list of everything that is not.

5. As a sociologist, you are constantly searching for social patterns to describe and analyze. In order to demonstrate your professional abilities, do a systematic analysis of the social patterns found while eating at a fast-food restaurant. Your analysis should include each of the five elements of groups and examples of each.

6. The following has been named the "Polite Stranger Experiment" by sociologist Harold Garfinkel. You may want to try it at home one morning or evening with your family. *Without telling anyone what you are doing, act as though you are a complete stranger in your own home. Address your parents as Mr. and Mrs. Introduce yourself to other people who may be there, including any sisters and brothers. Pretend you do not know any household routines — such as where dishes are kept, who sits where at the dinner table, and who washes the dishes. Ask permission to turn on the television or radio. Or ask directions to your room or the telephone. Keep this up as long as possible before letting the others in on your secret.* One of the purposes of this experiment is to show how much a certain status — in this case, son or daughter — determines what role behavior is expected of the person.

7. Prepare a portfolio of magazine advertisements that show people in at least three different statuses. What role behavior is depicted in the advertisements? Is other role behavior implied? If so, what?

8. In the *Sign of Four* by Arthur Conan Doyle, the great detective Sherlock Holmes makes the following statement: "While the individual man is an insoluble puzzle, in the aggregate, he becomes a mathematical certainty. You can, for example, never foretell what any one man will do, but you can say with precision what an average number will be up to. Individuals vary, but percentages remain relatively constant." Would a sociologist agree with Holmes? Give reasons for your answer.

9. A sociologist interested in studying your high school is given a copy of the most recent yearbook. She or he has not yet visited your school or talked with anyone familiar with it. What patterns of social behavior might a sociologist infer from looking at this book? Which of these observations would be confirmed by visiting your school this year? Which might be challenged?

10. Examine the photographs throughout the chapter for evidence of norms and values in our society. List as many examples of each as you can.

suggested readings

Baldridge, Letitia, and Amy Vanderbilt. *The Amy Vanderbilt Complete Book of Etiquette, A Guide to Contemporary Living.* (Doubleday, 1978.) Manners provide a fascinating insight into the folkways, values, and expected role behavior of a society. This edition of Amy Vanderbilt's classic book of etiquette explains proper procedures and manners for ceremonies and social events ranging from a formal wedding to going to the beach.

Huber, Betlina J. *Embarking Upon A Career With An Undergraduate Sociology Major.* (American Sociological Association, 1982.) A useful booklet which explains how the study of sociology can lead to a variety of careers.

Johnson, Allen G. *Human Arrangements.* (Harcourt Brace Jovanovich, 1986.) An excellent introductory sociology text. Chapters 1 and 3 contain particularly interesting sections on how sociologists search for social patterns.

Mills, C. Wright. *The Sociological Imagination.* (Oxford University Press, 1959.) One of America's greatest sociologists discusses the meaning and importance of the sociological imagination. Chapter One, "The Promise," is highly recommended.

Sillitoe, Alan. *The Loneliness of the Long-Distance Runner* (New American Library, 1971.) The title story in this collection of short fiction tells of the conflict in values experienced by a reform school student who gains self-respect through running and then is pressured by the authorities to represent his school.

Smith, Hedrick. *The Russians.* (Ballantine Books, 1984.) A *New York Times* correspondent to Russia has written a perceptive account of the people, institutions, and major issues in Russia. Chapter 2 is especially recommended for its account of the norms which define the routines of Russian consumers.

Smolan, Rick, and David Cohen. *A Day In The Life of America.* (Collins Publishers, 1986.) An outstanding collection of pictures which can be used to illustrate norms, values, roles, and other social patterns.

Editors of Time-Life Books. *This Fabulous Century: Volume 1, 1900-1910.* (Time-Life Books, 1985.) This richly illustrated volume provides a superb portrayal of the social patterns which defined the texture of life in America at the turn of the century. The chapters entitled "A Man's World," "The Kids," and "The Ladies" are excellent for a study of role behavior, while the chapter entitled "The Very Rich" contains fine material on social ranking and status symbols.

Modern technology has made surveys much more efficient.

chapter 2

methods

At the age of 21, Emile Durkheim was accepted into the Ecole Normale Superieure in Paris, one of the most elite schools in 19th-century France.

Durkheim was a sociology major. At this time, sociology was a new and undeveloped field of study, but this did not bother Durkheim. He thought that psychology, which was primarily concerned with the individual, was not useful in solving the problems of society. Durkheim believed that sociology offered an opportunity to use the scientific method to solve society's problems.

Although Durkheim did not graduate at the top of his class, he did impress his teachers and classmates as being a serious student. In fact, he was just beginning his academic career. Over the next five years, he took various teaching jobs to support himself. At the same time, Durkheim threw himself into the study of sociology, especially of the ways sociology could be applied to the problems he saw in society.

To Durkheim, sociology was not a study one undertook for idle interest. It had a direct relationship to the world he saw around him. "Although we set out primarily to study reality," he wrote, "it does not follow that we do not wish to improve it; we should judge our researches to have no worth at all if they were to have only a speculative interest."

Courtesy of the Bettman Archive

Emile Durkheim

It is to Durkheim that sociology owes much of its reputation as an independent social science. In this chapter, we will see how he went about studying a problem that was growing in Europe in the 19th century — suicide.

Durkheim's work is examined here for another reason, however. By seeing how he went about his study of suicide, we can learn much about the scientific method that sociologists follow. Durkheim worked from facts gathered by other people. This is called *secondary research*. Later in this chapter, we'll see other sociologists at work using other methods. We'll see why certain methods are best suited to particular situations. And we'll examine some of the ethical questions raised by some research.

The Scientific Method: Emile Durkheim's Study of Suicide

In Durkheim's time, it was widely believed that suicide was an individual act motivated by mental illness, inherited suicidal tendencies, or the effects of climate. Durkheim had a hunch, however, that there was a better explanation. If suicide was motivated by personal forces, he asked, why should the suicide rate be higher in some countries than in others? Durkheim believed that suicide was influenced by social forces and that a scientific investigation would show definite patterns and trends among suicides.

Although sociologists obviously cannot put people under microscopes or observe their behavior in a test tube, they employ many of the same objective procedures in conducting their investigations that all scientists use. These procedures are collectively called the *scientific method.*

The scientific method is designed to increase the probability that research will lead to valid and accurate conclusions, free of personal biases or wishful thinking. Sociologists attempt to deal in facts that can be observed, measured, and tested. The scientific method requires sociologists to collect data (factual material) systematically, state their findings precisely, and make their conclusions public. This is what Durkheim set out to do.

Durkheim began his investigation by checking the explanations of suicide against official records kept by a number of European governments. These records showed that suicide rates were highest in countries where the incidence of mental illness was lowest. Obviously, mental illness could not be singled out as the cause of suicide.

Durkheim also found that more men committed suicide than women. If suicide was caused by inherited tendencies, why shouldn't men and women be affected equally? For Durkheim, the higher rate of suicide among men ruled out heredity as a cause of suicide. Finally, Durkheim found that suicide was not directly related to variations in temperature or climate.

Having disproven the existing explanations of suicide, Durkheim began to test his own hunch that suicide is influenced by social forces. This he would do by applying the scientific method to the study of suicide.

1. Defining the problem. The first step in the scientific method is for the researcher to define precisely the problem that he is investigating. Durkheim defined suicide as "all cases of death resulting directly or indirectly from a positive or negative act of the victim himself, which he knows will produce this result." By a "positive" act, Durkheim meant suicide by jumping off a building, shooting oneself, taking poison, etc. By a "negative" act, he meant suicide by not taking essential food or medicine, not getting out of the way of a moving vehicle, or otherwise failing to protect oneself from danger.

The subject of a scientific investigation is called the *dependent variable*. The scientist wants to find out how the subject of the investigation will change, depend-

ing on other factors. In Durkheim's study, suicide was the dependent variable. He was looking for social forces that would change the suicide rate.

Factors which explain changes in the dependent variable are called *independent variables.* Durkheim next had to define the social forces that he believed would affect the suicide rate. These social forces would be his independent variables. He suspected that how closely a person was linked to other people would affect that person's inclination to commit suicide. So he picked religious affiliation, marital status, military or civilian status, and economic stability as social forces he would study in relation to the suicide rate. Since governments kept records on all these factors, he could analyze these records statistically.

2. Forming a hypothesis. Now Durkheim was ready to take the second step in the scientific method. In this step, the scientist makes a hypothesis. A *hypothesis* is an educated guess of how certain factors affect the subject of the investigation. A hypothesis must be tested against relevant data to check its validity.

Durkheim's hypothesis was that the suicide rate would vary by religion (Protestants, Catholics, and Jews); by marital status (single people and married people); by military status (soldiers and civilians); and by economic conditions (boom, bust, or stability).

❧ Test your understanding of these two steps of the scientific method with this example: You want to find out who is most likely to observe a stop sign in traffic. You suspect that whether or not a person stops may be affected by his or her sex. You guess that male drivers will be less likely to stop than female drivers.

What is the dependent variable in this example? What is the independent variable? What is the hypothesis of this example? Can you think of other independent variables that you might want to test? (Your teacher can tell you about an experiment that was conducted on this subject.*)

3. Collecting the data. The third step in the scientific method requires the researcher to collect and analyze the data that will either prove or disprove the hypothesis.

Durkheim found that, regarding religion, the records showed that the suicide rate was higher among Protestants than Catholics, and lowest among Jews. Regarding marital status, it was higher among single people than married people, and lowest among married people with children. In fact, the rate of suicide declined with each additional child a parent had.

Regarding military status, it was higher among soldiers than among civilians. It was also higher for officers than for enlisted men; and among enlisted men, it was higher for volunteers than for draftees.

Regarding economic conditions, the suicide rate was higher in times of economic depression than in more stable periods. The rate of suicide was also higher during economic booms than during more stable periods.

4. Analyzing the data. Given these facts, Durkheim had to interpret and explain them — the fourth step in the scientific method. Why did the suicide rate vary from one group to another? Durkheim had to find a way to explain all of the data he had collected. At this point, his work resembled a complex puzzle. When the pieces were in place, a social pattern should emerge.

As a sociologist, of course, Durkheim was committed to the idea that groups were very important to an individual's welfare. His explanation also showed that he had a very sophisticated understanding of scientific reasoning. His analysis of the facts he had collected led him to the conclusion that there was not one simple explanation for suicide. From his data, he was able to discern three distinct patterns of suicide, all of which were explained by the victim's relationship to the various institutions in his or her society.

Egoistic suicide. In the first category, which Durkheim called *egoistic*, individuals are not strongly supported by membership in a cohesive social group. As outsiders, they depend more on themselves than on group goals and rules of conduct to sustain them in their lives. In times of stress, they feel isolated and helpless. Sometimes these feelings lead them to take their own lives.

Shakespeare's Romeo and Juliet, who killed themselves rather than be separated by their families, offer a literary example of egoistic suicide.

The isolation of extreme individuals, Durkheim said, might explain why

---

*The teacher will find the necessary information in the chapter narrative of the Teacher's Resource Manual.

2

The Scientific Method

1 Define the problem.

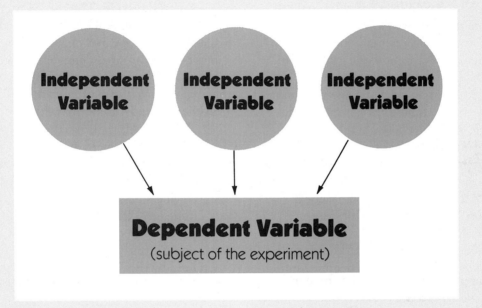

2 Form a hypothesis, an educated guess about how the independent variables relate to the dependent variable.

3 Collect the data. Use statistics, observe an activity, perform an experiment, or make a survey.

4 Analyze the data. What does this research show about the variables?

5 Form a theory. Does this research confirm the hypothesis? If not, what does it show? Record and publish the conclusions.

the suicide rate among Protestants was higher than among Catholics. Protestant faiths emphasize individualism and self-reliance, whereas Catholicism stresses both the authority and the supportive role of the church.

Why should Jews have the lowest suicide rate? Durkheim's explanation was that, as a result of persecution, Jews had become a closely knit social group. Durkheim's theory of egoistic suicide would also explain why single people were more likely to take their lives than married people. Single people often lacked the group ties provided by a mate. Similarly, each child that a parent raised strengthened the parent's ties to the family group.

Altruistic suicide. The second pattern of suicide that Durkheim observed differed sharply from the first. In this pattern, which Durkheim called *altruistic,* the individual is deeply committed to group norms and goals, and sees his or her own life as insignificant. Near the end of World War II, Japanese Kamikaze pilots dived their bomb-laden planes onto the decks of their enemies' ships. These men were quite willing to commit suicide for the sake of their country. Again during the war in Vietnam, Americans were shocked to see Buddhist monks set fire to themselves and commit suicide to express their opposition to the war. The Buddhist religion, however, places the individual ego in a less important role than do Western religions.

Durkheim's theory of altruistic suicide would also explain why the suicide rate among soldiers generally is higher than among civilians. In an army,

loyalty to the group is all-important; the significance of individual life declines. This would also explain why officers with their deeper commitment to the army are more likely to go on suicidal missions than enlistees.

Anomic suicide. The third pattern of suicide that Durkheim observed, which he called *anomic,* appeared chiefly during times of crisis or rapid change. At such times, customary norms may weaken or break down. With no clear standards of behavior to guide them, many people become confused, their usual goals lose meaning, and life seems aimless.

During the boom times of the 1920's, for example, quite a few men made fortunes in the stock market. When the market crashed in October 1929, many of these fortunes were wiped out almost overnight. Utterly confused and demoralized by the sudden, uncontrollable loss of their wealth, some men plunged to their deaths from Wall Street office buildings.

Ironically, the sudden acquisition of great wealth may also cause people to commit suicide. The reasons, Durkheim said, are essentially the same as for people who lose their money. The newly-rich also become confused, often not knowing what to do with sudden wealth. Their old goals — a $25–50-a-week pay raise or a new washing machine — now seem meaningless. Without new goals or norms to guide them, life appears aimless; and sometimes the result is suicide.

5. Formulating a theory. Durkheim concluded his investigation by formulating

2:A

Characteristics
of Four Sociological Methods

	SECONDARY RESEARCH	PARTICIPANT OBSERVATION	EXPERIMENT	SURVEY
Size of test group	Large	Small	Usually small	Can be very large
Usual cost	Very inexpensive	Inexpensive	Depends on equipment used	Depends on sample size and whether interview is used
Kind of interaction with subjects	None	Personal, informal	Personal, formal	Personal and formal if interview is used; impersonal if by mail
Where does research take place?	In a library or other research facility	In the field with a small group	In the laboratory	In the field, usually with a large group
Can the independent variable(s) be manipulated by the researcher?	No	No	Yes	Yes
Is there any way to check against error?	No	Yes; through testing and revision of theory	Yes; by random assignment to experiment and control groups	Yes; by careful sampling
Can results be generalized to a larger population?	Yes	Rarely	Rarely	Yes
Can results be influenced by the research itself?	Yes; by choosing a biased group of data	Yes; by the Hawthorne effect	Yes; by the Hawthorne effect	Yes; by the Hawthorne effect

a theory, the last step in a scientific investigation. (In science, a *theory* is a logical explanation of how some facts are apparently related to other facts.) Durkheim's theory was that suicide was clearly related to the links people have with social groups. Too little commitment to groups and group norms was likely to produce egoistic suicide. Too much was likely to produce altruistic suicide. Commitment shaken by rapid social change was likely to increase the chances of anomic suicide.

Critical assessment. Does Durkheim's work prove that personal unhappiness does not lead to suicide? Of course not. Durkheim would probably have been the first to admit that people who commit suicide may feel miserable. But as a sociologist, he was interested in the effects of group forces on suicide.

The sociological and psychological views of suicide do not oppose each other. Rather, each helps us understand the other. The sociologist can point out the social forces that will increase a person's probability of committing suicide. For example, a sociologist might predict that a single person will be more likely to commit suicide than a married one. But a sociologist would not attempt to predict which singles would be most likely to kill themselves. At this point, the psychologist's study of individual behavior would be much more useful.

Just how accurate was Durkheim's suicide theory? Like any scientist, a sociologist must produce work that can be duplicated in order to establish a theory. Over the years, many sociologists have attempted to repeat Durkheim's research on suicide. Many have criticized his methods. Can you think of any reasons why Durkheim's methods might have led to inaccurate conclusions? (Your teacher can tell you what some of his critics have said.)

In Durkheim's secondary research, he used data already collected by someone else. But sociologists have a number of methods of studying group behavior more directly, depending on the problem that they want to investigate. We'll look into three methods in this chapter. In a *participant observation,* sociologists become involved with a group and observe its activities as insiders. Or they might conduct an *experiment,* a method that allows them to study human behavior under controlled conditions in a laboratory or in real-life settings. Or they might undertake a *survey,* using questionnaires, interviews, or both. As you read about these methods, you may want to refer to Chart 2:A, which shows some characteristics of each.

Participant Observation

How do unusual and secretive religious cults operate from day to day? How do they recruit new members? How do they keep their faith when others seem to reject them? These were questions that intrigued John Lofland in the early 1960's when he was studying for his Ph.D. at the University of California at Berkeley. Lofland wanted to observe one of these cults closely, as an insider, taking part in its activities. It was the only way, he believed,

The Rev. Moon of Unification Church marries 2,200 couples in Madison Square Garden, NYC. Below, cult members rally in Yankee Stadium.

that he could come to understand their behavior.

So Lofland set out to find a suitable group for his study in the San Francisco area near the university. Of course, secretive religious groups were not likely to open their doors to an inquisitive sociologist.

Divine Precepts. In February 1962, after searching several months, Lofland finally found a group that seemed willing to admit him as an observer. He was invited to attend a meeting of the Divine Precepts, a cult that had originated in Korea. Its members believed that the successor to Jesus Christ had arrived in the world in the person of Soon Chang, a Korean engineer. (The names of the cult and its members are fictitious. Lofland, following scientific custom, did not report actual names.) They believed too that Judgment Day was soon coming, and that only the followers of Chang would rule over the perfect society under God that would shortly be established on earth.

On arriving at the group's quarters, Lofland was placed in a room — alone — to listen to a lengthy tape recording of the cult's "message." Afterward he was introduced to a Miss Lee, who described herself as Chang's missionary to America. So far, Lofland had met only two members of the group — the woman who had invited him there and Miss Lee. Seeing no others, he felt sure that they were the whole "movement." Such a group would be too small for the purposes of his study. As Lofland left, he felt quite discouraged.

But a week later, Lofland decided to visit the Divine Precepts again. This time he was surprised to find a room full of people. Miss Lee told him that the group had a core of at least a dozen members who lived communally and gave their full time to recruiting converts. The members were young adults, and several of them had given up family ties, including children, to join the group. They had been in San Francisco for almost a year. So far, they had acquired an apartment house and a printing press, and had published an English translation of their holy book. Now

they were looking for new members.

For Lofland, this would be an ideal group to study. Although he made it clear that he was interested in them only as a sociologist, they accepted him completely. (Eventually Lofland learned that the group believed he was divinely sent to them to become a convert.) Lofland immediately began to spend as much time with them as he could. He asked them several questions about their lives before they joined the Divine Precepts, their feelings about the group, and their daily activities. As soon as he was alone, he would make notes about all he had heard and seen. Sometimes he would record his observations on a tape recorder that he kept in his car. Lofland asked other sociologists to attend meetings of the Divine Precepts from time to time. Why do you suppose he did this?

A pattern emerges. Eventually, Lofland learned a great deal about the backgrounds of the cult's members. He discerned a pattern of characteristics and experiences that seemed to describe and perhaps explain why they had converted to an exotic religious group. Chart 2:B shows the seven steps of Lofland's hypothesis, or model, of the sequence of experiences that seemed to lead to conversion.

This model summarizes the main features of the converts' previous experiences and activities (Steps 1-4) and key events during contacts with the group (Steps 5-7). Because it was difficult to collect precise data in this setting, Lofland was not able to perform quantitative tests. His focus, rather, was on the *development* of a conception of how conversion occurs. Since Lofland's model was published in

2:B

A Person

Source: Society Today, Third Edition, Ziff-Davis Publishing Company, 1978

Predispositional Factors
Characteristics of individuals that they bring to the conversion process

1 The individual must experience an enduring, acutely felt tension or strain (for example, job failure or marital discord).

2 The person must hold a religiously oriented, problem-solving perspective. He or she may well have rejected conventional faith, but must still view the world in religious terms — see problems as having religious, as opposed to political or psychiatric, solutions.

3 On the basis of the first two characteristics, the person must be a religious seeker, one who is open to new religious outlooks.

4 When the person encounters the Divine Precepts group, he or she must be at, or very shortly coming to, a turning point in life. To convert, a person must be at a point in life when old lines of action and commitments are completed or have failed or been disrupted (or are about to be) and when the opportunity (or necessity) of doing something different arises. (For example, he or she may have just lost a job, been divorced, been graduated from school, or recovered from a long illness.)

Situational Factors
Characteristics of the interaction between an individual and the group

5 The potential convert must form or already possess a close, affective tie with one or more Divine Precepts members. Many converts already had such ties — they were married to, closely related to, or long-time friends with a Divine Precepts member. Others failed to convert until they had formed such a tie. In a sense, conversion meant coming to accept the beliefs of one's spouse, sibling, or friends.

6 Ties with persons outside the Divine Precepts group must be nonexistent or neutralized. Some probable converts were held back from conversion by the unwillingness of spouses to convert or by the counterpersuasion and pressure of friends and families. Converts typically lacked any ties that could restrain them, and, if they had ties, they were neutralized by distance.

7 To become an active Divine Precepts member, to move from verbal agreement to actually giving one's life to the movement, requires intensive, day-to-day interactions with group members. Some verbal converts whose physical circumstances prevent such interaction never become full converts. Others do so only when their circumstances change so that such interaction occurs.

A Convert

1966, however, it has been quantitatively tested by numerous other investigators with members of the Divine Precepts and with members of several other groups and has been found accurate.

Another observation. While developing and documenting his hypothesis about why people joined an unusual religious cult, Lofland also wanted to answer another question: How did a group like the Divine Precepts maintain its faith even when it failed to win new converts rapidly? Lofland believed that part of the answer lay in a pattern of activities that was repeated by the group again and again.

First, Lofland observed, the Divine Precepts would spend almost all their energies trying to recruit new members. When they had succeeded in getting about a dozen new people to attend their meetings, they would then concentrate on trying to convert them. After a few months, most (if not all) of the potential converts would drop out. When this happened, the members would begin an entirely different kind of project, one that would engross them for some time. At one point, they bought an old house and remodeled it. At another, they printed a book about their faith. The successful completion of one of these projects would give them renewed confidence in themselves. Then they would begin again the process of recruiting new members. It was this cyclical pattern, Lofland believed, that contributed to keeping the Divine Precepts going.

The most popular strategy of renewing their periodically failing hope was to disperse converts to nearby cities with orders to establish new centers and then to make new converts. At one point in their early years, the approximately 100 members they had acquired were scattered in about 25 cities. Such dispersal functioned not only to renew hope; it also contributed to making new converts. By 1977 the U.S. membership had grown to as much as 10,000 people living in 100 communes around the nation. However, in the 1980's membership began to decline and in 1987 was estimated to be less than 5,000.

The Sociologist as Experimenter

As a participant observer, John Lofland studied a religious cult in its actual environment. Sometimes, however, sociologists will *create* an environment in a laboratory in order to test its effects on human behavior. Laboratory experiments are designed to study social interaction under controlled conditions. In a laboratory, sociologists can reduce the number of variables affecting their studies and simplify them.

The Milgram experiment. In a laboratory experiment, Stanley Milgram learned that people are strongly inclined to be obedient to authority. After World War II, for example, many Nazis who had committed atrocities claimed that they were "only obeying orders." Usually people who are ruled by dictatorships obey orders without resisting. Milgram wondered whether people living in a free society would be more defiant if they were suddenly ordered to carry out cruel commands.

To find out, he designed a laboratory experiment at Yale University and tested more than a thousand people. Milgram advertised for volunteers in local newspapers. The ad said that they would be paid four dollars to take part in a one-hour "memory and learning test" conducted at Yale. It attracted people of many different occupations and ages to the plain basement of an elegant building on the Yale campus.

What happened when a volunteer arrived at Milgram's laboratory? He would first be introduced to a 31-year-old high school biology teacher who wore a white coat in his role as "experimenter." This was to enhance the experimenter's image as a scientist. Then the volunteer would be introduced to a second person, a 47-year-old accountant, who was also de-

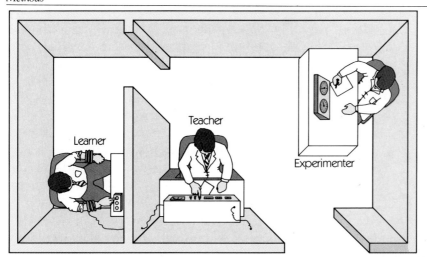

This diagram shows how Milgram set up his experiment.

scribed as a volunteer but was, in fact, Milgram's accomplice.

The experimenter would explain that he was testing the effect of punishment on learning and memory. The test, he indicated, was quite simple: One volunteer would serve as a "learner," the other as a "teacher." The learner would be required to memorize a long list of pairs of words, such as "slow-dance," "nice-day," and "blue-box." The learner was later required to pick the correct match from a list of several words read by the volunteer teacher. For example, the teacher would read: "Blue: sky, ink, box, lamp," and the learner was supposed to say, "Box."

Any time the learner forgot a word, the teacher would have to punish him with an electric shock. For each error, the teacher was instructed to raise the shock one level.

The experimenter then assigned the accomplice to be the learner and strapped him into an "electric chair." He assigned the real volunteer to be the teacher and seated him at the controls of an "electric-

The "shock generator" operated by the volunteer.

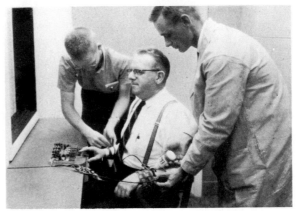

Strapping the accomplice into the "electric chair."

The volunteer-teacher gets his instructions.

The learner pretends great pain.

The teacher quits.

shock generator" in another room where he could hear but not see the learner. This generator, the experimenter said, could deliver shocks of from 15 to 450 volts to the learner strapped in the chair. The switches were clearly labeled from "Slight Shock" up to "Danger: Severe Shock," depending on their alleged voltage.

The volunteer teacher was then given a 45-volt sample of "slight" shock. It hurt considerably, and convinced him that more severe shocks would be terrible indeed. *This was the only real shock given in the entire test.*

Part of the transcript of Milgram's experiment follows. The teacher believes the learner is in great pain and has a bad heart. You may want to read the dialogue aloud with other classmates.

Learner *(whom the teacher can hear but not see)*: Ow, I can't stand the pain. Don't do that.

Teacher *(pivoting around in his chair and shaking his head)*: I can't stand it. I'm not going to kill that man in there. You hear him hollering?

Experimenter: As I told you before, the shocks may be painful, but —

Teacher: But he's hollering. He can't stand it. What's going to happen to him?

Experimenter *(in a patient, matter-of-fact voice)*: The experiment requires that you continue, Teacher.

Teacher: Aaah, but, unh, I'm not going to get that man sick in there — know what I mean?

Experimenter: Whether the learner likes it or not, we must go on.

From the film, OBEDIENCE, distributed by N.Y.U. Film Library, © 1965 by S. Milgram.

Teacher: I refuse to take the responsibility. He's in there hollering!

Experimenter: It's absolutely essential that you continue, Teacher.

Teacher (*indicating the unused questions*): There's too many left here. I mean, geez, if he gets them wrong, there's too many of them left. I mean, who's going to take the responsibility if anything happens to that gentleman?

Experimenter: I'm responsible for anything that happens to him. Continue, please.

Teacher: All right. (*He consults the list of words.*) The next one's "Slow: walk, truck, dance, music." Answer, please. (*A buzzing sound indicates the learner has signaled his answer.*) Wrong. A hundred and ninety-five volts. "Dance." (*Zzumph!*)

Learner: Let me out of here. My heart's bothering me!

(*Teacher looks at Experimenter.*)

Experimenter: Continue, please.

Learner (*screaming*): Let me out of here! You have no right to keep me here. Let me out of here, let me out, my heart's bothering me, let me out!

(*Teacher shakes his head, pats the table nervously.*)

Teacher: You see, he's hollering. Hear that? Gee, I don't know.

Experimenter: The experiment requires —

Teacher (*interrupting*): I know it does, sir, but I mean — hunh! He doesn't know what he's getting in for. He's up to 195 volts!

(*Experiment continues, through 210 volts, 225 volts, 240 volts, 255 volts,*

270 volts, delivered to the man in the electric chair, at which point the teacher, with evident relief, runs out of word-pair questions.)

Experimenter: You'll have to go back to the beginning of that page and go through them again until he's learned them all correctly.

Teacher: Aw, no. I'm not going to kill that man. You mean I've got to keep going up with the scale? No, sir. He's hollering in there. I'm not going to give him 450 volts.

Experimenter: The experiment requires that you go on.

Teacher: I know it does, but that man is hollering in there, sir.

Learner: Ohhh. I absolutely refuse to answer any more (*shouting urgently now*). Let me out of here. You can't hold me here. Get me out. Get — me — out — of — here.

Experimenter: Continue. The next word is "green," please.

Teacher: "Green: grass, hat, ink, apple." (*Nothing happens. No answering buzz. Just gloomy silence.*)

Teacher: I don't think he is going to answer.

Experimenter: If the learner doesn't answer in a reasonable time, about four or five seconds, consider the answer wrong. And follow the same procedures you have for wrong answers. Say, "Wrong"; tell him the number of volts; give him the punishment; read him the correct answer. Please continue, Teacher. Continue, please.

(*Teacher pushes lever. Zzumph!*)

Teacher (*swiveling around in his chair*):

Something's happened to that man in there. (*Swiveling back.*) Next one. "Low: dollar, necklace, moon, paint." (*Turning around again.*) Something's happened to that man in there. You better check in on him, sir. He won't answer or nothing.

Experimenter: Continue. Go on, please.

Teacher: You accept all responsibility?

Experimenter: The responsibility is mine. Correct. Please go on.

(*Teacher returns to his list, starts running through words as rapidly as he can read them, works through to 450 volts.*)

≈§ Why do you think the teacher obeyed the experimenter's instructions? What percentage of subjects do you think delivered the maximum 450-volt shock? Where do you think the largest group stopped? Your teacher can tell you Milgram's findings and conclusions.

The Hawthorne experiments. Some sociologists feel that experiments conducted in a laboratory do not accurately reflect real-life situations. They prefer to conduct their experiments in the field, that is, in actual prisons, factories, offices, etc., where variables may be observed in real-life settings.

Some of the most notable field experiments took place at the Western Electric Company's Hawthorne plant in Chicago between 1927 and 1932. These experiments, conducted by company personnel and a team of Harvard researchers, were first designed to find out whether there was a direct relationship between physical working conditions and the workers' rate of production. Would the workers produce more, for example, if the lighting was improved? To determine the effect of lighting on productivity, the researchers chose two groups of workers. For one, the test group, the amount of lighting was varied from time to time. For the other, the control group, the lighting remained constant. This was done to enable the researchers to make a comparison between the two groups.

Because of the precision and control with which researchers were able to conduct these experiments, they are considered classics in sociology.

To the researchers' surprise, they found that, no matter how they varied the lighting for the test group, its production increased. Even when the lights were extremely dim, the workers kept producing more! Just as surprising, the workers in the control group increased their production at the same rate as those in the test group.

The researchers came to the conclusion that the increased level of production in both groups had nothing to do with lighting. Rather it was due to the good feelings the workers had because they were receiving extra attention from the company. The effect of this extra attention was given a name which has become famous in the scientific community. It was called the *Hawthorne effect*. This term is now used to refer to any effect on an experiment caused by the experiment itself.

≈§ Can you identify the dependent variable in this experiment? The independent variable? What might the researchers have done to overcome the Hawthorne effect?

The Survey

When sociologists want to gather information about the opinions or behavior of large numbers of people, they conduct surveys. A survey may consist of questionnaires, interviews, or a combination of the two. Surveys are often used to predict how people will vote in elections, or to get people's opinions about various political and social issues.

The entire group that a researcher wants to study is called a *population*. There are limits, of course, to the number of people who can be questioned by a survey. If, for example, researchers wanted to find out what television programs high school students favored, it would be quite impractical to interview the entire population. The cost of such a survey would be staggering, and it would take a great deal of time.

As a result, sociologists generally question only a sample of the population whose opinions or views they seek. To make sure that the sample is representative and does not reflect any bias on their part, they use various techniques. One of them is similar to a lottery drawing. Sociologists select the survey group in a way that gives each person an equal chance of being chosen, such as drawing names from a box. Or they might take a long list of names — a voters' registration record, for example — and choose every fifth name. Both techniques are examples of *random sampling*.

A more sophisticated technique is to divide the number of people sociologists wish to learn about into a number of categories based on age, income, education, or other factors, and then pick a random sample from each. This is called *stratified random sampling*.

If you wanted to find the most popular television program with students in your school, which method would be most practical? A survey? A participant observation? A laboratory experiment? Why?

Faulty sampling can lead to erroneous conclusions, as this headline held by President Truman shows.

The Literary Digest survey. The accuracy of a survey depends not so much on the size of the samples as on the ability of the researcher to choose a true cross section of the group to be studied. In 1936, for example, a popular magazine called *The Literary Digest* attempted to predict the outcome of the Presidential election between Franklin D. Roosevelt, the Democratic candidate, and Alfred M. Landon, the Republican candidate. The *Digest* sent postcard ballots to 10 million people. About two million responded. When their ballots were tallied, Landon came out far ahead. The *Digest* predicted that Landon would win the Presidency by a landslide.

At the same time, George Gallup polled approximately 312,000 people and predicted that Roosevelt would win handily. Roosevelt, in fact, won every state in the nation except Maine and Vermont. The editors of *The Literary Digest* were shocked. How was it possible for a survey answered by two million people to be so inaccurate?

The fault, it was later discovered, lay in the technique the *Digest* had used to sample the voting population. The *Digest* had chosen the names of the people it polled from telephone books and automobile registration lists. During the Great Depression of the 1930's, when about one third of the population was living in impoverished circumstances, only middle- and upper-income people could afford to have telephones and cars. The well-off were mainly Republicans. As a result, the sample tested by the *Digest* was unrepresentative, despite its size. Those who were less well-off voted heavily in favor of Roosevelt, helping him to a landslide win. Although Gallup had polled many fewer people than *The Literary Digest*, he had used the stratified random sampling technique to obtain an accurate cross section of the entire voting population.

The accuracy of a survey depends not only on using scientific sampling techniques, but on the way that questions are worded. If people cannot understand the questions, or if their answers may be in-

interpreted in different ways, the survey is useless. For example, a survey should not include questions like: "What's wrong with city government?" or "Is garbage pick-up better than it used to be?"

Methods: An Evaluation

Choosing a method. In deciding how to study a particular subject, a sociologist is frequently faced with a number of difficult questions. Can human behavior be explained and predicted with the same precision, say, that a physicist can predict the movement of atoms? Sociologists would not make such a claim because people can consciously change their behavior, and atoms cannot. This does not mean that sociologists cannot make accurate generalizations about how groups of people will behave under certain circumstances, but simply that human behavior is more difficult to predict than that of atoms.

A major problem for sociologists is that when people are aware that they are being observed, they may not behave as they usually do. To get around the Hawthorne effect (described on page 44), sociologists occasionally mislead people. They may tell their subjects that they are studying one problem, while actually they are studying something else.

Stanley Milgrim, for example, told his subjects that they were taking part in an experiment to test the effect of punishment on learning, which was not at all true. He was really testing their willingness to obey authority. Later, other social scientists accused Milgrim of unethical

How to Read a Table

Sociologists often use statistical tables to report research findings. Newspapers, magazines, and textbooks publish tables showing the results of national and local surveys. Sociologists use the following six steps as guides for interpreting a table. The accompanying table is a model to help you apply these steps.

1. Read the title. The title tells you the subject of the table. Our table presents data on the willingness of Americans to vote for a woman for President.

2. Study the headnotes and footnotes. Many tables contain headnotes directly below the title. Headnotes may provide information about how data were collected, how large the sample was, and so on. The headnote in our table provides the question which the poll takers asked their respondents. Footnotes at the bottom of a table tell you the source of the data.

3. Read the headings for each column and row. The headings will tell you exactly what data are presented in the table. In our table, the column headings indicate that the researchers divided their data into three groups: national, women, and men. The row headings in our table tell you the years in which Gallup surveys were taken.

4. Examine the data. Carefully examine the data in the columns and the rows. Suppose you want to know what percentage of women would vote for a female president in 1971. First look down the rows to the left until you come to 1971. Then look across the columns until you find the one labelled "Women." By examining the data you will discover that 67 percent of women in 1971 would vote for a female for President.

5. Draw conclusions. As you examine the data, look for patterns that suggest possible conclusions. In our table, we can conclude that the percentage of people willing to vote for a woman for President has sharply increased since 1945. The data also shows that as many men as women would now vote for a female for President.

6. Pose new questions. Your conclusions can often lead to new research questions. Why, for example, did the percentage of women willing to vote for a female for President drop between 1955 and 1963? What caused the percentage of men willing to vote for a female president to rise during these same years? What impact did the 1984 vice-presidential candidacy of Geraldine Ferraro have upon the willingness of Americans to vote for a woman for President?

Thinking Critically

1. In what year did over half the population express a willingness to vote for a woman for President?

2. What conclusions do you think Democratic and Republican party leaders can reach from this table?

Willingness of Americans to Vote For a Woman President

Question: If your party nominated a woman for President, would you vote for her if she qualified for the job?

WOULD VOTE FOR WOMAN PRESIDENT (in percent)			
	National	Women	Men
1945	33	37	29
1949	48	51	45
1955	52	57	47
1963	55	51	58
1971	66	67	65
1978	76	77	75
1984	78	78	78
1987	82	83	81

SOURCE: Gallup poll.

conduct in duping his subjects.

Does a sociologist have the right to mislead people, or to risk exposing or hurting them in the name of scientific research? This question is controversial today on university campuses. Most universities now have human-subjects committees which decide if a sociologist's research is ethical. Ethical standards are still undefined, however, and many sociologists say that such committees restrain academic freedom. Most committees, however, insist that researchers explain the intent of their experiments to subjects and get their written consent to participate. If the committee agrees that some deception is necessary to perform an experiment, it usually requires sociologists to confer with their subjects at the conclusion of the experiment.

Now that you understand some of the ways in which sociologists go about their work, you are prepared to study some of their observations about patterns that human behavior can take. You can also use some of these methods yourself to make observations about the way people act and interact in groups.

application

To give you hands-on sociological experience, your teacher has instructions for conducting a survey.

summary

The **scientific method** is a set of procedures designed to increase the probability that research will lead to valid and accurate conclusions, free of personal biases or wishful thinking. The procedures consist of (1) defining the problem that is being studied; (2) forming a **hypothesis,** a statement that asserts a relationship between certain known facts; (3) collecting the **data,** or factual material, that will either prove or disprove the hypothesis; (4) analyzing the data; (5) forming a **theory,** or logical explanation of how certain facts are related.

Emile Durkheim, a French sociologist, was a pioneer in applying the scientific method to the study of human behavior. In his investigation of the causes of suicide, Durkheim formed the hypothesis that social forces influence the suicide rate. Durkheim investigated such social forces as religion, marital status, military status, and economic conditions. Durkheim used government records in his study. This method is called **secondary research,** because the researcher depends on someone else to collect the data he studies. Durkheim's analysis of official suicide records led him to the conclusion that there were three distinct patterns of suicide, which he labeled egoistic, altruistic, and anomic. These patterns described the way in which people were linked to social groups. Durkheim's theory was that suicide was clearly related to these links. Very little commitment to groups and group norms could produce **egoistic suicide.** Too much commitment could produce **altruistic suicide.** Rapid social change was likely to shake group links and increase chances of **anomic suicide.**

Since Durkheim's time, sociologists have developed new and more advanced techniques to explore the ways in which individual behavior is shaped by social groups. A sociologist who wants to study a group intensively will join it and take part in its daily activities; this method is called **participant observation.** A sociologist who wishes to study human behavior under controlled conditions will conduct an **experiment** in a laboratory or in the actual environment of the group being investigated. A sociologist who wants to gather information about a large group of people will conduct a **survey** consisting of questionnaires, interviews, or both. The accuracy of a survey depends on the ability of the sociologist to choose a true cross section of the group being studied. **Random sampling,** which is similar to a lottery drawing, gives every member of the group an equal chance of being selected and generally assumes that the sample will be representative. Sociologists try to frame survey questions that are easily understood and that can be answered as simply as possible.

Although sociologists strive for the same objectivity and accuracy in their research as all other scientists, their task is complicated by the fact that human behavior is quite changeable. Often, when people are aware that they are being observed, they do not react "normally." This is called the **Hawthorne effect,** in recognition of the studies in which it was discovered. Some sociologists have deliberately misled subjects about the nature of their investigations in order to obtain more valid results. Many sociologists deplore the use of deception in experiments, no matter how useful or humane the researchers' intentions may be. Increasingly, academic institutions have developed safeguards to protect the rights of individual subjects.

more questions and activities

1. List and explain five steps in the scientific method.

2. Name Durkheim's three categories of suicide and tell how each is related to group life.

3. Describe three types of research methods that sociologists use. Give an advantage and a disadvantage of each.

4. In 1984, 1,694 teenagers in the United States between the ages of 15 and 19 took their own lives. The suicides of teenagers and young adults was 40 percent higher in the 1980's than it was in the 1970's. Suppose you are a sociologist looking for causes of this increase. What would be your dependent variable? What independent variables would you investigate? What method would you use in your investigation?

5. In November 1978, U.S. Representative Leo J. Ryan was killed in Jonestown, Guyana, in South America, while investigating the People's Temple, a cult. Shortly afterward, the cult's leader, the Reverend Jim Jones, persuaded or coerced some 900 members of the cult to commit suicide with him. In what ways would your understanding of this event be increased by the research of Emile Durkheim and John Lofland? (You might examine magazine and newspaper articles about this event to give you more information about what took place.)

6. Obtain copies of *The American Journal of Sociology, Social Research, The American Sociological Review,* or other professional sociology publications. Make a list of subjects investigated by sociologists reporting to these journals. In each example, what method was used? Do you think the method was the only method that might have been used? If not, what other method could be used to research the same subject?

7. Conduct a participant observation of a school club, team, or musical group. What patterns of behavior can you find? Are they repeated and predictable? Do they apply to other organizations in your school?

8. In your school, conduct a survey to determine student opinion on some subject of common interest, such as the kind of food served in the school cafeteria or what kind of music should be played at school dances.

9. Conduct a class debate on the issue of deception or informed consent as a technique in conducting a scientific investigation.

10. Examine the photographs throughout the chapter. How many different methods of research can you find evidence of? Name them.

suggested readings

Cole, Stephen. *The Sociological Method.* 2nd ed. (Rand McNally, 1976.) A fine introduction to the basic concepts and logic of sociological research. Chapter One, "The Sociological Perspective," contains excellent summaries of several research projects, including Durkheim's study of suicide.

Light, Donald Jr., and Suzanne Keller. *Sociology.* (Alfred A. Knopf, 1985.) Chapter Two, "Science and Methods in Sociology," of this outstanding college- level introductory textbook is a clearly written and interesting overview of basic sociological methods.

Lofland, John. *Doomsday Cult.* (Prentice-Hall, 1966.) The full account of Lofland's participant observation of a radical religious group.

Marx, Gary T., ed. *Muckraking Sociology.* (Transaction Books, 1972.) An interesting collection of articles from the journal *Society* which illustrate how sociological research can be used to analyze important social problems.

Milgram, Stanley. *Obedience to Authority.* (Harper and Row, 1974.) Milgram's description of what happened and why in his famous experiment.

Plath, Sylvia. *The Bell Jar.* (Harper and Row, 1971; Bantam [paperback], 1975.) A bright young woman struggles for a self-identity and against the forces that led to a suicide attempt. This largely autobiographical novel demonstrates many of the dynamics of egoistic suicide that Durkheim documented.

Reynolds, P.D. *Ethics and Social Science Research* (Prentice Hall, 1982.) The author discusses the ethical problems which confront social researchers as they conduct their experiments.

Zimbardo, Philip, et al. "The Mind Is a Formidable Jailer: A Pirandellian Prison." (*The New York Times Magazine,* April 8, 1973.) A vivid description of psychologist Zimbardo's experimental study of the effects of prison on volunteers who played the roles of guards and prisoners.

A Yanomamo girl with cultural symbols of beauty.

chapter 3

culture

Imagine for a moment that you have just completed a three day journey deep into the jungles of southern Venezuela. After docking your small rowboat along the banks of a muddy river, you begin to follow a trail to a nearby Indian village. Soon your face and hands are swollen from the bites of small gnats. Your clothes are soaked with perspiration from the humid jungle heat.

When you finally reach the village wall, you push back the dry palm leaves. A dozen men with bows and drawn arrows greet you. These are the Yanomamo. They hunt wild animals and gather bananas and other fruits for food. Their clothes consist of a few cotton strings. They have not invented a way to write their language.

Fierce fighters, they are almost always at war with other villages. Violent deaths claim the lives of at least one-fourth of all adult male Yanomamos.

This was the experience of an American social scientist named Napoleon Chagnon. When Chagnon first visited the Yanomamo they had almost no contact with the outside world.

Judging from Chagnon's description of his first encounter with the Yanomamo you might conclude that they have no culture. But a sociologist would say that the Yanomamo are just as "cultured" as we are. Sociologists use the word *culture* to refer to a group's way of life — its knowledge, customs, values, beliefs, and material creations.

Left, Yanomamo child and man being painted. Bottom left, making a basket and meal. Above, Yanomamo couple.

The Impact of Culture

Ironically, although the impact of culture on behavior is enormous, for the most part, people are not even aware of it. We simply take for granted that our ways of doing things are "natural" without realizing that in other societies these ways might not seem natural at all.

In the United States, for example, we assume that monogamy is natural — a man has one wife, and a woman has one husband. To enforce this norm, we have laws forbidding bigamy. In Moslem societies, however, a man may have as many as four wives (if he can afford them). And in Jaunswar Bawar in the Himalaya Mountains, when a woman marries her fiancé, she automatically marries his brother as well. To our way of thinking, this may be "abnormal" and "immoral," but those societies consider it perfectly natural.

All people must eat, of course, but it is culture that largely shapes *what* and *how* they should eat. We might not understand the Hindus' aversion to eating beef, just as the Chinese find our aversion to eating dogs equally hard to understand. In most parts of the world, people must wear clothes, but it is culture that shapes what kind of clothes they wear, and what parts of the body are covered.

Because of the vast differences which separate the Yanomamo culture from our own, researchers who have lived with and studied the Yanomamo have faced a number of difficult decisions. For example: Should the Yanomamo be given steel tools and shotguns? Should they be given a ride in an airplane to see Caracas (the capital of Venezuela)?

You may want to think more about the Yanomamo as you read this chapter. In it we'll discuss how culture shapes our lives by giving meaning to the things we do and make. And you'll learn some of the concepts sociologists and anthropologists use to describe culture. (While sociologists have generally studied the way of life in modern, industrial societies, anthropologists have traditionally studied the way of life in nonliterate, simple societies. In more recent times, the two social sciences have grown closer together in the societies they study.)

⊷§ List as many different ways as you can that people in other cultures eat, dress, and build homes.

Culture shock. All human groups tend to believe that their way of life, which has been handed down from generation to generation, is the "right" way. Because their own values and norms are so ingrained, people of one culture sometimes become upset when they are confronted with those of another culture. Ordinarily, people can adjust fairly easily to variations in dress, eating habits, and daily routines. But if they visit or must live in another society where people's basic values and customs are drastically different from their own, they are likely to suffer severe stress, which sociologists call *culture shock*. An American might have culture shock living with the Yanomamo.

The following article, adapted from *This World*, the magazine of the *San Francisco Chronicle*, describes a Peace Corps volunteer's culture shock upon encountering life in a village in Ecuador:

I had become friendly with a farm family that also ran a little café out on the road where the buses stopped. One morning I was sitting around waiting for a bus to take me down to the next village, when one of the farmer's sons and his wife sat down by me. She was holding a baby in her arms who was dying of pneumonia, and I sat there listening to that unbearable gasping struggle for breath while the family calmly gathered around the child and watched. Only the mother seemed to be upset.

I was sure that they were waiting for the bus to rush the baby to a doctor, but as the bus came closer and into sight, they made no move. Suddenly, using the most beautiful Spanish of my life, completely out of control, I was screaming at them. "Your baby's going to die," I shouted. "You've got to get him to a doctor. Now. Now."

The young mother began to pant. Her husband looked to his father who simply nodded his

head in a sort of permission without saying anything, and the young couple ran down to the road and stopped the bus.

When I got back that night, they told me that the baby was dead. The next afternoon I was about a mile from town buying some pineapples from a farmer, just past the graveyard. As I was coming back, I met the funeral procession, the toylike coffin painted in white and sprinkled with a silver dust. . . . It was negligently packed on a farmer's shoulder.

Behind him, and strung out for a hundred yards, the family and their friends followed. The men carried bottles of trago [liquor], stumbling and reeling in the mud of the trail. But while they advanced with a sort of dignity, there was also something slapstick about it. Some of them stopped to offer me a drink.

The statistics, of course, I knew — in the country areas of Ecuador, three out of five babies die before their third year. And I was also aware that [the parents] believe that, when a baby dies, it dies in a state of grace and flies directly to heaven.

Within this framework, then, the death of a

Peace Corp worker in Ecuador.

child is something to celebrate; he has been released without sin from a life of suffering and poverty to become one of God's angels, but knowing
all this, I still could not accept it. Two mornings
later, drinking coffee in the same little café and
once more waiting for a bus, I had to leave and
stand in a drizzle of rain to keep from watching
another baby dying. The calmness with which they
accepted his death was obscene to me.

I began to develop a grudge against the town
and would make wild generalizations in my mind
about the town and the people in it. By the end of
the second week, I had pretty much decided that I
really didn't like the people and that it would be
impossible to work with them.

What I was going to do in that unrewarding
spot for 18 more months was something that,
when I seriously thought about it, sent me reeling
into a real depression. I locked myself into my
room for about three days. . . .

Well, I got straightened around, but it took
at least a month. And I write about this experience
now not because it is particularly interesting, but
because it is so typical of a volunteer's first reactions to another, a different culture.

⇥ Can you think of any situations in
which you experienced culture shock?
These need not be as severe as the one
experienced by the Peace Corps volunteer.
Simply visiting the city if you live in a
rural area, or visiting the country if you
live in a city might produce a mild culture
shock.

Culture as a system of meaning. The
culture of a society gives distinctive meanings to what its members do and the
things they make. These meanings may
differ greatly from culture to culture.

The Oglala Sioux, for example, traditionally arranged their tepees in a circle,

and sat in a circle at ceremonies. These
practices stemmed from a religious belief:
The Great Spirit caused everything in nature — the sun, the moon, the earth, the
sky — to be round. The circle, therefore,
was a sacred symbol to the Oglala Sioux.

In our society, the automobile is
more than just a form of transportation. It
embodies important American values such
as freedom, mobility, individualism, and
technological progress.

Culture has such a pervasive impact
on our lives that it gives meaning even to
our gestures. Often we assume that common gestures are "instinctive" and universal, but in fact they vary greatly among
different cultures. Americans who take the
meaning of their own gestures for granted
would be amazed to find how little the
same gestures would be understood in
other societies.

Our gesture for saying yes, for example, is to nod the head up and down. But
in northern Japan, the Ainu people bring
both hands up to the chest and gracefully
wave them downward. In India, a Bengali
swings his head in an arch from shoulder
to shoulder about four times.

⇥ What gestures would Americans use
to express the following:
    To say no?
    To show respect?
    To indicate an object across a room?
    To greet someone?
    Your teacher can tell you different
gestures that would be used for these purposes in other cultures.

    Just as culture gives distinctive mean-

The raised hand has many meanings in our culture. How many can you list?

ings to gestures, it may also define what is real and unreal in different societies. In the Western world, which exalts science and reason, we tend to believe that reality can be seen, touched, measured, and weighed. But what about things such as witches, demons, spirits, and black magic? Are they real or merely fantasies? In our culture, belief in them would probably be attributed to ignorance and/or superstition. Yet there was a time when witches and demons were terrifyingly real for people of the Western world, and they are today in many cultures.

Father Alphonse Sowada tells of the real consequences of black magic among members of the Asmat tribe in New Guinea. The following excerpt is from an article by Father Sowada in a book titled *Vanishing Peoples of the Earth:*

In my early days at Erma, Saati and others had told me that drugs — even the most powerful — could not counteract malevolent magic. Once under the spell, the victim "carried it around" until it produced death. No one could name a person who had survived its ravages.

Normally the older Asmat women possess the power of creating black magic. A woman sits quietly and meditates in an area behind her home, and at some point she may determine that she needs the aid of a companion. Men explained to me that the efforts of two or even three women together are better than those of one. The men had not learned all the ingredients for the potent mixture, but they knew some: dog's tooth and liver, snake's tooth and head, pig's hoof, bird's beak, frog's eye, man's hair and nail parings.

In proper sequence, the sorceress combines all or a selection of these in a small grass bag that she hides in the thatch of her house to "ripen."

Meanwhile, the malevolent power seeps into an imaginary arrow also in the bag. The female avenger patiently awaits the proper moment to inflict the magic on the victim, for sooner or later he must pass her home, and when he does, she shoots him with the invisible arrow. The news soon spreads, and the victim, hypnotized by fear, dies within a day, a week, or a month.

Dekes, a healthy man of about 25, had worked every day sawing lumber at a project started by the mission for the Asmat. One morning when he failed to report, I asked his whereabouts.

"He is sick," one of the men told me. "Very likely he will not be coming to work again."

"Why? What ails him?" I inquired.

"Dekes was inflicted with aro pok *(black magic) yesterday afternoon," he replied as he turned away.*

I immediately walked toward Dekes' hut; and as I neared it, I heard his female relatives wailing the death chant. When I climbed into the house, I found Dekes lying on a mat, immobile and deaf to my shouts. I began to slap his face, and soon his eyes fluttered open. I sat him up, rolled him some tobacco, and ordered him to smoke it.

Then I told him to follow me. I pointed to the lumberyard and commanded. "Now work; your sickness is gone." Dekes complied without any ill effects, much to the surprise, I'm sure, of some of his fellow villagers.

What do sociologists conclude from such phenomena as the belief in black magic? Regardless of what *actually* exists, they say, people act on the basis of what they *believe* exists. If men and women define a situation as real, they will act as though it is real, even though it has no reality by scientific standards. And it is the culture of a society that defines what is real at any given time.

The Elements of Culture

Symbols. The meanings that people attach to the things they do and make are conveyed by symbols. Words, of course, are our most important symbols. The word *school,* for example, immediately conveys an image of a building with classrooms, blackboards, desks, books, and other equipment for learning.

Yet many important symbols aren't words at all. A four-leaf clover symbolizes luck. A gold band worn on the third finger of the left hand is a symbol of marriage. Basically, a *symbol* is any object, gesture, color, design, sound, or word that represents something other than itself.

Symbols have particular meanings in each society, and these can change over a given time period. During World War II, for example, British Prime Minister Winston Churchill familiarly made a "V" sign with his fingers that stood for victory over the Nazi enemy, a gesture that was copied by Britain's allies all over the world. But in the 1960's, young men and women who opposed U.S. participation in the Vietnam War used the same gesture as a symbol for peace.

❧ Colors are another symbol whose meaning may change from culture to culture. The chart below shows what four colors mean in a variety of other nations. Can you tell what each color symbolizes in our culture?

Green — forgiving (France).
Yellow — envy (Italy, Germany).
Red — beauty and life (Russia).
White — mourning (Korea, China).

One Eskimo tribe has a dozen words for snow. *Top left,* oqaalugait *is hard enough for blocks.* Pukajaq, *top right, is soft for cooking and drinking. Above, symbols for* peace, money exchange, information, *and* ban the bomb. *Below, the Manual Alphabet for the deaf.*

A a B b C c D d E e F f G g H h I i J j K k L l M

Language. All culture is learned, and the chief vehicle of learning is language. *Language* is a system of verbal and, in many cases, written symbols. Language enables people to preserve meanings and experiences. Through words, the accumulated knowledge, beliefs, values, and technology of a society are passed on to each succeeding generation.

The study of languages often gives us insights into a group's culture. The number of words that people use to represent a particular object usually indicates how important it is to them. The Hopi Indians, for example, had numerous ways of describing water, which was a precious commodity in their desert environment. Among the Hanunoo of the Philippines, there are 92 ways to say *rice,* their staple food.

◄§ If this sounds absurd, name as many words as you can that we have to represent the automobile.

Language not only reflects a people's culture but, according to linguists Edward Sapir and Benjamin Whorf, it may also shape their thoughts as well. This assertion is known as the *Sapir-Whorf hypothesis.*

An experiment conducted among a group of bilingual Japanese American women seemed to support this hypothesis by revealing a definite connection between languages and the cultural ideals they expressed.

The women were asked a number of questions in Japanese. Later they were asked the same questions in English. The responses were quite different, depending

on the language that was used. One woman responded in this fashion:

1. When my wishes conflict with my family's . . .
   (the answer in Japanese) . . . it is a time of great unhappiness.
   (the answer in English) . . . I do what I want.
2. I will probably become . . .
   (the answer in Japanese) . . . a housewife.
   (the answer in English) . . . a teacher.
3. Real friends should . . .
   (the answer in Japanese) . . . help each other.
   (the answer in English) . . . be very frank.

Sapir and Whorf maintain that language accounts for many of the differences between cultures. The Japanese language, for example, is given to polite understatement. Because of this penchant for understatement, an interpreter must not only be skilled in the language, but must also be familiar with the culture.

In *Japan: The Fragile Superpower*, Frank Gibney tells how a Canadian sales manager in Japan once gave his employees a tongue-lashing for failing to meet their quota of orders. Speaking to them in English he said: "How can you people call yourselves salesmen? You don't know the first thing about selling. You've paid no attention to anything I've told you. I'm surprised that you can stand there and look me in the face. Now what do you plan to do about it?"

The manager's resourceful Japanese interpreter translated his words in this fashion: "I have the highest regard for your abilities. But I would not be completely honest if I did not permit myself to express disappointment in your recent performance."

Given the differences between the two cultures, the translation was quite accurate. Had the interpreter translated the manager's words literally, the sales manager would have appeared to the Japanese to have lost his senses. The salesmen would have been deeply humiliated. And the interpreter would have "lost face" for conveying the manager's insults.

Imagine that you are the interpreter for a group of Japanese baseball players. An American coach has given them the following speech: "Listen, you slobs. This sloppy playing has got to go. Mikado, you butterfingers, don't let me see you miss another fly ball, or out you go. Yukio, a baby could bat better than you did your last time up. OK now, you idiots, get out there and play ball."

Now you must translate this speech in order not to offend the players. How would you translate it into polite English?

The silent language of culture. Cultural differences, as we have seen, are often reflected in the ways that societies use language and other symbols. Edward T. Hall, an anthropologist, contends that cultural differences are also reflected in the ways that people perceive time and space. In his book, *The Silent Language*, Hall says that these perceptions "speak" as much as words and other symbols; they comprise, in effect, the silent language of culture.

Americans, Hall maintains, are a clock-bound people, acutely aware of time. We regard it as a commodity. We say, for example, "Time is money," and that time can be bought, sold, spent, wasted, lost, made up, and measured.

Sometimes we even regard time as a hostile force. An advertisement for an office dictation machine stated the case plainly. Featuring a close-up of a watch dial, it proclaimed: "This is the face of the enemy. Win the battle against time with the Lanier Action-Line Dictation System."

Not all cultures are as obsessed with "beating the clock" as our own. What happens when Americans find themselves in a society that has a more relaxed attitude toward time? The result may be culture shock.

This was the case when a new attaché of the U.S. embassy in a Latin American country made an appointment to visit a local official. Because Americans value promptness, the attaché appeared at the official's office a minute or two before the appointed hour. He was asked to have a seat and wait. After 15 minutes passed, the attaché reminded the official's secretary of his appointment. When 45 minutes had passed, the attaché became incensed. He informed the secretary that he had been "cooling his heels" for a long time and that he was "sick and tired" of such treatment. The secretary relayed this message to the official, whose answer, in effect, was, "Let him cool his heels."

The attaché was insulted and confused by this delay. What he failed to understand was that the local official was not acting impolitely according to his own standards. To the official, a wait of 45 minutes was the equivalent of only a five-minute delay in the U.S. He could not understand why the attaché was so unreasonable.

Attitudes toward space, or distance, also vary widely in different cultures. Americans, for example, are taught from early childhood to avoid body contact with strangers. When we ride a crowded bus or elevator, we try to "hold ourselves in" to avoid touching others, if possible. In many other cultures, however, people are much less squeamish about body contact; it may not bother them at all.

Hall identifies four distinct "zones" in which people in our culture communicate. The first, or *intimate,* zone ranges from a lover's embrace to about 18 inches. If a person in casual conversation comes closer than 18 inches, Hall says, someone in the U.S. will back away. Similarly, one can offend that person deliberately by invading the intimate zone. A military drill sergeant, for example, might yell at a recruit from a distance of a few inches in order to intimidate the recruit.

Hall's second, or *personal,* zone is from 18 inches to four feet. Most personal conversation takes place in this zone.

Although most people in our culture would not talk privately beyond four feet, Hall says, it would be permissible for guests at a large party or co-workers to converse across a space of four to 12 feet. He calls this third zone *social distance.*

What zones are illustrated in these photos?

Hall's fourth zone, 12 feet and beyond, is called *public distance.* From this distance, a speaker addresses an audience, but the speaker's voice becomes formal rather than conversational.

Hall's zones seem remarkably accurate in describing U.S. and Canadian customs; but, as any tourist can observe, people across the Mexican border converse, casually, well within the 18-inch intimate zone. Arabs operate on presumptions of distance that might seem strange to all North Americans. It is not unusual for Arabs to converse nose to nose; yet, when possible, they enjoy large, airy rooms and might sit down to talk in chairs 40 feet apart.

Norms and values. Every culture has rules that define appropriate or desirable behavior for its members. These rules, as you know, are called *norms,* and derive from the group's values. Yet what might be perfectly appropriate behavior in one culture may seem utterly shocking to members of another.

During World War I, for example, an anthropologist on a Pacific island described to a cannibal the terrible slaughter that was then taking place on European battlefields. Literally millions of soldiers, he said, had already been slain. The cannibal seemed puzzled and asked how Europeans could possibly eat so much human flesh. The anthropologist explained that Europeans did not eat the bodies of their enemies. The cannibal looked horrified. His voice shaking, he asked the anthropologist, "What kind of barbarians are you that you kill human beings for no good reason?"

Analyzing Cultures

Similarities in culture. The more we examine the world's cultures, the more we are struck by their great diversity. No two cultures, in fact, are exactly alike, and the variations among them are often startling. Yet if there are great differences, there are also basic needs common to all.

As we saw in Chapter 1, every society must meet certain needs if it is to survive. It must produce and train young people. It must find a way of enforcing its moral values and explaining existence; it must provide food and shelter; and it must maintain order and security. How a culture copes with the problems of survival depends to a great extent on the physical environment — location, terrain, climate, and natural resources.

For example, anthropologists were long puzzled by the fact that the ancient Aztecs, who developed a highly advanced civilization in Mexico, had no wheeled vehicles. Was it possible that such skilled artisans and builders did not know about the wheel? Then a number of Aztec children's toys with wheels were discovered. The Aztecs knew about wheels; they simply didn't find them useful in their mountainous terrain.

Variation in culture. Anthropologists have estimated that there are about 4,000 distinct human societies throughout the world. One way their culture patterns vary may be seen in a participant observation by Margaret Mead (1901-1978). She studied sex roles in three societies of New

Religion is part of every culture. Jews at the Wailing Wall in Jerusalem; left, Hindus at their sacred Ganges River in India; below, an American Christian prays.

Guinea — the Arapesh, the Mundugumor, and the Tchambuli. Her observations were recorded in a study titled *Sex and Temperament in Three Primitive Societies.*

The Arapesh, Mead said, are a very gentle people who regard competitiveness and aggression as abnormal behavior. They do not believe that there are temperamental differences between the sexes. Both men and women care for children, handling them with great tenderness. When a child cries, the nearest man or woman rushes to comfort it.

The neighboring Mundugumor are just as fierce as the Arapesh are gentle. Aggression and combativeness characterize the behavior of both sexes. The shy or submissive person, whether male or female, is regarded as a misfit. Hostility between members of the same sex is strong; a father considers his son a rival. Hostility between men and women is almost as marked. Women resent childbearing as a hardship and give their children very little attention. The children are expected to fend for themselves as soon as they can walk.

Among the Tchambuli, Mead found a complete reversal of the sex roles that prevail in Western societies. In this group, men are regarded as the weaker sex. Women do the fishing and farming, and decide how much money their husbands may spend. The men adorn their bodies and practice what we would call "feminine wiles." The women are kind and tolerant toward their men, but do not take them very seriously.

From her studies of these societies, Mead concluded that many characteristics that we ascribe to men and women as biological in their origin are "mere variations of human temperament to which members of either or both sexes may . . . be educated to approximate."

Though cultural variations such as Mead found in New Guinea may seem quite bizarre to us, anthropologists and sociologists take a more objective view of them. They see all cultural variations as different solutions to the common problems of survival.

Ethnocentrism. Every culture is inclined to believe that its own way of life is right and natural, while other cultures are rather odd, and sometimes downright uncivilized. When, for example, European nations began carving empires in China early in the 19th century, the clash of cultures was extremely pronounced. To the Chinese, the Europeans were little more than savages, hardly able to read, incapable of understanding the teachings of Confucius, and outrageously ill-mannered. To the Europeans, the Chinese were barbarians, who worshiped heathen idols and were unable to appreciate the blessings of Western technology. In short, each group saw the other as sadly lacking in "civilization."

The tendency to see one's own group as superior to all others is called *ethnocentrism.* It applies to whole societies as well. For example, we often use the term *American society* to refer to that of the United States, even though Canada and Mexico are also located on the North American continent. Feelings of superior-

Definitions of beauty tend to be ethnocentric. Beauty as defined by the culture of Morocco, above; French Guiana's Oyana Indians, left; South African Zulus, below left; and Japan, below.

ity based on race, religion, or national origin are common to numerous groups within the United States and many other societies. Ethnocentrism, in fact, pervades groups of every size and variety. It is our team, our school, our club, and our town that is the best — naturally.

When ethnocentrism is tempered, it can be a positive value, instilling pride in one's heritage and a sense of self-worth. It can boost a group's morale and help the group function together.

In its more extreme forms, ethnocentrism can be ugly and vicious. Often it leads to intolerance that may have devastating consequences for a society, or even the world. Adolf Hitler, the Nazi dictator, proclaimed in the 1930's that Germans were "the master race"; this belief was used to rationalize incalculable death, destruction, and suffering for those, particularly Jews, outside this "race."

🌿 After studying Chart 3:A, see how many ethnocentric attitudes you can add to each list. In each example, the idea is to describe the same thing; the attitude should be positive when it describes "us" and negative when it describes "them."

Symbolic clash of two cultures. What happens when two cultures with widely different customs collide? The following story by Lisa Hobbs, adapted from the *San Francisco Chronicle*, is an example:

Alice Springs, Australia — Here in the "dead heart" of Australia, where the desert is ochre-red and the air like an oven, people are talking about the case of Tjapaltjari.

Tjapaltjari is a 40-year-old aborigine not far removed from the Stone Age. Like all members of the Pintubi tribe, he has had no contact with the white man.

Until recently, Tjapaltjari hunted kangaroos with stone spearheads, dug in the hot sands for witchery grubs, and generally lived a life dominated by tribal custom. Today Tjapaltjari is in the Darwin jail . . . for manslaughter.

Last July, his young bride committed adultery with Tjangala, a young warrior of the tribe. According to tribal mores, the act was not only adulterous but incestuous. Death to both parties was the traditional penalty. So Tjapaltjari killed his wife with a 20-foot kangaroo spear. Tjangala fled to the security of white civilization after being speared in the leg by another male.

White territorial police charged Tjapaltjari with murder. Unaware of what was happening, the aborigine was taken to Darwin and tried in the Supreme Court.

3:A

Ethnocentric Attitudes

Our people are:	But their people are:
Good debaters	Quarrelsome
Patriots	Warmongers
Cultivated	Snobbish
Eccentric	Odd
True believers	Heathens
Robust	Fat
Athletes	Jocks
Restrained	Heartless

Many people here feel that the essence of the trial — the head-on collision between two unbridgeable cultures — was summed up in the first few moments. The judge appeared in the stifling little courthouse in traditional black robes and white, curled wig. The defendant appeared stark naked. Across his forehead he wore the distinctive red tribal band of the Pintubis; his long, matted hair was sleeked back by lizard fat. The judge ordered that the defendant be clothed, and Tjapaltjari was put into the only available garment — an old army greatcoat.

With the help of a Pintubi interpreter, the charge was reduced to manslaughter. Tjapaltjari was sentenced to one year in prison.' To this sentence was added a precedent-making rider. If imprisonment proves "harmful" to the defendant, he is to be released immediately.

. . . The judge's well intentioned rider has stirred a hornet's nest. Some people see the sentence as a sensible yet humanitarian step forward. Formerly, nomadic aborigines who fell afoul of the law were imprisoned even if confinement resulted in death. Others categorize the trial as a cruel farce and say that the ambivalence of the sentence proves it. Tjapaltjari committed no crime according to the laws of his own society. Why should he respect the laws of an alien society that has given him nothing?

◆§ What do you think?

Cultural relativity. The story of Tjapaltjari describes a conflict produced by widely varying cultural norms. Wide variations can be found in every area of culture, including marriage, values, religion, government, and economics. So, how can we judge what cultural customs are right or wrong, good or bad?

Many sociologists say that there are no absolute standards that can be used to evaluate them. Each must be viewed in the light of the whole culture and judged on the basis of the function it performs. Sociologists call this way of studying customs *cultural relativity.* It often leads to the conclusion that what may be unthinkable in one society may make a lot of sense in another.

For example, the fierce Yanomamo encourage young boys to strike their parents in the face! This practice, of course, seems outrageous to us. But when it is examined in the context of the Yanomamo culture, it becomes more understandable. The Yanomamo spend much of their time defending themselves against raids by enemy tribes, or carrying out raids of their own. If Yanomamo parents did not encourage aggressive behavior in a boy, he would be poorly equipped to survive in their society.

Cultural integration. When the people of "modern" societies attempt to "improve" the technology and customs of "backward" societies, though their intentions may be the best, the results are often disastrous.

The introduction of the steel ax to an aboriginal Australian group, for example, virtually destroyed its entire culture system. Like the Yanomamo, these people still employed primitive stone tools. To the aborigines, the stone ax was a rare and wondrous object. It was used in religious ceremonies as a symbol of their ancestry. Because of its great value, both as a symbol and a practical tool, it was entrusted to the safekeeping of a few elderly men of high rank. If a young man wanted to bor-

Cultural Integration in Japan

Arthur Golden, an American expert on Japanese culture, uses the following story to illustrate a central difference between Japanese and American values: "A Japanese friend told me of a class of third grade children who were given pencils and paper and asked to draw something. They responded by asking what they, as a group, were expected to draw, and would not begin until they received an answer."

The students in Golden's story behaved properly by Japanese standards. Rather than attempt to create unique individual drawings, they chose instead to display their group unity. Golden believes that the value placed upon group consciousness is responsible for the high degree of cultural integration that exists in Japan.

Japanese schools play an important role in teaching proper group behavior. For example, all students wear a common group uniform. First graders quickly learn to stand and bow when their teacher enters the room. Unlike American schools, which encourage students to think for themselves, Japanese classroom activities stress the importance of the group. "Students don't have to be able to discuss," a leading Japanese educator explains. "They just say, 'Yes, I understand.' The system does not encourage great creativity or individuality."

The best students in Japan aspire to work for the nation's giant corporations. These companies reinforce the classroom training in group unity. Corporations frequently require their employees to wear uniforms. Once on the job, workers address one another by the title of their position instead of by their names.

Japanese workers are expected to place their company's interest ahead of their own careers. Most employees work for the same company their entire career. They demonstrate their commitment by working long hours or staying on the job until their immediate supervisors have left for the day.

A typical business day usually includes a number of lengthy meetings. Participants do not claim credit for specific ideas or programs. Instead they strive for group consensus. Once a decision is reached, it becomes the group's opinion.

The high value placed upon group consciousness helps generate a number of important social norms. At parties Japanese hosts frown upon guests who break off into informal cliques. Social norms require everyone to stick together. Other social norms discourage bitter public disputes. People are expected to hide feelings which may cause ill will and therefore disrupt the group.

The Japanese provide sociologists with an example of a complex society that maintains a high degree of cultural integration. Their core of commonly held values and norms contributes to Japan's low crime rate and high industrial productivity. At the same time, they discourage individual initiative and creativity.

Thinking Critically

1. How do Japanese schools teach group unity? How do American schools emphasize individualism?

2. What are the advantages for the Japanese of having a high level of cultural integration? What are the disadvantages?

row it, he had to convince the elders that he was worthy of such a privilege. This meant, of course, that he had not violated any of the tribe's essential norms. So the ax was an important way of maintaining social control within the group.

Then Europeans brought with them modern technology — the steel ax. Any tribesman could obtain one from a trader or missionary, and it was superior as a tool to the traditional stone ax. Did life among the aborigines improve? On the contrary, the availability of steel axes produced a breakdown of authority and order that threatened the group's existence. The leaders could no longer control the young men by threatening to withhold the stone ax from them, and there was no other way to enforce social control.

The stone ax combined a number of elements in the aborigines' culture — its technology, norms, and religious beliefs. A change in one was bound to affect the others and throw the whole system out of balance.

In every society, whether simple or complex, the elements of culture are similarly meshed. The extent to which they mesh harmoniously is a matter that sociologists call *cultural integration.* Sociologists consider a culture well integrated when there are few contradictions between people's beliefs and their actions. If, for example, people believe in certain religious principles but find they must act differently in business or political life, their culture is not well integrated and contains built-in conflicts.

Can we assume, then, that a well integrated culture is good and a loosely in-

tegrated one bad? Not necessarily, according to many social scientists. They point out that a highly integrated culture like that of the Australian aborigines is extremely vulnerable to any kind of change. A complex, loosely integrated culture is likely to be more flexible, and therefore better able to adjust to change.

◦§ Consider again the Yanomamo. Do you think they should be given new tools? Medicine? Weapons? Should sociologists continue their participant observations of them?

The "flower children" of the 1960's and the Navajo woman preparing to weave a rug (next page) are both examples of subcultures in our society.

American Culture

Society in the United States is complex and diverse. Our people come from an extremely wide variety of cultural backgrounds, representing almost every area of the world. Our society has been enriched by the infusion of innumerable ethnic, racial, and religous groups, all of whom have brought new vitality to our arts and technology. Yet the diversity of our culture stems not only from our people of many heritages. Our customs vary from one geographic region to another, from urban to rural areas, and often from one occupation to another.

Subcultures. Some of the ethnic and religious groups that are part of our society have distinctive life-styles. Often they speak another language and have values that are somewhat different from those of most Americans.

Sociologists call any group whose patterns and beliefs differ noticeably from those of the dominant culture a *subculture*. In the United States, there are many varieties of subcultures. A youth subculture that evolved in the 1960's became identified with denim clothes, long hair, and rock music; heroes who rejected, or were rejected by, "the Establishment"; and attitudes about sexual freedom that differed sharply from those of their elders.

Clowns are a subculture in Japanese society, too.

Various occupational groups also constitute subcultures. Carnival workers, for example, are a subculture that has survived in the U.S. since the 1890's. "Carnies," as they call themselves, have an argot, or vocabulary, all their own. The carnival world has its own system of ranking that places owners of shows at the top and those who operate the rides at the bottom. Other "carnies" have ranks in between. Carnies rarely mix socially with people outside their subculture.

The trucker mystique. The following story, adapted from *Newsweek* magazine, describes the life-style of long-haul truck drivers, who also comprise a distinct subculture in our society:

It is 11 P.M. when Ben Rosson brakes his 18-wheeler and turns into the Union 76 truck stop in Ontario, California. He has been on the road for nine hours, bound for Suffolk, Virginia, with

43,000 pounds of almonds. Rosson hops down from his cab, orders 160 gallons of diesel fuel, and heads for his first full meal of the day: hamburger steak, fries, and four cups of "hundred-mile" coffee. . . .

For Ben, the night is just beginning. He slips his rig back onto Interstate 10 and flips on his CB radio. "Breaker 21, Breaker 21," he begins. "This here's the Midnight Man from Texas, eastbound on one-oh. Any Smokies come on?" A trucker heading west for Shakytown assures him that the stretch ahead is free of troopers. "Thanks for the info, good buddy, and we'll catch you on the flip side. We gone."

Ben Rosson sees himself as a hard-working family man who enjoys driving a long-haul truck. Most of the time, it is a tedious, wearying job. . . . But to millions of sedentary people, Ben's life on the road is the stuff of a legend. The lonely gearjammer has suddenly re-emerged as a romantic folk hero and pop-culture phenomenon. . . .

For a fast-growing number of Americans, the trucker's prestige has come through the medium of citizen's-band radio — the nontrucker's most direct access to the world of the long-haul driver and his argot.

In part, the trucking mystique is evoked by the truck itself — a . . . symbol of burly masculine power. Much of the mystique also lies in the trucker's aura of blue-collar integrity and his cowboylike freedom to move along when he wants. In reality, however, the trucker's freedom is limited by weighing stations, speed regulations, the Interstate Commerce Commission, and the omnipresent threat from "Smoky Bears" — the police. Yet the cat-and-mouse games they play with the cops give the truckers an outlaw's romantic appeal. . . .

At 2 A.M., Ben Rosson suddenly finds himself in the middle of a convoy of eight trucks. His eyes light up. He greets each driver by his CB handle. "Night Owl," "Arizon' Eagle," "The Captain," and "Mr. Oakie" are among those in the convoy,

and they all have the same mission: find Smoky. Nobody knows exactly where Smoky is hiding, but guessing makes the night go faster.

Out of the dark . . . Ben notices a California highway patrolman bearing down on the convoy. "Smoky!" he shouts into his CB. "Looks like Smoky is out to get him a truck." A line of red brake lights flashes instantly in the night. Then a voice crackles over the CB. "Drive it safe, drive it clean, and hope you get the good numbers," the patrolman radios from his own CB. "This is Blue Grass. We gone."

For professional truckers like Ben Rosson, the CB radio is a helpful tool, used in earnest since the 1974 gas shortage when the speed limit was lowered to 55 mph. Without it, Rosson would never know when to speed up — which he must do, he argues, if he is to meet most schedules.

*Truckers often lose touch with their families.
. . . Increasingly, trucking wives who want to
save their marriages are joining their husbands as a
trucking team. . . .*

*After deducting $600 for fuel, permits, and
other costs, Ben Rosson will net $600 from this
haul. Then he'll flip-flop west. He trucks about
100,000 miles a year. But one run, he insists,
is never like another. "What excites me about
truckin' is that there is no routine," he says.
"I'd just go nuts if I had to sit and watch the
sun come up every morning in the same place."*

Why are the truckers considered a
distinct subculture? What other American
subcultures can you list?

Truckers' glossary. No doubt you have
heard truckers talking to each other if you
have used a CB radio. The following is a
short guide to the truckers' argot. Can you
add to it?

Do you copy? — Do you understand?
Double nickels — 55 miles per hour.
Ears — CB radio.
Flip side — return trip.
Gearjammer — trucker.
Good numbers — good luck.
Handle — CB name.
Shakytown — Los Angeles.
Smoky Bear — highway patrol.
We gone — Stopping our message;
we'll listen.

application

The customs of other societies often
seem strange or barbaric as compared with
our own. Sociologist Horace Miner has
written about a group called the Nacirema. If the rituals, or established ceremonies, of the Nacirema appear strange to
you, remember that every culture solves
the problems of survival in its own
fashion. These rituals may work very well
for the Nacirema.

*The Nacirema are a North American group
living in the territory between the Canadian Cree,
the Yagui and Tarrahumare of Mexico, and the
Carib and Arawak of the Antilles. Little is known
of their origin, although tradition states that they
came from the East. According to Nacirema*

mythology, their nation was originated by a culture hero, Notgnihsaw, who is otherwise known for two great feats of strength — the throwing of a piece of wampum across the river Pa-To-Ma and the chopping down of a cherry tree in which the Spirit of Truth resided.

Nacirema culture is characterized by a highly developed market economy, which has evolved in a rich natural habitat. While much of the people's time is devoted to economic pursuits, a large part of the fruits of these labors and a considerable portion of the day are spent in ritual activity. The focus of this activity is the human body, the appearance and health of which loom as a dominant concern in the ethos of the people.

The fundamental belief underlying the whole system appears to be that the human body is ugly and that its natural tendency is to debility and disease. Incarcerated in such a body, man's only hope is to avert these characteristics through the use of the powerful influences of ritual and ceremony. Every household has one or more shrines devoted to this purpose. The more powerful individuals in the society have several shrines in their homes; and, in fact, the opulence of a house is often referred to in terms of the number of such ritual centers it possesses.

While each family has at least one such shrine, the rituals associated with it are not family ceremonies, but are private and secret. The rites are normally only discussed with children, and then only during the period when they are being initiated into these mysteries.

The focal point of the shrine is a box or chest which is built into the wall. In this chest are kept the many charms and magical potions without which no native believes he could live. These preparations are from a variety of specialized practitioners.

The most powerful of these are the medicine men, whose assistance must be rewarded with substantial gifts. However, the medicine men do not provide the curative potions for their clients, but

decide what the ingredients should be and then write them down in an ancient and secret language. This writing is understood only by the medicine men and by the herbalists who, for another gift, provide the required charm.

Beneath the charm-box is a small font. Each day every member of the family, in succession, enters the shrine room, bows his head before the charm-box, mingles different sorts of holy water in the font, and proceeds with a brief rite of ablution. The holy waters are secured from the Water Temple of the community, where the priests conduct elaborate ceremonies to make the liquid ritually pure.

In the hierarchy of magical practitioners, and below the medicine men in prestige, are specialists whose designation is best translated "holy-mouth-men." The Nacirema have an almost pathological horror of and a fascination for the mouth, the condition of which is believed to have supernatural influence on all social relationships. Were it not for the rituals of the mouth, they believe that their teeth would fall out, their gums bleed, their jaws shrink, their friends desert them, and their lovers reject them.

The daily body ritual performed by everyone includes a mouth-rite. Despite the fact that these people are so punctilious about care of the mouth, this rite involves a practice which strikes the uninitiated stranger as revolting. It was reported to me that the ritual consists of inserting a small bundle of hog hairs into the mouth, along with certain magical powders, and then moving the bundle in a highly formalized series of gestures.

In addition to the private mouth-rite, the people seek out a holy-mouth-man once or twice a year. These practitioners have an impressive set of paraphernalia consisting of a variety of augers, awls, probes, and prods. The use of these objects in the exorcism of the evils of the mouth involves almost unbelievable ritual torture of the client. The holy-mouth-man opens the client's mouth, using the above mentioned tools, enlarges any holes which decay may have created in the teeth. Magical materials are put into these holes. In the client's view, the purpose of these ministrations is to arrest decay and to draw friends.

There remains one other kind of practitioner, known as a "listener." This witch doctor has the power to exorcise the devils that lodge in the heads of people who have been bewitched. The Nacirema believe that parents bewitch their own children. Mothers are particularly suspect of putting a curse on children while teaching them the secret body rituals. The countermagic of the witch doctor is unusual in its lack of ritual. The patient simply tells the listener all his troubles and fears, beginning with the earliest difficulties he can remember. The memory displayed by the Nacirema in these exorcise sessions is truly remarkable. It is not uncommon for the patient to bemoan experiences from his earliest childhood.

In conclusion, mention must be made of certain practices which have their base in native aesthetics but which depend upon the pervasive aversion to the natural body and its functions. There are ritual fasts to make fat people thin and ceremonial feasts to make thin people fat. The ideal shape is virtually outside the range of natural human variation.

Our review of the ritual life of the Nacirema has certainly shown them to be magic-ridden people. It is hard to understand how they managed to exist so long under the burdens which they have imposed upon themselves.

✺ How does the Nacirema way of life differ from our own? Do you think you would like to live among them?

summary

For sociologists, **culture** refers to the entire way of life of a society. It includes all of a society's knowledge, customs, values, beliefs, and material creations. The influence of culture is pervasive; it determines what is "right" or "normal" behavior for the members of a society. A culture's norms and values are so ingrained that most people take them for granted. As a consequence, when people of one culture are suddenly exposed to other cultures whose customs and beliefs differ radically from their own, they may suffer emotional stress. Sociologists call this **culture shock.**

Culture gives meaning to the things people do and the things they make. The meaning of gestures, for example, is not universal but varies from one culture to another. Culture also defines what is real in a society. If men and women believe that a situation is real, they will act accordingly, even if their beliefs have no reality by scientific standards.

The meanings that people give to the things they do and make are conveyed by symbols. A **symbol** is anything that represents something other than itself. Words are our most important symbols, but gestures, colors, designs, sounds, and material objects like wedding rings are also symbols that convey meaning. Symbols vary from one culture to another.

Language is a system of verbal and, in many cases, written symbols. It is the chief means of transmitting culture from one generation to the next. Language reflects a people's culture. The number of words that a culture has to represent a particular object indicates the object's importance to that culture.

Not all language is verbal. Gestures communicate, as do people's attitudes toward time and space. They comprise a kind of "silent language."

The more we examine the world's cultures, the more we are struck by their diversity. Yet certain needs are common to all. These common needs stem from the fact that all societies must perform the same basic functions if they are to survive.

There are about 4,000 human societies throughout the world, and no two of them have identical cultures. Widespread cultural variations may exist even among neighboring societies.

Ethnocentrism is the tendency to see all other cultures as inferior to one's own. Ethnocentrism can be a positive force, instilling pride in one's heritage. But in its extreme form, it fosters intolerance and may even lead to war.

Considering the many variations that exist in cultures, how can we judge what customs are good or bad? Many sociologists say that there are no absolute standards that can be used to evaluate them. A custom that may be unthinkable in one society may perform a useful function in another. This way of assessing the worth of customs is known as **cultural relativity.**

Elements of culture — symbols, language, time, space, norms, and values — are all interdependent. A change in one is bound to affect the others. The extent to which these elements mesh harmoniously within a society is known as **cultural integration.** Sociologists consider a culture well integrated when there are few contradictions between the principles people believe in and how they act.

The United States is composed of many ethnic, racial, and religious groups. Some of them constitute **subcultures;** that is, their patterns and beliefs differ noticeably from those of the dominant culture. Various occupational and other groups also have distinctive life-styles and comprise subcultures in our society.

more questions and activities

1. Explain the meaning that sociologists give to the word *culture*.

2. List three elements of culture and give an example of each.

3. Prepare a guide to your community for a guest from some other culture. In order to do this, you might consult guides written for travel in other countries.

4. Distinguish between *ethnocentrism* and *cultural relativity*, and discuss the Yanomamo from both points of view.

5. Make up a system of symbols — silent, written, or spoken — by which you can communicate with other members of your class. Can an outsider detect what you are communicating?

6. Invite a speaker who is skilled in communicating through the American Sign Language to visit your class. In what ways might this language shape a person's thoughts?

7. Watch a series of television commercials to see what values are projected? After you have made a list of at least 10 values, see which ones you would describe as "American." Are any of these values not widely accepted in our culture?

8. Do you think it is possible to eliminate ethnocentrism? If this were possible, what might be the consequences?

9. Suppose it is your job to brief ambassadors assigned to other countries before they begin their duties. What tips might you give to them about what they might experience from the following cultures? Latin America? An Arab nation in the Middle East? Japan? (You might want to research other cultural differences not discussed in this chapter.)

10. Julia Martinez, a member of the Santa Clara Pueblo in New Mexico, was prohibited by tribal law from passing along property to her children because she married a Navajo. She claimed the tribal ordinance discriminated against her because she was a woman. (A man in the same position could have willed property to his children regardless of whom he married.) The U.S. Supreme Court, however, ruled that the 1968 Indian Civil Rights Act does not authorize legal challenges to tribal ordinances in federal courts. How does this case resemble the case of Tjalpaltjari in Australia? In what way does the Supreme Court's view of American Indian culture differ from the Australian court's view of aborigine culture?

11. Plan a field trip to visit a subculture in your area or invite a member of one to speak to your class. Afterward, prepare a guide to the special vocabulary of this group.

suggested readings

Benedict, Ruth. *Patterns of Culture.* (Houghton Miffline, 1961.) A classic anthropological study that draws largely on Native American groups to illustrate how cultural patterns shape our personality and social behavior.

Chagnon, Napoleon A. *Yanomamo, The Fierce People.* (Holt, Rinehart and Winston, 1983.) Chagnon's colorful and often exciting account of his fieldwork with the Yanomamo. Chapter One contains a particularly vivid account of the cultural shock Chagnon experienced on his first day with the Yanomamo.

Hall, Edward T. *The Silent Language.* (Doubleday, 1959.) An insightful analysis of how manners and behavior differ from one society to another. Chapters One and Ten are especially recommended.

Harris, Marvin. *Cows, Pigs, Wars, and Witches: The Riddles of Culture.* (Random House, 1974.) Have you ever wondered why Hindus worship cows, Kwakiutl Indians deliberately destroyed their possessions in potlatch ceremonies, and Europeans believed in witches? Anthropologist Marvin Harris attempts to unravel these and other cultural riddles in this provocative book.

Hendrickson, Robert. *American Talk.* (Viking Press, 1986.) An interesting account of the development and contributions of regional dialects in America.

Malcolm, Andrew H. *The Canadians.* (Times Books, 1985.) A highly readable portrait of Canadian society and culture.

National Geographic Society. *Primitive Worlds: People Lost in Time.* (National Geographic Society, 1973.) A fascinating and superbly illustrated account of such vanishing cultural groups as the Yanomamo of Brazil and the Tifalmin of New Guinea.

Riding, Alan. *Distant Neighbors: A Portrait of the Mexicans.* (Knopf, 1984.) A detailed description of Mexican culture and institutions. Chapter One, "The Mexicans," provides an excellent description of many of the key cultural forces which define the Mexican character.

Stern, Jane. *Trucker: A Portrait of the Last American Cowboy.* (McGraw-Hill, 1975.) An interesting and well-illustrated account of the subculture of the estimated 350,000 long-haul truckers in the United States.

Zerubavel, Eviatar. *The Seven Day Circle.* (Free Press/Macmillan, 1985.) An interesting account of the ways in which the weekly cycle affects our lives.

A young boy's first haircut is an act of socialization.

chapter 4

socialization

A father initiates his son into the rite of shaving by giving him a bit of lather and a toy razor. A young girl watches her mother feed the new baby and imitates her by practicing on her doll. A class of young children follows its teacher in pledging allegiance to the flag. As we see young children practice being "grown up," we are often charmed.

For sociologists, however, these activities have another dimension. They see them as examples of a vital process called *socialization*. Through socialization we learn the physical, mental, and social skills that we need to become individuals and to function in society.

Socialization begins at birth and continues throughout all of life. During early childhood, we learn, most of all, from our parents who teach us the values, norms, and skills that they have already acquired. We learn not only by their instruction, but by observing and imitating them as well.

At the same time that we are learning skills through interaction with our parents, we are also acquiring a self-identity, a conception of who we are. We come to realize that as sons or daughters, brothers or sisters, students or friends, we play a number of roles, and that certain behavior is expected of us in each of those roles.

The Importance of Socialization

Vital to culture. Socialization is as important to societies as it is to individuals. It is through socialization that every society transmits its culture to succeeding generations. Through the continuing process of socialization, each generation acquires the elements of its society's culture — its knowledge, symbols, values, norms, and beliefs.

Socialization is the vital link between cultures. If this process of cultural transmission is disrupted, a culture disintegrates or even dies out. The so-called Dark Ages provide a dramatic example of what happens when socialization breaks down. People lived in Western Europe for approximately 500 years, largely unaided by the advances made by the Greeks and the Romans at the heights of their cultures.

Early socialization. The following excerpt from sociologist Harry Gracey's observation of a kindergarten class provides an excellent illustration of the socialization process at work in our society:

By 1:50 P.M. most of the children have finished their pictures and given them to Edith [their teacher]. She talks with some of them as she ties the bundle of pictures together — answering questions, listening, carrying on conversations. The children are playing in various parts of the room with toys, games, and blocks, which they have taken off the shelves. They also move from table to table examining each other's pictures, offering compliments and suggestions. Three girls at a table are cutting up colored paper for a collage.

Another girl is walking about the room in a pair of high heels with a woman's purse over her arm.

Three boys are playing in the center of the room with the large block set, with which they are building walkways and walking on them. Edith is very much concerned about their safety and comes over a number of times to fuss over them. Two or three boys are driving trucks around the center of the room, and mild altercations occur when they drive through the block constructions.

Some boys and girls are playing at the toy store, two girls are serving "tea" in the play kitchen, and one is washing a doll baby. Two boys have elected to clean the room; and with large sponges they wash the movable blackboard, the puppet stage, and then begin on the tables. They run into resistance from the children who are working with construction toys on the tables and do not want to dismantle their structures.

The class is like a room full of bees, each intent on pursuing some activity, occasionally bumping into one another, but just veering off in another direction without a serious altercation.

At 2:05 the custodian arrives, pushing a cart loaded with half-pint milk containers. He places a tray of cartons on the counter next to the sink, then leaves. His coming and going is unnoticed in the room (as, incidentally, is the presence of the observer . . .).

At 2:15 Edith walks to the entrance of the room, switches off the lights, and sits at the piano and plays. The children begin spontaneously singing the song, which is, "Clean up, clean up. Everybody clean up." Edith walks around the room supervising the cleanup. Some children put their toys, the blocks, puzzles, games, and so on back on their shelves under the windows. The children making a collage keep right on working. . . . At more urging from Edith, the rest of the children shelve their toys and work.

The children are sitting around their tables now, and Edith asks, "What record would you like to hear while you have your milk?" There is some confusion and no consensus, so Edith drops the subject and begins to call the children, table by table, to come get their milk. "Table one," she says, and the five children come to the sink, wash their hands and dry them, pick up a carton of milk and a straw, and take it back to their table. Two talking girls wander about the room interfering with the children getting their milk, and Edith calls out to them to "settle down."

Choose five activities of the children, and explain how each illustrates the socialization process. Then list the cultural values Edith is trying to teach.

Now that we have seen how socialization operates at one stage of childhood, we'll explore the question of what we might be without it. We'll begin our study by looking at human beings who have been isolated at a very young age. Next we'll find out what some sociologists say about the differences in the ways boys and girls are socialized in our culture. Institutions play a large part in our socialization, and we'll examine two — television (actually a part of the institution of the communications media) and education. We'll read an account of how TV is socializing American children, and then we'll read an account of how education socializes children in the Soviet Union. Finally, we'll see how a person's early socialization may be changed, or even reversed, through resocialization.

Imitation is a major way by which we become socialized.

The effects of childhood isolation. The boys and girls in Edith's kindergarten class were obviously being shaped by their experiences there; but from Gracey's observation, it seems that they brought some skills with them — the abilities to walk and talk, for example. What would happen if a child were isolated at birth from human group life? Would this child instinctively learn to walk? To talk? Would it recognize other humans and be able to interact with them?

These questions have puzzled human beings for centuries. They could see, for example, that young birds could fend for themselves a couple of weeks after they were hatched, and that they seemed to know instinctively how to build nests. But what about human beings? Were their activities governed by inborn instincts, or did they have to learn everything they knew?

In the days of absolute monarchs, it was not unusual for rulers to experiment with their subjects. In the 13th century, Emperor Frederick II of Germany conducted an "experiment" on the effects of childhood isolation that was recorded as follows by a medieval historian:

His . . . folly was that he wanted to find out what kind of speech and what manner of speech children would have when they grew up, if they spoke to no one beforehand. So he bade foster mothers and nurses to suckle the children, to bathe and wash them, but in no way to prattle with them or to speak to them, for he wanted to learn whether they would speak the Hebrew language, which was the oldest, or Greek, or Latin, or Arabic, or perhaps the language of their parents, of whom they had been born. But he labored in

vain, because the children all died. For they could not live without the petting and joyful faces and loving words of their foster mothers.

Modern social scientists also have been interested to find out what human beings might be like if they were isolated from others at birth, but ethical considerations prevent them from experimenting so drastically with human life. We can, however, learn much about the effects of isolation from case studies of children whose own families have mistreated them.

The case of Isabelle. One of these children, whose first name was Isabelle, was the illegitimate child of a deaf-mute mother. When the mother became pregnant at the age of 22, her family locked her in a dark room. After Isabelle was born, she was confined with her mother to this room for 6½ years. In November 1938, the mother escaped, carrying Isabelle in her arms. State authorities placed Isabelle in a children's hospital in Columbus, Ohio.

What was Isabelle's condition at this time? Because her mother had been unable to communicate with her except with gestures, Isabelle was also unable to speak. She was terrified of strangers, especially men, and her behavior was as hostile as a wild animal after its capture. Because of poor food and lack of sunshine during her confinement, she was suffering from rickets (a bone disease). As a result, her legs were so badly bowed that she was unable to walk. Even after she was calmed, her behavior generally was infantile.

At first she did not respond at all to speech, and it was assumed that she was deaf. When it was discovered that she could hear, and her reactions were still so poor, the doctors concluded that she lacked intelligence. They were convinced that Isabelle could not be educated and that any attempt to teach her to speak would end in failure.

Nevertheless, speech experts did attempt to teach her, relying at first on pantomime and dramatization. Soon afterward, Isabelle began to respond remarkably. Within two weeks, she was able to identify toys by name when they were presented to her. Within two months, she was able to speak simple sentences, write well, and retell a story after hearing it. By the time Isabelle was 8½, she had reached a normal level of development. In two years, Isabelle had learned as much as most children of her age usually learn in six years. She was a bright, cheerful girl who spoke well and was able to walk and run without difficulty. She was soon entered in a regular school where she continued to make progress.

Sociologists say that Isabelle and similar cases prove that children cannot develop the skills necessary to function effectively as human beings when they are denied interaction with others. Children are not born with biologically inherited patterns of behavior that help them survive. Rather, they must learn through the socialization process the appropriate skills which will enable them to cope with their physical and social environments.

Sex-Role Socialization

Had Isabelle gone to a kindergarten like the one visited by Harry Gracey, there are other things she might have learned. Reexamine Gracey's report to see the difference in behavior between the boys and the girls. Why do you suppose that only little girls wear high heels, serve "tea," and wash the baby doll? Are the little boys allowed to play more aggressively?

Until recently, it was believed that differences in behavior between boys and

Research on Identical Twins

Each year in August, over 1300 pairs of twins from around the world gather for an annual summer festival in Twinsburg, Ohio. They enjoy sharing experiences, posing for pictures, and competing in contests for the most and least alike. But the similarities and differences between twins provide more than fun and entertainment. Researchers believe that the study of twins offers important new insights into the age-old debate of "nature versus nurture."

As we have seen, sociologists believe that nurture or socialization plays the most important role in shaping our behavior. Scientists have long known that genes control physical characteristics such as hair color and height. Recent research on identical twins now provides evidence supporting the view that nature—that is, our genetic history— also shapes our development as human beings.

Identical twins account for about one of every 250 births. In a recent project, at the Minnesota Center For Twin and Adoption Research, scientists conducted an exhaustive study of 350 pairs of identical twins reared apart. Identical twins who are reared apart can provide important clues for understanding the factors that influence personality and behavior. Since they have the same genetic background yet live in different environments, these identical twins help clarify the influence of heredity and environment on a variety of character traits. Each pair of twins answered 15,000 items on a comprehensive Multidimensional Personality Questionnaire.

Investigators then compared these results with answers given by the general population.

The results suggest an important genetic influence on some personality traits. For example, on the basis of their tests, researchers estimate that 61 percent of extroversion is inherited. The data also indicated that the traits of conformity, optimism, and cautiousness were 50 to 60 percent inherited. Heredity played a less significant role in other traits. Aggressiveness, ambitiousness, orderliness, and social closeness were only 48 to 33 percent inherited.

Researchers emphasize that the Minnesota Center's report only examined 11 traits. They also point out that the findings only apply to large populations. No one can accurately predict what the percentages will be for specific individuals.

Other scientists stress that genes do not act alone. Identical twins are by no means always alike in their behavior. Our social environment can both enhance and suppress inherited tendencies. One researcher points out that, "Given the same genes, different circumstances—including different educational opportunities—will produce different results."

Thinking Critically

1. How do identical twins reared apart provide an important source of information on the influence of heredity and environment?

2. What conclusion, if any, do you feel is justified by the data on twins research?

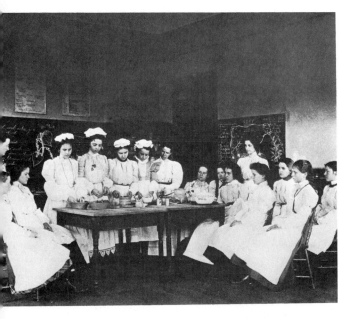

girls, and men and women, were "inborn" and "natural." Biological factors determined the abilities, interests, and traits of the sexes. Biology not only made men bigger and stronger, generally, than women. It also endowed them with instincts for hunting, fighting, and organizing. Biology gave women the ability to bear children, and instincts to complement it — gentleness and domesticity.

These ideas were widely accepted until anthropologists such as Margaret Mead studied primitive societies where sex roles differed sharply from those found in Western society. As you read in the previous chapter, Mead observed that in one tribe men and women were equally "maternal" toward children; in another, both men and women were fierce and aggressive; and, in a third, women were dominant and men were submissive. Mead concluded that masculine and feminine behavior was not inborn but was learned. Socialization, rather than biology, determined behavioral differences between men and women. Although the truth probably lies somewhere between the two explanations, there is mounting evidence that upbringing may have more impact than biology in shaping sex roles.

Gender training. Training children in behavior thought to be appropriate to their sex begins in infancy and continues into adolescence. Almost unconsciously, at first, parents usually handle baby girls more warmly and affectionately than boys and are more tolerant of physical aggressiveness in boys. Quite soon, however, the pattern becomes deliberate. Usually, little

In the 1890's, home economics classes were essential for girls; dressing or playing "like a boy," unthinkable.

boys are expected to act like "big boys"; behavior that is dependent or "sissyish" is actively discouraged. If a three-year-old boy cries, his mother is likely to say to him, "You don't see your daddy cry, do you?" Gradually the boy learns that only girls are allowed to cry.

Dependent or clinging behavior on the part of a little girl is more likely to be accepted by her parents. She is expected to be docile and compliant. Her presents probably will include a doll and carriage and toy dishes; she is already being socialized for the role of mother and housewife. A boy's presents probably will include toy soldiers, a toy truck, and a football. He is being socialized to be aggressive, adventurous, and competitive.

The message is unmistakable: To be feminine, a girl must be sweet, pretty, and passive; to be masculine, a boy must be rugged and fearless.

Mass media. Television, radio, movies, books, magazines, and records — the mass media — play an enormous part in shaping public consciousness about how men and women should act. Until the 1970's, the mass media presented traditional sex roles almost exclusively. Positive portraits of sensitive, nurturing men or assertive, self-sufficient women were conspicuously absent by today's standards.

Whether in drama, fiction, comedy, advertising, or pop music, the ideal woman of the 1950's and 1960's was beautiful and emotional, capable of running a perfect house by day and turning into a sex object by night. The ideal man was strong, professionally successful, and intelligent but able to show affection or strong emotion only with great difficulty.

Conditioning to traditional sex roles began early in children's television programming, in comic books, and in storybooks. A 1972 study of prize-winning children's books by sociologist Lenore J. Weitzman and others indicated that girls were "simply invisible" in a large number of the books they examined. Books about boys outnumbered those about girls by a ratio of three to one. Pictures of boys outnumbered those of girls by an even larger margin, eleven to one. The impression that both boys and girls received from such disproportionate representation, the authors of this study maintained, was that girls were not very important.

Boys were almost invariably portrayed as intrepid adventurers. They accompanied explorers to remote parts of the world, encountered wild animals, captured cattle rustlers, weathered tornadoes and tropical storms. They were cowboys, astronauts, scientists, soldiers, and doctors.

In most of these books, little girls sat in the safety and comfort of their homes and *watched* boys playing outside. Occasionally they ventured outdoors and discovered a box. Then they decided to "play house" in it. When girls did anything more daring, they were led by boys and quite often had to be rescued by them.

In the late 1970's the mass media began to reflect a wider variety of acceptable roles for both males and females. By the 1980's women were often portrayed in tradional male roles, such as detective, lawyer, adventurer.

The Self as a Social Product

Today the great majority of sociologists believe that neither biology alone nor socialization alone explains human behavior. Rather, it is the way that each culture shapes the biological drives of people that distinguishes the behavior patterns of one society from another, and one individual from another.

But social scientists are by no means agreed on *how* culture shapes the behavior of human beings. In the following sections, we will examine four of the theories about how this shaping takes place, how we become who we are.

Charles H. Cooley: the looking-glass self. As children come to distinguish between themselves and others, they also become aware that these others are judging their appearance and behavior. Others may indicate to children that they are clever or dull-witted, charming or boring, well-mannered or boorish, handsome or ugly. Although these judgments are not necessarily objective, the children tend to see themselves through the eyes of others. If, for example, a young boy's mother continually tells him that he is a bad boy, he will learn to think of himself as a bad boy. If, on the other hand, his mother continually tells him that he is the best of all possible boys, he may develop an inflated image of himself.

According to the sociologist Charles H. Cooley (1864-1929), all of us, from childhood on, develop a self-image that is largely a reflection of the way others see

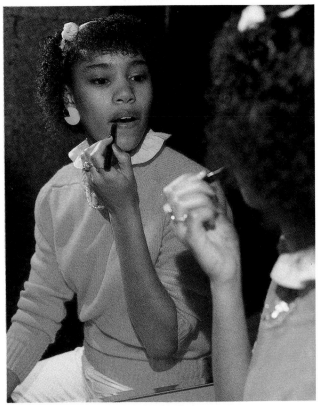

What does this photograph suggest about this girl's "looking glasses"?

us. Cooley called this image the *looking-glass self*. It is comprised of three principal elements: the way we think we appear to others, the way we think they judge our appearance and behavior, and how we react to their judgments about us. In short, we evaluate our behavior through the responses of others. If we think that others approve of our appearance and actions, then we will probably also approve of them. The "self," Cooley maintained, is a social product formed by interaction with others.

Being "realistic." In his 1965 autobiography, Malcolm X, the late black nationalist leader, described with bitterness a looking-glass experience that changed his life:

> . . .*One day, just about when those of us who had passed were about to move up to 8-A, from which we would enter high school the next year, something happened which was to become the first major turning point in my life.*
>
> *Somehow, I happened to be alone in the classroom with Mr. Ostrowski, my English teacher. . . . I know that he probably meant well in what he happened to advise me that day. I doubt that he meant any harm. It was just in his nature as an American white man. I was one of his top students, one of the school's top students — but all he could see for me was the kind of future "in your place" that almost all white people see for black people.*
>
> *He told me, "Malcolm, you ought to be thinking about a career. Have you been giving it thought?"*
>
> *The truth is, I hadn't. I never have figured out why I told him, "Well, yes, sir, I've been thinking I'd like to be a lawyer." Lansing [Michigan] certainly had no Negro lawyers — or doctors either — in those days, to hold up an image I might have aspired to. All I really knew for certain was that a lawyer didn't wash dishes, as I was doing.*
>
> *Mr. Ostrowski looked surprised, I remember, and leaned back in his chair and clasped his hands behind his head. He kind of half smiled and said: "Malcolm, one of life's first needs is for us to be realistic. Don't misunderstand me, now. We all here like you, you know that. But you've got to be realistic about being a nigger. A lawyer — that's no realistic goal for a nigger. You need to think about something you can be. You're good with your hands — making things. Everybody admires your carpentry shop work. Why don't you plan on carpentry? People like you as a person — you'd get all kinds of work."*
>
> *The more I thought afterward about what he said, the more uneasy it made me. . . . I was smarter than nearly all those white kids. But apparently I was still not intelligent enough, in his eyes, to become whatever I wanted to be. It was then that I began to change — inside.*
>
> *I drew away from white people.*

✑ What was the "looking glass" Mr. Ostrowski held up to Malcolm X? Why do you think Malcolm X reacted as he did? Do you think most young people in his situation would have accepted Ostrowski's looking glass? Why?

Malcolm X being interviewed.

Sigmund Freud: the psychoanalytic view. While Cooley had many insights into social relationships that were original in his time, he made no attempt to organize them into any set of theories that might explain human behavior in its entirety. But while Cooley was teaching sociology at the University of Michigan, there was a doctor in Vienna, Austria, who was undertaking such an ambitious task. He was Sigmund Freud (1856-1936), and no one who has seriously studied human behavior in the 20th century has been able to ignore his theories.

Freud did not believe that human behavior was random, and he sought to apply the scientific principles of cause and effect to the human mind. Although Freud had studied the human nervous system in a laboratory, he did not attempt to study the mind in the same way. Instead, he encouraged his patients to relax (first through hypnosis and later by simply reclining) and recall events from their early lives that might shed light on their emotional state. He called this process *free association,* a part of his treatment called *psychoanalysis.*

From such examination of his patients, Freud developed his theories about human behavior. Essential to these theories is Freud's division of the human personality into three parts, which he called the *id,* the *ego,* and the *superego.*

The *id,* Freud said, consists of inborn sexual and aggressive urges as well as hunger and warmth drives. Basically it is the part of the personality that seeks to gratify bodily wants. (Freud's insistence that sexuality was present even in infancy shocked and enraged most people when he formulated his theories in the 1890's.)

The *superego* acts as the conscience, or censor, that seeks to repress these pleasure-seeking urges. It develops as children learn from their parents and others that they cannot gratify all their urges at will, and that sexual and aggressive impulses especially are "no-nos" that may be punished severely. When the superego checks the pleasure-seeking impulses of the id, it usually drives them "underground" into the realm of the subconscious mind. But they continue to trouble the person as they seek some form of conscious expression, Freud said.

In the struggle between the id and the superego, the *ego* steps in as a kind of mediator, or umpire, seeking to find a healthy balance between their conflicting demands. In well-adjusted personalities, according to Freud, the ego redirects the lustful and sometimes antisocial impulses of the id into socially acceptable patterns of behavior so that the child, and later the adult, may function without emotional conflicts that produce stress.

In the following fictional example, Freud's followers might say that John's id, ego, and superego are all at work. See if you can identify the drives of each of them.

John plays basketball in the gym after school. He likes it very much and plays on the school team during the regular season. Tom frequently plays on the opposing team after school. At first John thought it was accidental that Tom bumped into him. Now he is convinced that Tom shoved him deliberately. One afternoon as John dribbles fast down the court, Tom tries to trip him. The second time he tries it, John falls and hurts his leg. He's not going to let Tom get away with it. John gets up and moves toward Tom. Just as he draws back his fist to hit Tom, he remembers how much Coach Johnson hates fighting. John still wants to give Tom a hard punch, but he worries that the coach might see him. He drops his fist and decides to take a break until his temper cools.

Erik H. Erikson: the eight stages of life. Freud's pioneering theories about the human personality have since been built upon by a number of scholars including Erik H. Erikson (b. 1902), one of Freud's most distinguished disciples. Erikson has expanded Freud's basic theories to include ideas of his own.

    Whereas Freud maintained that the human personality develops during childhood and adolescence and then becomes more or less fixed, Erikson contends that the process of socialization continues throughout life. Erikson says that failures at one stage of development can be rectified by successes at later stages. Erikson also places more emphasis than Freud on the role of culture in forming the individual's personality.

    According to Erikson, there are eight stages from infancy to old age, and we face a major crisis in each of them. Each crisis is brought on by the need to adapt to the changes in ourselves and in our social environment. Erikson sees the eight stages as follows:

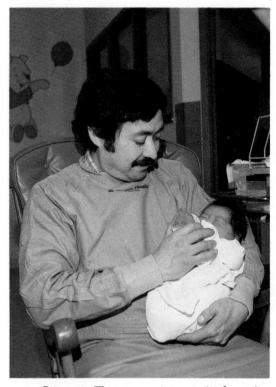

Stage 1. Trust v. mistrust (infancy). In the first year of life, our main problem consists of developing trust. If our needs are met promptly and lovingly, we learn to regard the world as a safe place, and find that people are dependable. If our needs are met inadequately or are rejected, we become fearful of the world and people. Our initial attitude, whether trust or mistrust, will carry on through later stages, but can be changed. For example, if we have learned to mistrust adults in infancy, we may change when we enter school and meet teachers whose behavior encourages trust. Or, if we developed a sense of trust during infancy, we may later become mistrustful if, for example, our parents undergo a bitter divorce.

Stage 2. Autonomy v. doubt (early childhood). During the second and third years of life, we develop new physical and mental skills. We can walk, climb, grasp objects, push and pull, and, of course, talk. We are proud of these accomplishments and would like to do as many things as possible by ourselves. The crisis that now arises stems from the growing desire for autonomy. If our parents accept our need for doing whatever we are capable of, then we will develop a sense of autonomy, the confidence that we can control our bodies, our impulses, our environment. But if our parents insist on doing everything for us, or are harshly critical when we attempt things and fail, then we will develop doubts about our abilities and feelings of shame about our "failures." If our sense of autonomy has been reinforced by parental encouragement, we will be well prepared for independence in later life.

But if we come out of this period burdened with self-doubts, we will be handicapped as we strive for independence later on. Again, however, Erikson emphasizes that we can be changed either positively or negatively by subsequent events.

Stage 3. Initiative v. guilt (the play stage). During the fourth and fifth years of life, our physical capacities develop to the point where we can initiate play activities, rather than merely follow other children. We often engage in play-acting, imagining ourselves in a variety of adult roles. We also begin to ask many questions, a sign of intellectual initiative. If our parents respect these efforts, our sense of initiative will be enhanced; this will be an asset in our later life. If, however, we are made to feel that our activities are "bad," our play-acting absurd, and our questions a nuisance, we will develop a sense of guilt about self-initiated activities that will be detrimental in later life.

Stage 4. Industry v. inferiority (school age). Between the ages of six and eleven, we experience a new socializing agent — school. As we begin to acquire new skills, we are also developing a sense of industry. This is the age when we begin to make all sorts of things — model airplanes, tree houses, "creepy crawlers," cookies, and clothes. Our major problem now derives from these efforts to create things. Our sense of industry will be reinforced if our parents praise and reward creative impulses. But if our parents scold us for "making a mess" or being mischievous, they will instill in us a lasting sense of inferiority. During these years, however, school experiences also play an important part in developing our personality. If our sense of industry is stifled at home, it may be stimulated in school by understanding teachers. Or, if we encounter repeated failures in school, we may develop feelings of inferiority even if our creative impulses have been encouraged at home.

Stage 5. Identity v. role confusion (adolescence). The adolescent years, from about 12 to 18, are often described as the period when we mature physically and begin to seek a romantic partner. In Erikson's view, however, adolescents are more concerned with the question of *who we are* than with attraction of the opposite sex. No longer young children, but not yet adults, as adolescents we are groping for a sense of identity, trying to find a continuity between what we have learned and experienced as children and what we are learning and experiencing as adolescents. At this stage of our lives, we are very much involved with peer groups. *Peer groups* are made up of companions of a social status similar to our own and usually of the same age. When we are searching for a sense of who we are, they help us overcome our uncertainties. By assembling all the images of ourselves that we have acquired as a son or daughter, student, worker, and friend, we not only arrive at a sense of who we are, but of where we are going as an adult. If we had an unfortunate childhood that produced feelings of mistrust, guilt, and inferiority, we will have difficulty in attaining a clear sense of identity. Erikson calls this *role confusion.* We may be tempted to seek a negative identity, one that is opposed to what our parents or friends prescribe for us, such as a delinquent.

tionship, whether with a friend or a marriage partner. However much we may desire love and companionship, we will shrink from intimacy with another person rather than risk being "swallowed up." If the fear of intimacy is greater than our need for it, we will end up being lonely and isolated.

Stage 7. Generativity v. self-absorption (middle age). In middle age, our greatest satisfaction probably will come from helping young people. We don't have to be parents to achieve this gratification. Anyone who is concerned with the well-being of the young, and works to improve the society in which they will live and work as grown-ups, can achieve it. Erikson calls this active concern for young people *generativity.* If we help the young, we will have a good feeling about ourselves and will work productively and creatively. But if we become completely absorbed in our own personal needs and comforts, we will probably stagnate both mentally and physically.

Stage 6. Intimacy v. isolation (young adulthood). The crisis that confronts us as young adults derives from our efforts to share with, and care about, another person. If we are unsure of ourselves, we will probably feel threatened by a close rela-

Stage 8. Integrity v. despair (old age). The last stage of life, when we must come to terms with dying, is a time of reflection and evaluation. If we can look back on the past and feel that our lives were not wasted, we will experience a sense of self-acceptance that Erikson calls *integrity.* But if we see our lives as a series of missed opportunities, we will probably give in to despair.

Chart 4:A gives a concise statement of Erikson's theory.

Behaviorists. The most serious challenge to the psychoanalytic point of view has come from a school of social scientists called *behaviorists.* Behaviorists believe that all human behavior is learned and can be controlled through the presence or absence of rewards and punishments.

American behaviorists were influenced by Russian psychologists, among them Ivan Pavlov (1849-1936). Pavlov conducted a famous experiment which demonstrated that much behavior among animals was learned rather than instinctive. Before his experiment, it was assumed that dogs salivated "instinctively" when they saw or expected food. Pavlov conditioned a number of dogs to associate feeding with the ringing of bells. After a while, the dogs would salivate when they heard bells, whether or not food was there. If salivation could be taught, said the behaviorists, then it was not instinctive.

4:A
Erikson's Eight Stages of Life

Age	Crisis	Main Social Setting
Infancy	Trust v. mistrust	The family
Early childhood	Autonomy v. doubt	The family
4 to 5	Initiative v. guilt	The family
6 to 11	Industry v. inferiority	The school
Adolescence	Identity v. role confusion	Peer group
Young adulthood	Intimacy v. isolation	A couple
Middle age	Generativity v. self-absorption	New family, work
Old age	Integrity v. despair	Retirement

American psychologist John B. Watson (1878-1958) applied this line of reasoning to human behavior. Watson believed that human beings could be socialized in any direction through learning. In 1924 he declared: "Give me a dozen healthy infants, well-formed, and my own specified world to bring them up in, and I'll guarantee to take any one at random and train him to become any type of specialist I might select — doctor, lawyer, artist, merchant-chief, and, yes, even beggar and thief, regardless of his talents, penchants, tendencies, abilities, vocations, and race of his ancestors."

Watson's ideas had a great influence on the thinking of B.F. Skinner (b. 1904). Skinner's own experiments and writings have made him the leading advocate of behaviorism in our time.

Skinner developed his own approach to behaviorism through a series of experiments with rats and pigeons. For these experiments, he designed what became known as the "Skinner box." It was a soundproof container that dispensed food when a rat pressed a lever or a pigeon pecked a key. Skinner was able to control the behavior of these animals by using food pellets to reinforce behavior which he desired. For example, he taught pigeons how to walk in the design of a figure eight by using the following process:

"I watch a hungry pigeon carefully. When he makes a slight clockwise turn, he's instantly rewarded for it. After he eats, he immediately tries it again. Then I wait for more of a turn and reinforce again. Within two or three minutes, I can get any pigeon to make a full circle. Next

B.F. Skinner and pigeon, above.

"Boy, have I got this guy conditioned! Every time I press the bar down, he drops in a piece of food."

Jester for Columbia University

I reinforce only when he moves in the other direction. Then I wait until he does both, and reinforce him again and again until it becomes a kind of drill. Within 10 to 15 minutes, the pigeon will be doing a perfect figure eight."

An outgrowth of Skinner's research is the widespread use of behavior modification, a kind of human psychotherapy that molds behavior with positive sanctions.

This example from a *Time* magazine article shows how this therapy is sometimes used:

> . . . *A point system for good behavior was set up for juvenile offenders — armed robbers, rapists, and murderers — in the Robert Kennedy Youth Center in West Virginia. Though no requirements were imposed on the delinquents, they earned points if they voluntarily picked up books, or went to lectures and managed to learn something from them. With the points, they could buy such rewards as better food, a private room, or time in front of the TV set.*
>
> *"All their lives," says Skinner, "these boys had been told that they couldn't learn and that they were useless. But under conditions that reinforced them every time they progressed, their morale improved enormously. Moreover, the return rate to the school dropped from 85 percent to 25 percent after the method was instituted."*

How do you think a behaviorist might advise a teacher to handle the following situations?

• Teacher wants all homework turned in the next day.

• Three students always monopolize class discussion.

• A student who finishes assignments quickly disturbs others who are still working.

The Agents of Socialization

The process of learning the mental, physical, and social skills that enable us to function effectively as human beings probably makes its strongest impressions in childhood, although, as we have seen, it continues throughout life. Traditionally, children in our society were almost entirely socialized by their families until they entered school and were influenced by that institution, by classmates and friends, and by religion.

Television. Since the 1950's, television has played an increasing role in the socialization of children, frequently from a very young age. In the following article, excerpted from *U.S. News and World Report*, James Mann discusses television as an agent of socialization:

> *Soon after 28-year-old David Radnis watched the movie "The Deer Hunter" on TV in his Chicago-area home, he was dead— one of at least 29 viewers in the U.S. who shot themselves imitating the show's Russian-roulette scene.*
>
> *When Hoang Bao Trinh fled from Vietnam to Silver Spring, Md., he spent months baby-sitting his grandchildren in front of the TV set. Soon the whole family was speaking English, much of it learned by imitating speech heard on the televised programs.*
>
> *Such cases reflect TV's increasingly pervasive influence on America, both for good and bad.*
>
> *Others in the industry are worried that what author and actor Steve Allen calls the "amoral force" of TV and other popular me-*

The panel's conclusion: *"Is television a cause of the SAT-score decline? Yes, we think it is . . . Television has become surrogate parent, substitute teacher."*

As TV's [first] children graduated in the 1960s and '70s, an Adult Performance Level test found that "20 percent of the American population could not perform the basic kinds of reading, writing or computing tasks. . . ." The result, says Paul Copperman, president of the Institute of Reading Development in San·Francisco, is that "society may be compelled to support an increasing percentage of dysfunctional or only marginally functional citizens."

[But] even the severest critics admit that television has achieved unprecedented results in making the public aware of a huge variety of developments—from war in Lebanon . . . to the plight of migrant workers.

. . . Television's broadening of perspectives also is credited with boosting worthwhile causes and diminishing the ethnic, religious and geographic prejudices that have plagued American history. Cited as a key example are the "freedom marches" that caught the attention of TV viewers in the early 1960s. Laws were then passed guaranteeing civil rights that blacks had sought for more than a century.

The medium also provides an invaluable window on the world for invalids and the elderly. Steve Allen recalls a series of visits he made to hospitals where Vietnam veterans were being treated: "What was helping to pull them through the day was television. The television set does provide company for lonely people, a voice in the house."

. . . Until recently, there was little research on how the human brain absorbs information from TV. Many scholars long have

dia is helping to weaken old values. . . .

A report released in May by the National Institute of Mental Health says that "violence on television does lead to aggressive behavior by children and teenagers who watch the programs." In one five-year study of 732 children, "several kinds of aggression—conflicts with parents, fighting and delinquency—were all positively correlated with the total amount of television viewing."

. . . A panel of educators appointed to study the decline [in Scholastic Aptitude Tests] noted that by age 16 most children have spent 10,000 to 15,000 hours watching television — more time than they have spent in school.

been convinced that viewers retain less from television than from reading, but evidence was scarce.

Now, a research project by Jacob Jacoby, a Purdue University psychologist, has found that more than 90 percent of 2,700 people tested misunderstood even such simple fare as commercials. . . . " Only minutes after watching, the typical viewer missed 23 to 36 percent of the questions about what he or she had seen.

. . . Another difficulty is the rapid linear movement of TV images, which gives viewers little chance to pause and reflect on what they have seen. Scientists say this torrent of images also has a numbing effect. . . .

The result is shortened attention spans — a phenomenon increasingly lamented by teachers trying to hold the interest of students accustomed to TV. . . .

Other researchers have found unrealistic career expectations among young people who watch a lot of TV. Frustation of these expectations, according to social scientists, can spill over into communities, helping to fuel destructive outbursts, ranging from disruption of schools to ghetto riots. Once civil disturbances are telecast, they may spread through imitation. . . .

. . . Fresh criticism is being leveled at the potential for abuse in two-way cable systems spreading across the country. These systems allow viewers with home computers or pushbutton consoles to communicate with central computers in requesting data, ordering merchandise, conducting banking transactions and responding to opinion polls.

. . . "Two-way systems are hitched to computers that scan each household every 6 seconds, recording all manner of informa-

tion," explains Les Brown, editor of Channels of Communication magazine. "They know what we watch, what we buy through television, how we vote in public-opinion polls."

More than 90,000 homes now have two-way systems, and rapid expansion into a fully "wired society" is expected eventually. Already, there are TV alarm systems tied to police stations and customers' homes that can turn on TV sets and record when people enter or leave a home. Although these processes are now aimed solely at detecting intruders, the possibility of other uses is alarming to some observers.

. . . Despite the uncertainties, there is widespread hope that the new video age will . . . do the country far more good than harm.

As Benjamin Barber, a Rutgers University professor of political science, observes: "It is difficult to imagine the Kennedy generation, the '60s, Watergate, the Woodstock generation or even the Moral Majority in the absence of national television."

Now, he adds, those concepts "belong to history, for we stand — prepared or not — on the threshold of a new television age that promises to revolutionize our habits as viewers, as consumers and ultimately as citizens."

≤§ Do you think this article is a fair interpretation of television as an agent of socialization? Explain your answer.

In the 1970's, the Federal Communications Commission made its first rules about what may be shown on programs during hours when children watch most. There was pressure too for the FCC to make rules about advertising shown during children's programs.

The atmosphere in this contemporary U.S. classroom is considerably less formal than that in many classrooms around the world.

Education. The education — and socialization — of children through public schools, on the other hand, has been a matter of public concern for many years. Free public education became available in every state by the end of the 19th century. Today all states have laws requiring children to attend school until they reach the age of 16.

When children enter school, they experience a drastic change from their lives at home. In the home, they obey their parents because they love them and recognize their dependence on them. The relationship between children and their parents is based on personal and emotional ties. In school, however, children learn to obey rules not because they love their teachers, but simply because rules must be obeyed. Students are judged not only on their academic abilities, but on how well they obey regulations, follow directions, show self-control, and get along with others. It is in school that they first learn to adjust to the impersonal authority of society.

As you read the following account of Soviet school life, you may want to jot down on a separate piece of paper some of the differences and similarities between it and life in U.S. schools.

Soviet education. Suppose you were consistently late for school or absent more than you should be. If you were a student in the Soviet Union, you would be judged and punished, not by adults, but by your own classmates.

The role that Soviet school children play in disciplining their peers stems from values that are basic to Soviet society. The Soviet Union is above all a collectivist state; that is, one that emphasizes organized group activity rather than individual initiative. In the Soviet Union, all activities, whether work, school, or play, are conducted by groups that are sponsored and controlled by the state. In the Soviet Union, a state system of nurseries and schools plays an important role in the upbringing of children.

Because Soviet schools are chiefly responsible for socializing the young, they give as much emphasis to "character building" as they do to formal academic studies. At the core of the character building process is the organization of the school into collectives.

In the classroom, for example, each row of double-seated desks constitutes a collective, and each child in that row is a member. The rows are strongly encouraged to compete with one another in every phase of activity and behavior, including discipline, personal grooming, community service projects, taking care of school property, gardening, shop work, sports, and others. ("Socialist competition" is also encouraged between larger educational collectives — classes, schools, and school districts.) Charts are displayed in the classroom indicating how each row,

called a *link*, stands in these activities, and one chart indicates their overall standing. "Who is best?" the chart asks. No individual names appear, only the numbered links or collectives.

At first the teacher sets the standards for the children and judges their performances, but very soon the teacher has helpers — the children themselves. Because the status of the children depends on the performance of their collective, it is to their advantage to watch over their neighbors, to help them when they are not doing well, to encourage good behavior, and to help punish bad behavior. Each collective also has an official monitor, whose responsibility is to keep track of the members and to criticize publicly any of them whose work, behavior, or grooming is found to be deficient. Although this sounds very much like tattling, Soviet school authorities claim: "The youngsters are not offended by this procedure. They understand that the leaders are . . . simply fulfilling their duty."

When a Soviet child consistently pulls down the performance of the collective, the collective meets and proposes various remedies, including sending the child to the director's office or temporarily exiling the child from the classroom, or even from school. If the discipline does not get results, the entire class meets to deal with the problem.

Urie Bronfenbrenner is a child psychologist who describes a typical case of collective discipline in his book, *Two Worlds of Childhood: U. S. and U.S.S.R.* This scene took place in a fifth-grade classroom.

"A Pioneer tells the truth and treasures the honor of his unit," says the Soviet classroom poster above. At right is a secondary geography class in Karaganda, Kazakhstan (Soviet Central Asia).

A month ago, Vova had been warned that he was doing poorly in arithmetic and pulling down his link. There had been no improvement.

After some discussion, Lyolya [the class monitor] proposed: "I think this problem is serious enough to require action by the entire collective [the class]. We can call a special meeting for this afternoon."

At the class meeting, Vova, a handsome lad in a white shirt, is called forward and asked what he did yesterday upon returning home from school.

"As always, I cleaned house so that Mother wouldn't have to do it when she got home. Then I did my homework."

"What subjects?"

"English, history, some drawing for shop."

As no mention is made of math, the class officers exchange significant looks. In a stern voice, Chairwoman Lyolya reminds him: "A month ago, you were warned to work harder on your math, and now you don't mention it."

Vova: "I didn't have any math homework that night."

A voice from the class: "You should have studied it anyway."

Lyolya asks the class for recommendations. After some discussion, a girl with a blue hair ribbon asks for the floor.

"I propose that we designate two of our class-mates to supervise Vova as he does his math home-work every night and give him help as needed."

Vova objects: "I don't need them. I can do it by myself. I promise."

But Lyolya is not impressed. Turning to Vova, she says quietly: "We have seen what you do by yourself. Now two of your classmates will work with you and when they say you are ready to work alone, we'll believe it!"

As a rule, Bronfenbrenner says, the collectives prefer to reward good perfor-mance rather than punish poor perfor-mance. But in either case, the children's collective, acting as the agent of adult society, is chiefly responsible for control-ling behavior. Rewards for the best link include pennants, a group photograph that appears in the school newspaper, or the privilege of leaving the classroom first after the bell. When praise is given to an individual, it invariably makes some refer-ence to the group. For example, "Today Pyotra helped Katya and, as a result, his unit did not get behind the rest."

Does the Soviet system of collectivist upbringing work? Generally, Bronfen-brenner says, Soviet children are quite well-behaved, attentive, and industrious. They appear strongly motivated to learn and to serve their society. On the other hand, the system also fosters conformity and discourages individual expression.

⋑ In your opinion, how do Cooley's, Freud's, Erikson's, and the behaviorists' theories of socialization contribute to an understanding of the Soviet approach to education? Explain your answer.

Resocialization

Although socialization continues throughout life, the basic values and behavior patterns that we learn during childhood seldom change radically. Usually adult socialization builds on what we have already learned. But sometimes major changes in attitudes and behavior do occur; people alter their lives, or their lives are altered for them, in ways that are quite inconsistent with their previous upbringing. This process is known as *resocialization.*

A moderate kind of resocialization occurs when young men or women join a military service. Soon after the recruits don uniforms, they acquire a new image of themselves, learn to obey orders without question, and value group cooperation rather than individual achievement. People are also resocialized when they convert to a radically different religious faith or political philosophy; when they undergo treatment for drug addiction, alcoholism, or mental illness; or when they are sent to prison. In each case, former values and patterns of behavior are usually replaced by new ones.

An extreme form of resocialization to which political prisoners and prisoners of war may be subjected is popularly called *brainwashing.* Developed first in the Soviet Union and later refined by the Chinese Communists, this radical resocialization process has two main objects. One is to make innocent people confess publicly, and in all sincerity, that they have committed serious crimes against the state.

Resocialization is usually a part of conversion to any religious group. The Hare Krishnas, above left, Roman Catholic nuns, below left, and Church of God members at the baptism below all show evidence of resocialization.

*Entering the military, whether the Naval
Academy or the Marines, leads
to intense resocialization.*

The other is to make people change their political views. Many of these tactics have since been adopted by other governments and by a variety of cults.

This technique essentially breaks down the prisoners' former personalities by creating the helplessness and confusion of childhood. Then it offers a new and approved way of putting the pieces together again. According to psychologist Albert P. Somit, these are the tactics:

1. *Total control.* Prisoners are made to feel completely dependent on their jailers. They cannot eat, sleep, go to the toilet, or leave their cells without permission. They are constantly harassed by the guards.

2. *Uncertainty.* Prisoners are not informed of the specific charges against them. When they ask what they are accused of, they are told that they know very well the nature of their crimes and that they had better confess. The prisoners are faced with a terrible dilemma. They can neither defend themselves nor confess because they do not know what they are alleged to have done.

3. *Isolation.* The prisoners are completely cut off from the outside world, including, usually, fellow prisoners. The only information they receive about their families is what the guards see fit to give them. Without the support of relatives and friends, each person's self-image begins to break down. Meanwhile the guards constantly tell them that they are despicable criminals.

4. *Torture.* Prisoners are tortured both mentally and physically. They may be told that their spouses have divorced

them or that their best friends have testified to their guilt. They will be questioned for hours at a time and subjected to terrible pain. The process is constantly repeated, and the prisoners allowed little or no sleep.

5. *Physical weakening.* The prisoners' allowance of food is limited so that they rapidly lose weight and strength. Inadequate diet, lack of sleep, and torture weaken them to such an extent that they are no longer capable of making the mental effort to defend themselves against any accusations.

6. *Personal humiliation.* Prisoners are constantly degraded and stripped of all sense of dignity. As old identities are destroyed, they begin to see themselves as their guards do — as traitors and enemies of the people.

7. *Certainty of guilt.* Eventually the prisoners' belief in their innocence is completely shaken by the unyielding conviction of their jailers that they are guilty. They even begin to justify in their own minds the measures their captors have taken to obtain a confession from them.

The case of Dr. Charles Vincent. How brainwashing techniques make innocent people confess to crimes and reshape their political views may be seen in the case of Dr. Charles Vincent, a French physician who lived in China for 20 years. Look for the seven steps mentioned above as you read this section.

Early in the 1950's, Vincent was arrested on the streets of Shanghai and taken to a "reeducation center," or jail. He was placed in a cell with eight other prisoners, all of them Chinese. These prisoners were fairly advanced in the process of "reforming" themselves and were eager to please their jailers by helping to reform Vincent. They formed a circle around Vincent, denounced him as a "spy" and an "imperialist," and demanded that he "confess everything." The more Vincent denied being a spy, the more he was accused of lying. This procedure was known as a *struggle.*

After several hours, Vincent was taken to a small room to be questioned by a "judge." He was asked about his activities, his professional associations, his friends, and his connections with foreign governments.

"This government knows all about your crimes," the judge told him. "That is why we arrested you. It is now up to you to confess everything to us. In this way, your case can be quickly solved, and you will soon be released." When Vincent denied that he had committed any crimes, the judge ordered guards to put handcuffs and chains on him. About 6 A.M., after 10 hours of questioning, he was returned to his cell.

"When you get back," Vincent recalled later, "your cellmates receive you as an enemy. They start 'struggling' to 'help' you. The struggle goes on all day to 8 P.M. that night. You are obliged to stand with chains on your ankles and your hands behind your back. . . . You eat as a dog does, with your mouth and teeth. You arrange the cup and bowl with your nose to absorb broth twice a day. . . . In the W.C. [toilet] someone opens your trousers and after you are finished they clean

you. . . . They continuously tell you that if you confess all, you will be treated better."

Vincent was called for further questioning at night. This time he invented an American spy ring that he said he belonged to. When pressed for details, he was unable to substantiate his story, so he was sent back to his cell for more "struggle." Questioned again on the third night, Vincent began to reconstruct and "confess" every conversation with friends and associates he could remember. By now he was fairly sure that he was suspected of being a spy.

For eight days and nights, Vincent was not allowed to have any sleep at all. The questioning became increasingly demanding. Occasionally Vincent would be taken out for a very fast walk. The purpose was to keep him awake. If the chains dug into his ankles and caused him great pain, so much the better. During the day, he was required to dictate to another prisoner everything he had confessed the night before.

"You are annihilated, . . ." Vincent recalled. "You can't control yourself or remember what you said two minutes before. You feel that all is lost. . . . From that moment, the judge is the real master of you. You accept anything he says. . . . You just wonder when you will be shot — and begin to hope for the end of all this."

Gradually a "full confession" began to take shape, one that was filled with lies, distortions, and exaggerations. Vincent had to compile lists of everyone he had known in China and everything he knew about their activities. After two months of writing and rewriting his confession, he began to get better treatment. The handcuffs and chains were removed, and he was permitted to sit in the presence of the judge, who now adopted a friendly tone. He told Vincent that the government regretted the "difficult" time he had gone through. It really wanted to help him. It would treat him more kindly if only he would make an absolutely complete confession and then work hard to reform himself. For the first time, Vincent felt some hope for the future.

Though his guards continued to address him by his prison number only, and the food he received was just enough to keep him alive, in other respects Vincent was treated more leniently. Soon he began to participate in his cell's "reeducation" program. It consisted of group study sessions that lasted from 10 to 16 hours a day. One prisoner would read aloud from Communist publications, and afterward each prisoner in turn would have to comment on the material. However, he had to express himself from the correct, or "people's," viewpoint.

All the while, Vincent would hear about men who were released because they had accepted their reeducation, and others who were shot because they had resisted.

After three years of intensive reeducation and polishing his confession, Vincent still had not been sentenced. He began to wonder how long he would be imprisoned. "Now you know that you will not be shot. . . . But you are thinking that your crimes are very heavy."

Soon after Vincent was told that his attitude had improved and he was granted a few privileges: an hour of outdoor exercise every day and permission to teach medicine to other prisoners.

Finally Vincent was called before a judge and heard both the charges against him and the sentence. For espionage and other crimes against the people, he was sentenced to three years in prison. However, the judge ruled that he had already served his sentence.

A few people have resisted brainwashing. One of them is a Chinese woman named Nien Cheng, who in 1973 amazed Westerners with her account of six and a half years of survival without surrender.

Nien Cheng

application

On February 5, 1974, Patty Hearst, the 19-year-old daughter of a wealthy California newspaper publisher, was kidnapped by members of a small revolutionary group called the Symbionese Liberation Army. Soon afterward, the public was surprised by tape recordings in which Hearst earnestly professed her conversion to the political philosophy of her captors.

Weeks later, she was photographed taking part in the armed robbery of a bank with other members of the SLA. In a subsequent robbery, Hearst fired a weapon to help two of her colleagues to escape capture. When she was finally taken into custody by law enforcement agents, she described herself as an "urban guerrilla" and gave the clenched-fist salute of militant radicals.

At her trial, defense lawyers claimed that Hearst had been subjected to "coercive persuasion" — brainwashing — by her captors. She had been blindfolded, locked in closets for 57 days, and raped.

According to psychiatrists who testified in her defense, she was rapidly "dehumanized" and "developed a childlike dependency upon her captors." It was a case of either accept the SLA or be killed. Hearst, they said, could not be held responsible for her criminal activities.

Psychiatrists who testified for the prosecution declared that Hearst was a willing convert to the revolutionary group. They said that a pampered upbringing had kept her from developing a strong self-image.

As you look at these pictures of Hearst, see how many of Cooley's "looking glasses" you can identify in each stage of her life. From the brief description of what happened to her, would you say that she had a strong ego? What portion of her behavior would you attribute to her id? To her superego? In which of Erikson's eight stages of life would you say Hearst was when she was captured? Do you think she remained in that stage through her trial? Applying Somit's criteria, would you say she was brainwashed?

With husband, Bernard Shaw, in 1986.

First communion, age 8.

At 19, with fiancé Steven Weed.

One month after kidnapping, with gun and SLA symbol.

With guard at her trial two years later.

summary

Socialization is the process by which people learn the physical, mental, and social skills that enable them to become individuals and to function effectively in their society. Without human interaction, socialization would be impossible. Children who grow up in relatively isolated circumstances suffer severe handicaps that must be remedied before they can function as social beings. Although socialization is a life-long process, it predominates during childhood when we are completely dependent on our parents. The long period of dependence stems from the fact that, unlike most animals, humans are not born with biological instincts for survival but must be taught how to cope with their environment. But humans are born with biological drives, or impulses, and potentials, including the need to be fed, to be kept warm, and to be loved. Later they experience a sexual drive. How are these drives to be satisfied? Ultimately it is culture that shapes the biological impulses of the young into socially acceptable patterns of behavior through the process of socialization.

Through interaction, we not only acquire skills, but a sense of **self-identity,** an awareness of who we are as individuals. Newborn babies have no self-image. Over a period of months, however, as their biological and emotional needs are being gratified, they learn to distinguish between themselves and others. Later they become aware that these others are judging their behavior and appearance. According to Charles H. Cooley, children develop images of themselves that are largely a reflection of the way others see them. Cooley called this image the **looking-glass self.**

Sigmund Freud, the founder of psychoanalysis, emphasized the importance of inner biological and emotional drives in the socialization process. Freud said that inborn sexual and aggressive drives, the **id,** are later repressed by the conscience, or **superego,** which develops as we learn of society's demands for self-control. The conflict between our emotional drives and the desire to be "good" (the conscience) is resolved by the **ego,** the part of the self that channels our drives into socially acceptable patterns of behavior.

Building on Freud's theories, Erik Erikson developed a view of the socialization process that encompasses the entire life span. Erikson maintains that human beings go through eight distinct stages of development from infancy to old age. In each of these stages, they are confronted with a major crisis that is brought on by the need to adapt to changes both within themselves and their social environment.

The most serious challenge to the psychoanalytic point of view comes from **behaviorists,** who believe that all human behavior is learned and can be controlled through the presence or absence of rewards. The leading behaviorist of our time is B.F. Skinner.

The chief agents of socialization usually are the family, the media, the school, and peer groups. **Peer groups** are companions of similar social status and usually of the same age. The goal of childhood socialization is to teach self-control, basic cultural values, necessary skills, and appropriate role behavior. At home, children obey their parents because they love them and also recognize their dependence on them. Of all the media, television is the most powerful force in socializing children, encouraging — along with its benefits — both passive and aggressive behavior. In school, children learn to accept the impersonal authority of teachers and the larger society.

Until recently, it was believed that biology determined differences in behavior between men and women. Biology made men bigger and stronger, generally, than women, and endowed them with aggressive instincts for hunting and fighting. Women, on the other hand, were endowed with gentle, maternal instincts. Today there is considerable evidence that socialization may have as much to do with shaping sex roles as biology. In the family, in books, and in school, boys are usually taught that to be masculine they must always be strong and fearless. Girls are usually taught that to be feminine they must be sweet, dainty, and compliant. Sociologists call these proscribed ways of behaving **sex roles.**

People sometimes change radically in later life, adopting values and standards of behavior that are incompatible with their previous upbringing. This process is called **resocialization.** The most extreme form of resocialization, popularly called **brainwashing,** is a form of coercive persuasion that makes prisoners confess to crimes they did not commit and convert to the political philosophy of their captors.

more questions and activities

1. Explain the concept of *socialization* and tell what its absence can do to human beings.

2. Briefly explain the four major theories of socialization discussed in this chapter. Give an example of each from the text.

3. Compare and contrast education as an agent of socialization in the United States and the Soviet Union.

4. From magazines and newspapers, collect examples of advertising that holds up social "looking glasses" of young people. Then make up a composite young man or woman as reflected in this advertising.

5. Jean Piaget is a Swiss scholar who has devoted many years of research to the social and psychological development of very young children — in much the same way that Erikson has studied the entire life span. Although Piaget's own writings are very difficult, you might consult a summary such as Mary Ann Spencer Pulaski's *Your Baby's Mind and How It Grows: Piaget's Theory for Parents,* published by Harper and Row. Report to your class on Piaget's stages of infant development.

6. For your personal use, list 12 traits of your own personality. Alongside each, write the name of the behavioral scientist or group whose theory best explains how this trait was acquired.

7. Visit a kindergarten, nursery, or other group of young children, and prepare a report similar to Harry Gracey's about the processes of socialization taking place.

8. Bring to class examples of religious publications prepared for young children. What values do they portray? In what ways might this literature be an agent of socialization?

9. "Our philosophy is that TV is neither good nor bad, but that it can be a window on the world. We must help children, parents, and teachers use it properly," says a Texas educator. With this view in mind, he and a group of teachers worked to develop a program to help young children view television in a critical sense. That is, children would be taught that not everything that appears on television is the absolute truth and how to evaluate persuasive messages such as commercials. Do you think such a program would be useful to young children in our society? Why or why not?

10. Discuss the process of resocialization as it applies to immigrants to this country. What are some of the problems? You might invite a recent immigrant to your class to share his or her experiences of resocialization. Be sure to ask in what ways people from our culture would have to be resocialized in this person's country.

suggested readings

Bronfenbrenner, Urie. *Two Worlds of Childhood.* (Russell Sage Foundation, 1970.) A comparative study of the socialization of children in the United States and the Soviet Union.

Cohen, Elie A. *Human Behavior in the Concentration Camp.* (Universal Library, 1953.) A former inmate's vivid description of life in a Nazi concentration camp provides considerable insight into the resocialization process.

Elkind, David. *The Hurried Child: Growing Up Too Fast Too Soon.* (Addison-Wesley, 1981.) A noted child psychologist examines the social pressures which influence how children are raised in the United States.

Elkind, David. "Erik Erikson's Eight Ages of Man." (*The New York Times Magazine,* April 5, 1970.) A clear and well-written introduction to Erikson's famous theory.

Shattuck, Roger. *The Forbidden Experiment.* (Farrar, Straus, and Giroux, 1980.) A fascinating account of the discovery and subsequent life of the "wild boy" who was discovered in France in 1799.

Spiro, Melford. *Children of the Kibbutz.* (Harvard University Press, 1975.) Spiro's study of the socialization of children who are raised in agricultural communes in Israel.

Editors of U.S. News and World Report. "Children Under Stress." (U.S. News and World Report, October 27, 1986.) An excellent overview of the social forces which affect the way children are socialized in America.

Warner, Steven. "A Conscientious Objector At Parris Island." (*The Atlantic,* June 1972.) A first-person account of how the Marine Corps transforms raw recruits into first-rate military units. This article gives a particularly good example of how resocialization works.

Winn, Marie. *The Plug-In Drug.* (Viking, 1985.) An examination of how television influences the values and outlook of children.

Sociologists would call this girls' chorus a secondary group.

chapter 5

groups

"I went to jail today."

That's the way football player Jerry Kramer described the first day of an eight-week Green Bay Packer training camp when he was playing for Vince Lombardi, the late coach.

"The worst part of it is that you're completely a captive of Lombardi and of football," continued Kramer. "It's not like you put in two hours in the morning, two in the afternoon, and two in the evening. You're required to attend breakfast at 7 A.M., ride in the bus over to the stadium and back again, dinner, meeting, curfew. If you're lucky, you get an hour-and-a-half or two hours a day to do whatever you want."

In *Instant Replay: The Green Bay Diary of Jerry Kramer,* Kramer describes how Lombardi took about 70 players, 35 of whom had never played for the Packers, and shaped 40 of them into a unique professional team.

One way Lombardi built his team was by drilling the players relentlessly, far beyond what other professional coaches demanded of their players. Kramer recalled: "The grass drills are exquisite torture. You run in place, lifting your knees as high as you can for 10, 20, sometimes 30 seconds. When Lombardi yells, 'Down,' you throw yourself forward on your face, your stomach smacking the ground, and when he yells, 'Up,' you get up quick and start running in place again. We call the exercises 'up-down,' and when Vince is in a good mood, he gives us only three or five minutes of them. If he's upset, he'll keep going till someone's lying on the ground and can't get up, till everyone's on the brink of exhaustion."

For Lombardi, whose motto was "Winning isn't everything; it's the only thing," the Packers were successful that year. In 1967 they won their third straight National Football League championship.

If sociologists had studied the Packers, however, they would have been less interested in their won- lost record than in how they functioned as a group. From a sociological point of view, a *group* consists of two or more people who interact with each other and engage in a common activity.

In this chapter, we will see how sociologists distinguish between and among groups. Among the kinds of groups they have labeled are peer groups, in-groups and out-groups, primary and secondary groups, and self-help groups. Groups exert enormous social pressure on individuals, some of which is obvious and

Kramer hoists his coach after the Packers win the Super Bowl, above. Below, quarterback Bart Starr leads his teammates in practice.

some of which is subtle. In this chapter, one woman tells how she was influenced during the 1960's by peer groups in her high school. In two other examples, we'll see how group norms can either stifle or encourage an individual's performance. Every group, of course, has its leaders. We'll see what some sociologists have said about various types and styles of leadership. Competition and cooperation are two important dynamics of group life. We'll see how both can work for or against a group's best interests. Finally, in the Application, your class will participate in an experiment on group behavior.

Why do sociologists attach so much importance to groups? As we have seen, group life is essential to human development and well-being. After six years of isolation, Isabelle had not acquired a human personality. Not until she was placed in a social environment and exposed to group experiences did this happen. Chinese Communists were able to break down Dr. Vincent's self-image by isolating him from his family, friends, and associates. Durkheim's study of suicide revealed that people who lack strong ties to social groups are more likely than others to take their lives in times of stress.

Groups, then, not only shape our values, attitudes, and behavior; they offer us vital emotional support by linking our "selves" to the "outside world." Through membership in groups, individuals are able to multiply their productivity and influence in society. Although group influence on an individual can sometimes be quite damaging, all human beings need some group contact to survive.

Types of Groups

Peer groups. As Erik Erikson observed, peer groups are an important agent of childhood socialization. As students, children meet many others of their own age and social position — their peers. Frequently, they form cliques, clubs, and gangs that have very strong appeal. For in these groups, young people are among equals rather than in the subordinate positions they occupy at home (to their parents) and in school (to their teachers).

While providing companionship and enjoyment to their members, peer groups work to socialize their members throughout life. Social clubs, athletic leagues, and civic groups play an important part in the continuing socialization of adults. Although some peer groups foster negative behavior such as drug use and delinquency, most perform a useful function. Cliques, gangs, and clubs satisfy the need for both social acceptance and codes of approved behavior. And by aligning themselves with their peers at a time when they are still dependent on their parents, young people achieve a sense of autonomy, an important step toward becoming adults.

In-groups and out-groups. For Jerry Kramer, who was entering his 10th season as a Green Bay Packer in 1967, there was little risk that he would be cut from the team. As a result of his years of playing, Kramer considered himself a Packer. That was not so for the 35 rookies who entered the Packer training camp for the first time. Kramer recalled a conversation he had with a discouraged rookie:

"It brought back to me the difficulties a rookie faces trying to make a pro football team. It's not only the newness of the whole system, learning the plays and the players. There's also the attitude among the veterans, the feeling of togetherness that makes the rookie feel like an outsider. He's away from home, away from a familiar setting, and often away from a wife he's just been married to for a little while. It's a miracle that any of them make it. In the past year, we've had lots of rookies 'domino' out on us, just pack up in the middle of the night, sneak out the door, and go home. The strain is brutal, going through all the incredible torture we go through and wondering if you're going to make the club."

The kind of exclusiveness that Kramer describes here illustrates an impor-

tant distinction that sociologists make between in-groups and out-groups. An *in-group* is one that a person feels he or she belongs to and identifies with. Whether the group is occupational, fraternal, political, ethnic, or religious, it is one in which the person feels at home. It consists of all those people, themselves included, whom they usually refer to as "we." Among in-group members, a person feels a sense of solidarity, loyalty, and cooperation. The Packers were Kramer's in-group.

An *out-group* is one to which a person does not feel she or he belongs. It consists of all those people a person describes as "they." Out-group members are "different." Among them, one may feel uncomfortable, competitive, or hostile. For example, during training camp, rookies were an out-group to the veteran Packers.

Clothing is a boundary that distinguishes the Hell's Angels, just as it distinguishes the students below.

Initiations can be as casual as a handshake or as formal as this 1905 ceremony at Vassar College.

Boundaries. How does an in-group distinguish between members and non-members, insiders and outsiders? Usually, a group has a clearly defined *boundary*. It may be territorial as in the case of a street gang, but more often it is symbolic. An athletic letter, for example, is a symbolic social boundary. Those who own one are "we"; those who don't are "they." An athlete who gives his letter sweater to a girl friend symbolically extends the boundary of his team to include her. A school decal on a car windshield is a social boundary; it differentiates between insiders and outsiders. Uniforms, hairstyles, clothes, and occupational speech are other ways of setting off one group from another.

☙ What kinds of social boundaries define groups within your school?

Getting inside. How does an outsider get to be an insider? Usually, one must go through some sort of *initiation rite* — a handshake or an introduction; the awarding of a letter by an athletic team; the presentation of a diploma or a certificate; receiving the special insignia of a military group. The Green Bay Packers marked their acceptance of a rookie by awarding him a nickname.

In his book, *Down These Mean Streets,* Piri Thomas describes the initiation rite that he experienced when he moved to a new block in Spanish Harlem, a neighborhood of New York City. This passage is adapted from the book.

Moving into a new block is a big jump for a Harlem kid. You're torn up from your hard-won turf and brought into an "I don't know you" block where every kid is some kind of enemy. Even when the block belongs to your own people, you are still an outsider who has to prove himself. . . .

As the moving van rolled to a stop in front of our new building, number 109, we were all standing there, waiting for it — Momma, Poppa, Sis, Paulie, James, Jose, and myself. I made out like I didn't notice the cats looking us over, especially me — I was gang age. I read their faces and found no trust, plenty of suspicion, and a glint of rising hate. I said to myself, "These cats don't mean nothin'. They're just nosy." But I remembered what had happened to me in my old block, and that it had ended with me in the hospital.

This was a tough-looking block. That was good, that was cool; but my old turf had been tough too. "I'm tough," a voice within said. "I hope I'm tough enough. . . ." I looked at the rulers of this new world and with a cool shrug of my shoulders I followed the movers into the hallway of number 109 and dismissed the coming war from my mind.

The next morning I went to my new school, called Patrick Henry, and strange, mean eyes followed me.

"Say, pops," said a voice belonging to a guy I later came to know as Waneko, "where's your territory?"

In the same tone of voice Waneko had used, I answered, "I'm on it, dad, what's shaking?"

"Bad, huh?" He half smiled.

"No, not all the way. Good when I'm cool breeze and bad when I'm down."

"What's your name, kid?"

"That depends. 'Piri' when I'm smooth and 'Johnny Gringo' when stomping time's around."

"What's your name now?" he pushed.

"You name me, man," I answered, playing my role like a champ.

He looked around, and with no kind of words, his boys cruised in. Guys I would come to know, to fight, to hate, to love, to take care of. Little Red, Waneko, Little Louie, Indio, Carlito, Alfredo, Crip, and plenty more. I stiffened and said to myself, "Stomping time, Piri, boy, go with heart. . . ."

Waneko, secure in his grandstand, said, "We'll name you later, panin [buddy boy]. . . ."

It wasn't long in coming. Three days later, at about 6 P.M., Waneko and his boys were sitting around the stoop at number 115. I was cut off from my number 109. For an instant I thought, "Make a break for it down the basement steps and through the backyards — get away in one piece!" Then I thought, . . . "I'm no punk kid. I'm not copping any pleas. . . . Walk on, baby man, roll on without fear. What's he going to call?"

"Whatta ya say, Mr. Johnny Gringo?" drawled Waneko.

"Think, man," I told myself, "think your way out of a stomping. Make it good." I said, "I hear you 104th Street [guys] are supposed to have heart. I don't know this for sure. You know there's a lot of streets where a whole clique is made out of punks who can't fight one guy unless they all jump him for the stomp." I hoped this would push Waneko into giving me a fair one. His expression didn't change.

"Maybe we don't look at it that way."

"Crazy, man," I cheered inwardly, "the [guy] is falling into my setup. We'll see who gets messed up first, baby!" I said, "I wasn't talking to you. Where I come from, the pres is president 'cause he got heart when it comes to dealing."

Waneko was starting to look uneasy. He had bit on my worm and felt like a sucker fish. His boys . . . were no longer so much interested in stomping me as in seeing the outcome between Waneko and me. "Yeah," was his reply. . . .

I knew I'd won. Sure, I'd have to fight; but one guy, not 10 or 15. . . . He would have to fight me on his own, to prove his heart to himself, to his boys, and most important, to his turf. He got away from the stoop and asked, "Fair one, Gringo?"

"Uh-uh," I said, "roll all the way — anything goes." I thought, "I've got to beat him bad and yet not bad enough to take his prestige all away. . . . Let him draw first blood, . . . it's his block." Smish, my nose began to bleed. His boys cheered, his heart cheered, his turf cheered. "Waste this chump," somebody shouted.

"OK, baby, now it's my turn, [I thought]. He swung. I grabbed innocently, and my forehead smashed into his nose. His eyes crossed. His fingernails went for my eye and landed in my mouth — crunch, I bit hard. I punched him in the mouth as he pulled away from me, and he slammed his foot into my chest.

. . . We rolled onto the street. I wrestled for acceptance, he for rejection or, worse yet, acceptance on his terms. It was time to start peace talks. I smiled at him. "You got heart, baby. . . . You deal good," I said.

"You too," he muttered, pressuring out. And just like that, the fight was over. No more words. We just separated, hands half up, half down. My heart pumped out, "Move over, 104th Street. Lift your wings, I'm one of your baby chicks now."

Five seconds later my spurs were given to me in the form of introductions to stardom's elite. . . .

"What's your other name, Johnny Gringo?"
"Piri."
"OK, Pete, you wanna join my fellows?"
"Sure, why not?"
. . . I was in; it was my block now.

Do you think Piri would have been accepted into the gang if he had beaten Waneko badly? If Waneko had beaten him badly? Explain your answers.

Reference groups. Suppose you received a grade of B in your sociology course. Would you consider it a good or a bad grade? Would you be pleased with it or displeased? According to sociologists, an important factor in your reaction would be the grades your friends received. If your friends earned C's, you would likely be delighted with a B. But if your friends earned A's, you would likely feel that you had done poorly. Usually we tend to judge ourselves in comparison with other members of our group.

But even groups that we do not belong to may set standards for us. If, for example, you are a high school freshman who aspires to approval from the senior athletes-and-ladies'-men clique, you will probably model yourself after its members in every way that you can — your clothes, your speech, your attitudes, and your manners. You may swagger a bit and boast of your popularity with the opposite sex.

Sociologists call any group that serves as a standard for evaluating yourself and your behavior a *reference group*. Usually the members of reference groups are people whom we admire and wish to emulate. Sometimes, however, a reference group may convey a negative image that we seek to avoid. If we don't like "freaks," for example, we may show our disapproval by dressing and acting according to quite conventional rules. On the other hand, if we believe that our parents and friends are too materialistic, we may wear old clothes and try to look less materialistic.

Reference groups can affect behavior in thoroughly unexpected ways. During

*Reference groups offer young people role models
and an opportunity to aspire to higher skills.*

World War II, for example, soldiers who were assigned to U.S. colleges for special training often became embittered and engaged in hostile acts against both Army and college authorities. One such case involved a unit of about 100 men who were assigned to study the Japanese language at a large Midwestern campus. These men had volunteered for the assignment and had qualified by getting high scores on general-aptitude tests. All had college backgrounds. At the university, they lived in attractive new dormitories, and enjoyed first-rate food. They wore uniforms, marched to breakfast each morning, and were under the authority of senior officers. However, discipline was very mild. The men could leave the campus after classes were over; no passes were required; and a curfew was rarely enforced. After a while, married men were allowed to take apartments and live with their wives in town.

Objectively, these men should have been delighted with their situation. They were a long way from the shooting war, living in comfortable surroundings, and enjoying privileges that were rare in regular Army camps. Yet before long, morale in this unit began to break down, and the men became increasingly negative in their behavior. They would skip classes, insult their civilian instructors, and accuse their officers of incompetence. Finally they drew up a petition demanding to be transferred overseas immediately!

Army authorities were baffled by this behavior. Any soldier who was living in a foxhole with bullets and shrapnel whizzing overhead would gladly have changed places with these men. Sociologists later

concluded that reference groups played a role in the behavior of the soldiers on campus. They were not comparing themselves to the men in the front lines. If they had, they would have felt no dissatisfaction. Instead, they compared themselves with the civilian students on the campus. Using the civilians as a reference group, they felt relatively deprived. By comparison, their own lot seemed mean and shabby, even though they were actually much better off than the vast majority of servicemen in World War II.

Primary groups and secondary groups.
When Jerry Kramer and his closest friends on the Green Bay Packers spent an afternoon playing golf or bowling, there was something special about their relationship. It was warm, personal, relaxed, and informal. They teased each other in a way no outsider would be permitted to get away with. In so doing, they filled their needs for intimate human companionship. Sociologists would call Kramer and his teammates a *primary group.* Similarly, families, a couple in love, street gangs, play groups, and some social clubs would also be defined as primary groups because of the high degree of intimacy in the relationship among members.

Other groups, called *secondary groups,* are organized around specific, impersonal goals rather than the need for personal interaction. The interpersonal relationships found within secondary groups are known as secondary-group relationships. For example, the Packers had a secondary-group relationship with their management. Management's goal was to make the highest profits possible by winning games and attracting fans to the stadium. Players such as Jerry Kramer were given contracts based on how well they performed, not on their personal characteristics. If they didn't perform well, they were cut from the team. The players' relationship with management was formal and impersonal. Almost all players negotiated their contracts through agents. Other secondary-group relationships would include workers and their supervisors in a large office, and a clerk and a customer in a store.

A primary group is judged by the quality of its human relationships. Emotional satisfaction was more important to Jerry Kramer and his golf buddies, for example, than who won at golf. A secondary group is judged by how well it performs a task or achieves a goal; a good professional football team wins games. In a primary group, members can express themselves with relative freedom. But a saleswoman in a department store, for example, is supposed to be polite and pleasant to customers even if she has a splitting headache and the customers are giving her a hard time.

Chart 5:A illustrates some of the usual characteristics of primary and secondary groups. See if you can categorize groups to which you belong that may not be listed on the chart.

5:A

	Primary	**Secondary**
Groups:	Family	School class
	Playmates	Political party
	Couple	Department store
	Gang	School band
Relationships:	Husband-wife	Class adviser-student
	Friends	Politician-party worker
	Sweethearts	Clerk-customer
	Gang leader-member	Conductor-musician
Social Characteristics:	Informal	Formal
	Feeling of freedom and spontaneity	Feeling of constraint
	Wide knowledge of other members	Limited knowledge of other members

The closeness of the primary group of teens is very different from that in a youngsters' dancing class, a secondary group.

Self-help groups. In our industrialized, mobile society, many people have abandoned—either voluntarily or through circumstances over which they have no control—many of the primary groups that were previously the support of their social lives. A young boy whose father dies, for example, may have no adult male relatives nearby to whom he can turn for friendship and guidance. A couple who might once have relied on a minister for help with marital problems no longer have a church membership. A farm family that moves to a big city finds it difficult to establish friendships with other families. It misses the camaraderie prevalent in its old and much smaller community.

As former patterns of social group life have faded, Americans have found a variety of substitutes—professional groups, charities, volunteer groups to help others, and even groups to help themselves. In the 1970's and 1980's, groups were organized to address almost every imaginable problem and need. For example, the young, fatherless boy might be assigned a "Big Brother" through an organization that pairs men with children who need male role models. His mother might join "Parents Without Partners" in order to meet more single parents and find out how they cope with child-raising. The couple with marital problems might join a therapy group to help them work out their difficulties. The farm family might make friends through a neighborhood group.

For many people, their commitment to self-help groups may be for a limited time. Their needs may be filled, or they may move on to other activities. In other groups, people who have learned to cope with a particular problem may turn around to help new members. The focus of groups may also change from time to time, too. Some groups (primary) spend most of their time discussing the individual problems of their members while others (secondary) seek remedies to common problems by trying to change society.

The following excerpt, adapted from a newspaper article, tells about self-help groups that meet to discuss common problems and to learn how to cope with them.

Across the country every week, some 12 million people participate in half a million support groups.

Their causes are varied. They discuss everything from claustrophobia to religion to child-rearing practices. But the purpose of the people who participate is the same: They seek moral support from others who are or who have been in the same psychic boat.

"The field is growing," says Margaret Duthie, education and outreach coordinator for the New Jersey Self-Help Clearinghouse. "We started in 1981 as a service provided by the Consultation and Education Department of St. Clare's Hospital. We were only supposed to be servicing Morris County."

That first year, Duthie says, the clearinghouse was inundated with 1,200 calls from people looking for groups for their particular problem. Seven years later, the clearinghouse gets 10,500 calls annually and services the whole state of New Jersey. The group's computer data base holds information on more than 3,400 self-help group meetings and hundreds of people who are interested in starting new groups in local communities.

There are groups for people with Lou Gehrig's disease, eating disorders, and addictions of every type. There are groups for short people, tall people, men who like to dress as women, women who love too much, and people with hundreds of other physical, mental and emotional issues they're dying to talk about. In addition, there are people trying to start groups in scores of other areas, from parents of hyperactive children to compulsive shoplifters.

Why are so many people anxious to join groups that deal with things that used to be reserved for the privacy of an analyst's couch? Duthie sees the groups as fulfilling a need that is neglected by other social and psychiatric services.

"One thing most therapists can't do is offer empathy," she says. "They can't say, 'I know exactly how you feel, because I've been there.' "

Tony, leader of a local chapter of Emotions Anonymous, a group for people with emotional problems, agrees. "Nobody can really understand a problem unless they've been through it themselves," he says. "It helps to see how your peers have faced a problem."

This peer-group approach owes a lot to Alcoholics Anonymous, the granddaddy of support groups. Alcoholics Anonymous, started in 1935 by "Bill W." and "Doctor Bob" (anonymity is a cornerstone of many of these groups, where last names are not used), emphasizes the fellowship of shared experience as the way to sobriety . . .

"In-groups have power," says Anne Baxter, director of the Rutgers University Personnel Counseling Service and an addiction specialist. "The group is greater than the individual. For instance, there is a networking effect, where members exchange telephone numbers. Then, if someone needs to talk they can just call up another member. There is no professional can give 24 hour service like that."

Baxter feels so strongly about support groups that she encourages her own clients to find a group for their needs. "When I run marital therapy groups, I encourage them to meet on their own, without me. Groups can counteract the impersonality of a professional. They are very cathartic."

Although there are tensions between the academic community and the support group movement—some professionals question the wisdom of all this soulbaring among untrained laypeople—the selfhelpers got a boost lately from none other than Surgeon General Dr. C. Everett Koop, who praised them at a workshop on self-help last October.

"I believe in self-help as an effective way of dealing with problems, stress, and hardship and pain," he said. Koop also called for a closer liaison between the self-help movement and public health agencies . . .

Some people don't see support groups as a new phenomenon at all, but rather a return to old traditions and support systems.

"People always got together in groups," says Dr. Brenna Bry, director of the psychological clinic and associate professor of clinical psychology at Rutgers University. "There were sewing bees, things like that. In a small town you had a stable group of neighbors who helped you. It's just that in this impersonal modern world people don't get that support anymore."

Helping Teens Fight Drunk Driving.
Over 40 percent of all teenage (15 to 19 year-olds) deaths result from motor vehicle crashes. Approximately ten 15 to 19 year-

olds die each day in alcohol-related traffic accidents. These tragic statistics became a terrible reality for Candy Lightner when a drunk driver struck and killed her 13-year-old daughter, Cari.

Vowing to do something about the problem, Candy Lightner formed a support group called Mothers Against Drunk Driving (MADD). Within a short time, MADD developed into a nationwide organizaiton headquartered in Hurst, Texas. Over half a million members now comprise 375 chapters in 48 states.

MADD volunteers have developed a number of programs to help teens fight drunk driving. Project Graduation, for example, attempts to unite students, educators, and civic organizations in a campaign "to insure that prom and graduation nights are memorable occasions, and not memorial ones." The project provides information about the dangers of drunk driving and sponsors poster contests. In addition, MADD organizes workshops for concerned citizens and offers guidance to high school students who are interested in organizing student groups.

Educational programs are only a part of MADD's total program. Local chapters also provide a number of special programs to aid the victims of alcohol-related crashes. Trained volunteers offer emotional support to help victims cope with their grief, anger, and confusion. Victims are also invited to attend meetings, where they can share their feelings with others who have had similar experiences.

Other self-help groups have also formed to help teens combat drunk driving. One year after Cari Lightner's death,

Students Against Drunk Driving is an important self-help group.

two teenage boys died in another tragic accident resulting from drunk driving. Their teacher and coach, Robert Anastas, felt that something had to be done. "As I witnessed the behavior of fellow students at the wakes of these two boys," he explains, "it became apparent to me that there is a great deal of love and caring amongst teenagers toward each other. It also became clear to me that, if they cared about each other so much, they could certainly address this problem themselves."

In order to help teens and their parents solve the problem, Anastas formed an organization called Students Against Drunk Driving (SADD). SADD encourages parents and teenagers to work together to "eliminate this needless slaughter on our highways."

Like MADD, SADD promotes student organizations in high schools throughout the country. The SADD chapters strive to provide their members with "a sound background in alcohol awareness." SADD also encourages parents and teenagers to sign a "Contract For Life." In this contract, the teenager agrees to call the parent "for advice and/or transportation at any hour, from any place, if I am ever in a situation where I have been drinking or a friend or date who is driving me has been drinking." The parent agrees "to come and get you at any hour, any place, no questions asked and no argument at that time, or I will pay for a taxi to bring you home safely. I expect we would discuss this issue at a later time."

🖎 What functions do these groups serve in the lives of their members? How might they feel or act without such groups?

Group Dynamics

Group influence on behavior. Because group membership is so important to our well-being as humans, we are rarely totally free of the influence of some groups — a family, a peer group, or a reference group, for example. Sometimes we are aware of these influences; we hear the cheering of our teammates and the booing of our opponents. At other times, the group influence is so much a part of our lives that we are not conscious of it. Frequently, the pressures of one group of which we are members conflict with those of another that is important to us. Our peers, for example, may tell us that a C is a perfectly acceptable grade, and our parents may find only A's acceptable.

Philip Zimbardo and Floyd Ruch give the following example of the strength of the influence of groups on an individual in their book, *Psychology and Life:*

In some colleges there is a student norm that restricts student participation during lecture classes. In one notable case, breaching such a norm of "shutting up and letting teachers do what they are paid to do" had devastating consequences for an eager, naive student in an introductory psychology class. This young student, Charlie B., would not only answer questions at great length but would ask questions and volunteer information.

At first, when he rose to answer, those seated around him would poke each other, smirk, frown, and clear their throats. In time, these nonverbal comments turned into snickers, giggles, and shuffling sounds. Finally, as he was about to rise, the student on one or the other side would bump him accidentally, or in turning to look at him, would

Peer groups are very important to
most adolescents and usually encourage
a high degree of conformity.

knock down his books and jam his seat up. By the
middle of the year, Charlie never raised his hand
or answered when the teacher called on him. What
is more, two years later he told his teacher (during
a counseling session about graduate school): "I
never take lecture courses anymore, even if the
teacher is good: I don't know why, but somehow
they just make me feel uncomfortable and anxious."

The influence of a group on individual behavior can be both positive and
negative. William Foote Whyte studied an
Italian slum neighborhood in Boston while
he was a graduate student at Harvard.

Whyte's study, *Street Corner Society*,
shows how groups can boost or suppress an
individual's performance. Whyte was accepted into a street-corner group called
the "Nortons" and became very close to
its leaders. He recalls one experience he
had when he went bowling with the group:

"Here was the social structure in action right on the bowling alleys. It held

the individual members in their places —
and [me] along with them. I did not stop
to reason that, as a close friend of Doc,
Danny, and Mike, I held a position close
to the top of the gang and therefore
should be expected to excel on this great
occasion. I simply felt myself buoyed up by
the situation. I felt my friends were for
me, had confidence in me, wanted me to
bowl well. As my turn came and I stepped
up to bowl, I felt supremely confident that
I was going to hit the pins that I was aim-
ing at. I have never felt quite that way before — or since. Here at the bowling alley
I was experiencing subjectively the impact
of the group structure on the individual.
It was a strange feeling, as if something
larger than myself was controlling the ball
as I went through my swing and released it
toward the pins."

Although Whyte was not an outstanding bowler, he won the tournament
for the Nortons.

Among the Nortons, Whyte observed
that during an important game when
everyone participated, good bowlers who
were not considered leaders were razzed or
distracted, and the leaders, who might not
bowl as well, were given so much group
support that they tended to win. Whyte's
participant observation was done between
1937 and 1940. His conclusion that a person's performance is affected by his or her
status in a group has come to be called the
bowling score effect.

Have you observed negative group
pressures on individual performances in
your school? Any positive group pressures?
Name as many of each kind as you can.

High school group pressures. As we
noted, peer pressure is extremely important to adolescents. In the following selection, excerpted from *Looking Back: A
Chronicle of Growing Old in the Sixties,*
author Joyce Maynard recalls the strong
influence that groups had on her behavior
in high school:

*We knew each others' faces and bodies and
wardrobes so well that any change was noticed at
once, the fuel for endless notes. That's why I
dressed so carefully mornings. I was about to face
the scrutiny of 15 gossip-seeking girls and 10 only
slightly less observant boys ready to imitate my
voice and walk. At every moment — even at
home, with no one but family there — I'd be
conscious of what the other kids, The Group,
would think if they could see me. They ruled over
us all — and over each other — like a supreme
court. . . .*

*Although popularity is a word I've never
warmed up to, I recognized the results of it every
time we chose up teams in gym, every time there
was a dance or field trip. One could tell from
where we sat in the lunchroom — the tables of
girls with too-long dresses and hair that curled in
the bent, squared-off way that came from using
bobby pins; the tables of matching mohair skirts
and sweaters, and shoulder bags bursting with
notes and cosmetics — the girls who had only their
failures in common and the ones who sat together
in victory, feasting. . . .*

*How do kids decide, as they invariably do,
which people to admire and which ones to ignore
or laugh at? It's more than looks (good looks often
happen after popularity, in the happy confidence
that comes from admiration). Anyway, beauty
wasn't all that successful at my school, any more
than grades over B-plus were. Cuteness, on the
other hand, was fine — for girls and boys. . . .*

If nobody especially longed to be anything as

One's self-image and behavior are greatly influenced by peer group pressures.

uncomfortably extreme as beautiful, everybody very much wanted to be good-looking. Most of us thought it had a lot to do with clothes and makeup. But the instincts — to know which makeup, how to look as if you really didn't care and it was just by accident that peach blusher brushed across your cheeks — that was the rare thing that, unlike looks, you had to be born with.

Some girls would try too hard and end up with lipstick on their teeth and a place around the jawline where, like a mask, the makeup color ended and the skin began. . . .

I was aware of almost every step I took, imagined heavy clumping sounds. I envied ballerinas and studied the girls at school whose walking I admired to see just how they swung their arms and where they put their chins and shoulders.

That was something I did a lot — checking to see how the others, the very popular ones, did things — how they chewed their lunch-box carrot sticks, whether they wore loafers with pennies in them or not (not — penny loafers were corny), and whether, on rainy days, they put on rubbers or got their feet soaked. But no matter what I learned from my study of The Popular, I seemed to be forever one step out of time.

How are group pressures in your school like those that Maynard describes? How are they different?

Leadership and group dynamics. In describing a season with the Green Bay Packers, Jerry Kramer shows that there were definite patterns of interaction and personal relationships. Bart Starr was the team's quarterback. He had the closest relationship with Coach Lombardi, told the offensive team what the upcoming play would be, and was the person most sought for interviews. Willie Davis was captain of the defensive team. He was popular with

teammates and fans, and was skilled in story-telling and imitating people. His nickname was "Dr. Feelgood."

Within every group, whether a class in school, a construction crew, or a street gang, there are similar patterns of interaction and relationships that clearly indicate to sociologists degrees of power, influence, and friendship among the members and how these affect the group's organization.

In every group, there are people who influence the behavior of others — its leaders. As we have seen, Bart Starr was a leader of the Packers. But was he the most popular member of the group? If the players had been asked to name the individual whose company they would most prefer on a social outing, they probably would have picked Willie Davis. Davis was the most popular member of the group and also one of its leaders.

Such patterns of leadership are not uncommon. In most situations, a group will choose as its leader the person, such as Starr, who has the greatest ability to influence others to move toward its goals. Sociologists call such people *task leaders.* But once the leader begins to give directions, tensions may develop.

Although the Packers regarded Starr as one of their best players and a model in his off-field life, Starr was extremely quiet.

A person like Davis, whom sociologists call a *maintenance leader,* frequently emerges in groups to maintain harmony. Using humor, charm, or both, the maintenance leader keeps morale high so that the group will accept more readily the directions of the task leader.

☙ Analyze other groups of which you have been a member — on a job, in a club, or on a team. Can you identify the task leader in that group? What tasks did that person perform? Can you identify the maintenance leader? What tasks did that person perform?

Leaders and their styles. We sometimes say of people that they are "born leaders," but is there any evidence that this is accurate? Do leaders have distinctive characteristics that make them stand out from followers?

Several sociological studies indicate that leaders are generally taller, or stronger, than other group members, and are better-looking in the judgment of the group. They also tend to have higher IQ's, to be more sociable, determined, energetic, and self-confident. If a leader's IQ is too much higher than the others, however, relations between them will probably break down.

Other sociologists say that such studies have too many historic exceptions to be reliable. Some famous leaders, like Napoleon, were small. Abraham Lincoln was not handsome by the standards of his day.

Also of great interest to sociologists are the types of leadership styles that are most effective in holding groups together and seeing that they accomplish their goals. Does the *authoritarian* leader, who makes all the decisions himself and gives orders to the others, get the best results? Or the *democratic* leader, who seeks to win the approval and support of the members on a course of action? Or the *laissez-faire*

A democratic leader is likely to seek the response of group members, while an authoritarian leader is more likely to give orders.

(permissive) leader who is easy-going and makes little effort to direct the group?

To explore this question, social psychologists Kurt Lewin, Ronald Lippitt, and Ralph White conducted an experiment with groups of 10-year-old boys. Each group was given an adult leader with one of three styles. The authoritarian leaders barked orders: "Get your work aprons on. Today we've got to paint and letter the sign." The democratic leaders guided their groups by giving suggestions such as this one to a boy sawing: "Did you ever try going the other way — with the grain?" The laissez-faire leaders did not offer any advice unless they were asked for it. Then they gave it in a quite friendly way. After observing the three types of groups once a week for several months, the researchers came to these conclusions:

The groups headed by the democratic leaders were effective, efficient, and friendly. The groups headed by the authoritarian leaders sometimes produced more, but only when their leaders were present. The authoritarian-directed groups were generally hostile toward their leaders, and relations among the members were strained and tense. The least productive and efficient groups were those headed by the laissez-faire leaders. There, boys were friendly with their leader, but they "fooled around" so much that they accomplished very few of their work goals.

Resistance to leaders. Other experiments have shown that no matter how talented leaders may be, if they try to change their groups' customs too much, they will probably fail and lose their positions as well.

In one such experiment, groups of nursery-school children were allowed to develop customs and norms of their own — where they should sit, what games they should play, what toys individual members might play with. Once these customs were established, the experimenters put another child in each group. The new child was usually a little older and bigger than the others and had already shown strong leadership qualities. Would the new leaders be able to dominate the groups in which they were now placed?

Sociologist Ferenc Merei found that whenever these potential leaders tried to direct their groups in new activities, they were rebuffed. The more they persisted, the more frustrated they became. Some gave up trying to lead. Others, however, tried a different tactic. They would carefully observe what their groups were doing and then join their activities. Once they had conformed to their groups' norms, they were allowed to lead. This did not mean that they could now introduce wholly new activities; they could, however, make a few innovations in the old. The conclusion of the experimenters was, of course, that successful leaders must first become followers.

⌁ Given Merei's findings, suppose for a moment that you have just been elected mayor of your city. How might you go about promoting new programs with citizens who are reluctant to change?

Group norms. When a group of workers consistently produces much less than it is capable of, how can its performance be improved? Is more money the answer? During one of the Hawthorne experiments you read about in Chapter 2, the Western Electric Company offered bonuses to workers at its plant to encourage increased production. The offer had no effect at all. The workers continued to produce at their usual rate.

Then sociologists discovered that the group they were studying had established a norm for how much its members should produce. Workers who exceeded the norm were criticized as "speed kings." Workers who produced less than the norm were called "chiselers." Once the group had set production at a certain level, it pressured the members to comply.

What, then, was the solution to group pressure aimed at keeping production below capacity? Many companies confronted with the same problem wanted to find out.

At a pajama factory in Marion, Virginia, production slowed considerably when the company made a slight change in a work procedure. The company wanted women employees who pressed pajamas to stack them in boxes when they had finished, instead of placing them on a flat piece of cardboard. The company expected that production would decline until the women got used to the new procedure, but that afterward it would return to its former level. This didn't happen, however. Once the women began to work at a slower rate, a new norm was established and the group continued to enforce it. How could the original production level be restored or increased?

Social scientists Lester Coch and

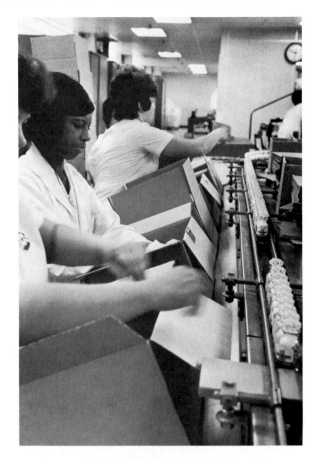

Group norms are important in determining the output of these vitamin packagers. Cooperation is essential in a group task such as the Amish barn-raising on the next page.

John French recommended an experiment to company officials. One group of women would be invited to meet with company representatives to discuss the purpose of the change and the relative ease with which it could be accomplished. Another group would simply be told that the change was necessary. The first group accepted the new procedure and soon exceeded its former rate of production. The second group quickly became hostile toward the company. Some of the women quit, and others filed grievances. Production remained low. The lesson of this and other industrial experiments was clear: When groups of workers are allowed to participate in decisions that affect them, they will be much more willing to accept changes, and morale will be higher.

Ⴠ The pajama workers, however, were not included in the actual decision-making process. Should they have been? Why, or why not?

Processes of group interaction. Groups are enormously diverse. Yet certain patterns of interaction appear again and again in all of them. Sociologists call the regularly recurring patterns of interaction that occur in human groups *social processes.*

Two of the most important social processes are cooperation and competition. When members of a group work together to achieve a common goal, they are *cooperating.* Among small, simple societies that obtain their food by hunting and fishing, these activities are likely to be carried out by entire communities.

Until recently, for example, the

people of the East African Ik tribe hunted together with nets. Typically, about 100 men, women, and children would move out onto the plains and set up a wide arc of nets attached to poles. The women and small children would then begin to beat the tall grass where animals grazed, driving them toward the trap. As the animals rushed headlong into the nets, they would be killed by the men and boys waiting there with spears and bows and arrows. Each member of the hunt then shared equally in the day's kill.

Competition occurs when two or more individuals or groups try to outdo each other to achieve a reward. In the 1960's, the Ik were driven off the plains where food was abundant and forced into the arid mountains above. (Their former lands were converted to national parks and preserves.) Faced with starvation, the Ik became very competitive. Food was not shared anymore, and often it was literally taken from the mouths of the old and the sick.

⮥ Refer now to the Arapesh in Chapter 3. Do you think these people would become as fiercely competitive as the Ik in the face of starvation? Why, or why not?

Who cooperates? As a rule, whether people prefer to compete or cooperate is determined by their culture. In her studies of New Guinea tribes, for example, Margaret Mead found that the Arapesh encouraged their children to get along with one another from a very early age. Cooperation was consistently rewarded, and competition discouraged.

In other New Guinea societies, however, children were taught that only by competing with each other could they obtain material rewards as well as the respect and approval of their elders (emotional rewards). Among the Dobuans, Mead found that competition was emphasized so strongly that even members of the same family were unable to cooperate.

Much of our society values competition highly. American children learn to compete for good grades in school, for prestige and leadership among their peers, and for a multitude of awards and honors.

Individuals and groups benefit from cooperation in many ways. "Many hands make light work," a saying goes, and it may apply to the building of a skyscraper or a group of neighbors helping a farmer to bring in his hay. Cooperative groups also provide security for members. A bushman hunter of southern Africa knows that, even if he fails to kill any game one day, his group will not let him starve. In industrial societies, a similar kind of security is provided by unemployment compensation and old-age pensions.

Though cooperation solves many problems, it may also create some. The Arapesh of New Guinea, for example, value cooperation so highly that an individual who shows outstanding skills or creativity is regarded with suspicion. Such a person appears to be "pushy." As a result, the Arapesh are rather passive and uncreative as compared with some of their more assertive neighbors. Their society remains static. The price of overemphasizing cooperation may be a society that is too static to adapt to changing conditions.

What do these photos suggest about the balance between cooperation and competition in our culture?

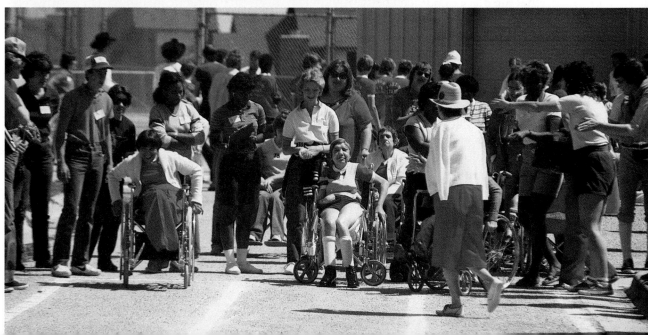

Competition's spur. Competition undoubtedly spurs both individualism and creativity, not only in business but in the arts and sciences, politics, sports, and many other areas. The competitive spirit primed the Industrial Revolution, which brought a higher standard of living to more people than ever before. Even in Socialist countries, which value cooperation highly, it has been found that productivity increases when factory and farm groups are encouraged to compete with one another.

An overemphasis on competition, however, can also create problems. Many people complain that competitive pressures in our society have made daily life a "rat race." In a competitive society too, people who are successful may look down on the less fortunate as "losers" who deserve only contempt. Though studies have shown that the majority of welfare recipients would much prefer to work and consider welfare degrading, many people simply regard them as "lazy" or worse.

🖎 Can you think of other stereotypes that are placed on uncompetitive individuals? What is the evidence that American culture places a high value on winning? What is the evidence that it does not?

War and other conflicts. Perhaps the greatest drawback of competition is that it may easily lead to another social process, conflict. In competition, rivals seek to outdo each other. In *conflict,* they seek to coerce, harm, or even destroy each other. Though conflict is often physical, it doesn't have to be. Conflicts between

labor and management may be settled by negotiations, and most strikes are peaceable. The danger of conflicts between groups is that, if they are not resolved quickly, they may lead to violence and destruction. The most destructive conflicts of all are wars; over the centuries they have caused untold human suffering. Today, a conflict fought with nuclear weapons could mean the end of all life on our planet.

Though conflict generally divides people, it can make members of a group unite against an external threat. Before the Japanese bombed Pearl Harbor in December 1941, for example, Americans were sharply divided in their attitudes about World War II. Some believed that it was "none of our business" and that the United States should stay out of it. Others believed that we had to help the victims of German and Japanese aggression or become victims ourselves. When the Japanese attacked the U.S. Pacific Fleet at Pearl Harbor, Americans forgot their differences and united against the common enemy.

Conflict can also have a positive effect by calling attention to serious social problems. The civil-rights movement of the 1950's and 1960's stirred up racial animosity that often led to violence. Yet it also brought about reforms that might never have been enacted unless blacks had confronted whites on the issues of prejudice and discrimination.

🖎 What examples can you think of in which conflict brought positive results? Negative results? How?

Reducing Intergroup Conflict

In one of his best remembered songs, John Lennon asked his listeners to "Imagine all the people living life in peace . . . Oh, you may say I'm a dreamer, but I'm not the only one . . ." For centuries many others have shared Lennon's dream of peace and, yet, repeated conflicts have marred this vision. What causes group conflicts and how can they be resolved?

These questions challenge researchers who specialize in studying group behavior. During the late 1940's and early 1950's, Muzafer and Carolyn Sherif conducted a series of new classic experiments which provide insights into both the causes and possible solutions of intergroup conflict.

The Sherifs conducted their experiments at summer camps in Connecticut, New York, and Oklahoma. Their subjects were 11 and 12 year-old boys. The Sherifs began by carefully testing the boys to make certain that they were all psychologically healthy. Posing as camp counselors, the experimenters then divided the youths into two groups. Each group received its own cabin and play area.

During the first week, the two groups separately participated in a number of activities including hiking, swimming, and boating. As a result of these cooperative experiences, the boys developed a strong attachment to their own group. They even gave themselves names such as the Bull Dogs and Red Devils.

After creating two tightly knit in-groups, the experimenters devoted the next week to a series of competitive activities. The two groups engaged in touch football games, a tug of war, and other contests. The Sherifs awarded attractive prizes and trophies to the winning groups.

At first, the groups emphasized friendly competition. However, this soon led to a fierce rivalry. The boys called each other names and blamed their opponents for starting a food fight. As tensions increased, each group exerted pressure on its members to see their rivals as the "enemy."

The Sherifs now attempted to reduce the high level of intergroup tensions. They began by giving lectures urging friendship. The boys rejected this advice, claiming that their opponents could not be trusted. The experimenters then tried to unite the groups by using visiting teams from nearby camps as outside enemies. The two groups did combine forces to defeat their "common enemy." However, once the visitors left, their rivalry resumed.

The experimenters finally reduced intergroup hostility by using *superordinate goals*. A superordinate goal is one that is attractive to both groups but cannot be achieved without a joint effort. For example, the Sherifs deliberately clogged the camp's water system, thus forcing the boys to work together to fix it. Cooperative activities such as this restored trust and helped build new friendships.

Thinking Critically

1. What conclusions about the causes of intergroup conflict can we reach from the Sherifs' experiment?

2. What are superordinate goals? What are possible superordinate goals which could reduce tensions between the United States and the Soviet Union?

application

Here is an experiment that your class can easily conduct with the help of your teacher. Suppose that you and your classmates are prisoners of war. Some of the group are in favor of trying to escape. Each member has to decide whether the risk is worth taking. If you stay where you are, you will probably survive the war, but you may be a prisoner for years. If you are caught trying to escape, you will be shot.

Now suppose that the odds of escaping range from one chance in ten (very risky) to nine chances in ten (fairly safe). At what odds would *you* be willing to risk an escape? One in ten? Three in ten? Nine in ten? Without any discussion among your classmates, write on a piece of paper the odds at which you would attempt an escape.

Your teacher can tell you what to do next.

summary

Sociologists focus most of their attention on **groups,** two or more people who interact with each other and engage in a common activity. In their studies, they identify a number of kinds of groups.

An **in-group** is one that a person feels he or she belongs to and identifies with. Members refer to themselves as "we." An **out-group** is one that a person does not feel he or she belongs to, nor identifies with. Members of an out-group are referred to as "they." Usually a symbolic **boundary,** such as a school decal, separates insiders from outsiders. To cross the boundary and become an insider, one goes through an **initiation rite,** which may be as simple as a handshake or as elaborate as a formal oath-taking ceremony.

Any group that serves as a standard against which one measures oneself is called a **reference group,** whether it is made up of one's friends or of people one admires.

The relationships that one finds in a family differ considerably from those, for example, in a large business organization. Families, friends, cliques, and other groups that are normally characterized by close, emotionally satisfying relationships are called **primary groups.** Groups, such as school classes, that are chiefly concerned with accomplishing a task, and are characterized by impersonal, formal relationships are called **secondary groups.**

Today many people complain that busy industrial societies offer fewer opportunities for traditional group life. In their search for greater intimacy and emotional security and to seek remedies to common problems, many people have started or participated in a variety of groups to help others and themselves. These may range all the way from Alcoholics Anonymous to neighborhood associations.

Within every group, there are usually people who are able to influence the behavior of others — its leaders. Some leaders, **task leaders,** are mainly concerned with getting things done; others, **maintenance leaders,** are more concerned with promoting good group morale. Studies have shown that leaders generally are taller or stronger than other group members, and are better-looking in the judgment of the group. Usually they also have higher IQ's, are more determined and self-confident. One experiment conducted in the United States revealed that **democratic** leaders got better results with their groups than either **authoritarian** or **laissez-faire** (permissive) leaders. Other experiments have shown that leaders who attempt to make substantial changes in the established norms of their groups will fail.

Certain patterns of interaction appear in virtually all human groups. These regularly recurring, common patterns are called **social processes.** Among the most important of them are cooperation, competition, and conflict. **Cooperation** occurs when members of a group work together to achieve a common goal. **Competition** occurs when two or more individuals or groups try to outdo each other to achieve a material or an emotional reward, or both. **Conflict** results when competitors seek to coerce, harm, or destroy each other. Though conflict usually divides people, it may unite a group against an external threat. Conflict may also have a positive effect by calling attention to serious social problems. When conflicts become violent, as in wars, they lead to heavy human suffering and destruction.

more questions and activities

1. Give the sociological definition of *groups* and explain why they are important to our individual social development.

2. In the example of Jerry Kramer, identify his peer group, his in-group, his out-group, his primary group, his secondary group, and his reference group.

3. Name three processes of group interaction and give an example of each.

4. Write a first-person account of peer group pressures in junior high school. You might also include social boundaries and what distinguished your in-group from your out-group.

5. Make a list of self-help groups in your community. You might visit one as a participant observer and find out how such a group functions.

6. Pick a group of which you are a member. Analyze the kinds of leaders it has and their styles of leadership. What social processes occur?

7. When you are in a group, do you tend to perform task or maintenance functions? Your teacher has a list of activities to help you decide.

8. A *sociogram* is a diagram that shows relationships between people within a group. In picture form, it attempts to illustrate who gets along well with other members and who is isolated. In the sociogram at the bottom of the page, each group member was asked to pick a first, second, and third choice of a swimming partner. After studying the sociogram, which person appears to be the favorite swimming partner? Which is least favored? You might attempt to draw a sociogram of some group with which you are familiar. If you prefer, you can identify the group members by numbers to assure that no one will be embarrassed.

9. You are President of the United States. You face an important strategic decision. You decide to call a meeting of your Cabinet and ask the members' advice. Perhaps a decision can be reached in the meeting. What sociological information about group decision-making would be helpful to you? How would you use it?

10. Analyze a current international crisis in terms of the social processes at work. What events or personalities appear to activate each process?

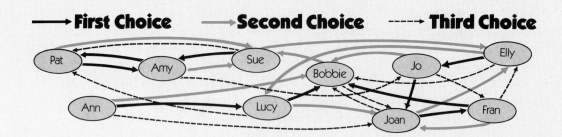

suggested readings

Boulle, Pierre. *The Bridge over the River Kwai.* (Bantam, 1970.) A fictional account of an authoritarian American colonel and his men who build a bridge while they are prisoners of war in a Japanese camp during World War II.

Finsterbusch, Kurt. *Sociology, 1987/1988.* (Dushkin, 1987). A fine collection of readings includes particularly strong sections on primary and secondary groups.

Gans, Herbert. *The Urban Villagers.* (Free Press, 1965.) Although primarily a study of a working-class Italian neighborhood in Boston, this well-known book also contains valuable insights into primary group-relationships and the adolescent peer group.

Golding, William. *Lord of the Flies.* (G.P. Putnam's Sons, 1959.) A fictional account about a group of young English school boys who are stranded on an uninhabited island, where they attempt to create a society. The chilling story of their failure illustrates many aspects of group dynamics discussed in this chapter.

Kramer, Jerry. *Instant Replay: The Green Bay Diary of Jerry Kramer.* (World, 1968.) Kramer's exciting account of a championship season with the Green Bay Packers contains many perceptive comments about group processes.

Olmstead, M.S., and A. Paul Hare. *The Small Group.* (Random House, 1978). A useful introduction to small group research.

Whyte, William Foote. *Street Corner Society.* (University of Chicago Press, 1981.) A classic participant observation of a street corner group. Part One, "Corner Boys and College Boys," is especially important for its insights into leadership roles in small groups.

How does this family compare with norms for the typical American family?

chapter 6

marriage and family

Kathy had just begun a new job at an advertising agency when a friend introduced her to Tom during their lunch hour. He was working as an accountant for a large company nearby. "It was just like you read about, but never thought would happen to you," Kathy recalls. "It was love at first sight. He was so handsome and interesting! I could barely keep my mind on my job."

Tom also remembered exactly how he felt when he first met Kathy. "To tell the truth, I was thinking about an important account and didn't even want to go to lunch. But when I met Kathy everything clicked. I knew I had to see her again. That same night I called her up. We went out the next evening and had a great time. I was so happy I could hardly keep from telling everyone at the office about her."

No doubt you've heard stories like this before, or perhaps you've felt the same way yourself. What Tom and Kathy describe is *romantic love*, a mixture of intense physical attraction and excitement, and a feeling that one has found the ideal mate.

In this chapter, we'll learn more about Kathy and Tom. In doing so, we will also examine American patterns of courtship, wedding celebration, marriage, and family life; and we will compare them to patterns found in other cultures. Among the changes in American family discussed are the increase in women working outside the home, the challenge to traditional sex roles, the high divorce rate, and the singleparent family. We'll also learn what population experts believe the U.S. must do to help solve these problems.

Selecting a Mate

Romantic love as a guide. Probably no
other society idealizes romantic love as
much as our own. "Love is the answer,"
we are told in songs, movies, romance
magazines, and even comic books: "Love
gives our lives purpose; without it, life is
empty." And how is love fulfilled?
Through marriage, of course. As a popular
song says: "Love and marriage go together
like a horse and carriage. A 1985 survey
conducted by the Roper Organization
asked, "What is the most important reason for marrying?" A great majority, 83
percent of men and women, answered,
"Being in love."

Kathy and Tom were no exception. A
year after meeting, they decided to get married. Since about 90 percent of all Americans marry at some time, their decision did
not surprise their family. Indeed, Kathy's
parents had become concerned that she
would never marry: "I was 24 and Tom was
26, " Kathy recalls. "My parents had begun
to wonder if I was ever going to marry. I
guess their concern was only natural. My
mother married when she was only 18 and
Dad was 20. I understand their concern but
times have changed. I wanted to finish college, get a job, and then settle down."

Tom agreed with Kathy: "My parents
understood that I wanted to go out on my
own for awhile. But, they really liked Kathy
and wanted me to marry her."

Kathy's and Tom's parents did not
interfere in their early relationship or plans
to marry. Such freedom is not the norm in
many other cultures.

*Romantic love has long been glorified in our
culture. The magazine cover above is from the
1940's. Below, a contemporary advertisement.*

Arranged marriages. In many societies throughout the world, parents still act as matchmakers for their children. They believe that young people are too impractical to be trusted with the choice of a mate. As a rule, parents who arrange their children's marriages look for mates of roughly equal social status. Why should they "throw away" their son or daughter on a mate who has no advantages except, perhaps, physical attractiveness?

An eligible son or daughter, they reason, has a certain market value. Often, in fact, an arranged marriage involves handing over a sum of money, or property, to one partner or the other. The exact amount may be arrived at after hard bargaining that requires the services of a mediator.

To us, the practice of arranged marriages probably seems quite heartless. Yet in societies where they are the rule, the children as well as the parents may favor them. In the 1950's, marriage counselors David and Vera Mace went to India, where marriages are usually arranged by parents. In their book, *Marriage East and West*, they record an interview with some teenage Indian girls. The Maces asked them how they felt about arranged marriages:

"Wouldn't you like to be free to choose your own marriage partners?" we asked.

"Oh, no!" several voices replied in chorus.

"Doesn't it put the girl in a very humiliating position?" one girl asked.

"Humiliating? In what way?" [we asked.]

"Well, doesn't she have to try to look pretty, and call attention to herself, and attract a boy, to be sure she'll get married?"

"Yes, I suppose that's what it amounts to."

"And if she doesn't want to do that or if she feels it's undignified, wouldn't that mean she mightn't get a husband?"

"That's possible."

"So a girl who is shy might not be able to get married. Does that happen?"

"Sometimes it does."

"Well, surely that's humiliating. It makes getting married a competition in which the girls fight each other for the boys. And it encourages a girl to pretend she's better than she really is. She has to make a good impression to get a boy, and then she has to go on making a good impression to get him to marry her."

Then another girl spoke. "In our system," she said, "we girls don't have to worry at all. We know we'll get married. When we are old enough, our parents find a suitable boy, and everything is arranged."

"Besides," said a third girl, "how could we judge the character of a boy we met? We are young and inexperienced. Our parents are older and wiser, and they aren't as easily deceived as we could be. . . . I could easily make a mistake if I had to select him myself."

One of these girls raised some interesting questions about marriage in the U.S.

"But does the girl really have any choice in the West?" she said. "From what I've read, it seems that the boy does all the choosing. All the girl can do is to say yes or no. She can't go up to a boy and say, 'I like you. Will you marry me?' can she?"

We admitted that this was not done.

"So," she went on eagerly, "when you talk about men and women being equal in the West, it isn't true. When our parents are looking for a husband for us, they don't have to wait until some boy takes it into his head to ask for us. They just find out what families are looking for wives for their sons, and see whether one of the boys would be suitable. Then, if his family agrees that it would be a good match, they arrange it together."

Above, Love at Harvest Time *by Eunice Pinney, painted about 1815. Right, a couple at the turn of the century. Below, students today.*

Social restrictions and pressures. Sociologists say that in every society there are patterns that guide the romantic impulses of the young toward "appropriate" marriages. The guidance may be very overt, as in those societies that favor arranged marriages, or it may be more carefully concealed, as in our society.

American parents may guide their children to make the right choice (from the parents' point of view) at an early age. They may move into neighborhoods and school districts where their sons and daughters will meet the kind of peers their parents prefer. Later they may send them to college where they are likely to meet a suitable mate.

🔊 In what other ways might American parents guide their children to make appropriate marriages?

Exogamy. In every society, the selection of a mate is limited by many restrictions and requirements. One restriction is universal. It is the prohibition of *incest*, that is, sexual relations within one's immediate family. In some cultures, this prohibition extends to one's own clan or tribe. Because incest is a taboo, people must marry outside their family, clan, or tribe. This requirement is called *exogamy*.

Most people assume that the incest taboo stems from the fear that inbreeding may produce abnormalities in children. But incest was forbidden long before the effects of inbreeding were recognized. The most likely reason for the taboo is that it prevents dangerous conflicts from arising within the family. Sexual rivalry between father and son, for example, could easily lead to bloodshed.

Endogamy. The selection of a mate is also limited by rules that encourage people to marry within their own social category. These rules tend to be flexible and are usually more a matter of custom than of law. The practice of marrying a member of one's own social category is called *endogamy*. Quite often, the mate we select is a lot like us and has the advantage of living nearby. For example, Kathy and Tom lived and worked in the same community.

Sometimes, however, people who live close together may be separated by differences in religion, race, ethnic background, and social status. These differences frequently become barriers to marriage. Studies show, in fact, that the great majority of married people found their mates within their own religious, racial, and ethnic category, and social class.

Although interfaith marriages, for example, are more common than they were in the past, people still tend to marry within their own religion. The U.S. Census Bureau included a question on religion in a 1957 population study, the first and only time it documented religious preference. At that time, it found that 21.6 percent of Protestants were married to someone outside their religious group, as were 8.6 percent of Catholics and 7.2 percent of Jews. Since the study has not been repeated, no one knows exactly what the interfaith marriage rate is today. One indication of an increase was found in a study of the American Jewish population between 1975 and 1985 by Dr. Egon Mayer of Brooklyn College. He found that 40 percent of Jews getting married during that period married someone outside their faith.

The tendency against intermarriage is much stronger among racial groups. In 1967, for example, the Supreme Court declared unconstitutional all laws prohibiting interracial marriages. (Seventeen states had such laws at the time.) Yet 20 years later, about one marriage in 300 was interracial.

Marriages between people of different social classes are more common than either interfaith or interracial marriages. (A *class* is a group of people with similar amounts of power, money, and prestige. We will read more about these distinctions in the next chapter.) Still, there is a strong tendency for people to marry within the same class.

What do sociologists conclude from these patterns? With remarkable consistency, people marry those whom they consider alike in important ways. Kathy and Tom, for example, were of the same race, religion, and social class.

According to sociologist Peter Berger, falling in love is actually a very selective process: ". . . In Western countries, and especially America, it is assumed that men and women marry because they are in love. There is a broadly based, popular mythology about the character of love as a violent, irresistible emotion that strikes where it will, a mystery that is the goal of most young people and often of the not-so-young as well. As soon as one investigates which people actually marry each other, however, one finds that the lightning shaft of Cupid seems to be guided rather strongly within very definite channels of class, income, education, and racial and religious backgrounds."

Name as many ways as you can through which institutions in our society promote endogamy.

The marriage gradient. There is one partial exception to the rule that "likes attract." That is the tendency of men to marry women who are slightly below them in social status. This tendency is called the *marriage gradient.* Many men, sociologists say, are willing to marry women of somewhat less education or social standing, provided they have other desirable personal characteristics. Tom, for example, had a higher income than Kathy when they met.

Interracial marriages are becoming more common in the United States.

The marriage gradient creates problems for men at the bottom of the social scale and for women at the top. The men have difficulty because there are few women left to marry. The women have difficulty because there are few men left who are socially superior or equal.

Age. Studies also show that people usually marry within their own age bracket. In about 80 percent of all American marriages, the groom, like Tom, is the same age or slightly older than the bride. According to the U.S. Census Bureau report of 1986, the average age difference between husbands and wives was only two years. The median age of men who got married that year was 25.3; the median age of their brides was 23.1. Only in one marriage out of 17 was the woman more than five years older than her husband.

One reason that women marry men who are slightly older has been economic. A somewhat older man has had time to start earning a living, and the marriage contract in this culture has placed the responsibility for financial support on the husband. However, the life expectancy of American men is about seven years less than that of women. When the average of two years difference in age between husband and wife is added to that, the result is obvious: Many American wives will outlive their husbands by about nine years.

≈∂ Can you think of any effects that women's increased earning capacity as a result of equal opportunity laws might have on the marriage gradient? Do you think women will continue to marry older men in our society? Explain your answer.

Weddings

With their parents' help, Kathy and Tom planned a big church wedding in June. According to tradition, Tom wore a dark tuxedo; Kathy, a long white gown. In a clear voice, Kathy and Tom affirmed their love by pledging, "To have and to hold, from this day forward, for better, for worse, for richer, for poorer, in sickness and in health, to love and to cherish, till death do us part."

In the U.S. During the 1960's and early 1970's, there was much talk about alternative kinds of weddings — outdoor settings, ceremonies written by the couples themselves, unusual attire, and guitar music. Some couples chose to live together without the benefit of any ceremony.

To what extent have these patterns of behavior become a part of the dominant culture? Although there has been a large increase in the number of people who stay single, demographers predict that nine out of ten Americans living today will get married at least once. In the 1980's traditional weddings regained mass popularity. Consider these facts from 1987:

• ninety-five out of a hundred couples who married for the first time had a religious ceremony.

• Virtually every couple has a wedding reception, averaging 207 people.

• More than four out of five first-time brides wore a formal wedding gown.

In *The Eternal Bliss Machine: America's Way of Wedding,* Marcia Seligson notes:

. . . We Americans are getting married almost precisely as we did a hundred years ago. We
are adorning ourselves in long, white, romantic
gowns, going to church or a hotel or country club,
repeating established vows that we have heard at
other folks' weddings for years, sipping cham-
pagne, cutting cake, dancing, tossing the bouquet,
posing for pictures, fleeing through a shower of rice
as we head for our Caribbean honeymoon — repeating, that is, all the clichés. We have invariably
spent more than we can afford and we will certainly tell ourselves that it was the most beautiful
wedding in history.

Although there is no such thing as the typical
American wedding — as many styles of weddings
exist as the styles of citizens giving them — every
single one possesses the same ritualistic ingredients,
the same replay of ancient custom and primeval
symbolism, the same predictable plot and standard
players. A wedding is, after all, a wedding.

Why do you suppose wedding traditions are so strong in our culture? What
values give rise to the norms of traditional
American weddings? Have these values
changed in the last 100 years?

In other cultures. A traditional wedding ceremony in some other culture, however, may be quite different from that of
Tom and Kathy, and millions of other
American couples.

In New Guinea, a Kwoma mother
gives her son a bowl of soup. He doesn't
know it, but the soup was prepared by his
girlfriend, not his mother. When he finishes the soup, his mother tells him he is
now the girl's husband. Such are weddings,
Kwoma syle.

In India, a wealthy Jaipur prince rides
a painted elephant to his bride's house.

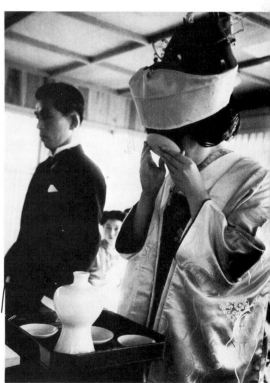

Weddings are a custom in every culture. On the opposite page, traditional American and English Royal weddings. Top left, a Hindu wedding. Top right, a Nigerian couple with dowry. Right, a Japanese wedding. Above, a Hasidic Jewish rite.

Richly dressed attendants walk beside him, while musicians play bagpipes, flutes, and drums. The ceremony takes place under a canopy strewn with flowers. Standing before a sacred fire, the bride and groom are joined together by priests as the families watch. Such are weddings, princely Jaipur style.

In Moscow, a couple may take a bus to a marriage bureau for a 10-minute civil wedding ceremony. Such are many weddings, Soviet style.

Whether simple or elaborate, weddings are one custom that every society observes. Each culture has its own particular rituals, but generally there is an exchange of gifts followed by a formal ceremony. The wedding ceremony is a public announcement that a man and a woman intend to live together and raise any children they may have in a socially approved manner.

It is also society's way of reminding the bride and the groom that obligations as well as rights are attached to their new status. The vows suggested in the *Anglican Book of Common Prayer,* for example, commit the couple to a permanent and exclusive relationship. Both the bride and the groom swear to love, comfort, and keep each other (forsaking all others) as long as they live.

The festivities that usually accompany weddings indicate the importance that people everywhere attach to marriage. The decision to create a family is, of course, a great turning point in life. But why must it be noted publicly and formally? A man and a woman can live to-gether and raise children without being married. Yet every society, from the simplest to the most complex, expects them to marry.

Many anthropologists and sociologists maintain that there is more at stake in marriage than the opportunity for a mutually supporting, loving companionship. They say that the primary function of marriage is to produce legitimate children, that is, children who are guaranteed a proper place in society. And this means that a child must be legally tied to both its parents and the parents' families. Marriage also provides for a distribution of family property through kinship lines. In other centuries, whole nations changed alliances and even boundaries as a result of the marriages of monarchs.

Family Patterns

After their wedding, Tom and Kathy continued to pursue their careers. Their long hours and hard work soon paid off. Both received promotions and raises.

Despite their high salaries, Tom and Kathy found that saving money was difficult. Purchasing a new home was even more difficult. "The price of new homes was just too high for us," Tom remembers. "Still we saved everything we could and finally managed to buy a condominium." Tom and Kathy decorated their new home and chose their furniture. "Some of it was a little old, but it was all ours," Kathy proudly recalls.

In short, Kathy and Tom lived a marriage style common to many young

Although these families show wide variations in size and life-style, sociologists would classify all of them as nuclear.

American couples. In some parts of the world, however, the idea of one man marrying one woman and the two of them setting up their own home by themselves might seem odd.

Monogamy and polygamy. Even marriages that appear to be "made in heaven" sometimes end in divorce, and either or both partners may remarry. In our society, however, no man or woman may legally have more than one marriage partner at the same time. This practice is called *monogamy*. Well, isn't it always this way? Not necessarily. Although a majority of marriages in the world are monogamous, 80 percent of the world's societies permit *polygamy*, that is, marriage in which a person has more than one mate. Polygamy has two forms. When a man is married to two or more women at the same time, the practice is called *polygyny*. When a woman is married to two or more men at the same time, it is called *polyandry*.

Throughout history, polygyny has been quite common. In ancient Israel and other Middle Eastern societies, to have more than one wife was a sign of high social status, prestige, and wealth. According to the Old Testament, King Solomon had 1,000 wives; poor Israelites had to be satisfied with one. In those societies that permit polygyny, the practice is still limited by the ability of a man to support more than one wife, as well as by the number of women who are available. While a majority of societies have no religious restrictions against polygyny, most of the world's husbands today can afford only one wife. Polygyny appears to flourish

Polygamy was made illegal by Congress in 1862, but sanctioned by the Mormon Church until 1890. Above, Mormon leader Brigham Young (1801-1877) and some of his wives.

more often in those societies where a wife, by raising food or tending herds, adds to a man's wealth.

Polyandry is much rarer than polygyny. Polyandry is linked usually with a very high proportion of males in the society, sometimes caused by female infanticide. In the polyandrous society of 60,000 Toda in India, for example, men outnumber women by four to one. When a woman marries, she becomes the wife of her husband's brothers as well. This prevents herds of sacred cattle belonging to a single family from being divided by the male heirs.

Why do you think monogamy is the norm in American society? Can you think of any circumstances in which polygyny or polyandry might be acceptable here? Explain your answers.

Extended, conjugal, and nuclear families. Family patterns vary not only according to the number of mates that a man or woman may have, but in their size and structure. An *extended family,* for example, consists of a mother, a father, their children, plus one or more blood relations, all living together. Some extended families may be very large. In pre-Communist China, 80 or more relatives might live together as a family. The family might include four generations, from a pair of great-grandparents down to their great-grandchildren. Extended families are still found in many parts of the world today, including India, Africa, and rural Japan.

When the United States was largely a nation of farms and small towns, extended families were more common in this country too. Grandparents might live under the same roof with their children and grandchildren. Unmarried aunts and uncles were also part of some households.

Although extended families are not very common in the United States today, it is not rare among some ethnic groups for relatives to establish separate households near each other so that they are close enough to see each other regularly. Sociologists call this family pattern of

Mobility has greatly influenced family patterns in our culture. Extended families are rare now.

separate households gathered together a *conjugal family*. A 1967 study by the National Opinion Research Center showed that 40 percent of Italian Americans and 29 percent of Polish Americans lived in the same neighborhood as their parents.

Today, however, most American families, like Tom's and Kathy's, consist solely of a husband, a wife, and their dependent children. This pattern is called a *nuclear family*.

Sociologists believe that the predominance of nuclear families in the United States today is due largely to the demands of our industrial society. In an industrial society, people tend to move wherever job opportunities are available. Many families shift from one job location to another every few years. This requires a high degree of mobility. The smaller the family, the easier it is to move to a new locale. The nuclear family meets the practical needs of an industrial age.

If the nuclear family is more mobile, it is also much more isolated socially. In the absence of parents, uncles, aunts, and others, a husband and wife are much more dependent on each other for protection and comfort than ever before. This increased mutual dependence is one reason that our society emphasizes romantic love as the foundation for marriage; it must provide the emotional support to sustain a couple that is removed from other family ties.

⋙ Can you think of other advantages and disadvantages of having an extended family? A conjugal family? A nuclear family?

Family Decisions

Having children. Three years after her marriage, Kathy gave birth to a little girl, named Robyn. Two years later, she had a baby boy, named Eric. Tom and Kathy agreed that two children were enough.

For a married couple in our society, having a child is probably the most significant step they will ever take. The decision requires a strong emotional commitment, for children make heavy demands on their parents' time, attention, and energies. It also requires a substantial financial commitment. In 1986, the Urban Institute, a research group, estimated that the cost of raising a child from birth through four years at a private university would be $135,000.

Until recently, having a large family was considered a marital duty. It was necessary in order to satisfy the most basic need of any society — to replenish the population in each generation. If couples chose otherwise, they were told that marriage was "incomplete" without children, that they were "selfish."

Most young couples in the U.S. today are choosing to have small families. In recent years, the average couple has had only two children. In 1972 the number of births was smaller than it had been for more than 25 years, and fell below the replacement level for the first time. What accounts for the trend toward smaller families? Some couples find it gives them more personal freedom. Others are concerned about the high costs of having children today. The fear of a runaway "population

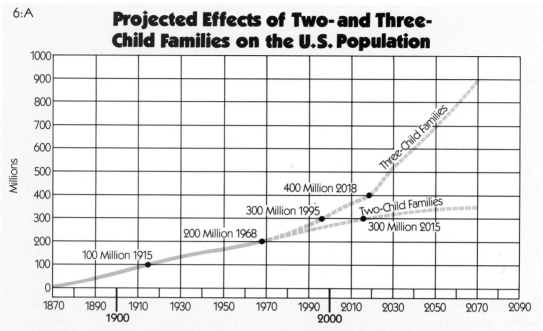

6:A

Projected Effects of Two- and Three- Child Families on the U.S. Population

Source: Population and the American Future, The Report of the Commission of Population Growth and the American Future (Washington, DC, Government Printing Office)

explosion" has also been an influence.

But if couples are choosing to have smaller families than was the custom in the past, only a minority of them plan to remain childless. Three out of four couples, in fact, have at least one child. The number of children that couples have also has important consequences for all of society. In 1986, the average birthrate per couple in the U.S. was 1.8 children. But what if the average should increase to three? It would soon have a drastic effect on the population of the United States, as Chart 6:A indicates.

◦§ What other changes might occur in U.S. society if the average family size jumped to three children? If it dropped to one?

Rearing children. What happens when a couple become parents for the first time? According to popular fiction, the newborn baby is invariably precious-looking and brings endless happiness to the mother and father. The truth, however, may be harsher than fiction. The needs of a newborn baby may be so great that they exhaust unsuspecting parents. The new parents may feel trapped in an endless round of baby care, worries about paying all the bills, and a sharp curtailment of freedom. Both parents may begin to think of all the pleasures they could have if it weren't for the baby. In short, the arrival of a baby sometimes produces stress in a marriage rather than the wondrous happiness depicted in movies and "soap operas."

The Birth Dearth

In 1957, at the height of the baby boom, the fertility rate reached an average of 3.7 births per woman. Thirty years later, the fertility rate fell to 1.8 births per woman. This downward trend alarms Ben J. Wattenberg, an expert on population changes. Wattenberg argues that the declining birth rate is producing a shortage, or dearth, of people. In his book *The Birth Dearth* he discusses the consequences of this trend and offers a number of controversial solutions.

Wattenberg believes that the birth dearth is already having an impact upon the U.S. economy. There are currently 3 million fewer Americans between the ages of 16 and 24 than there were in 1980. This shortage of young workers has created a demand for their labor. In the long run, however, a diminishing population means fewer consumers. Wattenberg points out that the decline in young adults will cause a sharp drop in home buying during the 1990's.

The author argues that the birth dearth will also have serious implications for the American family. Population experts predict that if the current trends continue, 50 percent of young American couples will have either no children or one child. Wattenberg believes that these couples will "live to regret" their choice. "When you are old, the people who will care about you most dearly, and the people whom you will care about most dearly—by far—will be your children, your grandchildren, sometimes your great-grandchildren. Growing old without offspring is, quite simply, quite sad for most people."

Wattenberg insists that the birth dearth's consequences will not be limited to the economy and family life. He notes that the U.S. fertility rate has fallen below the 2.1 average needed to maintain the present population. At the same time, the Communist-bloc nations have a fertility rate of 2.3 while the United Nations estimates that the Third World fertility rate is 4.1. If these trends continue, the U.S. and its allies will represent an ever declining proportion of the world's population. Wattenberg fears that this could result in a decline of America's cultural influence.

Wattenberg offers a number of proposals to reverse the declining birth rate. He suggests that large companies organize on-site day care centers for the children of their employees. This will make it easier for women to work and also have children. In addition, he recommends that the government encourage more births by providing a $2,000 per year cash bonus for each child under 16.

The ideas in *The Birth Dearth* have created a storm of controversy. Some critics emphasize that predicting future birth rates is difficult. Both the postwar baby boom and the recent "baby bust," for example, surprised most experts. Historians, furthermore, stress that a nation's cultural influence is not necessarily related to the size of its population. And, finally, many sociologists contend that Wattenberg's goal of maintaining America's global cultural dominance is ethnocentric.

Thinking Critically

1. According to Wattenberg, what impact will the birth dearth have upon the nuclear and extended family?

2. Are Wattenberg's goals ethnocentric? Explain your answer.

Although parenthood is one of our society's most important roles, we are frequently given little preparation for it. The stress which many first parents feel may be related to this lack of preparation. Like other young couples, Tom and Kathy spent years studying for their careers but devoted almost no time to learning about children.

In the past, the extended family provided new parents with much needed advice. In an age of highly mobile nuclear families this help has been reduced. Parents seeking assistance have turned to how-to-parent books and courses in effective parenting. For parents who are having special problems, networks of Hot Lines and TOT Lines, Families Anonymous and Parents Anonymous have opened across the country.

Even with all of this help, parents can still face a difficult challenge. "Parenting," says one expert, "means implementing a series of decisions about the socialization of your child—what do you do when he cries, when he's aggressive, when he lies, or when he doesn't do well in school?" Each of these questions demands an answer. Regardless of their approach, today's parents must try to find a consistent way to raise their children in a complex, ever-changing society.

≈§ If you become a parent, which of the following sources of guidance do you think you will use most? Explain your answer.
    Child-care books?
    Friends?
    Parents and relatives?
    Tradition?
    Child's physician?
    Something else?

Sex Roles in the Family

Traditional male and female roles.

Both Tom and Kathy have careers. Although common today, this pattern is relatively new. In 1950, 70 percent of all U.S. households consisted of a full-time working father and a stay-at-home mother.

According to tradition, when a man and woman marry in our society, the husband is the head of the household and is responsible for its support; the wife is responsible for the care of the children and for housekeeping services. This tradition is not only common in American society but in a majority of societies around the world.

The division of labor that makes the husband the "breadwinner" and the wife the "homemaker" is, like the nuclear family, tailored to the needs of an industrial society. In former times, the division of labor was less clear-cut. Most farms and many businesses were family enterprises in which wives, children, and grandparents were part of the work force. Extended families permitted grandparents, aunts, and uncles to help raise the children and do housekeeping chores.

But when industrialization created factories and businesses that were located away from homes, work roles and family roles tended to divide, especially among middle-class families. Increasingly, the husband became a wage-earner who labored in an office or factory, and the wife became a full-time mother and housekeeper; the nuclear family left no one else to care for the children.

Popular stereotypes of motherhood such as the one above have been challenged by the women's movement.

For many young women, the role of a full-time mother and homemaker often comes as a shock. Though she may have been trained to be independent, her new role may make her more or less submissive to her husband, for as a housewife her well-being depends on her husband's efforts, rather than her own. How much money she can spend, where they live, and where their children go to school usually are determined by her husband's earnings.

Men who have unhappy marriages may be compensated by rewarding careers. Until recently, at least, not many women have had this alternative. Numerous studies have shown that more wives than husbands consider themselves frustrated and dissatisfied with marriage. Similarly, more wives than husbands suffer from feelings of depression, anxiety, and passivity.

Many women find being a full-time housewife very rewarding, however. Sociologist Helena Lopata interviewed 571 housewives in the Chicago area and discovered that the most successful tended to be women with good educations, few financial problems, and the ability to take the intiative in a number of situations. These women valued their freedom to develop in many directions — as individuals, as neighbors and friends, and as citizens of the community. They tended to see their relationships to their husbands as complementary rather than competitive.

Wages for housework? Suppose housewives are to be compensated with salaries for the work they perform. Several attempts have been made to analyze the roles of housewife and mother according to what these jobs would pay outside the home. According to a recent estimate, the average value of housework in a family with two children is more than $26,000 per year. Chart 6:B gives a breakdown of the skills required.

✒ Why do you suppose housewives are not paid in our society? Do you think they are adequately compensated? Can you think of any system in which they might be treated differently?

Working women. The idea that women are too fragile to work outside the home gained popularity with the Industrial Revolution and remained conventional wisdom through most of the 19th century. In order for a woman to stay in the home, of course, there had to be adequate income to support the family. In some cases, it became a status symbol for men to afford to keep their wives at home. But poor women — married or not — always had to work. They often took menial jobs in factories and private homes. Single women often worked as factory hands, sales clerks, and school teachers; by the early part of the 20th century, it had become socially acceptable to the middle class for single women to hold these jobs.

World War II marked the first big influx of married women into the labor force. Between the start of the war and its end, the percentage of married women in the work force rose from 15 to 25 percent. It continued to rise into the 1980's when it exceeded 60 percent of all married women.

6:B
What's the Value of a Homemaker?*

	Hours per Week	Hourly Wage	Weekly Wage
Nursemaid	45.1	$ 4.12	$185.81
Dietician	1.2	6.10	7.32
Food Buyer	3.3	4.12	13.59
Cook	13.1	5.34	69.95
Dishwasher	6.2	4.27	26.47
Housekeeper	17.5	6.86	120.05
Laundress	5.9	4.57	26.96
Seamstress	1.3	5.34	6.94
Maintenance Worker	1.7	5.34	9.07
Gardener	2.3	5.34	12.28
Chauffeur	2.0	15.26	30.52
	99.6		508.96
			or
			$26,465.92 per year

*Based on wages in a large metropolitan area.
Combined sources: The Health Insurance Institute, Washington, DC 20006
The Bureau of Labor Statistics, 1986

This housewife was photographed in 1947 with her week's work load and cleaning aids. How might such a photograph today be different?

What accounts for the great increase in working wives during the last few decades? One reason is the trend toward smaller families. American couples are having fewer children than they did 50 years ago. The average married woman today has her first child at 24 and her last at 28. By the time she is 34, her children are in school and she is able to work at least part-time. Even if she waits until her last child leaves home, she will be in her forties and have many productive years of work ahead. By the mid-1980's, almost 60 percent of American mothers with children under 18 were in the work force.

When a married woman brings home a paycheck, she usually wields a greater share of power in making family decisions. The authority of her husband is often diminished. But working women rarely discard their familiar roles as housekeepers and mothers. One study revealed that many women who work 40 hours a week in an office or factory still manage to spend 39 hours a week at housework.

There is no evidence that children of working mothers are more likely to develop emotional problems than the children of full-time housewives. Another recent study, in fact, indicates that families are happier when the mother works by choice (not from necessity) than when she stays at home. This is particularly true after the children have entered school. Some sociologists maintain that the family will be strengthened, rather than weakened, if our society provides women with more rewarding and prestigious job opportunities.

Although women continue to be lower paid and have fewer opportunities for prestigious occupations, most of them "work for the money." The majority of working women are still employed in lower-paying, traditional female jobs such as sales clerks, waitresses, and secretaries. For some women, the income from these jobs keeps many of their families from the brink of poverty. For other families, the wife's income may mean the down payment on a house or the tuition for their children's college education. Inflation may make it necessary for two incomes to pay for what one income formerly supported.

Although money is the chief consideration when most women work, it is not the only one. Many women enjoy working outside the home. A recent survey, for example, asked working wives: "Would you continue to work if your family no longer needed the money?" The majority said they would, indicating that their jobs offer more than money. A job often makes them feel more important than they felt as full-time housewives. And it provides the company of other adults.

Dual-career marriages. What happens when the wife pursues a career as ardently as her husband pursues his? And what if she should earn more money than he does? Chances are the marriage will be seriously strained. According to one study of dual-career marriages, it takes a husband who is either very secure or closely identified with the efforts of his wife to allow her to equal or exceed his own accomplishments without major disruption in the relationship.

6:C

The Wage Gap

Women ▬   Men ▭

Median income of full-time workers	Women	Men
	$16,252	$24,999
Median income with four years of college	$21,389	$32,822
Persons earning $50,000 or more a year	1%	9.2%

In 1970, women working full time earned 59% of what men earned. The figure in 1985: 65%.

Note: All figures are for 1985.
Basic data: U.S. Census Bureau

6:D

New Opportunities

**Shares of jobs held by women
1972 ▭   1985 ▬**

	1972	1985
Lawyers	4%	18%
Managers, administrators	18%	36%
Securities brokers	10%	25%
Computer scientists	17%	31%
Engineers	1%	7%
Clerical workers	76%	80%

Basic data: U.S. Dept. of Labor

If the husband feels that his manliness is threatened, the wife may feel a serious conflict between the demands of her career and her role as a wife. If she has children, she may be troubled by a sense of guilt about "neglecting" them. As a result, most women who pursued careers in the past remained single.

Yet this situation appears to be changing rapidly. A 1985 Roper survey of American women, for example, indicated that 63 percent of all women want to combine marriage, motherhood, and a career. Since the early 1970's, the number of women attending professional schools has greatly increased, and many of these women want dual-career marriages.

Dual-career marriages don't *have* to be strained. Some, in fact, work out quite well. One career woman had this to say about her marriage: "Both of us look upon it as an absolutely 50-50 partnership. . . . One of the outstanding features of this situation is that we have a tremendous interest in common. We've never really quarreled over anything serious because we both realize it's a matter of deciding jointly, and we're prepared to compromise."

&§ Why do you suppose so many young women aspire to dual-career marriages in spite of the risks?

Changing male roles. The increase in working women and, in particular, dual-career marriages has had its effects on men — not only at work, but also at home, where once their word was law.

Some anthropologists maintain that historical evidence shows that there has never been a society which men did not dominate. Despite the findings of Margaret Mead that sex roles are largely learned and dictated by culture, these anthropologists argue that men are destined to rule over any society.

But contemporary evidence indicates that at least one group of men are adjusting to the demands of the feminist movement. Many well-educated men in their twenties or thirties are no longer insisting on traditional male roles. They are attempting to break cultural barriers that have denied them a full range of emotional expression. They are frequently present at the birth of their children and take a larger responsibility in their care. Some even challenge the mother's assumed right to custody of the children in the event of divorce. In 1986, 31 states had joint custody statutes, under which parents share care of their children.

These changes have not been easy. Nor are they spread throughout American society. Most older men and those of the working class still may be the undisputed "masters" of their castles. And even those who consider themselves "liberated" may not be consistent. Sociologist Mirra Komarovsky interviewed a large group of college males for her book, *Dilemmas of Masculinity.* Many of those interviewed had difficulty integrating their new values with reality. For example, they might say it was great for wives to work outside the home. But they also thought the wife's career should not rival her husband's or interfere with her housekeeping chores.

Morton and Marjorie Shaevitz, who counsel dual-career couples with problems, say it will take a while for men to adjust to women's new roles. Men, says Marjorie Shaevitz, "haven't had the role models. They are still responding to their fathers' ideas of what a husband is, and their fathers got the ideas from *their* fathers."

⊸§ To what extent do you think men's and women's roles will change in your lifetime? To what extent will they stay the same?

At home, sex roles are changing some, but television often fills in for working parents.

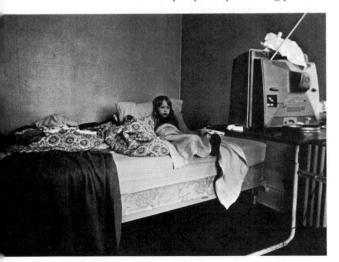

The Family in Crisis

Most young couples have high expectations for their marriages. Studies reveal that most Americans believe overall happiness depends more on marital happiness than on other aspects of life. And yet, the romantic love that binds most nuclear families together can lead to disillusionment.

After the birth of their two children, Kathy and Tom, the couple we met at the beginning of this chapter, began to experience problems. Kathy returned to work shortly after the birth of her second child. "At first I thought that I could do it all," Kathy recalls. "We placed Robyn and Eric in a day care center. But, while I was at work all that I could think about was how someone else was taking care of my children. When I was home with the children, I thought about all the work I had to do for my job. I felt terrible."

Kathy's sense of frustration and guilt deepened. The daily routines of trying to be a good wife, mother, and employee seemed endless. "I tried to be the best mother and the best employee possible," says Kathy. "I just couldn't handle the housework, diapers, bills, and reports for my boss. I needed help. But Tom just didn't seem to be there for me."

The birth of their two children also had an important effect on Tom. "Our two children meant new responsibilities and more bills than I ever thought possible," says Tom. "I took my role of breadwinner seriously, maybe too seriously. I put in extra hours at work and then came home exhausted. Kathy and I began to grow apart. The good times we had when we first met seemed like ancient history."

The problems which Kathy and Tom faced are not unique. As realistic problems begin to replace idealistic dreams, romantic love often begins to fade. The increasing numbers of women in the workforce has added new tensions. One social scientist calls today's working mothers "pioneers trying to find their way in the wilderness." The combination of dual-career marriages and children, raises new questions that previous generations seldom had to face. Can a woman successfully combine the roles of wife, mother, and employee? What adjustments will the husband have to make in his traditional role of breadwinner?

Finding the answers to these questions can test even the best marriages. At first, Kathy and Tom thought about giving up on their marriage. Kathy sadly remembers that "all we did was quarrel and shout at each other. Nothing improved and everything seemed to get worse. I really thought that we were headed for a divorce."

During the last two decades, millions of couples have used divorce to resolve their problems. "We thought seriously about it," Tom recalls. "But it seemed like we would be giving up too easily. We had worked too hard and come too far to just quit. When Kathy suggested that we see a marriage counselor, I said O.K."

Experienced therapists recognize that problems are inevitable at each stage of a marriage. Within recent years they have devised a number of strategies to help couples communicate their problems. For example, Kathy and Tom's marriage counselor asked them to become "listeners" and "speakers." As a listener, Tom heard and then summarized Kathy's view of their problems. Kathy then did the same for Tom.

As they "talked" and "listened," Kathy and Tom gradually realized that their problems could be solved. Kathy realized that she wanted to work, but also felt a strong responsibility to raise their children. Tom suggested that she start a small business.

After doing some research, they contacted the National Alliance of Homebased Businesswomen. They discovered that women now own about one-fourth of America's small businesses. Since she had always enjoyed cooking, Kathy began a small catering business. "Things are working out much better for us," Kathy says. "Tom has taken a real interest in what I'm doing. And the kids love helping. I'm so glad we had faith in our family and didn't give up."

Divorce. Like many other couples, Kathy and Tom worked hard to save their marriage. However, every marriage cannot be saved. The divorce rate in the United States has dramatically increased since the beginning of this century. In 1910, for example, fewer than nine percent of marriages ended in divorce. Sociologists point out that the United States now has the highest divorce rate in the world. About 50 percent of all recent marriages will end in divorce.

Although the divorce rate is high, Americans have not lost confidence in marriage. As you can see on the chart on the next page, the divorce rate has begun to decline. Of those who divorce, an estimated 79 percent will remarry.

6:E

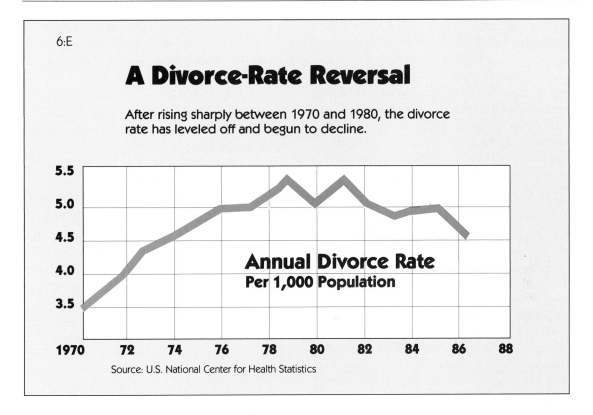

A Divorce-Rate Reversal

After rising sharply between 1970 and 1980, the divorce rate has leveled off and begun to decline.

Annual Divorce Rate
Per 1,000 Population

Source: U.S. National Center for Health Statistics

Some causes. Why do so many husbands and wives flock to divorce courts? Is it because people today care less about marriage? Ironically, some sociologists say that the divorce rate is high because people today care *more* about the quality of their marriages. Young couples enter into marriage nowadays with much higher expectations than their grandparents did. Their grandparents may have married for economic security, or for convenience. But young couples now expect marriage to bring "self-fulfillment." When they do not find this elusive goal, many choose divorce and look for fulfillment elsewhere.

Sociologists attribute the high rate of divorce today mainly to these reasons:

• The isolated nuclear family is less able to cope with the economic and emotional pressures of marriage than the extended family.

• More and more married women are entering the work force. With greater economic independence, it is easier for them to divorce their husbands if they choose to.

• Young couples today place a heavy emphasis on romantic love. When romantic love fades, they become disillusioned and view their marriages as failures.

Sociologist Ian Robertson has commented on our society's near addiction to romantic love as the basis for marriage:

Because Americans are so thoroughly socialized into an almost impossible ideal of lifelong romantic love with their chosen partners, they often experience severe disappointment when their married life turns out to fall short of their hopes. Romantic love is built on fantasy, mystery, spontaneity, bursting emotion, and surprise. It is meant to "sweep you off your feet," to make you "lose your senses," to make you "blind to all else."

When these expectations are confronted with the garbage can, the dishpan, and the diapers, they tend to shrivel. And when they do, millions of Americans assume that because the "thrill is gone" from their relationship with their spouses, the partnership must have failed. This is not necessarily true, for love takes many forms. Married love grows and changes as the partners grow and change; it is a love that may be mature, reasonable, realistic, and deeply fulfilling — but Americans are not socialized to expect it, to recognize it, or to appreciate it.

Thus, as long as the passions of romantic love continue to be extolled as the only viable grounds for a successful marriage, and as long as the fading of romance is considered to herald the fading of a marriage, the American family will have problems as millions of disillusioned couples discover that their dreams about their "one true love" are slowly disappearing in a pile of laundry, work pressures, and routine predictability.

Divorce patterns. Although it is difficult to predict which individuals are most divorce-prone, sociologists have identified six social characteristics by which they can predict with some accuracy which marriages are likely to endure. These characteristics are:

• *Age of partners.* The largest single group of divorces involves people in their twenties. The older the couple, the less their chances of divorce.

• *Length of marriage.* The longer a couple stays married, the less likely they are to seek a divorce. Most divorces occur within two years of marriage.

• *Number of marriages.* People who have been previously married are more likely to get divorced than people in a first marriage, although this gap is narrowing.

• *Social class.* Divorce is less common the further up the socioeconomic scale one moves. Much divorce may be due to unemployment and financial problems.

• *Education.* Divorce tends to decrease with formal education. Couples in which the man has more schooling are more stable than those in which the wife has more.

• *Religion.* Marriages between persons of different religions and between Protestants are more likely to end in divorce than those where both partners are Jews or Catholics. Highly religious people of any faith are less likely to get divorced than those who are not.

Single-parent families. Between 1970 and 1985, largely because of the high divorce rate, the number of single-parent families more than doubled. In 1985, single parents headed 26.3 percent of all families. About half the children born in the 1980's will spend part of their childhood living with one parent.

Most Americans raising their children alone are women. Today, about 26 percent of all families with children under 18 are headed by single parents. Eight out of ten single parents are women. This trend has been particularly pronounced among black families — one out of two black children live in homes where the father is absent.

As the number of single-parent families has grown, so has public awareness of the multitude of legal, financial, emotional, and social problems that confront single parents. The great majority of one-parent families face severe economic hardships. Generally, economic problems are the greatest for single mothers. Forty-seven percent of the children in families headed by women are living below the official poverty level.

One factor contributing to the poverty of families headed by single mothers is the number of fathers who default on their child-support payments. In the mid-1970's, the federal government opened a campaign to track down negligent fathers.

A major expense for most single parents — men as well as women — is child care. This is particularly true for single-parent families that fail to qualify for fed-

Single-parent families are a significant minority in our society today.

Wholesome, reasonably-priced day care is unavailable for many working parents today.

erally subsidized day care. Private day-care centers may charge anywhere from $60 to $150 a week per child. Moreover, they are hard to find. According to government estimates, care in licensed centers is available for only slightly more than one million children. It is estimated that more than six million preschool children and several million more school-age children need this service.

Despite the problems, the single parent's life is not all misery. Jane Schweiker, a divorced Washington, DC, mother with an eight-year-old son, told a *Washington Post* reporter:

"When your life is in order and you're happy, you can pay more attention to your child's problems. Though he has only one parent at home, he can still have a feeling of love and discipline. . . . Having one happy parent is beneficial to my son. Now my relationship with my child is not cluttered with somebody who puts my teeth on edge."

Increased social pressure. Women's changing place in society has greatly altered the ways of the American family. While women have been freed from constricting sex roles, they often must deal with added pressures, like wage discrimination and being a single parent with a career. What are the causes of these pressures and how can they be solved? A study conducted by two population experts, Suzanne M. Bianchi and Professor Daphne Spain addresses these issues. In 1986, they discussed the situation with the *New York Times:*

"The shift of women out of the home and into the labor force and out of marriages and into independent living arrangements represents changes which are out of step with the ability of social institutions to support the changing economic role of women," the study's authors . . . said.

As a result, three crucial issues confront society: wages, child care and housework, according to the study, entitled "American Women in Transition."

"If we want a productive labor force of female and male workers, but also value the family, work hours must be flexible, day care available and affordable and work within the home equitably divided," the authors wrote.

. . . Historically, men have held jobs outside the home while women tended to the house and family, the study noted, but that situation began to change when the baby-boom generation started to mature. . . .

By 1960 one-fourth of married women with children were in the labor force, and today the figure is more than half, the authors wrote.

But while most mothers hold jobs, adjustments at home have not been made. . . . They continue to do the majority of the housework, and day-care facilities for their children are often inadequate or . . . costly.

Complicating these problems are high divorce rates and delayed marriages, so more and more women are maintaining their own households, often trying to support themselves and children.

Women "who are divorced from their husbands are seldom divorced from their children; most children of divorced parents live with their mothers," Professor Spain and Ms. Bianchi wrote. The result is what many women term a "balancing act" in which they must juggle family and work responsibilities. . . .

While many dramatic changes have occurred for women, one area that has changed little is wages, Ms. Bianchi and Professor Spain noted.

"The ratio of female earnings to male earnings has remained remarkably stable over time," they said. "Women on average make 70 percent or less of what men make when both are working full time."

"Whatever the reason for the discrepancy," Ms. Bianchi and Professor Spain said, "the challenge for the future is to find a reconciliation between the roles of wife and mother and that of wage earner."

application

Which member of the family do you think should be responsible for chores in the home? Should this be determined by sex roles? Your teacher has a form to record your opinion on various chores.

summary

One of the most important decisions many young people have to make is their choice of a marriage partner. How do they make their choice? In our culture, most would probably answer, "By falling in love." Sociologists, however, say that people do not fall in love blindly. Our romantic impulses, they say, are guided by social patterns. These patterns are designed to ensure that we make "appropriate" choices. Every society imposes limitations on those whom we may marry.

One universal requirement is that people must marry outside of their immediate family, clan, or tribe. This requirement is called **exogamy.** The selection of a mate is also limited by rules that pressure people to marry within their own social categories. Although these rules are more or less flexible, the great majority of people do tend to marry others of the same race, religion, and social status. Whether they are conscious of it or not, most people prefer to mate with "alikes." The practice of marrying within one's own social category is known as **endogamy.** Although parents in the United States generally don't act as matchmakers, they influence their children's choice of marriage partners considerably. They may live in neighborhoods and send their children to schools where they are likely to meet their social peers. So when young people do fall in love, it is usually with someone from a similar background.

A **wedding ceremony** is a public announcement that a man and a woman intend to live together and rear any children they may have in a socially approved manner. Although wedding ceremonies vary throughout the world, every society observes them. Why do all societies acknowledge the importance of marriage? The answer, sociologists say, lies in the traditional function of marriage — to produce legitimate children who will be guaranteed a proper place in society.

Family patterns are determined by culture and differ considerably. In our society, no man or woman may have more than one marriage partner at a time. This practice is known as **monogamy.** Yet in 80 percent of the world's societies, it is permissible for a person to have more than one mate at a time. This practiice is called **polygamy.** Though it is fairly common for a man to have more than one wife **(polygyny),** it is much rarer for a woman to have more than one husband **(polyandry).**

For a married couple, the decision to have a child is probably the most significant they will ever make. Raising a child involves both a strong emotional commitment and a heavy financial responsibility. Most young couples today are choosing to have no more than two children, a marked decline from previous years. For these couples, smaller families mean more personal freedom and fewer financial burdens. Sociologists say many Americans are less able to cope with the decisions parents must make because of rapidly changing values and norms. Many turn to "experts" for help. Many who choose to have small families are also influenced by the fear of a runaway "population explosion."

Family patterns differ not only in the number of mates that a person may have, but in structure as well. A **nuclear family** consists solely of a married couple and their dependent children. An **extended family** consists of a nuclear family plus one or more relatives all living together. Extended families are somewhat unusual in U.S. society today, but they can be found commonly in parts of India, Africa, and Japan. More common in our society is the **conjugal family,** a group of related nuclear families in separate households who live near each other and visit regularly.

According to traditional family sex roles, the husband is the head of the household and responsible for its support. The wife is responsible for the care of the children and for housekeeping services.

For many women, the role of a full-time mother and housekeeper often comes as a shock. It may make them more or less submissive to their husbands, on whom they are dependent economically. And many feel trapped by the constant and monotonous routine of housekeeping, as well as by the demands of child-rearing. In recent decades, however, more and more married women have been entering the work force. This often enhances their sense of self-worth and gives them a greater voice in making important family decisions. Though most married women who work do so because they need the money, they tend to see their jobs as secondary to their role as housewives. But an increasing number of wives are pursuing full-time careers that are on a par with their husbands' occupations. The changes in women's work patterns have been accompanied by challenges to the traditional sex roles of husband and wife.

The high divorce rate in this country indicates that marriages today are less enduring than they used to be. Sociologists attribute the prevalence of divorce to our culture's emphasis on romantic love and self-fulfillment which often conflicts with the practical demands of marriage.

Divorce has been the chief reason behind a growing family form in the U.S. — the **single-parent family.** By 1985 one out of four households with children was headed by a single parent.

more questions and activities

1. Explain how *exogamy, endogamy,* the *marriage gradient,* and *age* guide the selection of marriage partners in the United States.

2. Explain the differences among *nuclear, conjugal,* and *extended* families. Tell which pattern is most common in the United States today and give at least one reason.

3. Define *monogamy, polygamy,* and *polyandry.* Which is the most common pattern of marriage in this country today? Why?

4. Interview your parents and grandparents in order to compare and contrast dating and courtship patterns in different periods of our history.

5. Within recent years, computer dating services have made a business of helping people find compatible partners. If there is such a service in your area, interview someone who works there to find out what factors are considered important in serving customers. If you cannot interview an employee, you might obtain a questionnaire given to customers to look for the same information.

6. In 1979 the U.S. Supreme Court struck down the alimony laws in Alabama because they applied only to husbands in case of divorce. The ruling was expected to affect alimony laws in Georgia, Idaho, Louisiana, Mississippi, Nevada, New York, South Carolina, South Dakota, Tennessee, and Wyoming as well.

In delivering the Court's opinion, Justice William Brennan wrote: "The old notion that it is the man's primary responsibility to provide a home and its essentials can no longer justify a statute that discriminates on the basis of gender." The Justice said that states should be able to write laws that provide alimony for the needier spouse in divorce cases without discriminating against men.

What do you think is the function of alimony payments? How long should they continue after a divorce? What is your opinion of the Supreme Court's ruling?

7. Many contemporary television programs attempt to portray American family life. Select a program and analyze it for patterns of family life discussed in this chapter. How does the program portray family roles? Parent-child relationships? The types of problems that real families face?

8. In the late 1970's and the 1980's, national attentions was focused on the problem of child abuse, an old but largely unexamined problem in our society. The National Institutes of Health estimated that approximately four percent of all children under the age of 17 were abused. Research and report to the class on the causes and consequences of child abuse. You might contact some organization, such as Parents Anonymous, to see what is being done to curb the problem.

9. In the 1980's, in an attempt to equalize the responsibilities of marriage, some couples drew up marriage contracts that made clear who was responsible for such duties as child care, shopping, making beds, taking care of the family automobile, and household repairs. Do you think it is a good idea for couples entering marriage to write a contract? If so, what conditions would you want covered in a contract you signed?

10. What do the photographs throughout the chapter suggest about changing family patterns?

suggested readings

Cleaver, Bill and Vera Cleaver. *Where the Lillies Bloom.* (New American Library, 1974.) Fourteen-year-old Mary Call keeps her orphaned brothers and sisters together in their Appalachian home.

Fallows, Deborah. *A Mother's Work.* (Houghton Mifflin, 1985.) A career woman describes her decision to leave work and raise a family.

Goldstein, Eleanor C., ed. *Family.* (Social Issues Resources Series, Inc., 1987.) An outstanding collection of articles drawn from popular sources and covering a variety of topics. New articles are added each year.

Guest, Judith. *Ordinary People.* (Ballantine, 1977.) Seventeen-year-old Conrad Jarrett's struggle back from mental illness has a shattering effect on delicately balanced family relationships.

Hennig, Margaret and Ann Jardin. *The Managerial Woman.* (Doubleday, 1981.) A study of the problems, achievements, and experiences of professional women.

Hood, J.C. *Becoming A Two-Job Family.* (Praeger, 1983.) A detailed study of 16 married couples in which both spouses work. Hood examines how these couples have adjusted to the demands of a dual-career marriage.

Melville, Keith. *Marriage and Family Today.* (Random House, 1987.) A widely used textbook which provides a useful sociological overview of the institutions of marriage and the family.

Pocs, Ollie. *Marriage and Family.* (Duskin, 1987.) An excellent collection of contemporary readings on marriage and the family.

Wietzman, Lenore. *The Divorce Revolution.* (Free Press, 1985.) A sociological study of the social and economic impact of divorce upon life in America.

Wernick, Robert and the editors of Time-Life Books. *The Family.* (Time-Life Books, 1974.) A highly recommended introduction to the family. Topics covered include the marriage ceremony, divorce, and alternative family structures.

What clues do each of these two women offer about their social class?

chapter 7

social stratification

A belief in equality has always been one of America's most basic values. "All men are created equal," Thomas Jefferson proclaimed in the Declaration of Independence, and Americans have echoed his words ever since. In some ways, American adults are equal. All are entitled to the same basic freedoms that are spelled out in the Bill of Rights. Each has one vote. But are Americans equal in other respects, such as wealth, power, and prestige? Read about the following three people and decide for yourself.

"There is no one my age who has accomplished more," boasts Donald Trump. Few would challenge this self-evaluation.

By his forty-first birthday, Trump controlled a financial empire with assets worth more than $3 billion.

Trump built his fortune with a combination of good luck, hard work, and talent. As he grew up, Trump learned about real estate business from his father, a successful New York builder. After graduation from the Wharton School of Finance, he plunged into the real estate business. Trump's driving energy, keen eye for a good deal, and bold ideas soon paid off.

The 68-story Trump Tower in New York City is a visible monument of his financial success. Tourists regard the Tower's pink marble lobby and $2 million

The lavish decors of these Trump Tower
apartments demonstrate the wealth of
the top social class in America.

waterfall as a must-see sight. Shoppers can browse for unique gifts in expensive boutiques. Famous celebrities live in lavish apartments priced at over $2 million each. Trump's wife and three children also live there.

The Tower apartment is not Trump's only home. On weekends he frequently uses his personal jet helicopter for a fast ride to his 10 acre 45-room estate in Greenwich, Connecticut. Or if he chooses, Trump can fly to his Palm Beach, Florida mansion in a private Boeing 727 jet.

Trump's empire also includes a 282-foot yacht, and 24,000 rental and co-op units in buildings throughout New York. Despite his success, Trump has plans for even more projects. He hopes, for example, to build a 150-story skyscraper in New York City. His three secretaries receive a constant flow of calls from politicians, business leaders, and celebrities who want to discuss ideas for new ventures.

In contrast, Carolyn Head does not have three homes or three secretaries. But like Donald Trump, she has achieved a great deal in a short time. As a young black girl living in Nashville, Head was not allowed to use the main public library. Today, she is the coordinator of branch services for the Memphis Shelby County Public Library. She is also one of the 12 members of the library's administrative cabinet.

Head attributes her success to hard work and a commitment to education. "It isn't easy and it didn't come easy," she recalls. First, she earned a bachelor's degree from Tennessee State. Next, she continued her education and obtained a master's in library science from Case Western Reserve, in Cleveland, Ohio. Her degrees, however, did not guarantee immediate success. Head worked at a number of library jobs before assuming her current position.

Head's new job supports a comfortable life style. She and her three children live in a pleasant neighborhood near Memphis State University. Her two oldest children attended a private school before going to the public high school. With her oldest son now going to college, Head knows that she has to budget cautiously.

Careful budgeting is a way of life for Glen and Darlene Whitbeck. Glen earns about $8,000 a year as a part-time worker at a fast-food restaurant in Tacoma, Washington. After paying for their rent, food, and other expenses, the Whitbecks' only have $8.00 a month left to spend.

Medical bills are the Whitbecks' greatest worry. Emergency-room treatments for Glen and his 5-year-old daughter cost the family $2,500 in one year. They don't have enough money to repay the bill or to buy their daughter a $60 pair of corrective shoes. "Katherine," Glen says sadly, "can't do most things others her age can do—like skip and hop."

Donald Trump, Carolyn Head, and Glen and Darlene Whitbeck clearly belong to three very widely separated social classes. Sociologists define a *social class* as a category of people who have about the same amount of property, power, and prestige. The pattern of social classes that results from the unequal distribution of property, power, and prestige in a society is called *social stratification*.

In this chapter, we will investigate

how property, power, and prestige are distributed in the United States. We will examine three of the methods that sociologists use to measure this distribution and see how their findings may be influenced by the methods they use. In contrast, we will take a look at stratification in the Soviet Union, which attempted to create a classless society. Returning our attention to the U.S., we will see how people move up and down the social ladder and discuss some of the factors that affect this movement. Finally, in the Application, we examine the question, How do we judge the value of a job?

7:A

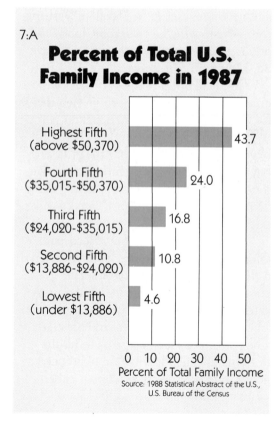

Percent of Total U.S. Family Income in 1987

Highest Fifth (above $50,370) — 43.7
Fourth Fifth ($35,015-$50,370) — 24.0
Third Fifth ($24,020-$35,015) — 16.8
Second Fifth ($13,886-$24,020) — 10.8
Lowest Fifth (under $13,886) — 4.6

0 10 20 30 40 50
Percent of Total Family Income
Source: 1988 Statistical Abstract of the U.S.,
U.S. Bureau of the Census

The Dimensions of Stratification

Economic inequality.

Income. In 1986 the median income of an American family was $29,458. That year 20.7 percent of American families earned more than $50,000. Thirty-seven percent earned $25,000 to $49,999; 19.5 percent earned $15,000 to $24,999; 9.7 percent earned $10,000 to $14,999. More than 12.4 percent earned less than $10,000.

Inequalities of income are even more apparent when families are divided into fifths according to income. In 1986, families in the top fifth received 43.7 percent of all income. Families in the lowest fifth received 4.6 percent. (See Chart 7:A for a further breakdown.)

Is the gap closing between high and low levels of income in the United States? Since the end of World War II, there has been almost no change in the distribution of earned income. However, earned income does not tell the whole picture. The federal government's "war on poverty," started in 1964, and various state assistance programs have had some effect on the distribution of money in our society. The poor and the aged have benefited the most. Aid in the form of food stamps, housing assistance, and various medical programs between 1964 and 1976 raised the *spendable* income of the lowest fifth of the population from 5.4 percent to almost 8 percent of the nation's total income. Taxes to pay for these programs cut sharply into the spendable income of the top 40 percent of the population. Between 1964 and 1976, this portion of the population lost almost 11 percent of its spendable income.

The standard of living in the United States was on the rise and benefited virtually every segment of our society between 1945 and about 1970. In 1959, for example, 39.5 million Americans lived in poverty. Ten years later, the number of poor had declined by 12 million.

By the 1970's, however, inflation had caught up with rising incomes to the extent that most Americans were unable to further increase their standard of living. The decline in the number of poor people in the United States tapered off in the 1970's, stopping at 23 million (or 11.1 percent of the population) in 1973. During the 1980's, the number of poor people rose steadily. In 1986, 32.4 million people (or 13.1 percent of the population) had incomes below poverty level.

How does the United States compare with other nations in terms of income distribution? Major industrialized nations such as Great Britain, West Germany, and Canada have similar income distributions. But all, including the United States, have greater equality than less-developed countries such as India, Venezuela, Brazil, and Mexico. In general, the greatest inequalities occur among the very poor and industrially developing nations of Asia and Latin America. Among Communist countries, there is generally more even distribution of income than among non-Communist countries, but in no society does everyone receive even approximately the same income.

Wealth. A family's income depends on what its members earn and what they own. Two families, for example, may have similar incomes; but one may come entirely from salaries while the other may come chiefly from owning stocks, bonds, or real estate. What people own is called *wealth,* and it may be inherited. The very wealthy derive only a small proportion of their income from salaries. Much of it comes from trust funds, stocks, and bonds. The distribution of wealth in this country is even more unequal than that of income. In 1972, economist James D. Smith found the top one percent of the population held 24.1 percent of the nation's personally held wealth. By 1976, the wealthy held 30 percent of bonds and 46 percent of stocks. The wealthiest 5 percent owned 52 percent of all bonds and 82 percent of all corporate stock. In 1981, 82 percent of all Americans owned no stocks or bonds at all.

Inequalities of power. Who wields the most power in the United States? Political leaders? Top military figures? The very rich? Labor leaders? Sociologists define *power* as the ability to control one's own life (personal power) and to control or influence the actions of others (social power). Unfortunately, it is much easier to define power than it is to measure or analyze it. People who wield great power usually don't open their doors to inquisitive sociologists. And even if they did, influence is very difficult to gauge. Power may not depend entirely on wealth. Martin Luther King, Jr., the late civil-rights leader, was a powerful man, though not a wealthy one.

Distribution of Income and Wealth in the U.S.

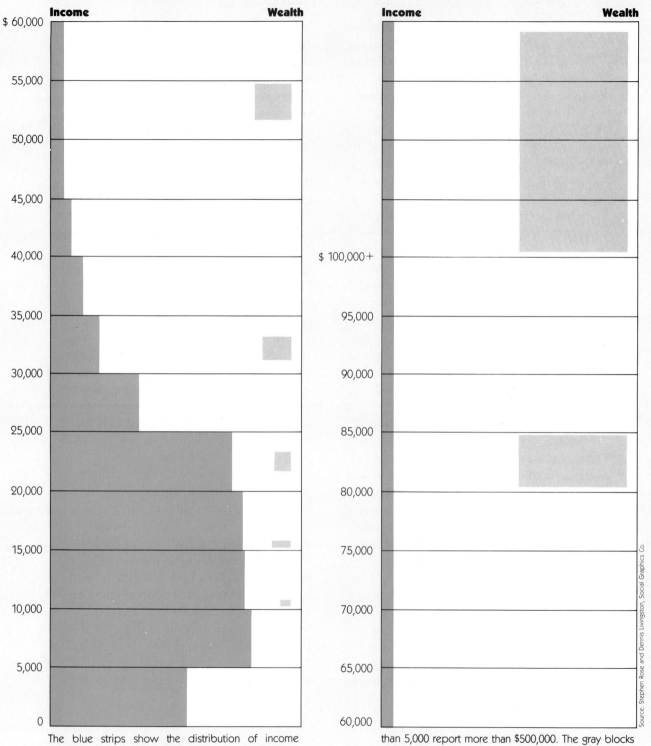

The blue strips show the distribution of income between $0 and $60,000 (left) and from $60,000 up (right). Roughly 1,100 people report income of more than one million dollars to the government, and less than 5,000 report more than $500,000. The gray blocks show the distribution of wealth among approximately corresponding population groups. Chart includes independent adults over 18 years old.

Source: Stephen Rose and Dennis Livingston, Social Graphics Co.

❦ Can you think of other people who have power and not money? Money and little power?

As a rule, however, sociologists associate power and wealth. Wealth can sometimes buy power. More and more political leaders, for example, seem to come from very wealthy families, like the Kennedys and the Rockefellers. And power often leads to wealth. Not many government leaders or important executives retire to a life of poverty.

On one point, almost all sociologists agree: The poor, many members of racial minority groups, most recent immigrants, and many of the aged are virtually powerless. They rarely influence others and often cannot control even their own lives. In many cases, they have no choice as to where they live and whether they are employed.

❦ Can you think of ways in which individuals and groups with little power can increase their power?

Inequalities of prestige. Prestige is an important dimension of social stratification. *Prestige* may be defined as the social recognition that a person or group receives from others. It can be influenced in a number of ways. In America, how we earn our money and how we spend it have been common indicators of prestige.

Occupational prestige. Because Americans attach great importance to how people earn their money, occupations are generally considered the best and most consistent measure of prestige in America.

The following conversation between anthropologist Elliot Liebow, who, in the 1960's, spent more than a year studying a poor neighborhood in Washington, DC, and a laborer named Tally Jackson clearly reveals the importance of prestige as a separate dimension of social stratification:

Jackson: You know that boy came in last night? That Black Muslim? That's what I ought to be doing. I ought to be in his place.

Liebow: What do you mean?

Jackson: Dressed nice, going to [night] school, got a good job.

Liebow: He's no better off than you, Tally. You make more than he does.

Jackson: It's not the money. (*Pause.*) It's position, I guess. He's got position. When he finish school he gonna be a supervisor. People respect him. . . . Thinking about people with position and education gives me a feeling right here (*pressing his fingers into the pit of his stomach*).

Liebow: You're educated too. You have a skill, a trade. You're a cement finisher. You can make a building, pour a sidewalk.

Jackson: . . . Anybody can do what I'm doing and that's what gives me this feeling. (*Long pause.*) Suppose I like this girl. I go over to her house and I meet her father. He starts talking about what he done today. He talks about operating on somebody and sewing them up and about surgery. I know he's a doctor 'cause of the way he talks. Then she starts talking about what she did. Maybe she's a boss or a supervisor. Maybe she's a lawyer and her father says to me, "And what do you do, Mr. Jackson?"

Liebow: . . . That happens to everybody. Nobody knows everything. One man is a doctor, so he talks about surgery. Another man is a teacher, so he talks about books. But doctors and teachers don't know anything about concrete. You're a cement finisher and that's your specialty.

Jackson: Maybe so, but when was the last time you saw anybody standing around talking about concrete?

🖝 What are the qualities that Jackson values in other occupations? How do they affect his own self-image?

Ranking occupations. In 1947 two researchers, Paul Hatt and Cecil North, compiled a list of 90 occupations and asked a cross section of Americans to rate each one. The ratings used for the survey ranged from "excellent" to "poor." Then the researchers gave a numerical value to each rating — 100 for excellent, 80 for good, and so on. Next they calculated the average rating for each occupation and ranked them accordingly. The survey was repeated in 1963 and 1977 with remarkably similar results.

🖝 Your teacher has a list of some of the occupations Hatt and North ranked. You may want to rank them and compare your results with theirs.

Later surveys tried to find out *why* people rated some occupations highly and

others poorly. The researchers concluded that generally people rank occupations according to their importance for society, the power and influence that they exert, their educational requirements, income, the nature of the work (white-collar or blue-collar), and the characteristics of the people who have chosen these occupations.

Occupational ratings are a useful device for sociologists studying stratification, but they do not tell the whole story. People rank one another in a variety of ways. In some communities, for example, family background is the most important indicator of a person's social standing. The chief value of occupational ratings is that they indicate quite clearly that prestige, like income and power, is shared unequally and that Americans are quite conscious of the differences.

🖝 In your community, what social characteristics carry the most prestige? Why? In your school, what social characteristics rank highest in prestige? Why?

Consumptive prestige. One conspicuous measure of prestige is how people spend their money. The very rich can afford to buy luxury items that are beyond the dreams of most ordinary mortals. These items become symbols of prestige. Two such symbols are the Jaguar and prep school student shown on the opposite page. What qualities of the automobile and prep school make them symbols of high status? What objects might be symbols of high status in your community?

Symbols of prestige.

The American Class System

Methods of determining class divisions. Let's look at two people in a small American city and try to fit them into appropriate social classes. One is a young lawyer who recently started her practice. In her first year, she earned $18,000. She lives in a small, rented apartment. The other is a 45-year-old plumber who earns $40,000 a year. He lives in a spacious new ranch house that he owns. Which one belongs to the middle class? Which belongs to the working class?

If it is difficult for you to decide, you are not unique. Sociologists also find it difficult to pinpoint exactly what social class some people belong to. The boundaries between classes are often blurred, or overlap. Prestige and income may vary widely in an occupation, for example.

In their studies of class divisions, sociologists use three principal methods which are described here:

1. *The subjective method.* Researchers using this technique simply ask a random sample of the population to name the class they belong to. If the information the researchers receive is accurate, they can then develop a clear picture of the class structure of the community they are studying.

Unfortunately, many people have a mistaken idea of their class status and tend to rank themselves higher than their incomes or life-styles would justify. Early surveys ran into serious problems on this score. In the 1940's, *Fortune* magazine conducted a poll in which people were asked to identify themselves as either upper class, middle class, or lower class. The great majority, 75 percent, answered "middle class." Only about 10 percent would identify themselves as "lower class."

Was this a true picture of the American class structure? Or did Americans prefer to believe that they were not "lower class?" In 1949 researcher Richard Centers decided to add another identity choice, "working class." He found that low-income Americans were proud to identify themselves in this fashion. Nearly half of those polled identified themselves as "working class." When a similar study was conducted in 1984, the number of people who identified themselves as "working class" was 46 percent. Only 4 percent said they were "lower class," reconfirming Center's theory that people don't like to think of themselves as "lower class."

2. *The reputational method.* Using this technique, researchers select a small town and ask a number of residents to assist them in their study. The residents are usually "old-timers" who know just about everyone in town by reputation. The old-timers are then asked to identify the social classes that exist in the community and to place each resident in one or another category.

When W. Lloyd Warner and Paul Lunt studied a small town in Massachusetts in 1941, they found that the old-time residents were quite class conscious. They described various townspeople as "old aristocracy," "the folks with the money," "nice, respectable people," "snobs trying to push up," "poor folks but decent," and "nobodies."

Based on their information, Warner and Lunt were able to analyze the town's social structure. It was divided, they said, into six distinct classes: an upper, a middle, and a lower, each of which contained an upper and a lower level.

The reputational technique often provides researchers with fascinating insights into small town class systems. Unfortunately, the technique cannot be applied to large cities where people do not know everyone else.

3. *The objective method.* In this technique, researchers divide people into social classes according to their income, occupation, education, and type of residence. This method is especially useful in studying large populations. Most of the information can be obtained from U.S. Census Bureau statistics, and it is quite precise.

Is the objective method more accurate, therefore, than the first two? Not necessarily. Sociologists often interpret information differently. Some might place a clergyman who earns $15,000 a year among the lower classes. Others might place him among the middle classes because of the high prestige of his occupation and the extent of his education. Obviously there is no cut-and-dried way to assign people to social classes.

≈§ Which method do you think would give the best analysis of stratification in your community? Explain your answer.

In 1937 photographer Margaret Bourke-White followed up on a 1929 study by sociologists Robert S. Lynd and Helen M. Lynd, Middletown — A Study in Contemporary American Culture. *The Lynds studied social stratification in Muncie, Indiana. Below, the Conversation Club.*

Above left, Wilbur E. Sutton, editor of the Muncie newspaper. Above right, workers at the Ball Jar factory. Below, Scott and Lizabelle Brandenberg in their one-room shack with the chickens they grow to eat. Into what class would you place each of these individuals and those on page 195?

Classes in America. Although class divisions are not precise, most sociologists would agree on their broad outlines, which are described here. The information was gathered by the objective method.

Upper class. The upper class is a very small one, comprising no more than three percent of the population, yet it owns about 54 percent of the nation's wealth and has great power in politics and the business world. Much of its wealth is inherited. Dividends from stocks, interest from bonds, and other investments in business are its main sources of income.

Members of this class, like Donald Trump, do not have to work. They can, if they wish, live as "the idle rich." However, many of the nation's wealthiest individual's continue to work (and earn more money) well into their old age. This is probably a result of the high value our society places on work.

Even the upper class is somewhat divided. The members of "old" families whose wealth was acquired a long time ago tend to look down on those whose money was recently acquired. Today, for example, the Kennedy family of Massachusetts is very rich and powerful. The Kennedys are upper class. Their fortune, however, was accumulated only about two generations ago. At the time of John Kennedy's election as President of the U.S., some members of old, aristocratic Boston families still regarded the Kennedys disdainfully as "shanty Irish."

Upper middle class. The upper middle class comprises about 27 percent of the population and consists mainly of business executives and professionals such as doctors and lawyers. Their income comes largely from profits, salaries, and fees. People in this class usually place great value on "proper" social behavior and respectability. Their moral attitudes and values have usually set the tone for most Americans. Members of the upper middle class often live in comfortable suburban homes, stress family "togetherness," and take an active part in civic affairs. They have high aspirations for their children and send them to college as a matter of course.

During the 1980's, an expanding black middle-class emerged as one of the fastest growing segments of the American economy. While the number of white families moving into the middle-class increased by about 20 percent, the number of middle-class black families jumped by almost 60 percent. By the late 1980's three out of every ten black families (compared with 44 percent of all white families) earned between $20,000 and $50,000.

Sociologists have identified a number of characteristics which distinguish the rising black middle-class. The civil rights movement of the 1960's helped create an expansion of opportunities. Like Carolyn Head, many blacks took advantage of these new opportunities by pursuing advanced college degrees. As a result, there has been a dramatic surge of blacks into managerial, professional, and governmental positions. In the past, the old black middle-classs of ministers, educators, and small businessmen served the black community. In contrast, the new professional elite now serves the society-at-large.

Women have played an important role

in the rise of the black middle-class. Robert B. Hill, an expert on social stratification in the black community, describes working couples as the "backbone of the black middle-class." They account for about four-fifths of all black middle-class families. The average working black wife earns about half of her family's income. In contrast, the average working white wife earns about one-third of hers.

Lower middle class. The lower middle class comprises about 25 percent of the population and consists mainly of people who own small businesses, sales representatives, office workers, and highly skilled craftsmen. They are usually "average" Americans as far as income is concerned. Like the upper middle class, they value proper social behavior, hard work, and success in their occupations. Because they must work hard to achieve and retain their middle-class status, they tend to be conservative politically.

Frances Swenson, a 50-year-old switchboard operator at a large motel, is a fairly typical member of the lower middle class. She described her job to author Studs Terkel in this excerpt from *Working:*

First thing I do is get my headset on, and I sit down at the board to relieve the girl that's been working all night. It's the type of chair that a stenographer would sit on. Believe me, after eight hours it's not a comfortable chair. (Laughs.) We are constantly kept busy. There isn't an idle moment.

I worked 125 hours the last two weeks. We asked the boss why we didn't get time-and-a-half overtime. He says, "Well, the girls at the front desk are getting it, I don't see why you don't. You'll get it starting the first of the month." We

were informed today we were not going to get it. The one that told us OK'd it, but there are two higher in the hotel than he. . . .

I'm tired at the end of the day. Say you pick up a thousand calls a day, and these cords are on heavy weights, they get pretty heavy by the end of eight hours. . . .

When you get up like in my age and go to work, it's a grind. We can't take even one break because we're constantly needed. If you got to go, you've got to come right back. 'Cause you don't get a 15-minute break. . . .

I think switchboard operators are the most underpaid, 'cause we are the hub of everything. When you call somebody, you want immediate service. Of course, I chose the job. If you choose the job, it's your responsibility. Just because I feel I'm not paid enough doesn't mean I'm not gonna give 'em good work. . . .

But I feel they need us badly. They need us to be polite and they need us to be nice. You cannot have a business and have a bad switchboard operator. We are the hub of that hotel. And we don't get respect. We don't get it from the bosses or the guests. Today communications is the big thing. So much business is over the phone. I really think we demand a little more respect.

Working class. The working class comprises about 32 percent of the population and consists of small shop owners, skilled or semiskilled laborers, and service workers. Their blue-collar jobs generally involve manual labor and have little public prestige. However, members of this class take great pride in the fact that they work with their hands and are respectable. Though their incomes are modest, they are very conscious of the differences that separate them from the poor. They are likely to take the view that people on welfare are lazy.

Hub Dillard, a 48-year-old construction worker in Chicago, also talked to Studs Terkel about his job. This excerpt from *Working* gives some insight into the lives of the working class:

There's no job in construction which you can call an easy job. I mean, if you're out there eating dust and dirt for eight, ten hours a day, even if you're not doing anything, it's work. . . .

The difficulty is not in running a crane. Anyone can run it. But making it do what it is supposed to do, that's the big thing. It only comes with experience. Some people learn it quicker and there's some people who can never learn it. (Laughs.) What we do you can never learn out of a book. You could never learn to run a hoist or a tower crane by reading. It's experience and common sense. . . .

The average . . . working man [lives to be] 72. The average crane operator lives to be 55 years old. They don't have the best sort of life. There's a lot of tension. We've had an awful lot of people have had heart attacks. Yeah, my buddy. . . .

There's a lot of times you have to take another man's word for something and a lot of people get hurt. I was hurt because I took another man's word. I was putting the crane on a lowboy — the tractor that holds it. The foreman told me to swing this stub section of the boom from the front of the lowboy to the back. I said it couldn't be done. He said it's been done a number of times. The lowboy wasn't big enough for the crane and the crane went over backward. They had some extra weight on the back of the crane, which is an unsafe practice. When the crane went over backward and threw me out, a 500-pound weight went across my leg and crushed my ankle and hip. I was in the hospital, had three operations on my leg, and was out of work 18 months. . . .

Trying to feed my family and make my house payments — which was very hard. My wife worked a little bit and we managed. The union gave us $31 a week, Workman's Compensation gave us $69 a week. And after I was off for six months, I received $180 in Social Security.

My father was a crane operator since 1923. We lived on a farm and he was away from home a lot. So I said I'd never do this. When I got out of the service, I went to school and was a watchmaker. . . . It was the same thing, every day and every day. It was inside. And being a farm boy.

. . . So I went to work with my father and stayed with it ever since. . . .

There's a certain amount of pride — I don't care how little you did. You drive down the road, and you say, "I worked on this road." If there's a bridge, you say, "I worked on this bridge." Or you drive by a building, and you say, "I worked on this building." Maybe it don't mean anything to anybody else, but there's a certain pride in knowing you did your bit.

The Poor. The poor make up about 14 percent of the population. Sociologists divide this class into two distinct groups. The working poor include households, like the Whitbecks', in which the wage earners work but still have incomes below the poverty line. In 1988 about seven million adults earned less than the official poverty line figure of $11,203 for a family of four.

The second group includes the welfare poor. In 1988, about four million adults received welfare. Plagued by illiteracy, poor health, and broken homes, many feel hopelesss about their condition and isolated from society. One woman on welfare summed up these feeling when she said, "You don't count at all. Except as a statistic."

Compare the power, prestige, and wealth of Donald Trump, Carolyn Head, Francis Swenson, Hub Dillard, and Glen Whitbeck.

Social Stratification in the Soviet Union

As we noted earlier, Communist societies tend to have the most even distribution in terms of income. However, equalities of wealth, power, and prestige are more difficult to maintain. As a correspondent for an American newspaper, Hedrick Smith had an opportunity to observe the dimensions of social stratification in the Soviet Union. The following passage from his book, *The Russians*, describes various inequalities in one Communist society:

Pick any weekday afternoon to stroll down Granovsky Street two blocks from the Kremlin, as I have, and you will find two lines of polished black Volga sedans, engines idling and chauffeurs watchfully eyeing their mirrors. They are parked self-confidently over the curbs, in defiance of No Parking signs but obviously unworried about the police. Their attention is on the entrance at No. 2 Granovsky. . . .

A sign, by the door, identifies the building simply as "The Bureau of Passes." But not just for anyone, I was told. Only for the Communist Party Central Committee staff and their families. An outsider, not attuned to the preference of Party officials for black Volgas and untrained to spot the telltale MOC and MOЦ license plates of Central Committee cars, would notice nothing unusual. Now and then, men and women emerge from the Bureau of Passes with bulging bags and packages wrapped discreetly in plain brown paper, and settle comfortably in the rear seats of the waiting Volgas to be chauffeured home. . . .

For these people are part of the Soviet elite, doing their shopping in a closed store deliberately unmarked to avoid attracting attention, accessible only with a special pass.

An entire network of such stores serves the upper crust of Soviet society — the bosses, or what one Soviet journalist irreverently called "our Communist nobility." These stores insulate the Soviet aristocracy from chronic shortages, endless waiting in line, rude service, and other daily harassments that plague ordinary citizens. Here, the politically anointed can obtain rare Russian delicacies like caviar, smoked salmon, the best canned sturgeon, export brands of vodka or unusual vintages of Georgian and Moldavian wines, choice meat, fresh fruit and vegetables in winter that are rarely available elsewhere. . . .

The store on Granovsky Street, which is only the visible tip of the valuable array of perquisites, epitomizes the system of privileges: By and large, these are favors money cannot buy. They are beyond the reach of ordinary citizens because they are a dividend of political rank or personal achievement in the service of the state. . . .

This privileged class is a sizable chunk of Soviet society — well over a million and, counting relatives, probably several million. Its precise size is one of many elusive things about Soviet society, since the Russians do not admit it exists. Officially there are only two classes, the workers and peasants, and a "stratum" of employees — white-collar workers and intelligentsia. It is only the upper portion of this intelligentsia which constitutes the real privileged class. Its core is the apex of the Communist Party and the Government, the political bureaucracy that runs the country, joined by the senior economic managers, most influential scientific administrators, and the princes of the Party press and propaganda. . . .

The one other avenue into the Soviet elite, the one other criterion of status and privilege in the Soviet system, is the ability of an individual to contribute to the power and prestige of the Soviet state in some demonstrable way. For outstanding service to the state, a leading scientist, prima ballerina, cosmonaut, Olympic champion, famous violinist, or renowned military commander can earn status in the Soviet elite — status, but not power, and that is the essential difference that marks off the political elite from all others. . . .

After the Revolution, Lenin decreed that talented specialists should be paid more than ordinary workers and that scientists should get special food rations, in spite of communism's egalitarian goals. . . . But it was Stalin who really developed the system of privilege and boldly defended it with capitalistic logic — on the grounds that certain people, certain groups, who were especially valuable to the state, merited special pay and rewards. . . .

The most conspicuous symbols of rank and privilege are the chauffeur-driven limousines of the nachalstvo [the bosses], with their gray curtains discreetly shrouding VIPs from curious glances. . .

The cream of the elite, about 20 people in all — Politburo members and national secretaries of the Communist Party — get to use black Zil limousines, handtooled and worth about $75,000 apiece.

As ostentatious tokens of rank and privilege, however, the chauffeur-driven cars are atypical. Generally, the Soviet political elite enjoys its privileged life in privacy and inconspicuous consumption, unseen by its own public. . . .

They dwell in exclusive residential ghettos, spend their leisure hours at their own holiday hideaways or in clubs segregated by rank. When they travel out of Moscow they use a special airport, Vnukovo II. The man in the street may be vaguely aware of their privileged existence, but he is kept well at a distance. . . .

The greatest perquisites of high status exist outside the city. The leaders and their families have entire communities of hideaway dachas [country houses]. . . . Practically any major

The dacha of one of the Soviet elite, above. Ordinary Soviet citizens like the woman and child below are probably unaware of such hideaways.

center in the Soviet Union, and many a minor one, has special state residences for the elite or high-level visitors — located out of sight, down a road, behind a fence, in a stand of pines. . . .

When it comes to travel or entertainment, not only Brezhnev, Kosygin, and Podgorny are given quick service or the royal box; but the larger political elite, and behind them, the cultural, scientific, and economic elites get their pick too. The Communist Party Central Committee, the Council of Ministers and other important agencies, for example, have special ticket offices where the upper crust can have aides make travel reservations or get them tickets to the top events, which are always in desperately short supply and for which people will commonly spend all night waiting in line. . . .

Equally important to some members of the elite is simply the right to enjoy things normally forbidden to others. . . . I knew of famous Soviet writers who have the banned works of Solzhenitsyn and other literary contraband quite openly on their bookshelves, a sin for which dissidents have been jailed. . . .

There is hardly any more striking double standard between the life-styles of the elite and ordinary Russians than the established access of the privileged class to things Western — magazines, books, movies, cars, travel. The privileged, I was told, can catch movies like Blow-up, Easy Rider, Midnight Cowboy, Bonnie and Clyde, The Conformist, or 8½ — which are banned by censors for normal Soviet eyes. . . .

For many, the system of direct privilege is reinforced by the informal network of connections that enable a general to call a scientist to get his son admitted into an institute, a scientist to wangle a draft deferment in return, or a movie scriptwriter who has produced a good Soviet spy film to call the security services to get permission for his wife and daughter to travel West. Blat, as the Russians call influence, is a constant, vital, and pervasive factor of Russian life. . . .

Russians themselves comment that the upper-class feeling today seems increasingly like Russia before the Revolution. An engineer observed to me that what Marx had predicted for capitalist society — increasing concentration of economic power in fewer and fewer hands and a widening gap between the elite and the masses — seemed to be happening in the Soviet Union today. . . .

Some Western sociologists have contended that the gap between the richest elements of the Soviet elite and the poorest Russians is still much less than the gap between the richest and the poorest elements in America. In pure money terms, that is surely true, though the hidden incomes of the Soviet elite in the form of their large discounts at special stores, the use of cost-free state cars, dachas, and other government facilities is hard to feed into a precise equation. In any case, money is an inadequate measure because the benefits enjoyed by the Soviet elite depend on influence, connections, and access that money cannot buy.

Social Mobility

*Only in America can a guy from anywhere
go to sleep a pauper and wake up a millionaire!
Only in America can a kid without a cent
get a break and maybe grow up to be President!*

This song, "Only in America," states a familiar refrain of American life — with hard work and perseverance, any poor boy (but not necessarily a girl) can become rich or powerful. America has had its share of millionaires who started out selling newspapers on street corners, and Presidents who were born in log cabins. America's fame as "the land of opportunity" drew millions of poor immigrants who

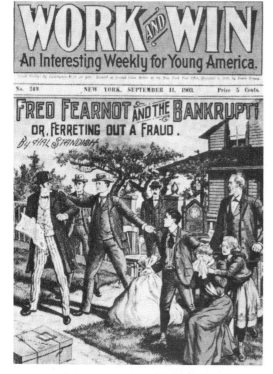

believed that in this country their labors would be rewarded with riches.

For many of these immigrants, as well as native-born Americans, the dream of wealth earned by hard work proved to be a myth. Often the reality they found was extremely harsh. Life in city tenements and factories, or in sod huts on prairie farms, was not the stuff of dreams. Yet some made it, or their children made it, and the dream persisted. It was nurtured by the rags-to-riches stories of popular fiction.

Types of social mobility. Sociologists call the movement of people from a lower social class to higher one *upward mobility.* In the United States, upward mobility, or success, is considered a right that belongs to everyone who is willing to work for it. Even more, upward mobility is considered a duty. Americans admire people who move up the social ladder. We call them "go-getters" and "self-starters."

Popular literature at the turn of the century exhorted young boys to work hard and grow rich. Below, immigrant millionaire Andrew Carnegie, whose real life imitated the Horatio Alger myth.

Conversely, we regard people who don't rise, or who move down, as rather unworthy. Such people, we say, lack "get-up-and-go." Americans are proud that their class system permits upward mobility and does not keep people "in their place." We all know of rock stars, TV personalities, and professional athletes who started out poor and are now earning astronomical sums of money.

The rise or fall of people within the class structure is known as *vertical mobility*. An attractive salesgirl who is "discovered" by a talent scout and becomes a movie star is an almost legendary example of upward mobility. If she should become an alcoholic, fade from the movie scene, and later be found working as a waitress, she becomes a classic example of *downward mobility*.

After World War II, a rising tide of economic prosperity helped lift many Americans into the middle class. As living standards increased, people came to expect that tomorrow would always be a better day. In recent years, however, a changing economy has shaken this expectation. The generation that entered the work world during the 1980's suddenly faced the real threat of downward mobility.

A rising cost of living now makes it more difficult to pay for homes, cars and a college education. For example, in 1970 the average family used 18 percent of their income to pay their mortgage. By the late 1980's, this figure had risen to almost 30 percent. During the same time, Americans also found that they needed more money to buy cars and to send their children to college.

As costs increased, incomes began to level off. Some economists believe that the shift from unionized factory work to service industry professions is causing a loss of jobs with middle-class salaries. Others point out that the postwar baby boomers entered the labor force in record numbers during the 1970's and 1980's. This created an oversupply of competent people competing for a limited number of middle-class jobs. "There are so many of us that you get to a certain point on the career ladder and there's nowhere else to go," complains one frustrated baby boomer.

Social mobility is not always upward or downward, nor is it always so dramatic. If a high school teacher should resign to take a job as a social worker, he or she remains in the same social class. The two jobs pay about the same and have the same amount of prestige. Such a move is an example of *horizontal mobility*. In society, horizontal mobility is much more common than vertical mobility.

✑ What other examples of horizontal mobility can you think of? List them.

Another form of mobility involves a change of status between parents and children. If a mail carrier sends his or her daughter to college and she becomes a psychologist, her social status will be higher than her parent's. This change is known as *intergenerational mobility*. As a rule, however, children tend to enter occupations similar in status to those of their parents. When children do move into another social class, it is generally only one level above (or below) their parents'.

Factors That Influence Social Mobility

Open and closed systems. Whether people rise or fall in a society, or remain in the same place, often depends on the society itself. In a relatively open society such as ours, people tend to move up or down the social structure according to their abilities and determination (or lack of them). In a relatively closed, or caste, society, children inherit the same social position as their parents and are more or less locked into it. In such a society, people are stratified according to such inherited characteristics as family origin, race, religion, and sex. Caste lines are rigidly drawn, and attempts to cross them may be punished by law.

Until recently, India was a major example of a legally enforced, closed society. The population was sharply divided into castes based mainly on family, religion, and occupation. Members of the lowest caste, the "untouchables," were excluded from temples and schools used by higher castes and were obliged to live in isolated villages. If a member of an upper caste came into contact with an untouchable, he was considered "polluted" and had to be "purified." Although the caste system is no longer legal in India, its effects linger. This 1973 story, adapted from *The New York Times*, cited an example:

> *Laxmi Rani is terrified to leave her mud hut in the morning and climb on her bicycle to pedal to school four miles away.*
>
> *"I will be beaten," the 16-year-old girl said.*

"I will be abused. I think the people are displeased. I think they do not want anybody of low caste to get an education."

Laxmi, the only untouchable in the mango-shaded village of 3,000 to attend high school — she is in the 12th grade — added: "I am missing my examinations now. What will happen to me?"

The girl has already been beaten by relatives of a high-caste, or Brahmin, landlord. Her fears are that the intimidation will continue.

"In this case they were trying to intimidate Laxmi Rani because she is the smartest girl in the village — smarter than the landowner's daughter — and they didn't want a harijan *(untouchable) who was smarter than a Brahmin. By shaming her, by harassing her, they wanted the girl to stop going to school or leave the village," said Chedi Lal Sathi, a Congress party official who works with untouchables.*

◄§ What might Charles H. Cooley say about this young woman? In your opinion, is she likely to achieve upward mobility? Explain your answer.

Industrialization. Rigid social systems are common in agricultural societies. When a society becomes industrialized, however, social mobility increases greatly. Advances in technology eliminate a large number of unskilled jobs and expand the number of technical, professional, and white-collar jobs.

The effect has been especially dramatic in the United States. In 1900 farm workers outnumbered professional and technical workers by more than ten to one. Today, professionals and technicians outnumber farm workers by almost two to one. The new high-level jobs created by industry require specialized skills, and the demand for educated workers increases. This provides greater opportunities for working-class and middle-class people, or their children, to move up the social ladder. Chart 7:C indicates that the United States leads all other industrialized nations in the advancement of blue-collar workers and the middle class into highly trained professions, such as lawyers, doctors, and engineers.

The data for Chart 7:C was collected in 1967 by sociologists Peter Blau and Otis Duncan. They noted that there is at least a grain of truth to the Horatio Alger rags-to-riches stories.

7:C
Social Mobility

Country	Manual Class into Elite* (percent)
United States	9.91
Japan	6.95
Netherlands	6.61
Sweden	3.50
Great Britain	2.23
France	1.56
West Germany	1.46
Denmark	1.07
Italy	.35

*Professional and high-level technical jobs.

Source: Adapted from S.M. Miller (1966) as revised by Peter Blau and Otis Duncan, The American Occupational Structure, Wiley and Sons, 1967.

Education. One of the most important ways to achieve upward mobility in this society has been to get as much education as possible. An advanced industrial society such as ours demands trained people. The more education one gets the more likely she or he is to qualify for a high-level occupation. And in our society, a person's occupation is an important factor in determining social status. As a rule, the jobs that confer high social status require the most amount of education.

One of the most dramatic examples of how education increases upward mobility took place after World War II. At that time, some 10 million veterans were offered the opportunity to attend colleges and universities at the U.S. government's expense. This program cost the government 19 billion dollars. Yet so many men were able to advance themselves as a result of this training that the government came out ahead. It gained about one billion dollars a year in additional income taxes.

The situation after the Vietnam War was different, however. Although the government provided tuition to returning veterans, many of them found it difficult to find work, whether or not they had college diplomas. The war's end brought an economic recession in which there were fewer jobs to be filled than qualified people to take them.

The 1970's marked the first time in recent American history in which the economic value of a college education was seriously questioned. Between 1975 and 1985, the number of household heads with college degrees more than doubled.

Risk Taking

Would you rather take the risk of starting your own business or work for someone else? Would you prefer an insecure job with a large income to a secure job with an average income? Do you have a high energy level? If you answered yes to these questions, you might have some of the traits of what Dr. Frank Farley calls the "Type T" personality.

According to Farley, Type T people ("T" stands for "Thrill") are creative risk takers. He believes that as much as 30 percent of the American public falls into this category. "They are the great experimenters of life," declares Farley. "They break the rules."

Creative risk taking plays an important role in promoting social mobility. Risk takers are frequently willing to finance bold projects and to invest in new ideas. If successful they can often earn huge profits.

Sociologists point out that our cultural values encourage risk taking. Americans have always believed that nothing ventured means nothing gained and that they should be ready in case "opportunity knocks." History tells of pioneers and inventors whose hard work and daring gambles opened the West and built industrial empires.

The public's admiration for risk takers does not stop with historic figures. Popular magazines and news broadcasts regularly publicize the exploits of risk takers. About 250 colleges and universities offer courses in entrepreneurship. Americans opened almost 125,000 new businesses each year during the late 1980's.

Creative risk takers experience both the rewards of success and the losses of failure. About half of all new businesses close their doors each year. Dr. Farley points out that Type T's rarely describe their mistakes as fail-ures. Instead they see them as temporary setbacks which can be overcome. Our culture encourages this attitude by emphasizing that, "If at first you don't succeed, try, try, again." Our greatest heroes are people like Thomas Edison and the Wright Brothers who triumphed over initial failures.

Researchers have identified two distinctive home environments which tend to produce creative risk takers. In the "suvivor pattern" children overcome the handicap of growing up in a poor or broken home by single-mindedly pursuing success. In the "high expectation pattern" families socialize their children to achieve high standards. Such families actively help their children to develop any unusual talents they may have.

Several areas in the country serve as subcultural centers which attract creative risk takers. New York City, for example, has historically been a breeding ground for gifted artists and writers. In recent years, the area around the University of Texas in Austin has become an important center for new ideas and research. The Silicon Valley near San Francisco now serves as a major creative hub for the U.S. computer industry. Risk takers in these and other areas help create the new ideas and technologies which promote economic growth and social mobility.

Thinking Critically

1. What values promote creative risk taking in our culture? Do we have any values which discourage creative risk taking?

2. Use your history texts to identify three creative risk takers who have made important contributions to American history. Does your text discuss any creative risk takers whose actions proved harmful?

Some economists predicted that a college education would no longer be the key to higher lifetime earnings.

These predictions proved to be wrong. In 1985, households headed by college graduates had average annual incomes 55 percent higher than households headed by high school graduates. As the level of education increased beyond a bachelor's degree, the earnings gap grew even larger. This gap becomes even greater as individuals enter the final stages of their careers.

The late 1980's and 1990's are expected to be a time of intense competition in the world of work. A college degree cannot guarantee an outstanding career. Nonetheless, the well-educated will be in the best position to take advantage of opportunities in a competitive job market.

Achievement motivation. Are the rewards of success so desirable that everyone will try to achieve them? Or will some people try hard while others feel the effort isn't worth it? Some sociologists believe that members of the middle class have a greater drive to succeed than members of the working class and the poor. Middle-class children are trained from an early age to excel in school or sports and to take risks. They are constantly rewarded for doing better than their peers. As a result, they are strongly motivated to work hard, go to college, and become upwardly mobile. A television program, *16 at Webster Grove,* studied the attitudes of middle-class fathers and sons toward higher education and social status. A portion of their comments follows:

Fred (*a son*): For the last five years at least . . . everything that I've done has been geared to being accepted into college because, "Son, if you don't go to college, you're not going to be anything in life."

Commentator (*speaking to Fred's father*): Are you worried about your son making good grades now so that he can go to college, so he can get a good job?

Father: Sooner or later, in all probability, he's going to get married and he's going to have to support a family. And he's going to have to have a decent job to support a family. In order to get a decent job, he's going to have to have the background, an educational background. It's just — that's it.

Do parents from working-class backgrounds pressure their children to do well in school to the same extent? Sociologist Joseph A. Kahl found that many of these parents do not. They believe that their children are more or less locked into their present social position, and that it would be futile for them to try to improve their status.

One working-class father, a bread salesman, described his attitude to Kahl: "I tried to tell [my son] he isn't going to be a doctor or a lawyer or anything like that. I told him he should learn English and learn to meet people. Then he should go out and sell something worthwhile. I suppose there are some kids who set their minds to some goal and plug at it. But the majority of kids I have talked to take what comes, just get along."

A mother working in a chain store

told Kahl: "I don't go to see the teachers. When I go up there I can't talk good enough. Some women go up there, and I don't know, they're so la-ti-ta, but I can't talk that way. Me, I'm just plain words of one syllable and that's all. I figure he'll get his knocks later on, and he should do what he wants now. I don't make him do homework or anything."

Other factors. Upward mobility may also be influenced by a number of other factors. Conventional good looks is one of them. Studies have shown, for example, that corporations often choose tall men to fill important positions in preference to shorter men. And a woman who is endowed with good looks may find them an asset in both a career and marriage. Since a housewife's social status is usually assessed by that of her husband, marrying the "right" husband may be especially important to her.

"Dumb luck" can also play a part in achieving success. In Horatio Alger stories, for example, luck seems to be just as important as hard work in rising to the top. Many an Alger hero gets his break when he finds a wallet and returns it to the owner, who just happens to be a mil-

Whether one repairs television sets or becomes a scientist in this society may depend on many factors — the status and aspirations of one's parents, education, looks, whom one marries, and just plain luck.

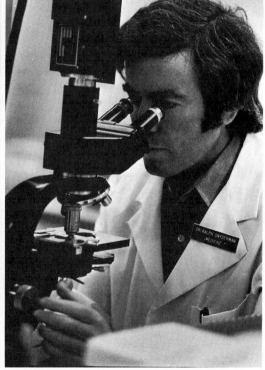

lionaire. The hero's reward, of course, is a good job and eventually marriage to the boss' daughter.

Becoming a millionaire. During the late 1950's, fascinated viewers turned on their TV sets each Wednesday evening to watch a program called "The Millionaire." Each week a wealthy philanthropist surprised a lucky person with a tax free check for one million dollars. The fictional characters of the program, enjoyed instant social mobility.

For most Americans becoming a millionaire is still the dream of a lifetime. However, for a small but growing number of people the dream has now become a reality. Sociologists calculate that there are more than a million millionaires in the United States. Who are these millionaires? What can a study of them tell us about social mobility in America?

Many people believe that most millionaires have inherited their wealth. Recent research reveals that this belief is a myth. About 80 percent of all American millionaires come from middle or working class families. "The real way people make money," concludes one expert, "is hard work for 30 years, six days a week." As a result, the typical millionaire is about 60 years old.

The path to becoming a millionaire frequently begins with college and ends with a business. Sixty-three percent of all millionaires attended college. Although professionals such as doctors and lawyers have prestigious jobs, 85 percent of America's millionaires are entrepreneurs who own a business or a share of a private company. Less than 1 percent of all millionaires

are entertainers and athletes.

Many of the nation's most successful businessmen and women share what one expert calls, "a nose for opportunity." Successful entrepreneurs pay close attention to finding better ways of satisfying consumer needs. For example, Judi Sheppard Missett once taught professional jazz dancing. After realizing that her students wanted to exercise and have fun, Missett developed a new program called Jazzercise. Fifteen years later, she had built a multi-million dollar business, with 3,000 franchised instructors who taught 350,000 students across the country.

Having worked all their lives to earn a fortune, millionaires are frequently reluctant to spend their money on a jet-set lifestyle. Although California, Texas, and New York provide popular settings for television programs about the wealthy, the highest concentrations of millionaire households are found in Florida, the District of Columbia, and Connecticut. The majority enjoy a stable homelife and have never been divorced.

Although financial success can provide security and freedom, it cannot solve every problem. Many millionaires worry that their children lack the necessary drive to succeed on their own. Less than 1 out of 10 children go into their parents' businesses. Jazzercise founder Judi Sheppard Missett speaks for many successful parents when she says, "I'd like to leave my children with the idea that dreams can come true, but that you first must be imaginative to dream dreams. Then, you need patience, perseverance and guts to work your derriere off and make it happen."

Who Gets What and Why

In 1986, the film star Sylvester Stallone earned 12 million dollars for making a movie. In the same year, veteran college professors in the United States earned an average of $44,600 a year. And Victor Posner, the chairman of DWG Corporation, earned almost 13 million dollars. The President of the United States earned $200,000 a year. Registered nurses earned $22,000 for a year's work. The average salary of major league baseball players in 1986 was $412,520. The average bus driver earned $16,000. The Pope does not earn any salary.

Do these income figures make sense to you? To some they seem ridiculous, to others they reflect the opportunity to succeed in the American economic system. To an economist, they reflect the economic principle of supply and demand for particular jobs and the value placed on certain kinds of work.

Why some people in our society get so much money, and others get so little, will always be something of a puzzle. Yet the fact is that every society contains inequalities, and not everyone thinks that this is bad.

Sociologists of the *functionalist* school believe that inequalities are necessary if a society is to work effectively. They say that some jobs are more important and

Supreme Court Justice Sandra Day O'Connor (right) earned $110,000 in 1987, while basketball superstar Michael Jordan (above) earned an estimated $4 million in 1987.

more difficult than others. To attract the most talented people to these positions, a society must offer them greater rewards.

If all people received the same amount of pay regardless of the work they did, who would want the jobs that require study and hard work as well as talent? One example of this theory concerns the late Russian opera star, Feodor Chaliapin. When the Communist Revolution took place in his country, Chaliapin was told he would get the same pay as the stage-hands. He replied, "Very well, but then I will work as a stagehand." As we have seen, Communists in the Soviet Union eventually offered rewards beyond salaries to people they considered important.

Another school of sociologists, the *conflict theorists*, believe that inequalities are not necessary and often prevent talented people from rising to important positions. They say that members of the upper classes usually get the most reward-ing jobs because their parents can afford to give them special advantages, particularly higher education. How many talented members of the lower classes do *not* be-come scientists and executives because their parents cannot afford to send them to college? Members of the upper class, these sociologists say, inherit their wealth and use it to maintain themselves and their children in high-status positions. So-cial inequalities exist not to reward talent but because the upper class keeps the lower classes "in their place."

⇛ After reading this chapter, with which group would you tend to agree? Explain your answer.

application

The following humorous story, pub-lished in *Social Policy* magazine and writ-ten by sociologist Herbert J. Gans, raises some serious questions: How do we judge the value of a job? Is manual labor less important than white-collar work? Who should get more money — people who have pleasant, interesting jobs; or people who do "dirty" work? Read the story and see what you think.

It was a small banquet as White House ban-quets go, but what mattered was that the President chose to memorialize the occasion and to honor the handful of old men able to attend. The men were the surviving members of DWW, the Dirty Work-ers of the World; the occasion, the 20th anniver-sary of the now almost forgotten Dirty Work Movement. The evening was highlighted by the is-suance of a new commemorative stamp showing the late Joe Green, the founder of the DWW, as he looked those days, lavatory mop held firmly in the revolutionary posture.

Mr. Green, older readers may remember, was a lavatory attendant at the University of California in Berkeley in the early 1970's; and one day, while cleaning the professorial facilities, he chanced on a newspaper headline about the Dirty Word Movement, which had flourished briefly in Berkeley in the mid-1960's. Not the best of spellers, he thought the headline referred to work and mentioned it to his colleagues later that eve-ning. A few days later, the entire Berkeley toilet staff walked off the job, saying they were fed up with doing dirty work.

The men came back when the university raised their wages and renamed them "personal service engineers''; but in a couple of weeks, they realized that they were still just cleaning johns, and walked off the job again. Soon lavatory attendants all over the country went on strike; and, finally, the President declared a National Pollution Emergency. He also called for volunteers to solve the problem, as was his fashion, and appeared on television mopping the floor of a White House staff toilet.

By then, however, other workers had begun to leave their jobs. The first to go were hospital orderlies and stockyard slaughterers. . . . In succeeding weeks, there were walkouts by dishwashers and garbage collectors; and when assembly line workers also quit, the economy just stopped altogether.

In the meantime, Joe Green had organized the Dirty Workers of the World. . . . And not much later, Joe Green came to the White House to negotiate.

Actually, there was nothing to negotiate; for with the economy at a standstill, the DWW held the trump card. Joe Green made only one demand: The dirtier the work, the more it ought to be paid. The President gave in, [and Congress passed the bill].

During the next year, life in America underwent drastic change. Toilet cleaners became a new economic elite, earning $20 an hour, with three months of paid vacation and a sabbatical every third year. Conversely, movie stars were working for $5 an hour and professors for $3 and Congressional salaries were reduced to $7,500 a year. This, in turn, produced many side effects. . . . Society pages were filled with accounts of lavish weekend parties given in the Bahamas by longshoremen, and Joe Green's son married a Philadelphia blue blood. . . .

By now, clean workers were becoming a new underclass, and hippies changed into white shirts to express their sympathies for them. Newspaper stories celebrated the courageous individualism of the few young people who still sought to

prepare themselves for clean jobs. . . .

These stories helped the clean workers retain their pride in being clean, but as their savings disappeared and their standard of living declined, so did their pride. Before long they began to demand change. The initial onslaught came from those in various occupations who argued that their work was actually dirty and required higher pay. The Army claimed successfully that its blood-letting activities were extremely dirty, and afterward the surgeons put in a bid for higher salaries . . . and executive secretaries pointed out that they often spilled coffee . . . on themselves while ministering to the needs of their bosses. Finally, the executives themselves sued for a salary increase, arguing that their work was tension-producing and thus psychologically dirty.

Although their case was bitterly contested in Washington, the Supreme Court ruled, in a landmark decision, that emotional factors also had to be taken into consideration in defining dirtiness. Soon after, the surgeons filed suit for another salary increase on the same grounds, so that, in the end, theirs was again the highest-paid occupation in the country. And when the clerk-typists went out on strike, claiming that their work, though clean, was boring, the economy was once more at a standstill.

History repeated itself as the head of the newly organized Clean Workers of America went to the White House to meet with the President. After she pointed out that her union, though barely three weeks old, already had five times as many members as the DWW, the President agreed to her demands, proposing a $10-per-hour minimum wage for clean work, and $20 for boring work. Congress passed his bill by acclamation, and thereafter the position of the dirty workers began to decline. The DWW fought hard to salvage at least some benefits, but the Republicans won the next election with a Keep America Clean campaign, and soon after, Joe Green died of a broken heart.

summary

Are all Americans equal? In some ways, they are. The Bill of Rights guarantees the same freedoms to all adults. Each has one vote. Yet Americans are not equal in other important respects. All Americans do not have the same income, wealth, power, and prestige. At the top of the social ladder in our society are some people who enjoy luxurious life-styles and have great influence in government and business. At the bottom of the ladder are people who subsist on welfare allowances and are almost powerless. In between are many people who are neither as rich or influential as the former nor as poor and powerless as the latter. Like all societies, the United States has a social class system. Sociologists define a **social class** as a group of people who have about the same amount of property, power, and prestige. The division of a society into unequal social classes is called **social stratification**.

When American families are divided into fifths according to income, striking inequalities are revealed. **Wealth,** the term for what people own, is distributed even more unequally. Power and prestige are distributed unequally in the United States, but they are more difficult to measure. One important indicator of prestige is a person's occupation. However, an occupation's status may vary, depending on where the ranking takes place and who does it. Researchers who have studied the American social structure say that essentially it is divided into five classes:

• The **upper class** comprises no more than three percent of the population, yet it owns about 54 percent of the nation's wealth. The main sources of its income are dividends from stocks, interest from bonds, and other business investments. Much of its wealth is inherited.

• The **upper middle class** comprises about 27 percent of the population and consists mainly of business executives and professionals. Its income is derived chiefly from profits, salaries, and fees. Traditionally, members of this class have valued occupational success and respectability.

• The **lower middle class** comprises about 25 percent of the population and consists mainly of people who own small business, sales representatives, office workers, and highly skilled craftsmen. Members of this class usually share the same values as the upper middle class.

• The **working class** comprises 32 percent of the population and consists of owners of small shops, skilled or semiskilled laborers, and service workers. Members of this class frequently take great pride in the fact that they work with their hands and are "respectable."

• The **poor** comprise 14 percent of the population and include unskilled workers with a high rate of unemployment, welfare recipients, and old people with little means of support. Many of them feel hopeless about their condition and isolated from the mainstream of society.

Although Communist countries have fewer inequalities of income, in no modern society is every person equal to everyone else. In the Soviet Union, where a rigid class system was destroyed by a revolution in 1917, there is a new group of elite citizens numbering well over one million. Although their salaries may not be extremely high, they have access to many privileges that money cannot buy in the Soviet Union — limousines, country houses, special stores, and books and films no one else is permitted to see.

Americans have always admired people who move up the social ladder, and rags-to-riches stories are a part of our folklore. Sociologists call the movement of people from a lower social class to a higher one **upward mobility**. Studies have shown that the opportunities for upward mobility in our society are greater than in any other. Almost 10 percent of American blue-collar workers, for example, manage to rise to elite professional and technical occupations. What accounts for the relatively high degree of upward mobility in the United States? One reason is industrialization. Advances in technology eliminate a large number of unskilled jobs and expand the number of technical, professional, and white-collar jobs. An advanced industrial society such as ours places a premium on education, for the new high-level occupations require considerable training.

Sociologists have long been puzzled by the inequalities that exist in our society as well as others. Why do some people get so much money and others get so little? **Functionalist** sociologists believe that inequalities are necessary if a society is to function effectively. In order to attract talented people to the most important and demanding jobs, a society must offer them greater rewards. **Conflict theory** sociologists believe that inequalities actually prevent talented people from rising to top occupations. Talented members of the lower classes are held back because they cannot afford higher education. Social inequalities exist, these sociologists say, because members of the upper class try to keep members of the lower classes "in their place."

more questions and activities

1. Explain what is meant by *social stratification.*

2. Explain what sociologists mean by a *social class* and list the three principal methods for analyzing class stratification in a community.

3. List five social classes in the United States and tell approximately what percentage of the population each includes.

4. Find a photograph or draw a picture of one status symbol for each social class you listed. You might play a guessing game with your classmates to see if they can determine which class each represents. Then prepare a bulletin board display of class symbols.

5. Author Barbara Tuchman once said: "Some people are of more value to society than others, Mozart, for example. If you insist on the theory that everyone is equal, then you are doomed to a lowering of performance, of achievement." What school of sociologists would agree with Tuchman? Do you agree with her or disagree? Why?

6. In a 1978 study of social stratification (*Social Standing in America: New Dimensions in Class*), Lee Rainwater and Richard Coleman report that many young Americans are pessimistic about future prospects for social mobility in America. The chapter you just read discussed several factors traditionally associated with high rates of mobility during the past century in America. Do you believe these factors are still important today? What other factors may be important in the future? Explain why you think young Americans should be pessimistic or optimistic about *their* social mobility.

7. At the beginning of a short story called "The Rich Boy," F. Scott Fitzgerald said: "Let me tell you about the very rich. They are different from you and me . . . in a way that, unless you were born rich, it is difficult to understand. . . . Even when they enter deep into our world or sink below us, they still think that they are better than we are. They are different."

How would you support or refute this statement? Is it possible for working or middle-class people to know what millionaires are like? Is it possible for the very rich to know what the poor are like? What role can sociology play in solving this dilemma for a democratic society?

8. Study several television shows to see if characters from different social classes are depicted. If so, how are their social classes made evident? Is it talked about by the characters? Is it intentionally made evident through styles of dress, manner of speech, or other status symbols? Prepare a report called "Social Classes Depicted During Prime-Time Television Programming."

9. Research and report on social classes during the Great Depression.

10. Prepare a report explaining why "Horatio Alger" is almost synonymous with "success story." Write your own modern version of this type of story.

11. Prepare a report comparing social stratification in the U.S. with that of two other countries.

suggested readings

Birmingham, Stephen. *Certain People* (Little, Brown, 1977). An interesting report on wealthy black families in America.

Chicago Tribune. *The American Millstone* (Contemporary Books, 1986). This collection of articles by writers for the *Chicago Tribune* examines the lifestyles and problems of Chicago's poor people.

Domhoff, G. William. *Who Rules America Now?* (Prentice-Hall, 1983). The author examines the power and privileges of a tiny upper class which influences key economic and political decisions in America.

Fussell, Paul. *Class* (Ballantine Books, 1983). A fascinating examination of the American status system. The author includes a discussion of how we rank clothes, colleges, and even sports.

Harrington, Michael. *The New American Poverty* (Holt, Rinehart, and Winston, 1984.) A news analysis of poverty in America by the author of *The Other America.*

Mills, C. Wright. *The Power Elite.* (Oxford University Press, 1956). In this volume, Mills presents his famous and controversial theory that a relatively small group of people exercise the real power in American society.

Terkel, Studs. *Working: People Talk About What They Do All Day and How They Feel About What They Do.* (Avon, 1974). A series of revealing interviews with working Americans of all social classes.

Wright, John. *The American Almanac of Jobs and Salaries.* (Avon, 1982). This volume describes who gets what and why.

Wriston, Walter. *Risk and Other Four Letter Words* (Harper and Row, 1986). A collection of essays by a former corporate executive which analyzes many of the factors responsible for upward mobility and corporate success.

How many racial and ethnic groups can you identify among these new American citizens?

chapter 8

ethnic and racial groups

Each year, Mrs. Jane Elliott, a third-grade teacher in Riceville, Iowa, conducts a classroom experiment on the effects of discrimination. First she divides her students into two groups based on the color of their eyes. In one group are the blue-eyed children; in the other are the brown-eyed children. Then she makes a short speech:

"Today the blue-eyed people will be on top and the brown-eyed people will be on the bottom. What I mean is that blue-eyed people are better than brown-eyed people. They are cleaner than brown-eyed people. They are more civilized than brown-eyed people. They are smarter than brown-eyed people. It's true. It really is."

Mrs. Elliott then gives the blue-eyed children a number of privileges. They will sit in the front of the room. They will be the first to go to lunch. They will have five extra minutes of recess. What about the brown-eyed children? They will not be allowed to drink directly from the water fountain. Instead, they will have to use special paper cups. They will not be allowed to play with the blue-eyed children during recess. And they will not be allowed to use the playground.

What happens during the day? The blue-eyed children have the time of their lives. They thoroughly enjoy taunting and "bossing" the brown-eyed children. As one blue-eyed boy said afterward: "I felt like a king — like I ruled those 'brown-eyes.' I felt like I was smarter, bigger, better, and stronger." The brown-eyed children become angry and frustrated. One of them later described her feelings.

The blue-eyed students line up first for lunch on the
first day, top. The drawings show how one student felt
about himself as a member of the dominant group (left)
and as a member of the minority group (right).
Below: left, blue-eyed Raymond Hansen, an eager discrim-
inator on Day One, turns gloomy on Day Two; center,
brown-eyed Julie Smith on the first day; right, Mrs.
Elliott hugs her students at the end of the experiment.

"I felt mad and I wanted to tie up the people with blue eyes," she said. "I felt dirty. And I did not feel as smart as I did before."

Feelings of inferiority affect the brown-eyed children in many ways. They begin to slouch and look depressed. They do not read as well as they did the day before; they make many mistakes in their work. The blue-eyed children, however, do better in their work than ever before.

The next day Mrs. Elliott switches the roles of the two groups. The brown-eyed children are now on top, and the blue-eyed children are treated as inferiors. The results are quite predictable. This time the brown-eyed group lords it over the blue-eyed group. The blue-eyed children feel miserable and do poorly in their work. The brown-eyed children excel in their work.

Mrs. Elliott describes the effects of the experiment as "frightening." The children apparently agree with her. They are so relieved when it is over that they hug and kiss each other with joy.

In this chapter, we'll look at discrimination as it affects two kinds of minorities — racial and ethnic groups. We'll see some ways in which these groups may be accepted by the mainstream of a culture and ways in which they may be rejected. We'll distinguish between prejudice and discrimination, and see their effects on a society. Finally, we'll see what sociologists have found about the causes of prejudice. In the Application, a Japanese American woman writes about the discrimination she experienced as a young person.

Kinds of Groups

Dominant and minority groups. No society is actually divided into blue-eyed and brown-eyed groups, but most societies do contain a mixture of people with different physical or cultural traits. The United States is one of the most "mixed" societies in the world. Its population includes an astonishing variety of ethnic and racial backgrounds. Some people believe that a mixture of different people in a country is good. Diversity, they say, enriches and stimulates a society. The ideal society is one in which people of many different backgrounds live in harmony.

Unfortunately, this ideal is hard to find. In many societies, tension, not harmony, prevails among members of different ethnic and racial groups. It exists, for example, between Protestants and Catholics in Northern Ireland; Moslems and Hindus in India; Jews and Arabs in Israel; blacks and whites in Zimbabwe and South Africa.

Frequently, when tension exists among groups with different physical or cultural traits in a society, one group is invariably dominant — it controls the other groups. The *dominant group* has more power, wealth, and prestige than any of the other groups. Its members live in better homes, go to better schools, and have better jobs. Dominant groups justify their privileged status by claiming to be "superior" in some way. They say they are more intelligent, perhaps, or stronger, or more moral. Conflict occurs when a subordinate, or underdog, group rebels against its inferior status. The underdog group claims that it should be on top or, at least, should be given equal status. Subordinate racial and ethnic groups are called *minorities*. Members of minority groups are singled out because of their physical or cultural traits and are subjected to unequal treatment. They regard themselves as victims of discrimination.

Minority groups are not necessarily smaller in numbers than dominant groups. Sociologists consider the black people in South Africa to be a minority even though the blacks greatly outnumber the whites in that country. The blacks are a minority because they are powerless and suffer discrimination. Minority groups are the underdogs in a society whether they comprise a small part of the population or actually constitute a majority.

List five groups that you consider to be minorities in the United States. What are your reasons for classifying them as minorities?

Racial groups. In southern India, most people have "black" skin but "white" facial features and straight hair. To what race do they belong? The Bushmen of southern Africa have yellowish skin and slanted eyes that look Oriental. To what race do they belong? Australian aborigines have dark skin and wooly hair that is often blond. To what race do they belong?

If you can't fit any of these people into neat racial categories, you are no different from anthropologists who study such matters. Many anthropologists, in fact, have come to the conclusion that there are so many variations in the human

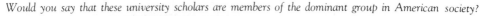

Would you say that these university scholars are members of the dominant group in American society?

species that people can't be classified into distinct races. For them, the term *race* has no scientific meaning at all.

Most sociologists would define *race* as a category of people who share a set of physical characteristics which are transmitted by heredity from one generation to the next. Rather than focusing on categories of human skin color, facial features, or hair texture, however, sociologists are concerned with what people believe about race and physical differences, and how they react to them.

What people believe about race often has no basis in reality at all, but their reactions may be devastating. The German Nazis, for example, believed in a "master race" composed of tall, blond, blue-eyed "Aryans." Actually, there is no such thing as an Aryan race. Yet the Nazis killed millions of "inferior" people who, they said, were a threat to their Aryan "purity."

Sociologists believe that most racial classifications are man-made and arbitrary. We call people "black," "yellow," or "white" even when the distinctions are quite blurred. For example, until 1960 the Census Bureau gave these instructions to its workers to help them decide who should be counted as "Negro":

"In addition to persons of Negro and mixed Negro and white descent, this category includes persons of mixed American Indian and Negro descent, unless the Indian ancestry very definitely predominates or unless the individual is regarded as an Indian in the community."

Though human beings have physical differences, these differences are less im-portant, sociologists say, than the meanings that people attach to them. This point is made quite clear in the following news story from the *Associated Press*:

Johannesburg, South Africa, . . .Sandra Laing is a girl whom no schools want.

Her parents won an 18-month struggle to have her officially declared white, only to discover that they can't find a school that wants her.

Parents in Sheepmoor, a tiny town in eastern

How might this girl's status as a member of a racial minority affect her opportunities for an education in South Africa? In the United States?

Transvaal province, have threatened to remove
their children from the local white primary school if
11-year-old Sandra is sent there as directed by the
education department.

South African schools are strictly segregated
along racial lines. Trouble occurs in borderline
cases where a child is of dark appearance, as
Sandra Laing is.

Sandra was going to boarding school in the
country town of Piet Retief 18 months ago.
Parents of other pupils objected to her presence,
children taunted her, and eventually she was sent
home by the school authorities.

Subsequently she was declared colored —
that is, mulatto — by a government-appointed
board, even though her parents are white. Then a
change in the law provided that descent and not
appearance is to be the deciding factor in borderline cases. She was reclassified white.

Sandra's storekeeper father, Abraham Laing,
decided not to send her back to the same boarding
school because of the scorn he felt she would meet.

He approached a number of convents, but
they turned him down. Some said they had no
vacancies. Others said that the Afrikaan-speaking
girl would find the English-speaking situation in the
convents difficult. [Afrikaan is a Dutch-based
language.]

Then the education department notified Mr.
Laing he must apply for Sandra to be admitted to
the Sheepmoor school, the school nearest her
home.

Principal L. Dreyer said: "This is a terrible
situation. I have my instructions from the education department to admit Sandra Laing. My hands
are tied. However, I have reason to believe that, if
this happens, most of the parents of the 53 other
children at the school will remove their children."

Mrs. E. Van Tender, mother of two pupils
at the school and a member of the school committee, commented: "The day Sandra Laing sets feet
in the school, my children will be taken home.
And they will stay home."

Abraham Laing doesn't know what to do
about his daughter.

❧ What meanings do you think white
people in South Africa attach to dark skin
color? Besides keeping Sandra out of
school, what other effects might their actions have on her?

Ethnic groups. Many groups are bound
together not by visible physical characteristics but by common cultural ties.
Physically, they may be no different in appearance from other members of the society. In Nazi Germany, for example, Jews
were forced to wear yellow Stars of David
because otherwise the Nazis could not tell
them apart from non-Jews.

Sociologists call people who are
linked by cultural ties, such as religion,
national origin, language, and customs,
ethnic groups. Such people usually have
strong feelings of in-group loyalty and
"we-ness." Because their customs, beliefs,
and traditions often differ from those of
the general culture, they may comprise
distinct subcultures.

In the United States, many ethnic
groups are linked by national origins —
Italian Americans, Irish Americans, and
Polish Americans, among others. What
does an ethnic identity mean to members
of these groups? In their book, *The Middle
Americans,* Robert Coles and Jon Erikson
report what one Polish American told
them:

My family has been here for four generations; that's a lot. My great-grandfather came over
here, from near Cracow. I've never been to Po-

land. *We're just like other people in this country, but we have memories, Polish memories, that's what my grandfather used to say: "John, don't let your kids forget that once upon a time the family was in Poland!"*

How could I forget? My wife won't let me. She says you have to stay with your own people. We don't have only Polish people living near us, but there are a lot. Mostly we see my family and my wife's family on the weekends, so there's no time to spend doing anything else. . . .

I don't know who's really an American. There are guys I work with, they're Italian and Irish. They're different from me, even though we're all Catholics. You see what I mean? We're buddies on the job. We do the same work. We drink our coffee together and sit there eating lunch. But you leave and you go home and you're back with your own people. I don't just mean my family, no. It's more than your wife and kids; it's everything in your life.

Distinctions between racial groups and ethnic groups sometimes tend to blur. In the United States, for example, blacks and Native Americans were long segregated on the basis of race (inherited physical characteristics). As a result of segregation, they have retained or developed distinctive cultural traits that are ethnic in character. Soul music and soul food, for example, are identified with black culture.

🦢 Are Jews a race or an ethnic group? If Jews are a race, then they all should have a set of common physical characteristics. Try this test on yourself. Look at the photographs on the next page. Write down the numbers of those people who you believe are Jewish. Your teacher will tell you the correct answers.

Three generations of an American Jewish family.

Racial and Ethnic Groups in the United States

Unlike many other societies, the United States is predominantly a nation of immigrants and their descendants. (The only native Americans, of course, are the people whom Columbus called *Indians.*) The first immigrants began to settle here in the late 1500's, and their numbers increased dramatically thereafter. The population of the original 13 colonies doubled every generation, mainly because of the steady flow of settlers from Europe and captives from Africa who were brought here as slaves.

The importation of slaves was banned by Congress in 1808, but immigration from Europe continued to rise. Between 1820 and 1860, five million immigrants arrived here, most of them from northern and western Europe. About two million came from Ireland, where the failure of the potato crop in the 1840's caused widespread starvation.

From 1860 to 1890, the number of immigrants doubled. Western states, such as Minnesota, Nebraska, and Iowa, at-tracted many immigrants from Sweden and Norway by advertising the availability of cheap farmland.

During the 1890's, the pattern of immigration changed. For the next 30 years, the majority of immigrants to the United States came from southern and eastern European countries such as Italy, Poland, and Russia. Altogether, more than 23 million people arrived here between 1880 and 1920.

Why did they come? For some, the United States was a refuge from the grinding poverty and hunger they had known at home. For others, it was a refuge from political oppression or religious persecution. Nearly all immigrants saw the United States as a country that offered a second chance — and land where they might prosper and be free. Pascal d'Angelo, a poet who arrived in this country in 1910, told why he and other Italians left their homeland:

"Our people have to emigrate. It is a matter of too many people and too little space. We feel tied up there. Every bit of cultivable soil is owned by the fortunate few who lord over us. . . . And what is it that saves the man and keeps him from

Students representing 19 ethnic groups at P.S. 1 in New York City lined up for this photograph in 1926.

New American immigrants from diverse lands.

8:A

Where the Immigrants Came From

1820-1984

Number	Country of Origin
7,014,160	Germany
5,331,392	Italy
4,977,606	Great Britain
4,730,227	Ireland
4,322,852	Austria-Hungary
4,157,129	Canada
3,418,826	Russia
2,489,251	Mexico
1,674,200	Other Americas
1,276,869	Sweden
860,637	Norway
758,842	France
51,950,000*	

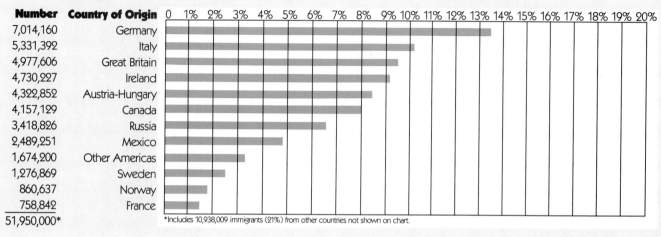

*Includes 10,938,009 immigrants (21%) from other countries not shown on chart.

8:B

1984

Number	Country of Origin
3,100	Italy
6,900	Germany
8,800	El Salvador
10,800	Canada
13,800	Iran
13,900	Great Britain
25,000	India
33,000	Korea
37,000	Vietnam
42,800	Philippines
57,600	Mexico
104,700	Other Asian countries
543,900*	

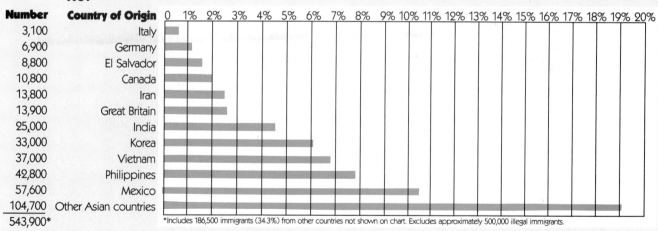

*Includes 186,500 immigrants (34.3%) from other countries not shown on chart. Excludes approximately 500,000 illegal immigrants.

being ground under the hard power of necessity? The New World!"

Fear and resentment of the foreign-born — by the descendants of earlier immigrants — led to the passage of laws in the 1920's that restricted the number of new immigrants to 153,000 a year. These laws established quotas which favored immigrants from northern and western Europe. In 1924 Congress passed the Oriental Exclusion Act, which banned all immigration from Asia. In the following years, these laws were only slightly modified, until 1965, when a more open law was passed.

The new law permitted entry each year of 170,000 immigrants from the Eastern Hemisphere and 120,000 immigrants from the Western Hemisphere. In 1978, these limits by hemisphere were replaced with a worldwide limit of 290,000. Three years later, this limit was lowered to 270,000. However, parents, spouses, unmarried children of U.S. citizens and refugees are exempt from quotas. As a result, over 500,000 people immigrated to the U.S. each year between 1980 and 1984.

Experts believe that another 500,000 illegal immigrants settle in the U.S. each year. They estimate that 6 million illegal aliens are currently living in this country. The overwhelming majority of these illegal aliens are from Mexico.

In 1986, Congress passed the Simpson-Rodino bill in an attempt to deal with the problem of illegal immigration. The new law offers amnesty to an estimated three million aliens who came to the U.S. before 1982. It also mandates stiff fines for employers who hire illegal aliens.

What immigrant groups are represented in your community? List them in order of size. Now compare your list to the Charts 8:A and B on page 229.

The Statue of Liberty greeted immigrants with these words inscribed on its base:

Give me your tired, your poor,
Your huddled masses yearning to breathe free. . . .

Once they landed, however, newcomers often got a hostile reception from native-born Americans. The Irish were one of the first white groups to experience severe prejudice; they were feared and despised for many years because of their Catholic faith. The arrival of approximately 100,000 Chinese on the West Coast between 1850 and 1880 created fears of a "yellow peril." Italians, who comprised the largest group of European immigrants in the 20th century, were often called "the Chinese of Europe." Typical of the attitude of many native-born Americans toward eastern Europeans was this comment about immigrants laboring in a field: "Animals, they work under the sun and in the dirt with stolid, stupid faces."

Today most white European ethnic groups have "made it" in the United States. To a large extent, they have been accepted as equals in our society. But other ethnic and racial groups still suffer severe discrimination, particularly black Americans, Native Americans, and Hispanic Americans. Let's take a look at some of these minority groups.

Black Americans. Black people comprise the largest minority group in our society. They number about 30 million or 12 percent of the total population. For more than 300 years, their history was one of almost unrelieved exploitation, poverty, and discrimination. Since the civil-rights movement of the 1960's, blacks have made important gains and have experienced a great awakening of ethnic consciousness and pride. Over 6,000 local elected officials are black, including the mayors of many large cities. Educated blacks are joining the middle class in increasing numbers. The number of black professionals and executives is growing. These blacks can afford to live in good neighborhoods and send their children to college.

In contrast, unskilled and uneducated blacks seem to be making little or no progress economically. Many live in decayed central cities where unemployment may be as high as 40 percent. They have little hope that they will ever escape poverty and discrimination. By the late 1980's nearly 30 percent of all blacks still lived below the poverty line. Additionally, there was a rise in violence against blacks.

In recent years, blacks have become increasingly aware of their cultural heritage. Some have diligently searched for their family roots. Toni Morrison, a black novelist and editor, vividly described her grandparents and their origins in an article in *The New York Times Magazine.* Part of it follows:

His name was John Solomon Willis, and when at age five he heard from the old folks that

Presidential candidate Jesse Jackson grew up at a time when racial segregation was very strict in parts of the United States.

Thomas Shedrick Small, shown here at a 1963 civil-rights demonstration, could trace his ancestors to South Carolina before the Declaration of Independence was written.

"the Emancipation Proclamation was coming," he crawled under the bed. It was his earliest recollection of what was to be his habitual response to the promises of white people: horror and an instinctive yearning for safety. He was my grandfather, a musician who managed to hold on to his violin but not his land. He lost all 88 acres of his Indian mother's inheritance to legal predators. . . .

He was an unreconstructed black pessimist who, in spite of or because of emancipation, was convinced for 85 years that there was no hope whatever for black people in this country. His rancor was legitimate, for he, John Solomon, was not only an artist but a first-rate carpenter and farmer, reduced to sending home to his family money he made playing the violin because he was not able to find work. And this during the years when almost half the black male population were skilled craftsmen who lost their jobs to white ex-convicts and immigrant farmers.

His wife, however, was of a quite different frame of mind and believed that all things could be improved by faith in Jesus and an effort of the will. So it was she, Ardelia Willis, who sneaked her seven children out of the back window into the darkness, rather than permit the patron of their sharecropper's existence to become their executioner as well.

They headed north in 1912, when 99.2 percent of all black people in the U.S. were native-born and only 60 percent of white Americans were. And it was Ardelia who told her husband that they could not stay in the Kentucky town they ended up in because the teacher did not know long division.

They have been dead now for 30 years and more and I still don't know which of them came closer to the truth about the possibilities of life for black people in this country. . . .

≤§ What current trends support an optimistic view of the possibilities of life for blacks today? A pessimistic view?

Native Americans. At least one million Native Americans lived in what is now the United States when the first Europeans arrived. As the pioneers moved westward, they defeated the Native Americans in battle and shattered their cultures.

Native Americans have suffered as much if not more than any other minority in American history. In 1871, all Native Americans were made "wards" of the federal government. They were forced to live on reservations controlled by the Bureau of Indian Affairs, which provided funds for food, housing, education, and health care. By 1890, only about 250,000 Native Americans still lived in the United States. They were finally granted U.S. citizenship and the right to vote in 1924.

Success of the black civil-rights movement inspired many Native Americans to become equally militant in their demands for equality. During the 1970's, an intertribal organization called the American Indian Movement campaigned for the right to self-rule on reservations. For many Native Americans, becoming a part of the larger U.S. culture was no longer a goal. They demanded greater respect for their own unique cultural traditions.

The protest movement helped to restore Native American pride. The Navajo, for example, are the nation's largest tribe. Their reservation in Arizona, New Mexico, and Utah covers 16 million acres. The tribe's council accepted a government offer to let them run their own reservation. In a short time, the Navajo built an electronics plant, opened a tribal museum, and planned a new town with modern housing. College-age students could attend Navajo Community College, the first institution of higher learning owned and operated by Native Americans.

The Navajo's success stimulated other tribes to strive for economic independence. In Oregon, the Wasco Indians operate a successful resort as well as logging and sawmill operations. Other tribes are beginning to exploit the mineral resources which lie under their lands. About one-fourth of the nation's 268 reservations may contain potential mineral wealth. An estimated five percent of the U.S. oil and gas, and one-third of its strippable low-sulfur coal are located on reservation land. These mineral riches could become a valuable resource for economic development.

Despite these recent gains and future opportunities, Native Americans are still our nation's poorest minority group. In the late 1980's, their family income was only about 60 percent that of white Americans. Almost one-third of all Native Americans were unemployed. Government reports also revealed that Native Americans have the highest infant mortality rate and the lowest life expectancy of any minority group.

A little over half of the nation's 1.5 million Native Americans still live on reservations. Many reservation dwellings are rundown and without water or electricity. On some reservations the jobless rate reaches 50 percent. Only about one-third of male Native Americans have graduated from high school. These statistics are tragic reminders of problems rooted deep in America's past. These problems present a challenge to the new generation of Native American leaders.

South Korean sisters Lucia and Angella Ahn came to America to study music. Rhodes scholar Hoang Nhu Tran left South Vietnam at the age of 9.

Asian Americans. The Immigration Act of 1965 has caused dramatic changes in the Asian American population. Prior to 1965, only a tiny trickle of Asians were allowed to enter the U.S. The new quotas established in 1965 reversed this pattern. During the last 25 years, almost one-third of America's immigrants have come from Asia. By the mid-1980's, the 3.6 million Asian Americans comprised about 1.6 percent of the total U.S. population. Immigration experts predict that the Asian American population will more than double by the year 2010.

The Chinese and Japanese have historically been the two most important groups of Asian Americans. Chinese immigrants first came to the U.S. between 1850 and 1880. Most settled on the West Coast where they took back-breaking jobs building transcontinental railroads and mining metals. A small number of Japanese also arrived in California. By 1900, there were about 25,000 Japanese and 90,000 Chinese living in the U.S. Both groups endured widespread discrimination. An example is the restrictive immigration laws which prevented their communities from expanding.

Chinese and Japanese Americans are still two of America's most important Asian subgroups. In recent years, they have been joined by increasing numbers of immigrants from Asia. During the last 25 years, more Filipinos have immigrated to America than any other Asian group. As a result, they are expected to become the nation's largest Asian community.

Asian Americans have achieved an impressive record of economic success.

The 1980 census revealed that the Japanese, Filipinos, Chinese, and Koreans all had median household incomes above the national average.

Sociologists have identified three key factors that are responsible for this rate of upward mobility. First, many Asians were highly trained managers or professionals in their native countries. Second, Asian Americans have demonstrated a willingness to begin small businesses. One writer noted, "Asian-owned fish markets, green groceries, and restaurants have breathed fresh life into fading inner-city districts."

A strong commitment to education is the third key ingredient in the Asian American success story. Asian cultures have traditionally placed a high value on education. Asian students have been accepted into every top university in America. In 1987, they comprised 11 percent of the freshman class in the prestigious Ivy League universities.

Hispanic Americans. Over 18 million people of Hispanic, or Spanish-speaking origins live in the United States. They are the nation's fastest-growing minority. During the mid-1980's, 42 percent of all legal immigrants were Hispanic. Many social scientists predict that if this pattern of growth continues, Hispanics will replace blacks as the nation's largest minority.

Mexican Americans make up the nation's largest Hispanic group. In 1985, it was estimated that they numbered 11 million, or about 60 percent of all Hispanic Americans. The overwhelming majority of Mexican Americans live in California, Texas, New Mexico, and Arizona.

The second largest group of Hispanics come from Puerto Rico. In 1985, they numbered over 2.5 million people, about 15 percent of the total Hispanic population. Half of all Puerto Ricans live in the New York City area. Cuban Americans comprise the third largest group of Hispanics. Eighty percent of the nation's one million Cuban Americans live in Florida.

Like other immigrant groups, Hispanics have had to work their way up the economic ladder. In 1985, 25.5 percent of Hispanic families lived below the poverty level. But this poverty was unevenly distributed. It included 43.2 percent of Puerto Rican families, 28.3 percent of Mexican American families, and 19.4 percent of the remaining Hispanic families (as compared with 11.4 percent of all American families). The average education for Cuban Americans was several years higher than that of Puerto Ricans and Mexicans in the U.S.

The Hispanic population is having a growing impact on American culture. Traditional Hispanic foods can be purchased in restaurants and supermarkets across the country. Hispanic musicians continue to influence American jazz and pop tunes. Hispanic athletes play a prominent role in boxing and baseball.

The blending of American and Hispanic cultures is particularly strong along the 2,000 mile border which divides the U.S. and Mexico. Seven million people live along this border. Citizens of both countries repeatedly cross the border to shop, work, and enjoy recreational facilities. In the process, they have developed what one writer calls, "a third country with its own identity. . . . Its food, its language, its music are its own." For example, many young Americans in the border area speak a combination of English and Spanish called "Spanglish."

The rapid increase in the Hispanic population has produced some social problems. As Hispanics move into cities such as Miami, Chicago, and Los Angeles, they inevitably compete with other minority groups for jobs and housing. In large cities such as these, the use of Spanish has become a source of controversy. Many Hispanics prefer to speak Spanish and have argued for bilingual education. Other citizens believe that the government should discourage bilingual programs.

Whether Mexican American, below, or Puerto Rican, Hispanic Americans take pride in their heritage.

Patterns of Acceptance

In every society, the treatment of minorities varies from at least partial acceptance to outright rejection. As a rule, societies that believe in equality and freedom strive toward accepting them fully. Let us see how minority groups may achieve equal status in such societies.

Assimilation. The United States has often been described as a "melting pot," absorbing people of many diverse cultures. Our public school system was especially designed to "Americanize" immigrants by teaching them our language and way of life. European immigrants who readily discarded their old language, customs, and dress, and adopted the dominant culture of native-born Americans had the best chance of being accepted here. The process of conforming to the dominant culture of a country is known as *assimilation*. Many native-born Americans asserted that assimilation was the only way that immigrants could gain acceptance here. Their attitude toward immigrant groups

was similar to the message that one sometimes sees on bumper stickers: "America — love it or leave it." One lifelong, small town New York resident expressed it this way:

"I am sure that foreign people make a mistake in keeping customs of their own land alive and featured in this country. If this country meets their expectations, they should forget the folklore of Europe, St. Patrick's Day parades, German Days, and get behind American things. If they can't do this, they should be returned to the land they love. This country is supposed to be the world's melting pot. If they won't melt, they should not belong."

In their eagerness to become assimilated and "make it" in the United States, many immigrants changed their "foreign-sounding" names or gave up the religion of their forebears. As much as possible, they sought to conform to the dominant Anglo-Saxon Protestant culture brought here by English speaking colonists.

✍ Can you find any evidence of assimilation in your community? If so, give examples.

The push toward assimilation was very strong at the turn of the century.

Amalgamation. Is assimilation truly a "melting pot" process? Some people say that it is more like camouflage — everyone takes on the appearance of the dominant group. In their view, a true melting pot is one in which all ethnic and racial groups merge biologically to form an entirely new hybrid culture. In this way, all physical and cultural differences disappear and there are no more dominant and subordinate groups. This process is known as *amalgamation.* It is occuring through intermarriage in places like Hawaii and Polynesia where three races — white, yellow, and black — have begun to blend into a single race. At one time it was believed that amalgamation would also take place on the U.S. mainland. This is what the writer Israel Zangwill had in mind when he likened America to a melting pot in 1909:

"There she lies, the great melting pot — listen! Can't you hear the roaring and the bubbling? Ah, what a stirring and seething — Celt and Latin, Slav and Teuton, Greek and Syrian, black and yellow — Jew and Gentile."

Zangwill's dream of a fusion of all ethnic and racial groups within the American melting pot remains just that — a dream. As we have seen in an earlier chapter, most Americans still prefer to marry and reproduce within their own racial, religious, and ethnic groups.

⊷§ Do you think that amalgamation is a good — or a bad — way to solve racial intolerance in our society? Why?

Cultural pluralism. In an area of New York City called the Lower East Side, a Puerto Rican barrio, a Little Italy, and a Chinatown are within walking distance of each other. Each neighborhood has its own language (in addition to English), its own distinctive customs, ethnic food stores, restaurants, and places of worship.

Ethnic neighborhoods, in fact, exist in almost every large American city. Despite strong pressures to assimilate, many ethnic groups have not disappeared into the melting pot. Instead, they have chosen to live together in close-knit communities where they still maintain some of their old traditions. A society in which different cultural groups are permitted to retain their own identities and life-styles without suffering discrimination is called *pluralistic.*

As a way of resolving the problems of ethnic and racial tension, some sociologists believe that cultural pluralism is superior to either assimilation or amalgamation. Ideally, they see the United States as a "nation of nations," in which there is a mutual respect for the ideas, values, and customs of all ethnic and racial groups. Whether this ideal will ever be fully achieved is uncertain. But there is no doubt that ethnic awareness and pride have been increasing in recent years and long-discarded traditions are being revived.

The struggle of earlier immigrants to win acceptance in the United States is being repeated by refugees from Asia, the Middle East, Mexico, and South America. Their lives are described in the following excerpt from *Time* magazine:

Apartheid in South Africa

"We aren't heading for a revolution in our country, we are already in the midst of one," says Johan Heyns, the leader of South Africa's Dutch Reformed Church. "And by that I mean, it's a revolution of ideas, a revolution of our system of values. We can't go on any longer as we did for the past three hundred years. We've got to change."

Change will not come easily for South Africa. The nation's government enforces a complex and controversial system of racial segregation known as apartheid. Under a law passed in 1950, all of South Africa's 35 million inhabitants are classified at birth into one of four groups: white (13 percent); Asian (3 percent); "colored," or people of mixed race (9 percent); black (75 percent).

Although a numerical minority, the whites are the dominant group in South Africa. The white population is split into two groups. The Afrikaners are the descendants of the original Dutch, German, and French settlers. They control the powerful National Party, and have governed South Africa since 1948. The English-speaking whites arrived from Great Britain during the nineteenth century. They have relatively little political power, but own about 80 percent of the nation's business and industrial wealth.

Shortly after gaining power, the Afrikaners passed a series of over 200 racial laws. This legislation created a system of apartheid designed to keep the four racial groups strictly separated. Each group has its own schools, neighborhoods, movie houses, and even cemetaries.

The Afrikaners believe that apartheid has helped make South Africa a strong and prosperous nation. They argue that South African blacks have a higher standard of living than blacks in other African nations. The Afrikaners also emphasize that South Africa holds important natural resources and occupies a strategic location, which must not fall under communist control.

South Africa's non-white majority point out that these arguments overlook the fact that apartheid denies them basic human rights. During the 1970's and 1980's, black leaders in South Africa denounced apartheid and demanded reforms. The government's refusal to carry out meaningful changes helped to spark a series of violent confrontations.

These demonstrations focused world attention on South Africa's racial policies. Both the United Nations and the World Council of Churches have called on the South African government to abolish apartheid. South African athletic teams are excluded from the Olympic Games. In 1986, the United States Congress banned new U.S. corporate investments in South Africa.

As a result of these internal and external pressures, the South African government has begun to make some gradual reforms. Although most South Africans anticipate further changes they do not yet share a common vision for their future. A building contractor sums up the confused feeling of many white South Africans when he says, "I don't want blacks to take over South Africa, but I don't like the way that [white] people treat blacks either."

Thinking Critically

1. What is apartheid? What are South Africa's four main groups?

2. What would be the advantages and disadvantages of assimilation, amalgamation, and cultural pluralism as new patterns of acceptance in South Africa?

New York children with a variety of
ethnic origins. Next page, an
American Indian in Chicago.

. . . "Los Angeles," says Rand Corporation Demographer Kevin McCarthy, "has become the natural embarkation point to the U.S. There's no question that it is the new Ellis Island." L.A. has no central processing facility like Ellis Island, or any Pacific Coast Statue of Liberty, no romantic symbol for every country's immigrants. But during 1982, according to Rand estimates, more than 90,000 foreign immigrants settled there and since 1970, more than 2 million. The exotic multitudes are altering the collective beat and bop of L.A., the city's smells and colors. And a deeper transformation is under way.

. . . The international hordes now streaming in from the West and South have . . . no-nonsense ideas about what they want: a chance to work hard and make money. The newcomers seem almost eager to endure adversity in pursuit of their American dreams. . . . Today in L.A., there are refugees from ugly politics—Soviet Armenians, Lebanese, Iranians. Most are not well-off and most came from countries of the "Pacific

rim": Mexico and El Salvador, across the ocean to Samoa, and still farther west to the Philippines, Taiwan, Vietnam and South Korea.

. . . Why L.A.? It is closer to Seoul, Mazatlan and Singapore than other big U.S. cities. The immigrants are reassured that the local climate, at least is not mean.

. . . What does a Taiwanese grocer living in Glendale have in common with a poor Guatemalan living in Boyle Heights? They may both watch the same local television, although the Guatemalan has Channel 34, in Spanish, and the grocer can stick to Chinese language Channel 18. But they most certainly share the sense of being quasi-Americans: every immigrant has to cope with pressures to assimilate. They are supposed to fit in, but they may never be wholly accepted. "We do not think in American terms of a melting pot," says Paul Louie, a second-generation Chinese American. "We prefer the metaphor of a rainbow or a salad."

Indeed, many of the new arrivals cling to their ethnic identity, preserving their usual customs and language, nurturing old prejudices . . . , developing new ones . . . . Whole neighborhoods seem to rub up against each other without mixing.

But the homogenizing melting pot remains a powerful national ideal. Regardless of whether the foreign-born Angelenos make peace with their extravagant, sometimes alienating new culture, they will likely watch their children turn into Americans.

&ʒ Would you say that the immigrant communities in Los Angeles are examples of assimilation, amalgamation, or cultural pluralism?

Patterns of Rejection

In some societies, minority groups may be tolerated very little, if at all. Rejection by the dominant groups often takes extreme forms. Let us see what some of these forms are.

Genocide. In a Nazi death camp, the prisoners were commanded by guards to line up. When the lines were formed, there was a harsh cry. "Jews to the right!" The Jewish prisoners knew what this meant. Once they were separated from the non-Jews, they were to be exterminated in gas chambers. This was Adolf Hitler's "final solution" for Jews, whom he regarded as a subhuman, inferior people. About six million Jews were killed before Nazi Germany was defeated in World War II.

The deliberate extermination of an entire ethnic or racial group is known as *genocide.* Genocide has been practiced throughout history by many dominant groups. The Native American population of this nation was almost exterminated by what amounted to a policy of genocide in this country. An attempted genocide was conducted by the Khmer Rouge regime in Cambodia (Kampuchia) from 1975 to 1979, when the North Vietnamese invaded and took control of the country. It has been estimated that as many as 2 million Cambodians were massacred during that period.

These men were among the survivors in the Buchenwald concentration camp when it was liberated at the end of World War II.

The expulsion of the Cherokee Nation from the Southeast is portrayed in this painting by Robert Lindneux. Only half of those who set out on the Trail of Tears survived the trip.

Expulsion. In 1838 U.S. Army troops rounded up the Cherokee Indians from their farms in Georgia, North Carolina, and Tennessee, and herded them into camps. The reason? President Andrew Jackson believed that the Cherokees and other tribes in the South would never be assimilated. Ironically, these tribes had already adopted much of the dominant white culture. With the approval of Congress, Jackson ordered these tribes removed to reservations in what is now Oklahoma. The Cherokees were marched westward under military guard. Along the way, more than 4,000 died of various diseases. An eyewitness reported that "even aged females, apparently nearly ready to drop into the grave, were traveling with heavy burdens attached to their backs." The Cherokees who survived called the forced march "the Trail of Tears."

The forcible removal of a racial or ethnic group from a society is known as *expulsion.* This form of rejection has also been prevalent throughout history. A more recent example was the expulsion of 55,000 Asians from Uganda by President Idi Amin in 1972.

Segregation. In a city of South Africa, a police car is cruising an all-white neighborhood. It is after dark. Suddenly the police see a black man walking down the street. They demand to see his passbook ID, which South Africans are required to carry at all times. "You know better than to be in a white neighborhood after dark," they tell him. "It's against the law." The man is arrested and put in jail without a trial.

The enforced separation of minority groups from the dominant members of a society is known as *segregation.* It may be enforced by law, by custom, or by both.

In the Middle Ages, Jews were forced to live in ghettos that separated them from the rest of society. The ghetto was a section of town that was surrounded by a high wall. Segregation is a very common way of dealing with minorities. For many generations, most black Americans had to live in all-black residential neighborhoods. Black children had to attend segregated schools. Although civil-rights legislation in the 1960's put an end to legally enforced segregation of the races, whites and blacks for the most part still live in separate communities.

Signs like these were prevalent in many parts of the United States before the 1960's, when Congress passed laws forbidding segregation in public places.

Prejudice and Discrimination

Martin Luther King, Jr., the late civil-rights leader, was making a speech in Atlanta, Georgia. Blacks, he said, needed laws to protect them. "The law may not make a man love me," King told his audience, "but it can restrain him from lynching me, and I think that's pretty important."

With these words, King was making crystal-clear a distinction between two terms that many people confuse — *prejudice* and *discrimination. Prejudice* is a hostile attitude that people have toward members of another group. This attitude is based on a prejudgment that all members of the group have highly undesirable qualities. "You can't trust any of them," the prejudiced person says. "They're lazy, they lie, and they'll steal anything that isn't nailed down." Even when prejudiced people are presented with evidence that contradicts their views, their attitudes will not change. To prejudiced people, "they" are all bad and always will be.

How is discrimination different from prejudice? *Discrimination* is an act against members of a group that one dislikes. A restaurant commits an act of discrimination by refusing to serve people because of their race or ethnic background.

The following interview with a prejudiced high school senior, conducted in the 1960's in a rural California city, is adapted from the book *Prejudice and Discrimination,* edited by Frederick Holmes:

Holmes: Do you have any minority groups in Hollister?

Student: Negroes? No, we don't have any of those.

Holmes: How about farm workers?

Student: Oh yeah, but they don't live here all year round. Oh, if you mean Mex Wetbacks, we got some of them. Some Mex families live here all year.

Holmes: What kind of work do they do?

Student: Stoop labor — that's man-killin' if you never done it — picking beans or berries. Some pick fruit. Some work on hay balers, but they're not too good. Too lazy.

Holmes: Too lazy?

Student: Yeah, can't stay workin' in the sun like a white kid.

Holmes: Why not?

Student: I dunno, probably not as well-fed, probably not in as good shape, maybe they're just weaker.

Holmes: Could they be?

Student: Yeah, I guess. They're always a lot smaller too. Probably why they always want to use a knife when they fight. Buddy of mine was caught by three of the Wetbacks and really cut up — no reason either. They're like that — cut you up for no reason at all!

Holmes: How do they do in school?

Student: Not much. The Wets don't go, and the ones that live here are kinda dumb.

Holmes: What about the houses they live in?

Student: Man, are those shacks filthy — even the ones that live here. They could at least get some whitewash and tarpaper.

Holmes: Do you know any of these Mex kids?

Student: No, man — you know that white kids don't hang around with Mex.

Holmes: Why not?

Student: They don't eat or drink like us, we like different music, and they can't talk worth a hoot 'n a holler. Tough to get on with them — they won't let any of their women go out with "the guys." I'm sure I don't have to take any of their guff. We've got them just where we want them!

Holmes: What do you mean, "just where we want them"?

Student: You know, as long as they stay in their place, it's OK, I like them fine. But not in the drugstore or where we play pool. . . .

List as many examples of prejudice on the part of the student as you can find in the reading. Can you find examples of discrimination?

Institutional discrimination. Is the life of a black child worth less in dollars and cents than the life of a white child? Strange as it may seem, insurance companies once put less value on the life of a black child. Elliot Liebow, a sociologist, recalls an example from the 1960's:

The six-year-old son of a woman on welfare was struck and killed by an automobile as he tried to run across the street. The insurance company's initial offer of $800 to settle out of court was rejected. In consultation with her lawyer, the mother accepted the second and final offer of $2,000.

When I learned of the settlement, I called the lawyer to protest, arguing that the sum was far less than what I assumed to be the usual settlement in such cases, even if the child was mainly at fault. "You've got to face the facts," he said. "Insurance companies and juries just don't pay as much for a Negro child." Especially, he might have added, a Negro child on welfare.

If the relative worth of human life must be measured in dollars and cents, why should the cash surrender value of a black child's life be less than that for a white child's life? The answer clearly has nothing to do with private prejudice and discrimination. . . . Damage awards are based primarily on the projected lifetime earnings of the individual; they are statements about his probable productivity, not about his skin color.

But this child, this Anthony Davis, was only six years old. On what basis do they make lowered projections of earnings for a six-year-old child, before he has accepted or rejected an education, before he has demonstrated any talents or lack of them, before he has even selected an occupation, or indeed before he has made a single life choice of his own?

. . . What is most important for us to know and admit is this: The insurance company was absolutely right. Anthony was more likely than his white, middle-class counterpart to go to an inferior school, to get an inferior job, to be last hired and first fired, to be passed over for promotion, and to live a shorter life. . . .

Liebow saw this story as evidence of how deeply discrimination was imbedded in our society. The insurance company knew this. It assumed that Anthony Davis would get unequal treatment in housing, health care, education, employment, and other important areas. Unequal treatment that is built into the entire structure of a society is called *institutional discrimination.*

⇚ Can you think of any ways that federal, state, and local governments are fighting institutional discrimination? Name as many as you can.

The Causes of Prejudice

Stereotypes. The California high school senior characterizes Mexicans as lazy, weak, treacherous, dumb, clannish, and dirty. In his view, they are all the same. His mental image of Mexicans is, of course, a gross distortion of reality. Artists would call such a ludicrous image a *caricature.* Sociologists call it a *stereotype.*

The tendency to picture all members of a group in an oversimplified or exaggerated fashion is a common cause (and result) of prejudice. In Northern Ireland, for example, Protestants and Catholics often use stereotypes to justify their hostility toward each other.

A Protestant housewife complains that Catholics "don't keep a nice little house. Why can't they just fix up their houses like decent people do? And their children always seem to be so dirty." One of her Catholic neighbors says: "We always lived within a stone's throw of Protestants, but neither me nor my brothers ever knew any. They always seemed different from the rest of us. They didn't laugh or joke like we always did."

⇚ Now look at the pictures on the next page. What stereotypes can you identify?

In-groups, out-groups, and ethnocentrism. Rudyard Kipling, an English writer, captured the feeling that most groups foster to some degree when he wrote:

All good people agree
and all good people say
All nice people like us, are We
and everyone else is They.

The belief that all groups or societies are inferior to one's own is, of course, an example of *ethnocentrism.* It applies not only to cultures but to racial and ethnic groups as well.

Isn't *our* school, *our* team, and *our* club superior to all others? Aren't "we" who belong to an in-group better than "they" who are members of out-groups? "We" are the good guys. We are stronger, braver, smarter, and cleaner than "they." Sometimes "they" are just plain lazy, stupid, and sneaky. So the human tendency to belong to groups, and to consider these groups as better than all others, may also lead to prejudice.

Authoritarian personality. Do some people have personality traits that make them more likely than others to be prejudiced? A researcher named Theodore Adorno tried to find the answer to this question in the 1940's. His study was motivated by the extreme prejudice shown by German Nazis toward Jews and other ethnic groups. Adorno tested people on their attitudes toward fascism (a dictatorship that stresses nation or race), ethnocentrism, and anti-Semitism (prejudice against Jews).

Adorno found that the three were closely related. That is, people who were anti-Semitic were also likely to despise other groups as "inferior," and to be sympathetic to fascism. Such people, Adorno said, had a distinctly authoritarian personality. Generally they were intolerant, highly conformist, submissive to superiors, and bullying to inferiors. These traits, of course, were highly characteristic of the Nazis. Later research has shown that the authoritarian personality is not confined to fascism; it can be found in political extremists of any ideology.

Scapegoating. Minority groups are often a convenient target for people who are troubled. Suppose, for example, that a man has been out of work for a long time. He is worried about his debts that keep piling up. In his frustration, he blames a minority group for his problems. "These days you've got to be black to get a good job," he might say. Or, "How can I get a decent job when a Mexican American will work for half of what I usually earn?"

Why doesn't he blame the business recession that has put him out of work, or the employer who has fired him? It is simply easier for him to direct his anger at defenseless minority groups. Sociologists call this *scapegoating.* The need of some people to find scapegoats for their troubles plays an important role in fanning prejudice.

In most cultures, some people blame their troubles on something else. The modern term *scapegoat* is derived from the ancient Hebrews who actually confessed their sins over a goat and drove it into the desert.

application

On December 7, 1941, Japanese carrier planes bombed U.S. Navy ships at Pearl Harbor, Hawaii. The next day, the United States entered World War II. Americans began to fear and hate the Japanese. Japanese Americans were suspected of helping the overseas enemy. Soon the United States set up internment camps for Japanese Americans. About 110,000 men, women, and children were sent to them.

Jeanne Wakatsuki was seven years old when her family was sent to a camp named Manzanar. Like other Japanese Americans, they were innocent of any crimes, yet they were treated as prisoners. Almost 30 years later, Jeanne and her husband, James Houston, wrote a book about life in the camp. It is called *Farewell to Manzanar.* Jeanne also described her life right after the war when she moved to Los Angeles. Here is that story, beginning with her first day back in public school:

Saluting the American flag at Manzanar.

When I entered the sixth-grade class, the other kids looked me over. I would have done the same thing to a new student. The teacher was a kind woman who tried to make me feel at ease. She gave me time to get used to the class. Later, she asked me to read a page aloud. I had not yet opened my mouth except to smile. I smiled wider, then read the page without making any mistakes.

Afterward a blond girl near me said, "Gee, I didn't know you could speak English."

She wasn't being mean. She was really surprised. I was shocked. I suddenly knew what having Japanese ancestors was going to be like. I would be seen as a foreigner, not as an American.

After that, part of me wanted to be invisible. I didn't want people to see me as a slant-eyed Oriental. If I couldn't be seen as an individual, I didn't want to be seen at all. But another part of me decided to prove that I wasn't different. For a long time I lived with two urges — to disappear and to be accepted.

At one point, I wanted to join the Girl Scouts. A friend of mine, Radine, belonged. She was the blond girl who was surprised at first that I knew English. Radine's folks didn't have much money. They lived in the same housing project that my folks lived in. So Radine and I walked home from school each day. She never talked about the

*Raising the flag at Heart Mountain
Relocation Camp in Wyoming, above.
A children's Bible class, below.*

Girl Scouts with me. But one day I asked, "Can I belong?" I added, "You know, I'm Japanese."

"I don't know," she said. "But I'll find out. Mama is the assistant troop leader." The next day she said, "Gee, Jeannie, no. I'm really sorry." I didn't hold this against her. It was her mother who had drawn the line, and I was used to that. If anything, Radine and I were closer now. If she'd catch someone staring at me, she'd growl, "What are you staring at? She's an American citizen. She's got as much right as you to be here."

Soon we were together all the time. I had learned how to twirl the baton from an older girl at Manzanar, and now I taught Radine. There was a Boy Scout marching band in the neighborhood. They wanted some baton twirlers to march in front of them in local parades. Radine and I tried out. We made it, along with another seventh-grade girl. She and Radine wore blue satin outfits. I was head majorette, and my outfit was white with gold trim.

Why was I allowed to perform with the Boy Scouts, but not allowed to join the Girl Scouts? The boys in the band loved having girls march in front of them — stepping high in short skirts. . . .

My older brothers teased me about my short skirts, but they went to the parades I was in and they were proud of me. Papa didn't share that pride. While I was trying to be Miss America of 1947, he wanted me to be Miss Japan of 1904. He would tell me it was wrong to wear short skirts and to smile so much. I wanted out of Papa's world. Being a majorette with Radine was what I wanted.

We stayed best friends until we went to high school. Then everything changed. She was asked to join girls' social clubs, I was not. The boys I liked flirted with me, but they never asked me out. They asked out girls like Radine — girls they could safely be seen with. I didn't want to change my face. I just wanted to be accepted as easily as Radine.

I often had a dream about this. In my dream, I saw a beautiful blond girl moving through a crowd of other teenagers. She is admired by both boys and girls, including me. But I am watching through a window. I am not angry at the girl. I don't even envy her. But I am apart and helpless. I want to cry out because she is something I can never be.

I was a senior when my family moved to San Jose. Since I had been to a big high school, I was sort of respected. It was a chance to start over, and I made the most of it. By the spring of that year, it was time to elect the carnival queen for the senior class. My homeroom chose me. I was one of 15 girls who would compete for the crown. The students — all of them — would select the winner.

I knew I couldn't beat the other girls at their own game. I couldn't look like a bobby-soxer. But I couldn't look too Japanese either. I decided to look different — but in an exciting way. I wore a low-cut sarong, and I was barefooted. I wore my hair loose, with a flower behind one ear. When I walked on stage, the boys whistled and yelled much louder than they had for the other girls. The next day it was announced that I had been chosen carnival queen. I couldn't believe it.

When I told the news to my family, no one cheered. Papa, in fact, was furious. "No wonder those white boys vote for you!" he shouted. "You show off your body. What Japanese boy is going to marry that kind of girl?"

In her quiet way, Mama supported me, in spite of Papa's views. Being accepted, she felt, was one way of surviving. Still, she agreed with Papa that I should be careful about the way I dressed. The four girls who would be my attendants were going to wear strapless gowns. Mama would not let me wear one. She picked out a long, frilly gown with a high neck. It seemed right to me. I had used a low-cut sarong to win the contest, but now I would be very respectable.

The night I was to be crowned, the gym was lit up like a church. The throne was flooded with light from the ceiling. A white carpet (made up of bed sheets) went from the door of the girls' locker room to the throne. The four attendants and I waited at the door for the music to start. Lois Carson, one of the attendants, wore an expensive strapless gown, "Jeannie," she said, "what a marvelous idea to wear a high neck. You look so — so proper. Just perfect for a queen."

The music started and I stepped out into the spotlight. I heard the applause and saw that the gym was packed. The lights on me were bright as I walked toward the throne. Suddenly I felt very hot. I imagined that everyone was murmuring about how old-fashioned my dress was. I kept walking slowly. I thought of the kids who had voted for me, and I didn't want to let them down. But in a way, I already had. They hadn't voted *for me in this old-fashioned dress. They had voted for somebody I wanted to be — and wasn't. I looked ahead at the throne, which was made of plywood and covered with purple cloth. It seemed farther away than ever.*

I wanted to laugh. I wanted to cry. I wanted the carnival to end so I could be alone and get out of my stuffy dress. But all eyes were upon me. It was too late not to follow this make-believe carpet to this make-believe throne. And I did not yet know of any truer goal.

❧ Is Jeanne a member of a racial or an ethnic minority — or of both? Why? What kinds of acceptance does she seek? What stereotypes of Japanese people are described here? Would you say that the discrimination against Jeanne is personal or institutional? Explain your answer.

summary

A diversity of racial, religious, or ethnic groups within a society often leads to strained relations among them. Wherever tension exists among groups with different physical or cultural traits, one group dominates the others. The **dominant group** has more power, wealth, and prestige than the others. The dominant group justifies its privileged position by claiming to be "superior" in some way. The subordinate groups are called **minorities**. Members of minority groups are singled out because of their special physical or cultural traits and are subjected to unequal treatment. They regard themselves as victims of discrimination. Minority groups are not necessarily smaller in number than dominant groups; they may actually be larger. What distinguishes a minority group is its inferior status within a society regardless of its numbers.

A **racial group** may be defined as one that shares inherited physical characteristics such as skin color, facial features, and hair texture. To sociologists, racial differences are much less important than what people believe about them and how they react to them. The Nazis, for example, killed millions of people whom they believed to be "racially inferior." Unlike racial groups, ethnic groups are not bound together by visible, inherited physical characteristics. **Ethnic groups** are linked by common cultural ties such as national origin, language, religion, or customs. When their beliefs and traditions differ noticeably from those of the dominant culture, they comprise distinct subcultures within a society.

Within a society, the treatment of minorities may range from at least partial acceptance to outright rejection. When a minority achieves acceptance by conforming with the norms and values of the dominant group, the process is called **assimilation.** When the ethnic and racial groups in a society merge to form a new culture, the process is called **amalgamation.** When ethnic and racial groups retain their own identities and life-styles without discrimination, the process is called **cultural pluralism.** On the other hand, a society may take extreme measures to reject minorities. The worst of these is **genocide,** a deliberate effort to exterminate a minority. On other occasions, dominant groups force a minority to leave a society. This process is called **expulsion.** When a dominant group forces minority groups to be separate — either by law or by custom — the process is called **segregation.**

Ethnic and racial minority groups suffer both prejudice and discrimination. Although the two terms are often confused, there is a clear difference between them. **Prejudice** is a hostile attitude toward members of a minority group. It is based on an irrational belief that all members of the group have highly undesirable qualities. **Discrimination** is an act against members of a minority group. If, for example, a restaurant refuses to serve people because of their race or ethnic background, it has committed an act of discrimination.

What are some of the causes of prejudice? One of them is the tendency of some people to form distorted images of minority groups. They picture every minority group member without exception as dishonest, lazy, dirty, or stupid. Sociologists call such a distorted and generalized image a **stereotype.**

The very human tendency to belong to groups may also lead to prejudice. Groups generate feelings of **ethnocentrism,** that is, the belief that "our" group is superior to "their" group. When such feelings become very strong, we are likely to develop stereotyped images of those outside our group.

Certain personality traits may make some people more prejudiced than others. According to studies, such people are usually highly conformist, submissive to superiors, and bullying to inferiors. Sociologists describe a person with such traits as having an **authoritarian personality.**

Another cause of prejudice is the need of some people to find some one else to blame for their troubles. The group or person who gets the blame is called a **scapegoat.** Some prejudiced people find it easier to blame members of minority groups for their problems than to search for the real causes.

more questions and activities

1. Explain what is meant by *dominant* and *minority* groups. Give the social characteristics of the dominant group in the United States and the dominant group in South Africa.

2. How do most sociologists define *race?* What is their primary concern when studying race?

3. Define *prejudice* and *discrimination.* Then give an example of each, illustrating the difference between them.

4. On the chalkboard list as many of the racial and ethnic groups represented in your community as you can. Divide them into categories according to the patterns of acceptance or rejection each has experienced in our society.

5. If you have ever felt the experience of being treated as a stereotype, put your reactions to this experience into a short story, poem, editorial, or nonfiction article. (If you are not a member of a racial or ethnic minority, you might have been stereotyped because of your age or some other social characteristic.)

6. Women are sometimes referred to as the "largest minority group in the United States." List the ways in which women — who make up 51 percent of the U.S. population — could be described as a minority group.

7. Do research to determine which group(s) of Native Americans inhabited your community or state before white settlers took over the land. Are there remnants of their culture in your community? If so, what are they? If there are still members of these groups in your community, invite a member to speak to the class. If there are none, try to trace the history of their displacement and their current location.

8. Watch several shows of a TV series that has regularly appearing characters who are members of racial or ethnic minority groups. How realistic are the characters? Are they stereotypes? If necessary, do research to find out if the characters are realistic members of those groups.

9. Debate: "Every kind of discrimination is a protection of the incompetent against the competent, with the result that the motive to become competent is taken away," G.L. Dickinson, *The Choice Before Us.*

10. Except for the descendants of Native Americans, the ancestors of every person in your school came to the United States from another country. First, take a poll to see how many members of your class know the origins of their earliest ancestors. Is there a pattern of immigration to your community revealed in the backgrounds of class members?

11. Research your cultural background. There are numerous books to help you do this; one excellent book is *Finding Your Roots: How Every American Can Trace His Ancestors — At Home and Abroad,* by Jeane Westin, 1977. Your school library probably has several others. Bring to class an object or describe a custom that is a part of your cultural heritage. Be prepared to give an account of its origin.

suggested readings

Allport, Gordon W. *The Nature of Prejudice.* (Doubleday, 1979). A classic study of the causes of prejudice.

Carlson, Lewis H., and George A. Colburn, eds. *In Their Place: White America Defines Her Minorities 1850-1950.* (John Wiley, 1972.) A collection of primary source readings which graphically illustrated examples of prejudice and discrimination directed at each of our major ethnic and racial groups.

Furman, Harry, Richard Flaim, and Edwin Reynolds, eds. *The Holocaust and Genocide.* (Anti- Defamation League, 1983). An outstanding collection of high interest readings designed especially for high school students.

Gambino, Richard. *Blood Of My Blood.* (Doubleday, 1974). A superb journalistic portrait of Italian Americans.

Kramer, Mark. "U.S.-Mexican Border: Life on the Line." (*National Geographic,* June 1985). An excellent photo essay on the unique life-styles and problems of the communities along the U.S.-Mexican border.

Namias, June. *First Generation: In the Words of Twentieth Century American Immigrants.* (Beacon Press, 1978). An interesting collection of interviews which reveal the difficulties, joys and cultural experiences of immigrants who came to America during this century.

Schoener, Allan, ed. *Portal to America: The Lower East Side 1870-1925.* (Holt, Rinehart and Winston, 1967). A poignant collection of photographs depicting the life of America's immigrants at the turn of the century.

Sowell, Thomas. *Ethnic Americans* (Basic Books, 1981). A concise history of ethnic and racial groups which includes chapters on black, Irish, Jewish, and Chinese Americans.

Time Editors. "Immigrants - The Changing Face of America." (*Time,* July 8, 1985.) A special issue of *Time* devoted to the impact which modern immigrants are having upon American life.

Marathon races are one example of collective behavior. Can you list others?

chapter 9

collective behavior

Was Paul McCartney of the Beatles really dead? In 1969 a rumor that the young rock idol had been killed in a car crash spread around the world. According to the rumor, the accident had occurred in 1966. But the Beatles' record company had ordered a cover-up; it wanted to make money from future Beatles albums. Under pressure, the remaining Beatles had hired a "double" to impersonate McCartney. The young man who now posed as Paul McCartney was a fraud.

How did the rumor of McCartney's death get started? No one is certain; but, according to one account, a college student invented the story and sent it to a disc jockey, who repeated it on the air. It was then reported by a number of newspapers and magazines. As the rumor spread, the details were embellished. Beatles John Lennon, Ringo Starr, and George Harrison had tried to be honest with their fans. They had secretly inserted some clues about McCartney's death into their albums to let the fans know the truth.

Soon Beatle fans were playing their idols' albums both forward and backward in a search for clues. Sometimes they thought they heard the evidence they were looking for. When a song entitled "Revolution No. 9" was played backward, for example, a ghostly voice was heard to say, "Turn me on, dead man." Album covers were also studied for clues. On one, *Magical Mystery Tour*, Lennon, Starr, and Harrison wore red carnations, but McCartney wore a *black* carnation.

The photograph on the next page appeared on the cover of a Beatles album called *Abbey Road*. Those who believed the rumor said the photograph resembled a funeral procession. John Lennon, in white, was the priest. Ringo Starr, in black, was the undertaker. McCartney, barefoot and out of step, walked with his eyes closed — the corpse. George Harrison, in working clothes, was the gravedigger. A car in the background had the license plate 28IF. It meant, of course, that McCartney would be 28 if he were still alive.

The Beatles' record company denied the rumor of McCartney's death again and again, but it kept spreading. Finally McCartney himself squashed the rumor with the following statement: "If I were dead, I'd be the last one to know about it."

Are sociologists interested in rumors about rock stars? They are when those rumors cause large numbers of people to behave oddly. As we have seen, sociologists usually study the regular, patterned behavior of people in groups. But people don't always behave the way we expect them to. Sometimes, as in the rumors of McCartney's death, they depart from usual norms of conduct and surprise or shock us.

Why, for example, should college students suddenly start swallowing goldfish or jamming themselves into telephone booths? Why should an enthusiastic crowd at a rock concert become transformed into an angry mob that smashes store windows and fights with police?

In these examples, large numbers of people engaged in conduct that is spontaneous, brief, and out of the ordinary. Sociologists call such conduct *collective behavior*. Some forms of collective behavior, such as riots, lynch mobs, and panics, are violent. Others, like fads, fashions, and crazes, are nonviolent. What they all have in common is that they are unpredictable and depart from regular norms.

In this chapter we will discuss a

number of forms of collective behavior. We'll also examine the role of public opinion in collective behavior, and see how some people attempt to manipulate public opinion through propaganda and how others seek to measure it with polls. Finally, we'll study a theory one sociologist has developed to explain how collective behavior occurs.

Rumors

On November 22, 1963, President John F. Kennedy was shot to death while riding in a motorcade through downtown Dallas, Texas. Within a very short time, hundreds of rumors began to spread throughout the nation. Among them were the following:

• Lee Harvey Oswald, the accused assassin, was an agent of the Cuban dictator, Fidel Castro.

• Oswald was an agent of the FBI or the CIA.

• Jack Ruby, the man who killed Oswald, was paid by the Dallas police to silence him.

Although none of these rumors has ever been confirmed, they persist today. *Rumors* are unverified reports that spread from one person to another.

Usually they arise in tense and confused situations when people are unable to learn all the facts or distrust the information they receive. The spreading of rumors is itself a form of collective behavior. Rumors also play an important role in influencing other forms of collective behavior. A rumor of police brutality, for example, may provide the spark that will ignite an angry riot.

A laboratory experiment. Social scientists have extensively studied the process by which rumors are transmitted. Controlled laboratory experiments and analysis of actual cases are the two major methods that have been used.

The best-known experimental study of rumors was conducted by Gordon Allport and Leo Postman in 1947. They began their experiments by telling a subject a complicated story. This story was frequently supplemented by showing the subject a drawing or photograph of the described event. The subject then had to relate what he or she had seen and heard to another subject who had no familiarity with this information. The second subject was instructed to repeat it to a third, and so forth. The researchers recorded the story each time it was retold.

Based on their experiments, Allport and Postman identified three steps in the process of rumor transmission. First, the story became shorter and shorter until only a few easily remembered details were retold. The researchers referred to this shortening process as *leveling*. As a result of leveling, the remembered details became emphasized and gained importance. They called this second step *sharpening*. But even the few leveled and sharpened details tended to change as they were passed along. For example, in over half of the retellings, a razor in a white man's hand moved to the hand of a black man.

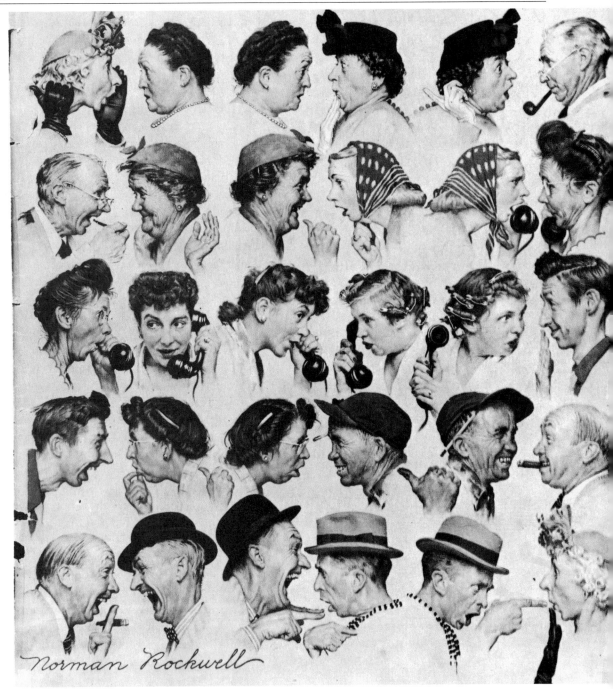

This 1948 Saturday Evening Post *cover illustrates the snowball rumor theory.*

Allport and Postman concluded that these distortions reflected the personal and cultural biases of the person telling the story. They called this step *assimilation.*

The following story from news reports shows how information can be distorted into an absurd rumor as it passes from one person to another:

For consumers, 1973 may go down in history as the Year of the Shortages. After waiting in line for gasoline, being warned against using too much electricity, and finding even onions in short supply, no wonder consumers were upset when they heard about the toilet paper "shortage."

The first hoarding started when news reports told of shortages in Japan. About the same time, a Wisconsin Congressman, Harold V. Froehlich, received complaints from some of his constituents that paper companies in his heavily forested district were selling their paper abroad to avoid federal price controls.

Upon investigating, the Congressman found that the government's National Buying Center had fallen 50 percent short in its attempt to get bids on 182,050 boxes of toilet tissue, a four-month supply for government and military workers. Representative Froehlich issued a press release which said in part:

"The United States may face a serious shortage of toilet paper within a few months. . . . I hope we don't have to ration toilet tissue. . . . A toilet paper shortage is no laughing matter."

The wire services and television networks picked up the press release. Radio stations and even foreign correspondents wanted interviews with Froehlich. Unfortunately, the fact that there was only a *chance* of a shortage got lost in many reports.

In Philadelphia, more responsible reporters contacted one of the nation's 10 biggest tissue manufacturers. Production there was reported normal — 7,500 miles a day — and consumers were urged to remain calm. If people bought normally, company officials said, there would be no shortage.

However, eight days after Representative Froehlich's press release, the rumor gained coast-to-coast credibility when television talk show host Johnny Carson told his sleepy audience: "But have you heard the latest? I'm not kidding. I saw it in the paper. There's a shortage of toilet paper."

The next day, a nationwide buying binge was underway. A concerned Seattle store-owner ordered 21 extra cases of paper. When he got only three, he rationed his supply to customers.

A Bronx, New York, food-store manager watched customers check out with up to $20 in tissue purchases.

"There are so many credibility gaps today, and we fell into one," said a paper company executive. A college professor of marketing, Stewart Henderson Britt, called the "shortage" a classic study in rumor. "Everyone likes to be the first to know something," he said, "It's the old 'did-you-hear-that' syndrome. In the old days, a rumor took a long time to spread. Now all it takes is one TV personality to joke about it, and instantly the rumor is in all 50 states."

Professor Britt said the story had all

the elements necessary for a rumor. It could affect everyone intimately. There was a Congressman, presumably an authority, talking about it, saying there could be a problem. The next person said there probably was a problem. The next person said there *was* a problem.

As the professor predicted, the "shortage" was over as soon as shoppers observed that empty shelves were refilled. There was enough toilet paper to go around again.

≈§ How was the toilet paper rumor leveled? What details gained importance as it was passed along? How was the rumor encouraged by current biases?

Snowballing. In their laboratory studies, Allport and Postman found that as rumors were transmitted, they tended to become shorter. Other studies, conducted where actual rumors took place, have revealed a different pattern. In this process, one rumor leads to another, setting off a chain reaction. This often happens in times of crisis, when people are desperately seeking answers for "unthinkable" calamities. When the Japanese bombed Pearl Harbor, for example, Americans were stunned by the disaster. How were the Japanese pilots able to carry out their attack so successfully? Hundreds of rumors developed to explain it. Researcher Tamotsu Shibutani described some of them and their consequences in his book, *Improvised News:*

How had the enemy been able to plan so carefully, catching the entire area off guard? Where had he gotten the detailed information necessary to execute the attack with such preci-

sion? The finger pointed directly at Hawaii's 160,000 residents of Japanese ancestry, and hundreds of rumors arose implicating them. Among the most widespread of these rumors were: a McKinley High School ring was found on the body of a Japanese flier shot down over Honolulu; the water supply had been poisoned by the local Japanese; Japanese plantation workers had cut arrows pointing to Pearl Harbor in the cane fields of Oahu; the local Japanese had been notified of the time of the attack by an advertisement in a Honolulu newspaper on December 6; local Japanese armed with machine guns drove up to the main gate at Pearl Harbor in trucks and, as the side panels dropped off, shot down Marines; automobiles driven by local Japanese blocked the roads from Honolulu to Pearl Harbor. . . .

Rumors developed among the Japanese that the U.S. Army planned to kill everyone of Japanese ancestry in Hawaii. Many fully expected retaliation from outraged Americans and were immobilized with fear.

Rumors of the complicity of local Japanese were immediately denied by military and civilian officials, and the denials were apparently accepted by most Hawaiians. On the mainland, however, the tales persisted; they were disseminated in newspapers and magazines and even incorporated into motion pictures.

Unfortunately, the rumors that Japanese Americans were spies and traitors became widely accepted in the United States. These rumors played a role in the sequence of events that led to the 1942 decision of the U.S. government to send all Japanese Americans living on the West Coast to inland prison camps. [See the story from *Farewell to Manzanar* in the preceding chapter.]

≈§ Track down a rumor that has been spread in your school or community, and analyze the process by which it was transmitted.

Fads, Fashions, and Crazes

Fads. In the warmer months of the mid-1980's, people on a boardwalk in Venice, California or on a New York City street were occasionally entertained by break-dancers. The dancers would place a stage of cardboard and a radio on the sidewalk and then dance in bizarre twists and gyrations. Street breakdancing would die down with the approach of cool fall temperatures. Sociologists were quick to label breakdancing a *fad*—a trivial variation in behavior that usually lasts a short time. Well-remembered American fads include flagpole sitting in the 1920's, marathon dancing in the 1930's, cramming into telephone booths in the 1950's, and disco dancing in the 1970's.

Why do people engage in fads? Sociologists and psychologists say that a fad is often a means of asserting one's identity. It is a way of showing that one is a little different from everyone else and is really worth noticing. Young people are especially susceptible to fads, for many of them have not yet established their personal identities. When a fad becomes so commonplace that it is no longer distinctive, it quickly loses its appeal.

Fashions. About 1968, women in Great Britain, Europe, and the U.S. started wearing shorter skirts. Soon it was not uncommon to see hemlines several inches above the knees, and many women wore them even shorter. The new garments were dubbed "miniskirts"; but by the early

This 1930's couple was participating in a marathon contest to see who could dance the most miles.

The 1980's had many fads, including aerobics, skateboarding, and specialty toys like the Cabbage Patch dolls. Rock stars inspired look-alike contests and fashions. One fad in the 1950's was telephone booth stuffing.

1970's, they had all but disappeared and were replaced by newer fashions. *Fashions* are currently accepted styles of appearance. Though they do not change as rapidly as fads, their popularity also tends to be brief. In general, women's fashions have changed more quickly than men's fashions in our culture. But the 1960's and 1970's brought changes in men's fashions too.

One reason that fashions soon become out-of-date is that our society values novelty; new things are considered desirable rather than a threat to established traditions. Another reason is that designers and apparel makers, who profit by producing popular new styles, encourage change. Finally, new fashions are a means of showing social status, as well as appearing attractive. The latest styles are adopted first by the wealthy who can afford them. Afterward inexpensive copies are made available to people of lower status. Sometimes, however, a reverse process

takes place. Blue jeans were for many years the traditional clothes of the working class. Today they have become very popular with younger members of the middle and upper classes.

Crazes. A *craze* occurs when a number of people share a short-lived, intense, and obsessive interest in something. A person who is learning the newest dance step (a fad) probably doesn't lie awake at night thinking about it. But a person who is involved in a craze may not be able to think of anything else. Get-rich-quick schemes often excite crazes. The discovery of gold in California in 1848 caused tens of thousands of prospectors to rush there from all over the world. All of them had visions of becoming millionaires overnight, but only a few lucky ones actually struck it rich.

One of the strangest crazes in history was the passion for tulips that swept Holland in 1634. Soon most of the Dutch people were buying and selling tulip bulbs for profit. Many even sold their homes to have more money to invest in tulips. At the height of the craze, a tulip bulb was literally worth its weight in gold. Then a rumor spread that the price of tulips was about to fall. Investors rushed to sell their bulbs while the price was still high, but now there were few buyers. The price of tulips collapsed, and thousands of people were ruined. But the tulip industry persisted in Holland. To this day, the Dutch are famous for their tulips. In this case, a brief episode of collective behavior had lasting social effects.

Fads, fashions, and crazes amuse their

followers, sometimes outrage their opponents, and frequently become remembered cultural landmarks. The following story, adapted from William Manchester's book, *The Glory and the Dream*, details the hula hoop fad of 1958-1959:

Zany as they were, the 1950's had witnessed nothing comparable to the ukulele or flagpole-sitting, until 1958 when the deficiency was spectacularly remedied by two young toymen in San Gabriel, California. Richard Knerr and Arthur Melin, co-owners of an enterprise called the Wham-O Manufacturing Company, had started making slingshots after World War II with less than $1,000 capital. In 1957 they had racked up their first big score with frisbees, light plastic saucers which could be skimmed slowly through the air from one thrower to another.

At a New York toy fair in March 1958, an acquaintance told them that large wooden hoops had achieved swift and startling popularity in Australia; children rotated them on their hips. Back at Wham-O, Knerr and Melin went into production with wooden hoops. After 20 or so they stopped; they didn't like wood and wanted to experiment with plastics. In May they had what they wanted: three-foot hoops of gaudy polyethylene tubing which could be marketed at 93 cents each, representing a 16 percent gross profit. Wham-O's new toy was christened the hula hoop.

Patenting the hoops was impossible and by Labor Day a dozen other firms were turning out imitations under other trademarks. Even so, by early September Wham-O had sold two million hoops for a net profit of over $300,000. Then adults started using them for calisthenics. Wham-O's bookkeeper couldn't keep up with the production figures. Workers went into three shifts. Counting the copies at home and abroad, hula hoop sales that autumn were reckoned in the tens of millions. So widespread was their use that European medical journals warned of injuries that

might be sustained by enthusiasts. It was a long list. In Leiden, Holland, a Dutch woman was being wheeled into surgery for removal of her appendix when her physician found that what was really wrong with her was a torn abdominal muscle, the result of strenuous gyrations inside a hoop. Japanese emergency wards were filling up with hoopers suffering from slipped discs and dislocated backbones. After a child was killed chasing a runaway hula, the hoops were banned from Tokyo streets. Nevertheless sales there passed the three million mark. Lines of Japanese waiting to buy more stretched down the Ginza [in Tokyo] for blocks, and Premier Nobusko Kishi received one as a gift on his 62nd birthday. . . .

Elsewhere the American fad swept on. . . . Germans who had no children, and therefore no easy explanation for buying toys, avoided embarrassment by having stores deliver them, wrapped, at night. A party of Belgian explorers leaving for the South Pole disclosed that 20 hoops were in their luggage; the expense was charged to morale.

In some countries hoop shortages were serious. . . . In Warsaw, a weekly newspaper for young Poles observed, "If the Ministry of Light Industry and the Chamber of Artisans do not embark upon the production of hoops, we will be seriously delayed in hula hoop progress, especially on the international level." The ministry and the chamber continued to be dilatory, so hulas were smuggled in through East Germany.

The [fad] receded as quickly as it had spread. By the summer of 1959 discarded hoops had begun to pile up in city dumps, but the rage had been a singular illustration of how great a grasp even the trivia of American mass culture had on the rest of the world.

⊷ What factors do you believe contributed to the success of the hula hoop? Why do you think it appealed to adults? Can you name some fads that have appeared since the hula hoop?

Panics

In December 1903, a fire broke out in Chicago's Iroquois Theater. Eddie Foy, a popular comedian who was appearing on stage at the time, described what happened in his book, *Clowning Through Life:*

As I ran around back of the rear drop, I could hear the murmur of excitement growing in the audience. Somebody had of course yelled, "Fire!" There is always a fool of that species in an audience, and there are always hundreds of people who go crazy the moment they hear the word. The crowd was beginning to surge toward the doors and already showing signs of a stampede. Those on the lower floor were not so badly frightened as those in the more dangerous balcony and gallery. Up there they were falling into panic. I began shouting at the top of my voice, "Don't get excited. There's no danger. Take it easy!"

. . . I stood perfectly still, hoping my apparent calm would have an equally calming effect on the crowd. Those on the lower floor heard me and seemed somewhat reassured. But up above, and especially in the gallery, they had gone mad. . . . The horror in the auditorium was beyond all description. There were 30 exits, but few of them were marked by lights; some had heavy [curtains] over the doors, and some of the doors were locked or fastened with levers no one knew how to work.

It was said that some of the exit doors . . . were either rusted or frozen. They were finally burst open, but precious moments had been lost — moments which meant death for many behind those doors. The fire-escape ladder could not accommodate the crowd, and many fell or jumped to their death on the pavement below. Some were not killed only because they landed on the cushion of bodies of those who had gone before.

But it was inside the house that the greatest loss of life occurred, especially on the stairways

The tragedy caused by panic during the Iroquois Theater fire resulted in increased safety precautions in theaters around the nation.

leading down from the second balcony. Here most of the dead were trampled or smothered, though many fell or jumped over the balustrade to the floor of the foyer. In places on the stairways, particularly where a turn caused a jam, bodies were piled seven or eight feet deep. Firemen and police confronted a sickening task in disentangling them. An occasional living person was found in the heaps, but most of these were terribly injured. The heel prints on the dead faces mutely testified to the cruel fact that human animals stricken by terror are as mad and ruthless as stampeding cattle. . . .

Never elsewhere had a great fire disaster occurred so quickly. From the start of the fire until all in the audience either escaped, died, or lay maimed in halls and alleys, took just eight minutes.

In that eight minutes, more than 500 people perished.

The Iroquois Theater fire represents a classic example of panic behavior. A *panic* is a form of collective behavior in which a group of people, faced with an immediate threat, engages in an uncoordinated and irrational response. Social scientists have identified five elements which characterize panic behavior such as that described by Foy:

• A sudden crisis such as fire, flood, military invasion, or widespread bankruptcy disrupts normal patterns of behavior.

• People perceive this disruption as a threat to personal safety.

• They react with intense fear, which expresses itself in an attempt to escape.

• Remedies, such as sufficient exits in case of fire, are not readily available.

• This causes a breakdown in mutual cooperation and an every-man-for-himself attitude.

⌐ Reexamine the Iroquois Theater fire story and identify each of these elements of panic behavior. In terms of these elements, what is the function of required school fire drills?

Fortunately, panics are the exception and not the rule when people face threatening situations. E.L. Quarantelli and Russell R. Dynes of the Disaster Research Center at Ohio State University report that "in at least 20 years, we have found only a few clear-cut examples of panic behavior in which more than three or four dozen people were involved."

Mass Hysteria

In 1692 the town of Salem, Massachusetts, was suddenly seized by a great fear of witches. Many people were found guilty of practicing witchcraft and wizardry, and 20 people were executed. In early September 1949, 29 people in Mattoon, Illinois, claimed that they were attacked by a "mad gasser" who sprayed them with a sweet-smelling gas that caused temporary paralysis. Newspaper headlines sensationalized the story and may have contributed to the fear and anxiety which gripped Mattoon. Despite a massive search by police, armed citizens, and scientific experts, no trace of the "mad gasser" or his gas was ever found. These two cases are examples of what sociologists call *mass hysteria*. Mass hysteria is a frightening delusion that is accepted and spread by a large number of people and provokes considerable anxiety.

War of the Worlds. Perhaps the most famous case of mass hysteria in the United States took place October 30, 1938. That night about one million Americans believed that Martians were invading this country and would soon destroy our planet. How were so many people deluded? In 1938 television was virtually unknown, but millions of Americans then listened to network radio shows. On Sunday night, one of the shows was *The Mercury Theatre of the Air*, which featured dramas. It was headed by Orson Welles, a young actor and director. Halloween was the next night, and Welles thought it

Above, South Vietnamese refugees panicked as the U.S. left the country in 1975. Below, an actual Mattoon headline.

DAILY JOURNAL-GAZETTE

WEATHER
ILLINOIS: Fair tonight and Sunday.
Warmer tonight. Little change in temperature Sunday.

Seventieth Year. No. 197   MATTOON, ILLINOIS, SATURDAY EVENING, SEPTEMBER 9, 194   All Phone 230   Price 5 Cents

"Mad Gasser" Adds Six Victims!

Stage Set for Siegfried Battle

5 WOMEN AND BOY LATEST OVERCOME

4 in One House; Another Home Visited 4 Times in 2 Nights

Springfield, Ill.—(INS)—Failure to identify the gas sprayed into Mattoon homes by a phantom-like "mad anesthetist" was announced today by Richard T. Piper, chief of the Bureau of Criminal Identification and Investigation of the Illinois Department of Public Safety.

Piper said that State Chemist John Fouler reported to him that evaporation of the chemical stains on a cloth used by the mad anesthetist in attacking his victims had made the drug impossible of identification. But-

STRENGTH OF LINE SOON TO BE TESTED

Tight Censorship Believed to Be Favorable Indication

BY J. C. OESTREICHER
(I. N. S. Foreign Editor)

The stage was set today for a week-end test of the war's greatest enigma—strength or weakness of the Siegfried line.

Four powerful Allied armies swept from the west and south against the

Doubts U. S. Land of Equal Chance

Chicago — (P) — W Lloy ner, University of Chicago ogist-anthropologist, contends it "mythical" to believe every American school boy has an equal chance to reach the White House.

It's mythical, he said, because the American school system operates as a conservative force to keep most people in the class from which they spring.

Professor Warner asserted that the schools fail to provide equal opportunity because America has a complex and varied class system, more subtle then the distinctions of wealth. The schools fail to break class barriers, he said, being designed to fit into the distinctions

VIET FORCES SWEEP INTO BULGARIA

Near Junction With Yugoslav Troops of Marshal Tito

BY NATALIE RENE
(I. N. S. Staff Correspondent)

Moscow—The rapidly expanding Soviet drive which has enveloped practically the whole of Romania swept into Bulgaria today on a 135-mile front, hammered westward at the gates of Yugoslavia and push-

Allied Leaders to Study Future of Italy

BY KINGSBURY SMITH
(I. N. S. Staff Correspondent)

Washington — It was learned authoritatively today that the future of Italy will be discussed at the forthcoming meeting between President Roosevelt and British Prime Minister Winston Churchill.

This conference between the two Allied leaders, which is expected to be held shortly in Canada, will deal with European political problems in addition to drafting plans for the final defeat of Japan next year.

Churchill, who recently visited Rome, is understood to favor a more lenient policy toward the Italians now. The British have been

ISOLATIONISM IS DEAD, SAYS GOV. DEWEY

G. O. P. Presidential Nominee Travels to Michigan

BY LEO W. O'BRIEN
(I. N. S. Staff Correspondent)

Aboard Dewey Campaign Train, Enroute to Michigan—Gov. Thomas E. Dewey traveled toward his native state of Michigan today for conferences and a week-end with his mother after telling the people that American Isolationism is dead and that isolationism must be lifted en-

125 RETAILERS HEAR SPEECH ON AVIATION

Douglas Representative Speaks at Fall Meeting

Geoffrey P. Morgan of Chicago, a member of the sales bureau of the Douglas Aircraft Company, thrilled 125 persons at the fall dinner meeting of the Retail Division of the Mattoon Association of Commerce in the Masonic Temple Friday night with an address on future aviation.

Mr. Morgan, introduced by H. B.

would be appropriate to scare people. The play he chose was based on a science-fiction novel, *The War of the Worlds.* Written by the late H.G. Wells, it tells how monsters from Mars attack Earth in rocket ships and destroy it.

Orson Welles wanted the story to sound as realistic as possible. It would be told as a series of news broadcasts, as if it were actually happening. Of course, Welles didn't want to frighten people *too* much. So when the program began at 8 P.M., the announcer said, "The Columbia Broadcasting System presents Orson Welles and the *Mercury Theatre of the Air* in *The War of the Worlds* by H.G. Wells."

Anyone who tuned in at the beginning knew it was only a play. But many people did not hear the show from the start. Most were listening to a popular comedy program, *The Charlie McCarthy Show,* or were turning their radio dials until they found a program they liked. Meanwhile *The War of the Worlds* had begun rather innocently with a dance band playing music from a hotel in New York. (Welles used fictitious names for the band and the hotel.) Suddenly the music was interrupted for "a special news bulletin." An announcer reported that several explosions had been observed on the planet Mars. The band resumed playing, but not for long. According to another "special bulletin," a huge flaming object had fallen on a farm near Trenton, New Jersey. It was believed to be a meteor, the announcer said. Soon more and more "news bulletins" began to crowd out the music. Each new report was more frightening than the last. The "meteor," the an-

nouncer said, was really a rocket ship from outer space, probably from Mars! An "on-the-spot" newsman described the first Martian to emerge:

"Good heaven! Something is winding out of the shadow like a gray snake. But the face — I can hardly force myself to keep looking at it. The eyes are black, and they gleam like a serpent's. The monster is raising himself. The crowd falls back. I can't find words. . . . I'll have to stop. . . . Hold on, will you please? I'll be back in a minute!"

Meanwhile millions of people who were restlessly turning their radio dials (some had lost interest in *The Charlie McCarthy Show*) began to pick up the broadcast — too late to know that it was a play. Many of them thought the "Martian invasion" was the real thing. And what they heard was terrifying. The Martians had brought with them huge machines that shot out flames, heat rays, and poison gas. They killed people in an instant. In a few minutes, they wiped out an entire U.S. Army troop sent to stop them.

Now the Martians were moving toward New York, destroying everything in their path. The "Secretary of the Interior" appealed to the nation to stay calm. There was still hope, he said, that the armed forces might stop the Martians. He asked the people to put their faith in God and to unite against the enemy.

Many listeners were sure that the end of the world was near. Here are a few of the things that happened during the broadcast:

Thousands of people in New York and New Jersey got in their cars and raced away from the invading Martians. Many others crowded into buses that were leaving for the West. Police stations, newspapers, and radio stations were flooded with phone calls. "Do the police have any extra gas masks?" the callers asked. "Should we close our windows?" "What can we do?"

In one New Jersey town, the police told callers: "You know as much as we do. Keep your radio on and follow the announcer's advice." (The announcer was telling people to run for their lives.)

On one street in Newark, New Jersey, 20 families rushed out of their homes. All had wet towels over their faces to protect them from "poison gas." Many other people hid in cellars.

In Providence, Rhode Island, people asked the electric company to turn off all lights. They hoped to save their city by "blacking out."

In Minneapolis, Minnesota, a woman ran into a church shouting: "This is the end of the world! I just heard it on the radio!"

In Pittsburgh, Pennsylvania, a man found his wife about to swallow poison. "I would rather die this way than be killed by men from Mars!" she told him.

All over the country people called their relatives to bid them farewell. Others simply prayed and waited for the end. One girl later told a reporter: "I kept saying, 'Where can we go? What can we do?' My two girl friends and I were crying and holding each other. We felt it was awful to die so young. I was sure the end of the world was coming." And a man said: "I was waiting for death to strike. I could almost smell the gas."

After the broadcast, Welles was questioned by New York police for hours.

Left, a man awaits the Martians. Right, Welles in the studio.

They wanted to know just what he thought he was doing. Welles told them that it was only a Halloween joke, that he had no idea people would take it so seriously.

For two weeks, newspaper stories described the shock and terror that had overcome radio listeners. Later a team of researchers talked to hundreds of people who had heard the broadcast. The researchers wanted to know why so many listeners that night believed the story of a Martian invasion. Many people said that they were fooled by the technique of presenting the play in the form of news broadcasts. At that time, Europe was on the brink of World War II, and radio listeners were used to having regular programs interrupted by special news bulletins. As a result, *The War of the Worlds* seemed quite realistic.

The researchers also wanted to know why some listeners (about one million) succumbed to hysteria while others (about five million) did not. The researchers concluded that the listeners could be divided into four groups:

Group 1. These people were able to figure out that the broadcast was only a play. After all, how could the Martians reach Earth, defeat an army, and attack New York in less than one hour? One woman said, "It sounded just like Buck Rogers to me." (Buck Rogers was the hero of a science-fiction comic strip.)

Group 2. These people were suspicious of the "news" they were getting. They checked the radio listings in their newspapers or called radio stations, and found out that the broadcast was only a play. Others concluded it was fiction when they turned their radio dials and found no other stations reporting a Martian invasion.

Group 3. These people tried to find out if the Martian attack was real, but they didn't use much sense. Most of them just looked out of their windows to see if there were any Martians around. When they did not see any, they concluded that the invaders hadn't reached their town yet. If they saw a lot of traffic, they assumed that people were fleeing the Martians. (Some were.)

Group 4. These people made no attempt either to check the broadcast or to look for signs of an invasion. According to the researchers, most of them were so frightened "that they either stopped listening, ran around in a frenzy, or exhibited behavior that can only be described as paralyzed."

Crowds

Which of the following groups would you describe as a crowd?

• Ten or more people who have gathered on the street to watch firemen put out a blaze.

• Eighty thousand people watching the action at a Super Bowl football game.

• Three hundred thousand young people attending a rock festival at Woodstock, New York.

• Twelve hundred inmates rioting in a prison.

Adopting Fads and Fashions

What clothes will parents buy their children? What foods will appeal to customers at their local restaurants? In short, what's in and what's out? The answers to these seemingly simple questions can mean huge profits for American businesses. These questions also pose a fascinating challenge for sociologists. For example, how do fads and fashions begin? Is there any pattern to the way in which they spread?

In their book, *Communication of Innovations*, Everett Rogers and F. Floyd Shoemaker, provide a model which we can use to examine the way in which innovations such as fads and fashions spread through our society. Rogers and Shoemaker note that not everyone buys the same product at the same time. They suggest there are actually five different types of adopters, each of whom plays a special role in the success or failure of a new fad, fashion, or idea.

Rogers and Shoemaker call their first category *innovators*. People in this category love adventure and have a strong desire to experiment with new products. If their ideas become fasionable, innovators experience the thrill and status of being "in." However, since many ideas will not catch on, they must also have a willingness to accept occasional failures. Innovators are a small group which include only about 2.5 percent of the population.

Each major industry contains a few successful innovators. Famous chefs, for example, can create new fashions in foods. When Paul Prudhomme, a famous chef at the Cajun restaurant in New Orleans, cooked in New York City, a critic compared his visit to "a rock star making his tour." Cajun cooking soon caught on and became very popular across the country.

Cajun cooking became more popular because a second category called *early adopters* decided to give it a try. Early adopters are respected leaders of their local groups. Studies have shown that they are well-educated, widely travelled, and exposed to information from a variety of sources. Rogers and Shoemaker place 13.5 percent of the population in this category.

As more restaurants and fashionable stores offered Cajun cooking, a third group, called the early majority, carefully made up their minds. The *early majority* is a deliberate group which rarely takes the lead but still thinks of themselves as being a "part of the times." Since they comprise 34 percent of the population, the early majority can either stop or accelerate a new fad or fashion.

When a new idea becomes acceptable, a group called the *late majority* may reluctantly try it. Rogers and Shoemaker note that the people in this group are skeptical and cautious. They include another 34 percent of the population.

Rogers and Shoemaker label the final group *laggards*. They are traditional and tend to be suspicious of change. By the time the laggards tried Cajun cooking, the innovators were already moving on to a new food fashion called "spa cuisine," which emphasized healthy foods.

Thinking Critically

1. What are the characteristics of each type of adopter?

Actually, all of them are crowds. *Crowds* are temporary collections of people who are physically close together, share a common focus or interest, and are conscious of and influenced by one another's presence. Crowds are characterized by relatively short life spans, by simple role structures which rarely make distinctions between followers and leaders, and by a sense of anonymity among their members.

Types of crowds. Despite their common characteristics, crowds vary greatly in their patterns of behavior. In an essay entitled "Collective Behavior," sociologist Herbert Blumer identified four types of crowds:

• *Casual crowds* are the ordinary kind that gather in the street after a traffic accident or, perhaps, to listen to a peddler making a sales pitch. Members of these crowds have little involvement with what they are watching or with one another.

• *Conventional crowds* include spectators at sports events, theater audiences, and shoppers at a bargain day store sale. These crowds are planned, rather than spontaneous, and their members behave according to established norms. People in conventional crowds may interact only slightly.

• *Expressive crowds* behave in ways that normally would be considered "far

A Mets baseball audience at Shea Stadium, in the 1980's was typical of expressive crowds. Right, this antiwar protest at the University of Wisconsin in 1969 turned from an expressive to an active crowd.

out." At events such as a Mardi Gras, a rock concert, or a big New Year's Eve party, people discard everyday social controls. The object of these crowds is to "let go."

• *Acting crowds* engage in extreme forms of behavior such as rioting, lynching, and destruction. They are angry mobs aroused to violence. Often their behavior is provoked by rumors spread during tense situations.

Blumer emphasized that a crowd can turn very quickly from one type to another. For example, a conventional crowd of sports spectators can become a destructive, active crowd under certain circumstances.

In the following article, excerpted from *Mademoiselle* magazine, Eula A. Morrison recalls from her childhood an incident which took place in her hometown in 1917. It provides a vivid account of the furor of an acting crowd:

As I walked along the dusty sidewalk toward home, swiping at the sweat running down my face, my pinafore limp in the still heat, I played a wishing game. I was wishing the trouble in town would go away.

Late summer enclosed the small mining town in junglelike heat. It was the year America entered the First World War; I was seven.

There was a strike on among the miners. Ordinarily a rough but kindly lot, the continuing strike was making them nervous and resentful, restless with inactivity. Now the strike had been complicated, its direction changed by the inexplicable murder of two little girls who had been friends.

No one knew who the murderer was. Within a short time, suspicion and distrust spread, and the "native" Americans were pitted against the

"foreign-born." Reason disappeared as people tormented one another with name-calling. The least excuse served for violence. Attempts by the authorities to discover the truth were fruitless, and rumors began to be accepted as fact.

Two days before at our house we had celebrated my brother Sandy's fifth birthday. But it hadn't been much of a celebration, not with the police trucks rumbling past, stirring up the dry road so that the dust filtered through the screens of the open windows and settled all over Sandy's cake.

Oddly, this afternoon there didn't seem to be any trucks or police around. A strange quiet lay over Tenth Street, a quiet that made me glance uneasily behind, as if someone might be stealing up to grab me. A door banged along the street, empty of children and women, empty even of the few automobiles that customarily joggled along it to town.

Something about the place — the silence, the suggestion of lifelessness behind the green shades drawn to the very bottoms of the windows, the closed doors ordinarily ajar for the passage of a breeze — made me shiver. I turned, scanning the area. Every front door was closed.

Then, down the way in the direction from which I had come, I heard another bang. A man appeared from somewhere, but I couldn't see which door had closed behind him. Another man joined him. Two came from the alley and walked behind them. The miners didn't greet each other, the way people usually did — just went along as though they were angry. Five other men from various spots fell in line with the four, all shambling in a half march behind me. More swung in from here and there.

I began running. I felt an urgency to keep ahead of them. My breath began coming in gasps, then whistles. . . .

Our house came in sight, its gray and white paint beginning to dull beneath the onslaught of soot that bathed it daily. . . .

As I ran to our sidewalk, I heard voices.

Looking up, I saw Mother and the mayor's wife sitting behind the partially closed front porch. They were sewing and talking. . . .

Mother glanced my way, breaking off. "Why, honey," she called, "don't you know better than to run like that on such a hot day?"

"I — " I looked over my shoulder. The men were scuffing determinedly along, closing the distance between me and them.

Mother's glance followed mine. Wordless, she rose and studied the silent group. Then, laying her sewing aside, she said, "Mrs. Coxley, I think there's going to be trouble of some kind. You'd better call your husband. He can get in touch with the police." To me, she said, "Go inside — and see that Sandy stays with you." Instead, I went just beyond the door and remained in the living room, watching Mrs. Coxley . . . run across the road to the mayor's dingy brown house. In it was the only telephone on the block. As the screen door shut behind her, the men neared the edge of our property. One detached himself from the rest, increased to 12 now, and crossed the road as though given an order; yet there appeared to be no leader. Skirting a wall of the mayor's house, he ran his hands along its side, yanking at something. Then, plodding like a stray animal joining a herd, he melted into the group — trotting now — and began trotting too. There was something horrible about that silent trotting bunch. They went past our place . . . past all the houses until they reached the corner. I lost sight of them as they turned.

Mrs. Coxley called on a note of hysteria: "The telephone's dead! I can't get Mr. Coxley — I can't get anyone!"

"Then we'd better find another telephone," Mother said in a calming voice. "I'm afraid that mob's going to a certain — "

"The Patricellis', I bet!" I burst out. "Ange's papa said he wouldn't be scared away by no one. Kids say Mr. Patricelli's got a still — in his cellar."

Mother turned, her face paling. "A still's as good an excuse for that mob as any," she said tautly. (Our prohibition laws made a still illegal.) . . .

"Where's Sandy?" Mother asked then. Aghast, my face screwed up with panic. Without replying, I sprinted through the living room to the back of the house, calling him. There was no answer. . . . Not telling Mother what I feared, I hurried through our backyard . . . and raced to where the men had turned earlier. The Patricellis lived a street over. As I rounded the corner, I heard a muttering. There was an animal snarl to it that reminded me of dogs growling before a fight. And there, skipping along, was Sandy, his body bent forward in an excited way, his face turned toward the muttering men.

"Sandy!" I called. "Come home!" There was taunting now, angry taunting: "Yah-yah!" "Foreigners!"

. . . I paused to get my breath. . . . As I watched, the crowd surrounded the Patricelli house, milling past a woodpile outside the kitchen door. . . . An ax stuck up from a chunk of wood, its blade sunk deep in the grain.

The shattering of glass, the pressing forward of the mob, as if it would squeeze out the people in the house by sheer weight of numbers, sent me tearing downhill. There was a shouted, "Patricelli! Come out! Murderer!"

As I ran, a rock hit another window and the shrill cry of a woman rose above the sound. "Go 'way!" she screamed. "Go 'way. He not here!"

. . . Mrs. Patricelli came from the doorway to the [porch] railing, a baby in her arms. Everyone knew it was only three days old. Now, Mrs. Patricelli was standing there, weak and white-faced, staring defiantly at the crowd. Huddled against her side was Ange, sister to the baby, her face set with fear.

. . . Another window broke. At the same time, as if at some signal, the mob surged forward. The men streamed up the steps, pushing Mrs.

Patricelli aside, and poured into the house. High
above that angry clamor, Mrs. Patricelli was crying, "No! No!"

As I hurried forward, frantically trying to
reach Sandy, Mrs. Patricelli ran to the sidewalk,
Ange with her, the baby crying. Then I heard
Sandy yelling my name from behind the woodpile.

Forgetting Mrs. Patricelli and the new baby,
forgetting everything except that Sandy must be got
away from there, I leaped over the wood chunks
and grabbed his hand. . . .

Suddenly there was something like a chuckle
behind us, not a merry sound, but chilling. The
mob was spilling out the back way. High on someone's shoulders was a man. He was handed from
one shoulder to another, never falling to the
ground. Mrs. Patricelli ran toward them, with
Ange still holding to her skirts. "He do no
wrong!" Mrs. Patricelli was crying.

The ax that had been sticking up in the chunk
of wood gleamed in the sunlight as it was lifted
high in the air. Then the ax came down. A hush
came over the men. The low despairing cry of
Mrs. Patricelli was clear in that stillness.

"My man! They've killed my man. . . ."

Sick, terrified, I put an arm around Sandy
and stumbled home.

A few weeks later the real murderer of the
two children was discovered.

∾ What tensions in the town helped
create a climate for starting mob violence?
What role do you believe rumors played in
triggering the violence? Keep this story in
mind as you read the following theories
about crowd behavior.

Theories of crowd behavior.

Contagion theory. What makes a
usually shy young girl shriek at a rock concert and hurl herself at the performers?
What makes a normally peaceful man join

a mob and take part in a lynching? Some
sociologists believe that people are transformed in crowds; they do things that they
wouldn't even consider if they were alone.
In a crowd, individuals generate a mood
of excitement that becomes contagious.
As the excitement builds, the crowd develops a sense of power. One girl at a rock
concert told a reporter: "I just had the feeling that, wow, there are so many of us,
we really have power. I felt, here's the
answer to anyone who calls us deviates."
Finally, the members of a crowd get
carried away and indulge in extraordinary
behavior.

Game theory. Other sociologists reject the contagion theory as an explanation of crowd behavior. They say that, far
from being carried away, a member of a
crowd carefully weighs all the consequences of his actions. He plays a kind of
game. Say, for example, that his object is
to loot a store of goods that he cannot afford to buy. The "reward" for such an action would make it quite worthwhile. But
what if he were caught? The "cost" of his
action would be too high. However, if he
senses that other members of the crowd
have the same idea, he may decide to take
the risk. For if everyone joins in the loot-
ing, then the chances of any one person
being arrested are much less. According to
this theory, members of crowds judge the
risks of their action and take them only
when the odds seem to be favorable.

∾ What does each of these theories
contribute to our understanding of the
crowd's behavior in the killing of Patricelli?

Public Opinion

Sociologists call a large group of people who share an interest in some issue a *public*. What its members think about an issue is called *public opinion*. Today, when public opinion can be measured quickly and accurately by polls, it has become a powerful influence on collective behavior.

For example, a dramatic change in public opinion contributed to the downfall of a U.S. President. In January 1973, 68 percent of the voters polled by the George Gallup organization approved of the way President Richard Nixon was handling his job. In March 1974, after the Watergate affair had been widely exposed, only 25 percent approved of the President's record. Commenting on this rapid shift of opinion, George Gallup said: "The approval rating is really a confidence rating. Clearly Nixon has lost the confidence of the American people." A few months later, under threat of impeachment, President Nixon resigned from office.

Formation of public opinion. How much do television news broadcasts, newspapers, and magazines affect public opinion? Sociologists believe that the media influence is considerable. The media not only report news; they select the stories that they think are worth reporting and also interpret them. As writer Gay Talese has said: "News, if unreported, has no impact. It might as well not have happened at all. . . . Each day, unhaunted by history, plugged into the *instant*, journalists of every creed, quality, and

quirk report the news of the world as they see it, believe it, understand it. Then much of it is relayed through America, millions of words a minute."

Most people tend to believe the information they get from the media, and to react accordingly. When, for example, a TV documentary focuses on an issue such as child abuse, viewers are bound to ask, "Why isn't something done about it?" Many may demand action to remedy the situation.

Often, however, the news media may not be as influential as one's family, friends, or co-workers in forming opinions. A movie critic may turn "thumbs down" on a new science-fiction film; but if your friends enjoyed it, you'll probably want to see it too. People are also influenced by their membership in social groups. If, for example, the head of the local Chamber of Commerce endorses candidate Jones for mayor, smaller business owners will probably support Jones. Similarly, if the head of the local Council of Trade Unions endorses candidate Smith, many union members will get behind Smith.

Measurement of public opinion. In recent years, public opinion polls have become increasingly accurate in predicting the outcome of elections. It is now possible to foretell the results of a Presidential election using a well-chosen sample of only 3,000 voters. Some political observers fear, however, that polls may do more than measure public opinion; they may actually influence it. Suppose, for example, a preelection poll indicates that candidate A is ahead of candidate B. This could

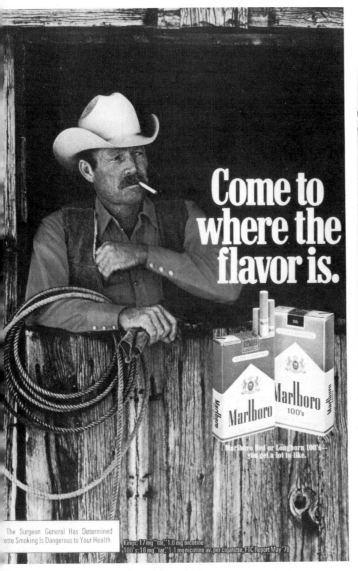

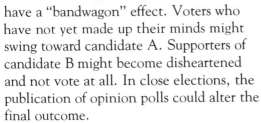

have a "bandwagon" effect. Voters who have not yet made up their minds might swing toward candidate A. Supporters of candidate B might become disheartened and not vote at all. In close elections, the publication of opinion polls could alter the final outcome.

Propaganda promoting and combatting smoking with a "macho" stereotype and beautiful actress Brooke Shields.

Propaganda and the manipulation of public opinion. The description beneath Paul Revere's engraving of the Boston Massacre described the British troops as savage bands and "fierce barbarians grinning over their prey."

Immediately after the battleship *Maine* was sunk in the Havana, Cuba, harbor, the New York *Journal*'s headlines screamed: "Destruction of the warship *Maine* was the work of an enemy; the whole country thrills with war fever."

During World War I, the British and French circulated stories about German soldiers who chopped off a baby's hands during the "rape" of Belgium and who shot down a French boy who aimed his toy gun at them.

The above "reports" were one-sided, over-simplified appeals to the emotions, attempts to influence public opinion. In fact, the British were under extreme provocation when they killed five Bostonians. Even today, no one is sure who sank the *Maine* and why. And the atrocity stories about the Germans in World War I were later admitted to be false. The term *propaganda* refers to attempts to manipulate information and influence public opinion by appealing to emotions and prejudice.

Propaganda techniques. In their book, *The Fine Art of Propaganda*, Alfred McClung Lee and Elizabeth Bryant Lee identify seven common propaganda techniques. The list below is adapted from their work:

1. *Glittering generalities.* Surrounding a policy, person, or product with words that get a favorable response. For example, politicians might claim to be "God-fearing," "honest," and "hardworking" because they know Americans value these qualities. These adjectives may actually obscure less desirable qualities.

2. *Name-calling.* A negative tool used to associate one's enemies with some very unfavorable cause. In the 1950's, many people were labeled "red" or "pink" by name-callers attempting to associate them with the Communist party.

3. *Transfer.* A tool by which approval is sought for a policy, person, or product by associating it with something known to get a positive public response. For example, attractive models might be used to sell automobiles. People buying such an automobile might be led to believe it will draw attractive people to them, or that they will be judged attractive if they drive it.

4. *Testimonial.* Using a famous or respected person to make public statements in favor of or against something. Political movements, for example, often seek celebrities to endorse their causes.

5. *Plain folks.* A method of promoting persons, policies, or products by associating them with "ordinary" people. For example, a very wealthy person might campaign for public office in work clothes.

6. *Card stacking.* Arranging a large amount of data in such a way that it points to only one logical conclusion. For example, a drug company might cite five studies to show that its pain reliever is effective but not use other studies that showed its competitors were equally good.

7. *Bandwagon.* Building support for a point of view or policy by convincing

people that "everyone is doing it." An advertiser might seek to promote a new product by implying that many people are switching away from established brands to the new one, for example.

Propaganda in action. In 1924 Congress debated and eventually passed a new, highly restrictive immigration law (see Chapter 8). During the debate, Alabama

Senator James Thomas Heflin gave the following speech, excerpted from the *Congressional Record.* It shows how a skilled orator can influence public opinion through propaganda.

Less than 10 days ago in New York City, the metropolis of America, an American boy bearing an honored American name — William Clifford, Jr., a name as old as the government itself —

This cartoonist used the card-stacking technique to make his point that the "real American" in the center was becoming a minority surrounded by immigrants in his own country.

while walking with his father along the streets of his home city, in his native land, was attacked without a moment's warning, stabbed in the back, and murdered before his father could realize what had happened.

His assailant was a 12-year-old boy not long in our country. He is the poisoned product of a stupid and dangerous immigration policy. His name was Paul Rapkowskie. He had just robbed a store, had committed the double crime of burglary and larceny, and among other things that he had stolen was a dirk knife, and when asked why he had murdered young Clifford he replied: "I just wanted to see how deep I could drive the dirk into his back."

Mr. President: I am thinking of that brutal and barbarous crime against this American boy, of the crime against his father and mother, and of the crime against the institutions that the dead boy's forebears have loved and supported for 100 years and more.

They were soldiers in the War of the Revolution. A distinguished American by his name, Nathan Clifford, was once a member of Congress, later Attorney General under President Polk, and for 20 years a Justice of the Supreme Court, of the United States. But William Clifford, Jr., descended from a long line of American patriots, is dead as the result of our unsound and dangerous immigration policy.

No more his welcome footfall is heard in the doorway of the Clifford home. Hushed is the music of his merry laughter in the American home place now so sad and sorrowful. . . .

What are the facts? The young criminal from a foreign country . . . came into our country under an immigration law passed by Congress and approved by the President, or some unfaithful and corrupt immigration officer in violation of the law accepted a bribe and permitted him to come in, and in so doing he admitted into the sacred precincts of our dearest inheritances a moral degenerate and a dangerous enemy. The passport thus

bartered to this young European criminal was not paid for alone in money. It cost an American boy his life, struck down and destroyed one of the indispensable forces in the national defense, and left in the heart of an American father and mother an aching void that the world can never fill. . . .

There is nothing more interesting, more fascinating and promising than a plain, sincere, and upstanding American boy. His . . . courage and patriotism must be relied upon to defend [our country] in the hour of its peril. . . .

Mr. President, in behalf of the American boy and his sister, I appeal to the Senate to close our immigration doors. If I have my way about it, no immigrant shall come into the United States in the next 12 months. I would close the doors for a period of two years at least and wait until we assimilate these who are here. I would wait until we taught them to speak English and taught them American ideals. I would work to the end of making of them law-abiding American citizens.

I would want by the principles of right and the laws of justice to educate out of them the spirit of the Bolshevik. I would want to crush the spirit of the Communist, which is the deadly enemy of the American home and the Christian civilization. I would try to get those who are criminals out of the ranks of the peaceful, law-abiding people, and into the penitentiaries so that boys like young Clifford, who sleeps in a grave not yet 10 days old, may be safe as they walk the public roads and the streets of the towns and cities of their homeland.

This boy has not died in vain. In his name and in the name of the father and mother who weep for him, I ask the Senate to wake up on this question and take the American view of it and close the doors for the good of our American country. . . .

⊷ How many of the seven propaganda techniques did the Senator use? List each one and give as many examples as you can find.

A Theory of Collective Behavior

As we have seen, collective behavior takes many diverse forms, ranging all the way from fleeting fads to monstrous riots. This diversity presents a challenge to the sociologist's search for social patterns. But sociologist Neil Smelser has developed a theory that he says encompasses all forms of collective behavior. In his book, *Theory of Collective Behavior,* Smelser identifies six basic conditions which he says are necessary for any form of collective behavior to occur. Adapted here, Smelser's conditions are these:

1. A society must be *structured* in such a way as to make collective behavior possible. For example, in order for mass hysteria to occur in reaction to Orson Welles' account of *The War of the Worlds,* it was necessary for a national radio network to broadcast that play to a very large audience.

2. That society must be *strained* by pressures such as discrimination, uncertainty about the future, or even boredom. In September 1938, when *The War of the Worlds* was broadcast, the world was on the brink of war as a result of Hitler's demands in Czechoslovakia.

3. A large number of people must share some general *belief* about the situation. The mass hysteria brought on by the Welles' broadcast was made possible by the general beliefs that radio was a medium to be trusted and that it was possible for life to exist on Mars.

4. An incident takes place that *triggers* collective action. In a tense racial situation, for example, an arrest by a police officer may be enough to touch off a riot. Welles' announcement of a Martian invasion set off a massive hysterical reaction.

5. People must be *mobilized* to act by spreading the news of the triggering incident. For example, the woman in Minneapolis who ran into church shouting, "This is the end of the world! I just heard it on the radio!" was spreading news that would mobilize people. Rumors are the most common means by which people are mobilized to act.

6. Whether collective behavior is suppressed, quickly checked, or gets out of control depends on the various agents of *social control.* In case of a threatened riot, how effective are the police and community leaders? If they are too weak, the violence may continue until it runs its course. If they react too strongly, they may provoke further violence. In the case of *The War of the Worlds* broadcast, social control was faulty. Listeners at the beginning and at intermission were told that they were hearing a play. But these announcements failed to reach listeners who had switched from *The Charlie McCarthy Show* on another station.

application

Use Smelser's theory to analyze some of the examples in this chapter. How might the six steps apply to the "death" of Paul McCartney? To the hula hoop fad? To the killing of Patricelli?

summary

Sociologists generally study the regular, patterned behavior of people in groups. But people don't always behave the way we expect them to. Sometimes they depart from the usual rules of conduct and surprise or shock us. College students have engaged in such bizarre behavior as swallowing goldfish and cramming themselves into telephone booths. Normally peaceful, law-abiding citizens occasionally turn into angry mobs and riot in the streets. In each of these cases, large numbers of people have engaged in conduct that is spontaneous, unpredictable, brief, and irregular. Sociologists call such conduct **collective behavior**.

Collective behavior takes many forms and may be violent or nonviolent. Some of the principal forms follow.

In tense or confused situations, when people are unable to get accurate information, they are likely to spread rumors. **Rumors** are stories that circulate from one person to another and are assumed to be true, even though they cannot be verified. As a rule, the more a rumor is repeated, the more distorted it becomes.

Fads are trivial variations in behavior that usually last a short time. They include such momentary diversions as hula hoops, skateboards, "streaking," or a new dance step. Many people engage in fads to show that they are a little different from everyone else. As soon as a fad becomes so commonplace that it is no longer distinctive, it is quickly abandoned.

Fashions are currently accepted styles of appearance. Though they do not change as rapidly as fads, their popularity also tends to be brief. One reason that fashions soon become out-of-date is that our society values novelty. Americans regard new things as desirable, rather than a threat to established traditions.

Crazes are felt more intensely than fads. They become obsessions. People who are involved in them can't think of anything else. Get-rich-quick schemes often excite crazes. The discovery of gold in California in 1848 started a wild rush of prospectors from around the world. All of them had visions of becoming millionaires overnight, but only a few lucky ones struck it rich.

Panics sometimes occur when people in a crowd feel threatened and entrapped. Instead of cooperating with each other, they lose their self-control. For example, in a building fire, they stampede toward the exits, which soon become clogged. The results can be disastrous.

Mass hysteria is a form of irrational behavior caused by anxiety — a fear that has little or no basis in reality. People who succumb to mass hysteria simply let their imaginations run away with them. In October 1938, for example, about one million Americans believed that a radio drama about an invasion from Mars was actually true. According to researchers, most became so frightened "that they either stopped listening, ran around in a frenzy, or exhibited behavior that can only be described as paralyzed."

Crowds are collections of people that form and disband within a short time. Though all crowds are temporary, they vary greatly in other respects. **Casual crowds** are those that gather spontaneously to witness an event, such as an accident. **Conventional crowds** are those that are planned for, such as spectators at a sporting event. **Expressive crowds** behave in ways that usually would be considered "far out." They are found at such events as a Mardi Gras, a big New Year's Eve party, or a rock festival. Their object is to discard everyday social controls and "let go." **Acting crowds** engage in extreme forms of behavior like rioting, lynching, and destruction. They are angry mobs aroused to violence. Often their behavior is provoked by rumors spread during tense situations.

Now that public opinion can be measured quickly and accurately, it has become a powerful influence on collective behavior. A shift in **public opinion** — what people think about a particular issue — can have dramatic results.

Sociologist Neil Smelser formulated a theory about conditions that lead to collective behavior. First, he said, the society must be structured in such a way as to make collective behavior possible. Then, that society must be under some strain, which can be as great as war or as trivial as boredom. Next, many people must share some general belief about the situation. Then, some incident must trigger collective activity. Once the activity starts, people must be mobilized. Rumors usually serve this purpose. Finally, whether the collective behavior is checked or spreads depends on the effectiveness of various agents of social control.

more questions and activities

1. Define and give examples of *collective behavior.*

2. List and give examples of Blumer's four types of crowds.

3. Define *propaganda* and list seven of its commonly used techniques.

4. Explain why collective behavior might be difficult to study through the methods — participant observation, experiment, and survey — described in Chapter 2.

5. Use old high school yearbooks to find examples of fads, fashions, and crazes that have swept through your school in the past 20 years. Take note of the years in which there was an extraordinary amount of such behavior. Can such years be accounted for by events within the school alone, or are there parallels between the collective behavior and events in the community (or world) at large?

6. Use news magazines, newspapers, or history books to prepare a sociological case study of an example of panic or riot. Are each of the five elements of panic listed in your text present in the example? Possible examples for analysis could include: the stock market crash of October 1929; the riots in Newark, New Jersey, and Detroit, Michigan, of July 1967; the riots associated with the Democratic National Convention of July 1968 in Chicago; and the electrical blackout in New York City in 1977.

7. Analyze news or historical accounts of potentially dangerous situations in which people did *not* panic or riot. Again check the five steps listed in your text to see which were present. Possible examples for study could include: the assassination of President John F. Kennedy in November 1963; the march on Washington led by Dr. Martin Luther King, Jr., in August 1963; the electrical blackout in New York City in November 1969; and the Republican National Convention in Miami Beach in August 1968.

8. Attempt to start a fad in your school. Your teacher can tell you one theory about how fads spread.

9. An article in the *Village Voice* (a newspaper published in New York City) on February 12, 1979, began with this paragraph: "*Disco* is the word. It is more than music, beyond a beat, deeper than the dancers and their dance. Disco names the sensibility of a generation, as jazz and rock — and silence — announced the sum of styles, attitudes, and intent of other ages. The mindless material of the new disco culture — its songs, steps, ballrooms, movies, drugs, and drag — is denounced and adored with equal exaggeration. But the consciousness that lies beneath the trendy tastes is a serious subject and can hardly be ignored, for it points precisely where popular culture is headed at the end of the American seventies."

Write an analysis of the disco phenomenon including such subjects as its type of collective behavior, its similarity to or difference from other musical trends, its economic impact, and its fashion impact. Do you agree that the "consciousness . . . beneath the trendy tastes is [was] a serious subject"? Analyze the extent to which disco pointed where American culture was "headed at the end of the American seventies."

10. How many different kinds of collective behavior can you identify from the photographs throughout the chapter? List them.

suggested readings

Clark, Walter Van Tilburg. *The Ox-Bow Incident.* (Signet, 1960.) An exciting novel about the fury of an acting crowd in the Old West.

Erikson, Kai T. *Everything in its Path.* (Simon and Schuster, 1976.) A sensitive study which examines the sociological implications of a devastating flood on a West Virginia mountain community.

Koch, Howard. *The Panic Broadcast: Portrait of an Event.* (Little, Brown, 1970.) A vivid account of the panic created by H.G. Wells' famous "War of the Worlds" broadcast.

Kunhardt, Philip, ed. *Life, The First Fifty Years.* (Time Inc., 1986.) An outstanding pictorial review of the period from 1936-1986. A special section lists the leading fads during each of the fifty years covered in this book.

Editors of Life Magazine. *The Best of Life.* (Time-Life Books, 1973.) This book contains superb pictures of many of the forms of collective behavior discussed in this chapter.

McGinniss, Joe. *The Selling of the President 1968.* (Trident, 1969.) A behind-the-scenes description of the use of political propaganda in the 1968 Presidential election.

Editors of Newsweek Magazine. "What A Doll!" (*Newsweek,* December 12, 1983.) Do you remember when the Cabbage Patch doll craze swept the country? This article explains the origins and spread of one of the most memorable fads of the 1980's.

Pugh, Meredith D. *Collective Behavior: A Sourcebook.* (West Publishing, 1980.) A fine collection of readings on collective behavior.

Sann, Paul. *Fads, Follies and Delusions of the American People.* (Crown, 1967.) Sann uses a witty narrative style and numerous illustrations to bring his subject to life.

The Megabytes are one artist's view of the high-tech American family.

chapter 10

social change

What if someone asked you to paint a picture illustrating how a modern family lives today? Would you choose a nuclear or extended family? How many members would the family have and what would they be doing? The American artist Kinuko Craft attempted to answer these questionss when she painted the picture "Meet the Megabytes," shown on the opposite page.

A careful examination of the Megabytes reveals that they have been shaped by a number of social patterns which we have previously studied. Mr. and Mrs. Megabyte are clearly a dual career family. Mr. Mega-

byte is probably talking with a business associate on his wireless telephone. Mrs. Megabyte's business suit and briefcase are status symbols which suggest that she is a career woman. As we have learned, Americans place a high value on being prompt. Perhaps Mrs. Megabyte is gazing intently at her watch because she has a meeting to attend.

Like many dual career couples, the Megabytes have only one child — a son. The youngest Megabyte seems comfortable with the family's home computer on the table to his right. He listens to music on his

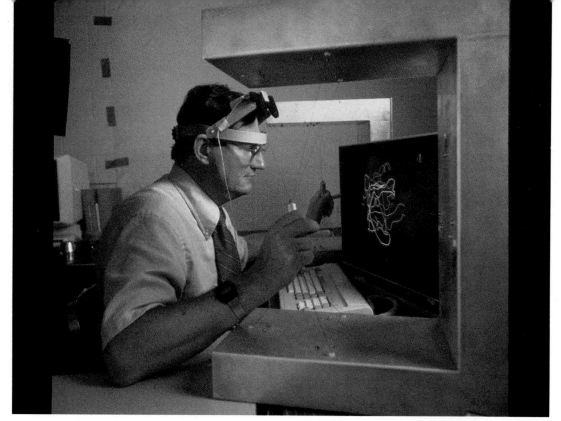

Above, a scientist maps a molecule on a computer. Below, a machine uses lasers to analyze a DNA molecule. Next page, a superconductor at absolute zero degrees repels a magnet.

portable headset while bringing along a soccer ball for exercise.

A glance out the window reveals that the Megabytes live in a development located in an area which was recently farmland. The Megabytes probably left a nearby city to enjoy the pleasures of living in a more rural setting. The offices where they work may be located just beyond the hill in an office complex, alongside a super highway.

A number of sweeping social changes have made the Megabytes' lifestyle possible. Sociologists define social change as a shift in widely accepted norms, values, roles, and institutions. Many experts believe that there has been more social change in the last 30 years than in any other time in our history. Sociologist predict that the pace of these changes will become even swifter in the coming decade.

In this chapter, we will examine four fundamental causes of social change. We will begin with science and technology. The pictures on this page and the opposite page, illustrate some of the exciting research which modern scientists are conducting. Their study of organic molecules, DNA, and superconductivity will affect how long we live and the way we use energy.

Although important, science and technology are not the only sources of social change. We'll also look at how population growth, cultural diffusion, and social movements have shaped our lives. And, finally, we will examine some of the consequences of these forces in this century and for the future.

☙ What additional adjustments could you make in the painting "Meet the Megabytes"?

Science, Technology, and Social Change

Science and technology. What would our lives be like without cars, television, computers, jet planes, and skyscrapers? We who live in a modern, industrial society would hardly be able to imagine doing without them. We take them for granted, unaware, perhaps, that less than a hundred years ago none of them even existed. What accounts for their development in recent times? Most of us would probably attribute them to modern science and technology, which we tend to assume are one and the same. In fact, however, there is an important distinction between them. *Science* is knowledge that is obtained through the use of systematic methods. *Technology* derives from the practical application of such knowledge

Is it possible for science and technology to exist separately? In many societies, they have. In ancient Greece, for example, scientists understood the principles of the steam engine and even built small models that worked. But the ancient Greeks never put the steam engine to any practical use, for a variety of reasons. For one thing, power for the Greek economy was supplied by the muscles of slaves and animals, and there was no shortage of either at the time.

In some societies today, simple technology exists without science. People in simple societies can make bows and arrows, dugout canoes, and huts. But this ability comes from experience, rather than a knowledge of scientific principles. Austra-lian aborigines, for example, know how to light a fire, but they probably do not know why it burns or why some substances burn and others do not.

In modern industrial societies, however, science and technology have been combined to produce astonishing results. The automobile, airplane, radio, and television could not have been invented without a knowledge of the scientific principles that apply to them. Since the beginning of the century, the number of scientists has vastly increased. It is estimated that 90 percent of all the scientists who ever lived are still alive today! The United States alone now has more than 300,000 professional scientists, and the great majority are engaged in research that aims at the development of useful inventions. The merger of science and technology in recent times has changed societies all over the world.

The impact of science and technology. Not only has the world changed enormously in the 20th century, but the rate of change is rapidly accelerating. Each advance in technology seems to trigger others, with less and less time between each.

This accelerated pace may be seen in the development of transportation. About 6000 B.C., the fastest means of traveling over long distances was camel caravan. It averaged about eight miles an hour. More than 4,000 years passed before the chariot was invented, increasing the speed of travel to about 20 miles an hour. This speed generally was not exceeded until the 19th century, when steam locomotives gradually pushed the limit to 100 miles an

Computers and Social Change

In late 1946, scientists at the University of Pennsylvania watched in amazement as a new machine called ENIAC needed just 30 seconds to calculate trajectory tables for artillery guns. Previously, trained mathemeticians had needed seven to 20 hours to make the same calculations. ENIAC (Electronic Numerical Integrator and Calculator) was the world's first all electronic digital computer. It weighed 30 tons, contained 18,000 vacuum tubes, filled an entire room, and cost half a million dollars.

For many years, computers remained a scientific tool used by a small group of experts. As recently as the mid-1970's, there were only about 500,000 computers in use in the United States. However, revolutionary developments in the production of transistors and silicon chips enabled manufacturers to mass produce small, powerful personal computers, which could be purchased for less than $3,000.

The computers used in our schools, homes, and offices today are well over a million times faster than ENIAC. In a very short time they have brought changes to virtually every area of American life. Businesses use computers to process checks, keep tabs on inventory levels and buy or sell stocks. Computers aid consumers when they check out groceries or book seats on an airline. At schools, students are using computers to learn how to write music, correct spelling errors, and locate places on a map.

Although computers have touched many aspects of our lives, their greatest impact is being felt in the workplace. Over 10 million office employees use computers to word process, file reports, and calculate statistical data. Until recently, workers had to remain in their offices to perform these tasks. However, since computers can now be connected to existing telephone and television systems, many employees can perform their jobs at a home computer linked to their office.

Computers are also at the cutting edge of high technology — the application of electronics to industry, communications, medicine, and other aspects of life. The use of computer-generated imagery (CGI) provides an example of how high technology is revolutionizing many industries. For example, artists can now use CGI to help make animated TV commercials.

Computers are creating both new opportunities and new problems. As our economy shifts from manufacturing to services, many industrial jobs are being lost. For example, American automobile companies expect to have 21,000 robots in use by 1990. Each robot costs about $6.00 an hour to operate and can replace two workers. Many experts believe that the loss of high paying manufacturing jobs is a primary cause of downward mobility. Others point out that in the long run high technology will create new jobs while making our economy more competitive.

Thinking Critically

1. What impact are computers having upon the workplace?

2. List at least three ways in which computers affect your daily life.

hour. By 1938 some airplanes were capable of flying more than 400 miles an hour. In the 1980's it was possible to travel from the United States' east coast to Europe in less than four hours, while spacecraft were circling the earth at 18,000 miles an hour!

The same pattern of acceleration appears in practically all fields of technology, including communications. Writing did not develop until about 5,000 years ago when people in Mesopotamia (present-day Iraq) began using symbols that were scratched into clay. The invention of papyrus and then paper simplified writing, but no really significant changes took place until 500 years ago when Johannes Gutenberg invented a method of printing with movable type. By 1850 it was possible to send code messages in seconds by means of the telegraph. In 1876 Alexander Graham Bell demonstrated the telephone at the Centennial Exposition in Philadelphia. Radio broadcasting began in 1920, and by 1950 television aerials were sprouting all over the country. Today space satellites make it possible to view events that are happening thousands of miles away. Computers, which first came on the scene in the 1950's, can store, analyze, and produce enormous quantities of information at astonishing speeds.

Advances in communications have greatly increased our store of knowledge, and this in turn has led to advances in many other areas of science and technology. Before the invention of movable type, books were produced in Europe at the rate of 1,000 titles a year. In the 1960's, the world production of books was nearly 1,000 titles a day. The number of scientific journals and reports doubles every 15 years. Today nearly 100,000 scientific journals are published, and more than two million scientific papers appear each year. The greatest breakthrough in the acquisition of knowledge, of course, has been the computer, which has led to ever-increasing technological innovations.

How do new advances in technology produce social change? To cool themselves in the summertime, Roman emperors had snow brought down from the mountains to their gardens. Today, with air conditioners, we can turn a switch and cool our homes, cars, and offices in a matter of seconds. The air conditioner has affected not only how we live, but where we live. In recent years, there has been a massive population shift to America's "Sun Belt" — the South and the Southwest. This movement of people is partly a result of air conditioning, which has tamed the summer heat of those regions. Two of the country's fastest-growing cities, Phoenix and Houston, have been made vastly more attractive by air conditioning. It has also had a great effect on our architecture. The glass-enclosed office buildings that dominate our largest cities today owe their design to central air conditioning.

⊷ What other inventions have changed our society in recent decades? In what ways?

New frontiers of science and technology. What can we expect from technological advances in the future? One possibility is that people will live and work at the bottom of the sea as well as on land. In his book, *Future Shock,* Alvin Toffler tells what this might mean:

"Within 50 years," says Dr. F.N. Spiess, head of the Marine Physical Laboratory of the Scripps Institution of Oceanography, "man will move onto and into the sea — occupying it and exploiting it as an integral part of his use of this planet for recreation, minerals, food, waste disposal, military and transportation operations, and, as populations grow, for actual living space."

More than two thirds of the planet's surface is covered with ocean — and of this submerged terrain a bare five percent is well mapped. However, this underwater land is known to be rich with oil, gas, coal, diamonds, sulphur, cobalt, uranium, tin, phosphates, and other minerals. It teems with fish and plant life.

These immense riches are about to be fought over and exploited on a staggering scale. Today in the United States alone more than 600 companies . . . are readying themselves for a monumental competitive struggle under the seas.

The race will intensify year by year — with far-reaching impacts on society.

Technologically, novel industries will rise to process the output of the oceans. Others will produce sophisticated and highly expensive tools for working the sea — deep-diving research craft, rescue submarines, electronic fish-herding equipment, and the like. The competitive struggle will spur ever-accelerating innovation.

Culturally, we can expect new words to stream rapidly into the language. "Aqua-culture" — the term for scientific cultivation of the ocean's food resources — will take its place alongside "agriculture." Along with a new vocabulary will come new symbols in poetry, painting, film, and the other arts. Representations of oceanic life forms will find their way into graphic and industrial design. Fashions will reflect dependence on the ocean. New textiles, new plastics, and other materials will be discovered. . . .

Most important, increased reliance on the oceans for food will alter the nutrition of millions — a change that, itself, carries significant unknowns in its wake. What happens to the energy level of a people, to their desire for achievement, not to speak of their biochemistry, their average height and weight, their rate of maturation, their life span, when their society shifts from a reliance on agriculture to aqua-culture?

The opening of the sea may also bring with it a new frontier spirit — a way of life. . . .

What other social change might result from increased use of the oceans? Would you like to be a pioneer in the development of undersea settlements?

Problems of scientific and technological change. Modern societies are quick to accept technological innovations that appear useful or desirable. It takes longer, however, for societies' norms and values to adjust to the changes created by new technologies. This delay, which sociologists call *cultural lag,* often creates problems.

When, for example, inexpensive cars were produced by assembly lines, they soon became an indispensable part of American life. A national system of roads and highways was built that increased travel enormously. Suburbs and shopping centers sprang up everywhere as a result of the new mobility. So did drive-in theaters, banks, and even churches.

But cars have also had some effects that are far from desirable. Thousands of people are killed or injured in accidents every year. Traffic chokes our cities. Automobile junkyards, service stations, and billboards disfigure the landscape. Car exhausts pollute the air. As our petroleum

Society's failure to anticipate the safety problems of the auto was the result of cultural lag. So was its inability at the turn of the century to foresee the dangers of using children like these young miners as workers in an industrial society.

resources dwindle, some cars are criticized as being inefficient "gas-guzzlers."

In the 1960's, for the first time, the automobile-based way of life was challenged. In an effort to alleviate air pollution and other problems caused by cars, the U.S. government sought to reduce the number of parking spaces in 30 large cities. Many car owners reacted hostilely. Their attitude was expressed by a city councilman in Boston who swore that no one was going to tell him where or when to drive his car. So, the greatest obstacle to cleaner air and less traffic congestion stemmed from a cultural lag — the unwillingness of many people to accept any limitations on the use of their cars.

The social control of science and technology. The automobile caused serious problems that were not foreseen at the time of its invention. This has been true of many other technological innovations. For example, it was found that gases from some aerosal cans interfere with the earth's ozone layer and allow dangerous radiation to reach this planet. It was also suspected that certain additives used to make food last longer and look better contributed to human cancers. Disposing of radioactive wastes from nuclear reactors has become a serious problem in our time.

These and other problems stemming from technological innovations have raised a number of serious questions. At the present time, our society has few means of monitoring and controlling the effects of scientific research. Yet these effects, as we have seen, can sometimes be quite dangerous.

Many people, including scientists, are deeply concerned about the problems arising from scientific research. They fear that in the future science and technology may change our society in ways that would be quite undesirable. For example, scientists are now working on techniques that may enable parents at some future time to choose the sex of their children. Does this sound like a good idea to you? If it does, think about this: Opinion polls have indicated that a majority of parents would prefer to have boys rather than girls (although a major student poll has shown this preference is not as strong among younger people). If parents could pick the sex of their children, the result might be a society in which males would considerably outnumber females. How might this affect family patterns?

Another controversial field of research involves the rearrangement of living molecules, especially the DNA molecule that determines the hereditary characteristics of all living things. Scientists who support this research say that it could lead to cures for cancer and for inherited diseases such as diabetes and hemophilia. Scientists who oppose it fear that the risks of experimenting with DNA molecules outweigh the possible benefits. The danger is that rearranged DNA molecules might create new strains of bacteria to which human beings would have no natural immunity. What if some of these bacteria should escape from the laboratory and infect human beings? The result might be a worldwide epidemic of some baffling new diseases which scientists could not control. Some scientists believe that existing safety procedures for DNA research are inadequate. They have called for a complete ban on it.

◦§ Do you think we should impose restrictions on scientific research? If so, what kind? Who should have the responsibility for decisions about new research? A government agency? A committee of prominent scientists? A "science court" with full legal powers to restrict research of certain kinds? Or someone else?

Population and Social Change

The world population explosion. The rapidly accelerated growth of science and technology in modern times has been paralleled by an equally dramatic growth in the world's population. It is a second major cause of social change.

The rate of growth of a population depends on changes in the birthrate, the death rate, and the rate of movement of people into or out of a country or region. The recent dramatic increase in world population is the result of sharp decreases in world death rates largely because of advances in agriculture, sanitation, and medical science. DDT sprayed from airplanes, for example, has been a potent factor in curbing malaria which once caused countless deaths.

In industrial nations, birthrates have also been declining, though not as fast as death rates. In developing countries, however, birth rates generally are unchanged. People in these countries are having as many children as earlier generations, but many fewer of them die at birth or in their early years. The result is runaway population growth.

A sharp rise in population in any country produces great pressures for social change. The economy must produce more food, clothing, and homes. More schools and hospitals are needed. Governments must expand their activities. In developing nations, rapid population growth may cause startling changes. To increase the food supply, wealthier farmers turn to improved technology — machinery and chemical fertilizers. Poorer farmers, whose small plots barely grow enough food to feed their families, move to towns and cities. If these societies cannot produce enough for all, famine and hardship may result in both cities and rural areas.

In recent decades, the increase in the world's population has been so rapid that it is sometimes described as a *population explosion.* We can understand why if we take a brief look at how the number of people in the world has grown since the time of Jesus:

In Jesus' lifetime, the world's population was about 250 million. By the year 1650, it had doubled to 500 million. Only 200 years later, in 1850, it had doubled again to reach slightly over one billion. It doubled again in just 80 years, reaching two billion in 1930. The next time it doubled was in 1976, only 46 years later. At the present growth rate, it is estimated that the population will double every 35 years. In short, the time that it takes the human population to double has decreased from 16 centuries to just one generation.

Chart 10:A shows how the world's population has grown in the last 10,000 years. Notice how the line sweeps upward in modern times.

The human population is currently increasing at an average of two percent a year. This may not seem like much; but because of the large number of people already in the world, it is truly "explosive." Chart 10:B shows how the population of the world's 10 most populous nations would grow by the year 2000, based on their recent rate of increase.

What do you think life might be like

10:A

World Population Growth Through Time
8000 B.C. to 2000 A.D.

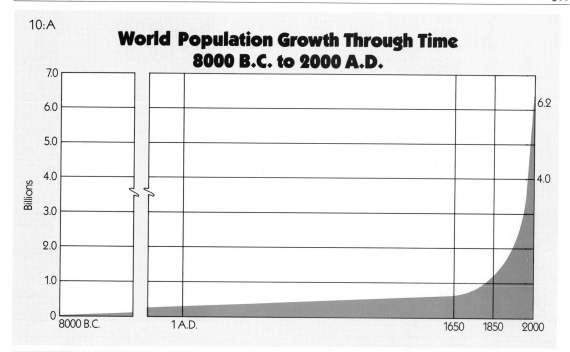

10:B

Estimated Population of the World's 10
Most Populous Countries (in millions)

1932		1976		2000	
China	425	China	837	China	1126
India (BR)	360	India	621	India	1051
USSR	160	USSR	257	USSR	314
United States	125	United States	215	United States	263
Japan	66	Indonesia	135	Indonesia	230
Germany	66	Japan	112	Brazil	208
Indonesia (Neth.)	63	Brazil	110	Pakistan	146
United Kingdom	46	Bangladesh	76	Bangladesh	145
France	42	Pakistan	73	Nigeria	135
Italy	42	Nigeria	65	Mexico	134

Source both charts: World Population Council

Reminders that overpopulation is a serious world problem: traffic in Tokyo (above); a drought victim in Niger, West Africa (left), and a sign in New Delhi, India.

PRACTISE FAMILY PLANNING ▼

in the not-too-distant future if the world's population continues to increase at its present rate? It might be very similar to what Paul Ehrlich, a scientist and author of *The Population Bomb,* saw on a trip to India:

I have understood the population explosion intellectually for a long time. I came to understand it emotionally one stinking hot night in Delhi a couple of years ago. My wife and daughter and I were returning to our hotel in an ancient taxi. The seats were hopping with fleas. The only functional gear was third. As we crawled through the city, we entered a crowded slum area. The temperature was well over 100, and the air was a haze of dust and smoke. The streets seemed alive with people. People eating, people washing, people sleeping. People visiting, arguing, and screaming. People thrusting their hands through the taxi window, begging. People defecating and urinating. People clinging to buses.. People herding animals. People, people, people, people.

As we moved slowly through the mob, hand horn squawking, the dust, noise, heat, and cooking fires gave the scene a hellish aspect. Would we ever get to our hotel? All three of us were, frankly, frightened. It seemed that anything could happen —but, of course, nothing did. Old India hands will laugh at our reaction. We were just some overprivileged tourists, unaccustomed to the sights and sounds of India. Perhaps, but since that night I've known the feel of overpopulation.

As the world's population has increased sharply in modern times, so has the number and size of its cities. Rapid population growth, in fact, is one cause of urbanization. In 1850 only four cities in the entire world had a population of one million or more people. By 1970 there were more than 120. And in 1986 at least

50 cities had populations of more than 2 million. The number of people who live in cities has been growing at a much faster rate than the general population. In 1982, 65 percent of the population lived in a city with 100,000 or more people. Urban population is doubling worldwide about every eleven years.

Many scientists are deeply concerned about the population explosion. Unless it is checked soon, they say, the future of the human race is very bleak. They predict mass starvation, overcrowding, and a general impoverishment of life. Ehrlich made the following comment in 1970:

"Somewhere between one and two billion people are today undernourished or malnourished. Somewhere between four and ten million of our fellow human beings will starve to death this year. . . . We have an inadequate loaf of bread to divide among today's multitudes, and we are quickly adding more billions to the bread line."

⊰ Do you think that predictions of mass starvation and poverty will come true? What do you think might happen to prevent such conditions? How would you solve the problem of overpopulation?

Population and social change in America. The birthrate in the United States is presently at an all-time low. As we have seen, many young couples today are choosing to have small families. In the late 1980's, the birthrate per couple was 1.8 children. This does not mean that our population will soon level off. Even if the birthrate remains at present level, the population of the United States will continue to grow for several decades because the number of women of childbearing age is still increasing, the result of the "baby boom" from the end of World War II until 1957. As we saw in the chapter on the family, the effect on the population would be enormous if young couples were to have an average of three children. At the rate of two children per couple, the population of this country would rise to 307 million by the year 2020. But at the rate of three children per couple, it would rise to 477 million.

What would an increase to 477 million people mean? This was one of the questions studied by the Presidential Commission on Population Growth and the American Future. The commission, which was appointed by President Richard M. Nixon, made its report in 1972. It said that an increase in population to 477 million would have the following effects:

• Living standards would decline for most American families.

• Cities would become extremely overcrowded.

• There would be shortages of water, petroleum, natural gas, and other resources.

• Food supplies would rarely be enough to meet the demand, and food prices would rise drastically.

• Pollution of the environment would increase substantially.

The commission concluded its report with these words: "We have found no convincing argument for continued national population growth. On the contrary, the pluses seem to be on the side of slowing growth and eventually stopping it altogether."

What will happen if the birthrate continues at its present level in the next few decades? There will be many more middle-aged and older people, and fewer young people. In 1976, for example, the median age of Americans was 28.1. By the year 2000, it will reach 35; and by 2030 it will be almost 40. The number of people over 65 will more than double to 52 million — one out of every six Americans. This "graying" process would produce great changes in the United States. this article, excerpted from *Newsweek* magazine, describes them:

> . . . *The transitions forced by these demographic population shifts are likely to be painful. The burden will fall most heavily on those born during the 1947-1957 baby boom. "It's a kind of doomed generation," says Rand Corporation population analyst Peter Morrison. There are so many people in the baby-boom generation that they will be competing with each other every step of the way. "A million and a half people who graduate from college in this decade will never get jobs at their level of expertise," predicts Basil Whiting, who oversees demographic research at the Ford Foundation. "That may not sound like a lot, but they will be bumping out high school graduates from jobs they would otherwise have gotten — and so on all the way down the line."* . . .
>
> *But one generation's loss will be another generation's gain. "The 'baby-bust' group 20 years from now will be in [an excellent] position," Morrison says. "There will be a large number of people in their fifties heading for retirement with not many to follow them." At that point, older workers who want to continue on the job will probably have little trouble persuading their bosses to let them. Companies may even offer in-*

centives to keep workers from retiring — a trend that would help ease the economic burden of pensions and Social Security. . . .

Though some experts fear that zero population growth will lead to economic stagnation, demographers note that a stable population is at least 60 years away. In the meantime, the population will grow from a total of slightly more than 215 million to between 245 million and 287 million by the end of the century, depending on future fertility rates. That is a potential new consumer market about the size of England or France.

It also promises to be a lucrative market. The fastest-growing segment of the population over the next two decades will be the 24- to 44-year-olds, who account for the bulk of new household formations and buy most of the durable goods that underpin the nation's economic growth. . . .

The soft drinks, blue jeans, and records that symbolize the youth market are not likely to be in such great demand in a predominantly middle-aged society. No one is quite sure what will be. . . .

Clearly, companies whose products do not appeal to more mature tastes and needs will find themselves plagued with a shrinking share of the economic pie. And already, a number of firms are scrambling to adjust to the new demographic realities. Johnson & Johnson has started trying to persuade adults to use its baby shampoo and baby oil. . . .

Even Levi Strauss, which prospered by clothing a generation of teenagers in denim, is changing with the times. It is marketing a three-piece suit and its "Levis for Men" line is "cut more fully," explains marketing director John Wyek, "to accommodate the guy who has stopped playing football and started watching it."

. . . Recognizing a trend when it sees one, RCA Corporation is now promoting remote-control TV sets. The idea, says a spokesman, "is to appeal

Once babies were Gerber's only business, but today the company seeks a wider—and older—market.

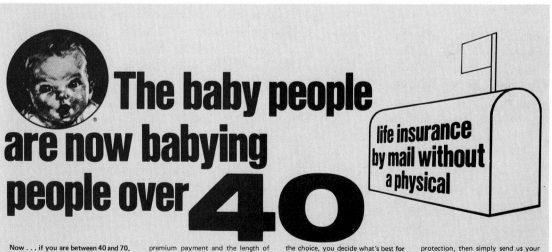

to the older people who don't want to get up."

As the U.S. becomes increasingly a nation of middle-aged and older people, cultural values will probably change too. America's frantic worship of the young, the new, the different, is bound to decline. "An aging population is likely to have the effect of damping down the speed of change in cultural ideas, political ideas, and the like," predicts political scientist Philip E. Converse of the University of Michigan. "We've been through a pretty rapid evolution of mores in recent years — and it seems almost certain that a graying population is going to slow that rate of change very significantly."

. . . "Senior Power" and "Gray Panther" political organizations are already gathering steam. . . . The American Association of Retired Persons furiously lobbied the Georgia legislature for a bill that would allow druggists to fill prescriptions for older people with generic drugs instead of higher-priced brand names. The rise of such action has been aided by the growth of community centers and other programs for the aged . . . . The result, says executive director Jack Ossofsky of the National Council on the Aging, is likely to be a new political touchstone: "The 1960's were the time of civil rights [for minorities]. The 1970's emphasized women's rights. I think the 1980's will be the time for the rights of the aged."

Old age may never be revered in America as it was in ancient China. But the shifting demographic balance may well erase the stigma the young in America have attached to age and aging. As the ranks of the middle-aged swell in the next few years — while the number of young people continues to drop — it's even possible that a new ethic could emerge. Youth may still be served, but by dint of sheer numbers it will be their elders who will be heeded. And as they blossom into the best-educated, best-financed, healthiest — and biggest — group of post-65-year-olds the nation has ever seen, their vision of America will begin to set the economic, political, and cultural tone.

List some consequences that the "graying" of the U.S. may have for people your age.

Population movements and social change. Not only is the size of a population important, its distribution and movements throughout a nation influence social change too. Immigration to the United States has had profound effects on our society, spurring its economic growth and enriching its culture. Equally important in producing social change has been the movement of large numbers of people *within* our country. In the last century, many people moved to the West, and many others moved from farms to cities. In the 20th century, Americans have been as mobile as ever, but different patterns of migration have occurred. One major pattern was the movement of rural, Southern blacks to Northern cities. Another was the movement of middle-class whites out of the cities to the suburbs. In recent years, the migrations have been to the Sun Belt, and back to rural areas. While people and industries are leaving Northeastern and North Central states, Arizona, Florida, Nevada, Idaho, and Colorado are rapidly growing. Scores of small towns in the Sun Belt and the West are either booming or feeling the pains of sudden growth, or both. Millions of Americans have profoundly altered their way of life. One man who moved from Los Angeles to Santa Rosa, a much smaller city, said: "In Los Angeles, you could never get away from the freeway roar. Here, there is silence. And you see the stars when you go out at night."

Cultural Diffusion and Social Change

In Japan, American cowboy films are quite popular on TV. The cowboys, of course, all speak fluent, dubbed-in Japanese. In the United States, Italian-style dinners are readily available at supermarket frozen-food counters. In many countries, the Mercedes-Benz, a German car, is a highly visible status symbol. These are examples of *cultural diffusion* — the spread of cultural traits from one society or group to another. Diffusion takes place whenever people of different cultures come into contact, and is responsible for much social change. Invariably, it is a two-way process. Native Americans, for example, introduced corn, potatoes, and tobacco to the first European settlers who came here. The settlers, in turn, introduced horses, beads, whiskey, and rifles to them. As a rule, when two cultures come into contact, the one with the simpler technology adopts more from the other. Cultural diffusion has been the major force in spreading science and technology around the world.

Americans who believe that our culture is unique would be surprised to learn how much of it has been borrowed from other societies. Ralph Linton, an anthropologist, describes this cultural diffusion in an article that is ironically entitled "One Hundred Percent American":

German cars on a Baltimore dock. Foreign automobiles are commonplace in the United States.

There can be no question about the average American's Americanism or his desire to preserve this precious heritage at all costs. Nevertheless, some insidious foreign ideas have already wormed their way into his civilization without his realizing what was going on. Thus dawn finds the unsuspecting patriot garbed in pajamas, a garment of East Indian origin, and lying in a bed built on a pattern which originated in either Persia or Asia Minor. He is muffled . . . in un-American materials: cotton, first domesticated in India; linen,

domesticated in the Near East; wool from an animal native to Asia Minor; or silk, whose uses were first discovered by the Chinese. . . . If the weather is cold enough, he may even be sleeping under an eiderdown quilt invented in Scandinavia.

On awakening he glances at the clock, a medieval European invention, . . . rises in haste, and goes to the bathroom. Here he must feel himself in the presence of a great American institution: He will have heard stories of both the quality and frequency of foreign plumbing and will know that in no other country does the average man perform his ablutions in the midst of such splendor. But the insidious foreign influence pursues him even here. Glass was invented by the ancient Egyptians, the use of glazed tiles for floors and walls in the Near East, porcelain in China, and the art of enameling on metal by Mediterranean artisans of the Bronze Age. Even his bathtub and toilet are but slightly modified copies of the Roman originals. . . .

In this bathroom the American washes with soap invented by the ancient Gauls. Next he cleans his teeth, a subversive European practice which did not invade America until the latter part of the 18th century. He then shaves, a masochistic rite first developed by the heathen priests of ancient Egypt and Sumer. The process is made less of a penance by the fact that his razor is of steel, an iron-carbon alloy discovered in either India or Turkestan. Lastly, he dries himself on a Turkish towel. . . .

§ List other examples of cultural diffusion that this man may encounter during the day. Then list several American norms and inventions that someone in another culture might encounter.

A Disney theme park in Japan and an Italian pizza parlor show cultural diffusion.

Social Movements and Social Change

Let's turn back the clock to the year 1937. The United States is still in the throes of the Great Depression. Millions of workers are unemployed, and their misery is widespread. According to President Franklin D. Roosevelt, one third of the nation is ill-housed, ill-clothed, and ill-fed. Even workers who have jobs are experiencing hard times, for wages are very low.

In Flint, Michigan, workers at the General Motors factories earn only about $1,000 a year. To make matters worse, there is a speedup on the assembly line. The workers have to do their jobs very quickly, and the strain on them is severe. Many belong to a new union, the United Automobile Workers, but officers of the General Motors Company refuse to meet with their representatives. Finally the workers vote to go on strike.

Strikes are common in the 1930's, but this one is something new. It is called a *sit-down strike*. The men remain inside the factories, but do not work. This way, strikebreakers cannot be brought in to replace them. At night the men sleep on the floors of new cars. Food is passed to them through the factory windows. The strikers are orderly and carefully protect the company's property. No drinking is allowed.

The strike drags on for weeks. The men keep their spirits up by singing union songs. One of them has the following words:

When they tie the can to a union man,
  Sit down! Sit down!
When the speedup comes, just twiddle your
  thumbs,
  Sit down! Sit down!
When the bosses won't talk, don't take a walk,
  Sit down! Sit down!

Meanwhile the company is trying to force the men to leave. Heat is shut off in all the factories. It is the middle of winter, and the men are cold, but they refuse to budge. The police try to storm into one of the factories, but the workers drive them back with flying soda bottles, coffee mugs, iron bolts, and door hinges. The police return armed with tear gas. The workers drive them back again by turning fire hoses on them.

Finally a court orders the strikers to leave the factories. They have to get out by 3 P.M. on February 3. The National Guard is authorized to back up the court's order. But the workers insist they will not leave. Outside the factories, thousands of union workers and relatives gather to support the strikers.

Three o'clock — zero hour — arrives on February 3. But Governor Frank Murphy of Michigan decides not to order the National Guard to attack. A confrontation is avoided. President Roosevelt asks for a peaceful end to the strike. A week later, General Motors agrees to bargain with leaders of the United Automobile Workers. The union has won a big victory.

The strike of General Motors workers was part of a great social movement that swept the United States during the Depression. It was the drive of millions of in-

dustrial workers to join unions to obtain
better wages and working conditions.
Sociologists define a *social movement* as a
form of collective action that seeks to
promote (or to resist) social change.
Sociologists have classified social movements into the following four broad
categories, although many movements are
a combination of types.

Reform. The General Motors sit-
down strike is an example of a social
movement whose goal is to attain some
kind of *reform.* Reform movements generally seek to improve a society by changing
certain conditions with which they are
dissatisfied. They do not wish to change
the entire structure of the society. Reform
movements predominate in democratic
societies where people have considerable
freedom to criticize existing conditions.
Our society has had many historic reform
movements which have caused reforms
such as the abolition of slavery, women's
suffrage, and the prohibition of liquor. In
recent years, the efforts of minority groups
to achieve equal treatment have been reform movements. Other reform movements have been organized to oppose U.S.
participation in the Vietnam War, and to
protect our natural environment.

Revolutionary. During the reign of
Czar Nicholas II (1894-1917), the great
majority of people in Russia were extremely poor and illiterate. Reformers had
long urged the czars to make political and
economic changes to improve living conditions, but their pleas were rejected. As a
result, more and more Russians turned to
the revolutionary parties in the country for
help. In March 1917, during World War I

Reform: Suffragettes advocating
the right to vote, around 1900.

and amid widespread hunger, they over-
threw the government of the czar. A few
months later, the Communist party seized
all power in Russia. Under Communist
rule, Russian society was completely re-
vamped. Factories, mines, farms, and all
other means of production, once privately
owned, became the property of the state.

The goal of a *revolutionary movement*
is to overthrow the existing social structure and to replace it with an entirely new
one. Unlike the reformers, revolutionaries
do not believe that the existing system is
worth saving.

Resistance. On a raw, windy night in
1915, 16 men stood on top of Stone
Mountain, Georgia. They wore white
robes, and their faces were covered with
hoods. One of them touched a match to a
gasoline-soaked cross. It quickly went up

Revolution: Storming the Russian winter palace at Petrograd, 1917. Below, the Ku Klux Klan, a resistance movement.

in flames. The Ku Klux Klan, dormant since 1871, was reborn.

The Klan was first organized after the Civil War to keep former slaves "in their place." It terrorized blacks in the South who wanted to vote or become educated. Following an investigation of the Klan's violent activities, Congress outlawed it in 1871. Revived in 1915, the Klan became a nationwide movement. It was hostile not only to blacks, but to immigrants, Catholics, and Jews as well. It regarded all of them as threats to the dominant Anglo-Saxon Protestant culture of this country. In the early 1960's, the Klan opposed the civil-rights movement.

Most social movements strive for change. But some, like the Ku Klux Klan, arise to prevent change or to abolish change that has already taken place. These are called *resistance movements*. In a democratic society, periods of rapid social change stimulate resistance movements. In 1954, for example, the U.S. Supreme Court ordered an end to racial segregation in the schools. The order led to the formation of many "backlash" organizations determined to resist integration.

Expressive. Some social movements believe that it is hopeless to try to change society. Instead, they seek to change the inner, spiritual lives of their members. Called *expressive movements*, they include most of the religious cults that sprang up in the U.S. in recent years, such as the Hare Krishna sect and the Scientologists. They offer members the emotional support of warm, personal relationships, an identity, and a distinct life-style.

The development of social movements. How does a social movement get started? How does it choose leaders and organize to achieve its goals? How does it decide what tactics to use? A brief look at the early development of the civil-rights movement, adapted from Ira Peck's *The Life and Words of Martin Luther King, Jr.*, is revealing:

>   When the Reverend Martin Luther King, Jr., and his wife, Coretta, moved to Montgomery, Alabama, in 1954, it was a peaceful town. But it was peaceful because hardly anyone there challenged the system of racial segregation. Some blacks were afraid to challenge it. They might lose their jobs, or suffer violence. Others just thought it was hopeless to fight the system.
>   A few brave men did speak out against racial segregation. They were able to build a slow fire of

Martin Luther King, Jr., a charismatic leader of the civil-rights movement.

discontent among Montgomery's blacks. But so far, it was all beneath the surface.

Then, on December 1, 1955, something happened in Montgomery that would change the lives of its 50,000 black people. Within a few years, it would affect the lives of all Americans, black and white.

That day, Rosa Parks, a black woman, was seated just behind the "white" section on a bus. By law, whites sat up front, blacks in the back. Mrs. Parks was going home from her job as a seamstress. Several white people got on the bus. There were no more seats in the "white" section. So the bus driver ordered Mrs. Parks and three other blacks to move to the rear of the bus. The bus was now full, and Mrs. Parks would have to stand. The other blacks obeyed the driver, but Mrs. Parks said no. She would not give up her seat. (Her feet hurt, she said later.)

Why was this so unusual? When Mrs. Parks said no to the bus driver, she was breaking the law. The law in Alabama said that she had to move to the back of the bus. If she did not obey the driver, she could be arrested and fined — or maybe go to jail. Mrs. Parks was arrested on the spot.

Mrs. Parks was well known among Montgomery's blacks. She had once been secretary of the local chapter of the National Association for the Advancement of Colored People. The news of her arrest spread like wildfire. Everyone began calling everyone else on the telephone. "Have you heard the news? Rosa Parks was arrested. She wouldn't give up her seat on the bus!"

That evening a group of black women leaders met and agreed that a boycott of the buses would be an effective way to protest. They wanted all of Montgomery's black leaders to consider it. King offered his church as a meeting place. The following evening, more than 40 black doctors, lawyers, teachers, businessmen, and ministers came to the meeting. A minister proposed a one-day boycott of the buses on December 5. That night there would

be a big meeting, open to all. Then they would decide what to do next.

The leaders agreed to this plan. They also agreed to print leaflets telling about the boycott.

That night King was so excited he could hardly sleep. But he went to his church early the next morning to see that the boycott leaflets were printed. The leaflets said: "Don't ride the buses to work, to town, to school, or anywhere on Monday, December 5. If you work, take a cab, or share a ride, or walk. Come to a mass meeting Monday night at 7 o'clock at the Holt Street Baptist Church."

An army of women and children began handing out leaflets. The Montgomery newspaper made the boycott front-page news. Still, King was worried. Would the boycott work? Would the people have the courage to protest? King wasn't sure.

The boycott proved to be almost 100 percent successful. Driving around town that morning, King counted only eight blacks riding the buses. Buses that were usually crowded with blacks were running nearly empty.

That afternoon, the black leaders held another meeting. They decided to form an organization to head the protest movement. It was called the Montgomery Improvement Association (MIA). Then King was taken by surprise. Before he could say no, he was elected president of the MIA. He really didn't want the job. He felt he needed more time for his church work. But now he couldn't refuse — it was too late. So Martin Luther King, Jr., became the leader of the black protest movement in Montgomery. It was the beginning of his career as a civil-rights leader.

The Holt Street Baptist Church was packed that night. Thousands of blacks stood outside the church to hear the speeches over loudspeakers. The meeting began with the hymn, "Onward Christian Soldiers." Then King got up to speak. He talked about the bad treatment blacks got on public buses. They were sick and tired of being pushed around and insulted by the drivers. The time had come to protest. But, he said, the protest must be guided by law and order. They must never copy the violent methods of the Ku Klux Klan. King repeated the words of Jesus: "Love your enemies, bless them that curse you." This was the cornerstone of King's philosophy of nonviolence.

When King finished, the crowd stood up and cheered. Rosa Parks, who was free after paying a fine, was also cheered.

Finally, the Reverend Ralph Abernathy spoke. He proposed that the boycott should continue until blacks got better treatment on the buses and a number of black drivers were hired by the bus lines. Abernathy then said, "All in favor, stand."

Every person in the crowd stood up. Cheers rang out from inside and outside the church. The blacks had voted solidly not to ride the buses.

That day, King said, was Montgomery's moment in history. The black people there had started a movement that would bring new hope to blacks everywhere.

Victory did not come to the blacks easily.

The boycott dragged on for months while lawyers for the blacks challenged Alabama's bus segregation laws in the courts. The resistance of some whites in Montgomery was fierce. The homes and churches of black leaders were damaged or wrecked by bombs. One night the Ku Klux Klan made a show of force. Forty cars full of hooded Klansmen rode through the black section of town. In the past, the blacks would have gone inside their homes, locked the doors, and turned off the lights. Not this time. They sat on their porches with the lights on. Some even waved at the Klansmen. The KKK couldn't believe it. They quit in disgust after riding a few blocks.

More than a year after the "one-day" boycott began, the blacks won a complete victory. The U.S. Supreme Court ruled that Alabama's bus segregation laws were unconstitutional. From then on, the civil-rights movement, headed by King, rapidly gained momentum. It achieved its greatest victory when Congress passed the Civil Rights Act of 1964. The law, which was signed by President Lyndon B. Johnson, prohibited discrim-

Attorney General Ramsey Clark, King, and the Reverend Ralph Abernathy singing "We Shall Overcome," the song identified with the movement.

ination in public facilities, in voting, and in job hiring. It was a historic step toward meeting the demands of blacks for an end to unequal treatment.

Life cycle of social movements. The civil-rights movement emerged slowly and painfully from feelings of resentment that had been pent-up for a long time. The development of any social movement, sociologists say, is usually a gradual, step-by-step process. In his book, *Sociology: A Critical Approach to Power, Conflict, and Change*, sociologist J. Victor Baldridge lists these seven steps:

1. *Premovement social conditions.* Most social movements have their roots in the oppression of a group. Conditions of poverty, prejudice, and discrimination usually create discontent and a desire for social change. When the fortunes of a group are at their lowest ebb, however, the members are usually too concerned with the problems of everyday survival to consider organizing a protest movement. After a brief period of progress and improved conditions, the hopes and expectations of an oppressed group rise rapidly. If these expectations are not realized soon, the group's dissatisfaction intensifies. The Montgomery bus boycott came at a time when blacks had been encouraged to expect better treatment. The post-World War II economic boom, President Truman's integration of the U.S. Army, and the 1954 Supreme Court decision that outlawed racial segregation in schools fueled these expectations.

2. *Agitation and awakening.* Leaders are especially important in transforming a large number of discontented people into an organized social movement. A magnetic or "charismatic" leader stirs people to action by verbalizing their oppression and hope, and becomes a symbol of the movement. Such leaders appear to their followers to have superhuman qualities.

3. *Organizing a social movement.* It takes a charismatic leader to arouse oppressed people and start a social movement. Once the movement gets under way, however, it needs another kind of leader — an administrator — if it is going to flourish. While the charismatic leader gives speeches and leads marches, the administrator handles the practical work of organizing the movement, raising money, and "getting things done." The administrator welds the movement's followers into a strong political force and directs their actions toward concrete goals. Ralph Abernathy and others served in this capacity in the civil-rights movement.

4. *Ideology and goals.* As the movement grows, it must develop an *ideology* — a set of beliefs. An ideology binds people together in a cause and prepares them to make sacrifices for it. It provides a sense of "we-ness," setting the members apart from the out-groups. The out-groups are "the enemy." Depending on the social movement, the enemy may be racists, male chauvinists, "the Establishment," Communists, Jews, or atheists, among others. After a while, members need more than an ideology to unite them. They must have some limited, specific goals that can be achieved by direct action. Vague calls for "liberation" may give way to demands for laws against discrimination.

Above, workers at General Motors' Fisher Body
plant "sitting down" on automobile seats, January
1937. Below, National Guardsmen celebrate
the peaceful end to the strike a month later.

Calls for "world socialism," for example, may be narrowed to demands for workmen's compensation and unemployment insurance.

5. *Tactics.* As a social movement develops its goals, it also evolves tactics. Tactics vary widely, from prayer and fasting to the hijacking of airplanes, but basically there are three main kinds:

Many social movements seek to win public support for their programs by *educational means.* Members hand out leaflets or make speeches on busy street corners. They may also give away buttons, posters, and bumper stickers containing their slogans. Leaders often appear on radio and television interview programs.

Social movements often seek changes by exerting *political pressure.* They may start letter-writing campaigns urging legislators to pass laws that favor their goals, or they may support candidates who are sympathetic to them. Holding mass meetings in Washington, DC, and delivering petitions to public officials are other forms of political pressure.

If education and political tactics fail to accomplish their objectives, social movements may resort to *direct action.* In such cases, members confront "the enemy." Strikes, picketing, boycotts, sit-in demonstrations, and marches are all forms of direct action. Revolutionary movements resort to more drastic kinds — terrorism and armed insurrection.

6. *Response of authorities.* Social movements call for basic changes in a society. Their demands, if met, would lead to shifts in distribution of power, wealth, and prestige. How do authorities react to such demands? Do they promote or hinder social change? People in power often feel threatened by social movements. They tend to respond slowly, or not at all. Women began to campaign actively for equal rights in the United States as early as 1848. Their chief demand, the right to vote, was not granted in most states until 1920 when the 19th Amendment was ratified. But the right to vote did not alter women's status in other respects. Today women's rights advocates are campaigning for a new amendment to the Constitution that would guarantee them full equality under the law.

Authorities are sometimes quite hostile to social movements. Police action has been used to subdue strikers, civil-rights demonstrators, feminists, and student activists. Yet authorities may also protect members of social movements. In the 1960's, federal troops and marshals were called on many times to safeguard civil-rights demonstrators.

7. *Results.* Only a few social movements grow, prosper, and make important changes in society. Many die after a brief existence without making any impact at all; some linger on after having made a modest impact. In the United States, labor unions, the civil-rights movement, and feminists have succeeded in bringing about major reforms, and are still powerful forces in our society today.

How many of these seven steps can you identify in the life cycle of the civil-rights movement as told in the reading about Martin Luther King, Jr.? Give an example for each step you list.

application

A person born in the late 1980's has a good chance of living until the end of the 21st century. But what will the person's life be like? In the following article adaption, two well-known futurists speculate on the changes which await us.

Isaac Asimov:

Assuming we don't blow ourselves up with nuclear weapons, we're going to have a world that's completely different from anything we've known — and infinitely better.

For thousands of years, a great many human beings have been doing the kind of work that seriously underuses their brains. They push, they pull, they dig, they hack. But now we're going to have robots taking over these dull, repetitive, and undemanding tasks. And human beings will be free to do truly creative work.

Education will also become creative — a game more under the control of the person being educated. In addition to going to school, youngsters will hook up their home computers to the contents of a huge computerized library. This will allow them to explore whatever they want — to work at their own speed, in their own way, on subjects of their choosing. Everyone will have a chance to discover exactly what he or she enjoys.

Space will be the new frontier. Mankind has already filled the earth. And, if we insist on staying here, we will only create a prison for ourselves. We're simply wearing the earth out, using it up, and not treating it properly. Space is our one great hope.

The shuttle makes it feasible to build large space stations that can be continuously occupied by relays of astronauts. These astronauts will put together the first structure in orbit — perhaps a solar power station that can convert sunlight into electric current and beam an endless supply of energy to the nations of the earth. We'll build factories and laboratories in space, and settlements of tens of thousands of people. These space settlers will be pioneers of the future. Inspired by the frontier spirit, they'll be able to undertake long space journeys without physical or psychological discomfort. Someday, they or their children will venture into the outer reaches of the solar system and beyond — to the stars.

Dick Teresi:

By the year 2000, scientists will develop vaccines to prevent heart disease and many cancers. By 2030, there's a good chance they'll discover how to stop and even reverse the aging process. The result? People will routinely live 100 or more years, and 80-year-olds will have the bodies of 30-year-olds.

But not every part of your body will be your own. When a kidney, heart, or liver goes bad, you'll get either an artificial or genetically engineered [a clone] replacement. As cloning becomes more common, some braindead bodies will be grown only for their parts. If you lose an arm or a leg, your clone will provide a new one.

Some of the biggest breakthroughs will be in the area of drugs. Scientists have already discovered the receptors and chemicals in the brain that control sleep, aggression, depression, and anxiety. In the 21st century, there will be smart pills to enhance your memory and boost your IQ. Wake-up pills will have the power of 1,000 cups of coffee but won't give you jitters.

And power pills — made of the brain chemical serotin — will turn you into Henry Kissinger. I also envision creativity drugs and antiwar drugs.

◄§ Which of Asimov's and Teresi's predictions do you agree with? Which do you disagree with? What do you think the world will be like in the early 21st century?

summary

The 20th century has been a time of revolutionary changes in social patterns. Many observers say that norms, values, roles, and institutions have changed more since 1900 than in the previous 50,000 years. And they are continuing to change at an accelerating rate. Shifts in widely accepted norms, values, roles and institutions are called **social change**.

The growth of science and technology in modern, industrial societies has caused considerable social change. **Science** is the knowledge obtained through the use of systematic methods. **Technology** derives from the practical application of such knowledge. Inventions like the automobile and the air conditioner have greatly affected the way America lives. Cars have given us greater mobility than ever before and were responsible for the enormous growth of suburbs. However, the automobile brought with it some problems — accidents, pollution, and a dependence on decreasing oil supplies among them. The auto's advocates were slow to recognize these problems. Sociologists call this delay between the acceptance of a new technology and adjustment to its accompanying norms and values **cultural lag**.

The rapid growth of science and technology in modern times has been paralleled by an equally dramatic growth in the world's population. At the present rate of increase, it will double every 35 years. A sharp rise in population creates great pressures for social change. The economy must produce more food, clothing, and homes. More schools and hospitals are needed, and governments must expand their activities. In developing nations, runaway population growth may result in widespread hunger and privation. Many scientists fear that unless population growth is checked, the future of the human race is very bleak. They predict mass starvation, poverty, and extremely overcrowded cities. The number of people who live in cities is increasing at a faster rate than the general population.

Worldwide, the urban population is doubling about every 11 years.

While people in developing nations are having as many children as previous generations, in modern industrial societies birth rates have been declining. In the United States, the birth rate is at an all-time low. Young couples are having an average of 1.8 children. What would a continuation of the present low birth rate mean? In the next few decades, there would be many more middle-aged and older people, and fewer young people. By the year 2030, the number of people over 65 would more than double to 52 million. One out of every six Americans would be a "senior citizen."

The movement of large numbers of people within our country has caused social change. In this century, many rural, Southern blacks have moved to Northern cities, while many middle-class whites have moved to suburbs. In recent years, migrations have begun to the Sun Belt and back to rural areas.

Another cause of social change is **cultural diffusion** — the spread of culture traits from one society to another. American cowboy films are very popular in Japan, for example, and are often shown on TV. At the same time, small Japanese cars have become quite popular in the United States.

A well-organized social movement may also produce changes in society. Sociologists define a **social movement** as a form of collective action that seeks to promote (or resist) change. Four types of social movements studied by sociologists are **reform**, in which participants seek to change conditions in society without changing its structure; **revolutionary**, in which the goal is to overthrow the existing social structure and create a new one; **resistance**, in which the goal is to stop change; and **expressive**, in which members seek to change their inner spiritual lives without changing society.

All social movements develop by a gradual process. The phases in a movement's life cycle may be described in these steps: Premovement social conditions such as poverty and oppression create discontent; expectations rise if these conditions improve even slightly. A charismatic leader agitates and awakens the discontented people to see the need for the movement. An administrative leader helps the charismatic leader build an organization and raise money. The group develops beliefs (ideology) and goals that set it apart in the culture. It develops tactics through educational programs, political pressure, and direct action, such as boycotts and strikes, to reach its goals. Authorities respond either by repressing or encouraging the movement. Through these steps, a few social movements achieve widespread social change while others settle for more limited results, or die without accomplishing any of their goals.

more questions and activities

1. Explain the difference between *science* and *technology.* Give one example of a development in each that has brought change in your lifetime.

2. Define *cultural lag* and tell how it sometimes creates social problems.

3. List seven steps in the life cycle of social movements as labeled by sociologist J. Victor Baldridge.

4. Make a list of at least eight social movements and divide them into the four categories described in the chapter.

5. List five major causes of pressure for social change and discuss to what extent any or all of these pressures exist in your community.

6. Debate the pros and cons of zero population growth as a desirable national goal.

7. Use the most recent volume of the statistical abstract of the United States to prepare a demographic analysis of your state. The analysis should include information about age, birth and death rates, internal migration, immigration, etc.

8. Use your local community as an example for a study of the impact of population changes on social change. You may want to use government census data, and interview local government and planning officials.

9. During the last 10 years most states and the District of Columbia have passed some sort of legislation affecting smoking in public areas. How well is the antismoking movement doing today? Prepare a report on the history, effectiveness, and probable future of the antismoking movement. Which of the four categories of social movements does it fit into? Has its development followed the seven steps described in this chapter? Answer for each step. What values and norms is it trying to change? What social forces are working with and against this movement? You might contact such organizations as the Tobacco Institute and Action on Smoking and Health for propaganda on both sides of this movement.

10. As an example of *cultural diffusion,* analyze the significance and impact of the 1979 opening of trade and diplomatic relations between the United States and the People's Republic of China. For example, we sent them Coca-Cola, and they introduced us to acupuncture. What long-range effects, if any, might this cultural diffusion have on both societies?

11. Social change is not always seen as "progress" by everybody. Many people advocate a return to earlier, simpler times. Others say that the future will be exciting. If you were able to enter a time machine and go back into the past or forward into the future, which way would you go? What would you find in the period you choose? How would you change your values and norms of behavior to fit into that time period? If you could take five things with you — into the past or future — what would you take? Why?

suggested readings

Jones, Landon Y. *Great Expectations.* (Coward, McCann, and Geoghegan, 1980.) A fascinating study of the impact of the baby boom generation upon American culture and institutions.

Nesbitt, John. *Megatrends.* (Warner Books, 1984.) A popular account of how a number of major trends are re-shaping American life.

Norris, Frank. *The Octopus.* (Bantam, 1958.) This novel, originally published in 1901, shows how the coming of the railroad affected forever the social fabric of the Old West.

Rogers, Everett M., and Floyd Shoemaker. *Communications of Innovations: A Cross-Cultural Approach.* (Free Press, 1971.) A well-documented theory of how innovations diffuse within and between societies.

Editors of Time-Life Books. *This Fabulous Century.* (Time-Life Books, 1985.) Each volume in this eight-part series contains excellent photo essays on the technological developments and social movements which have shaped American society.

Toffler, Alvin. *The Third Wave.* (Morrow, 1980.) A highly readable account of social change in America.

Editors of U.S. News and World Report. "Ten Forces Reshaping America." (The U.S. News and World Report, March 19, 1984.) An excellent survey of how the computer revolution, foreign competition, medical miracles, and other forces are changing our society.

Williams, Juan. *Eyes On The Prize.* (Viking, 1987.) An outstanding history of the civil rights movement from 1954 to 1965.

PART
TWO

social

problems

High crime rates have made Americans less trusting.

chapter 11

crime

"I found myself walking down the street one day thinking about being shot. I realized how stupid this was, so I angrily stomped along, determined not to die. But you are aware of crime all the time here. Life could end any time."

This statement by a teacher reflects the fear of violent crime—murder, rape, robbery, and assault—that grips so many Americans today. As a resident of one of the nation's most violent cities, this woman was no doubt aware that the rate of crime in our society has been growing very rapidly since the 1960's. It would probably be of little comfort for her to hear that by the mid-1980's the growth rate of crime had begun to slow down. Reports of violent crime reached an all-time high of 1,361,820 in 1981. In 1985 reports of violent crime decreased three percent from the 1981 reports. And reported property crime — burglary, larceny, and theft — decreased eight percent.

Probably much more prominent in the teacher's mind are highly publicized stories about young criminals like Bobby. Bobby was nine years old when he was arrested for shoplifting. The Los Angeles police spoke sternly to him and released him. Three months later, Bobby was arrested for burglary and was released with a warning. Bobby's 16th arrest — at the age of 12 — earned him his first jail term, two years at a California Youth Authority camp, from which he escaped four times. A few days after his release, at age 14, he killed a man. By the time Bobby was 18, he had been charged with 26 crimes, including murder; but on his 18th birthday, under California law, he was legally responsible for none of them.

Frightening as stories like Bobby's may be, they represent only a small part of the widespread problem of crime in our society. *Crime* is the violation of a law — any law. It confronts us not only on the street but, as we shall see, in business, and even in our homes.

In this chapter, we will look at crime in our society and see how we try to measure it. Next, we'll examine four different types of crime — juvenile delinquency, organized crime, white-collar crime, and so-called victimless crime — and see how they affect us. Who are the criminals? We'll try to break them down by sex, age, race and ethnicity, and social class. Finally, we'll examine several well-known sociological theories which attempt to explain the causes of crime. We'll conclude our chapter with a consideration of differing views of what can be done to reduce crime in the United States.

The Problem

The extent of crime. The most detailed statistics on crime in this country are contained in the *Uniform Crime Reports* *(UCR)* published each year by the Federal Bureau of Investigation (FBI). These statistics are based on crimes reported by citizens to local police and sent monthly and yearly to the FBI. Although the *UCR* presents data on 29 categories of crime, it concentrates on seven serious crimes against people and property. These seven crime categories are known collectively as the *Crime Index* offenses. They are:

1. *Murder and nonnegligent homicide* (all willful homicides, as distinguished from deaths caused by negligence).

2. *Forcible rape* (including assault to rape and attempted rape).

3. *Robbery* (stealing, or taking anything of value, by force or threat of force).

4. *Aggravated assault* (assault with intent to kill or to do great bodily harm).

5. *Burglary* (breaking, or unlawful entry, into a structure with the intent to commit a felony or a theft; includes attempts).

6. *Larceny-theft* (theft of items without force or threat of force, or by fraud; excludes embezzlement, worthless checks, and forgery).

7. *Auto theft* (stealing, or driving away in, a vehicle without lawful consent).

The FBI calls the first four offenses *violent* crimes and the last three *property* crimes. Chart 11:A compares the number of *Index* crimes and the number of crimes for each 100,000 people (the crime rate) for selected years from 1960 to 1985.

What do these figures tell us about crime in the U.S.? They indicate that:

• The number of reported offenses in these seven categories more than tripled for that period.

• The crime rate for these crimes almost tripled for that period.

• Crimes against property greatly outnumbered those against people. (Although most Americans fear violent crime the most, it comprised just over ten percent of all serious offenses in 1985.)

᠎᠎ What other facts about crime can you deduce from this chart? What crimes have increased the most? The least?

In order to dramatize the frequency with which crime occurs in the U.S., the FBI always includes what it calls *crime clocks.* In 1985 the *UCR* crime clocks showed that a larceny-theft occurred every 5 seconds, a burglary every 10 seconds, an auto theft every 29 seconds, and aggravated assault every 44 seconds, a robbery every 63 seconds, a rape every 6 minutes, and a murder every 28 minutes.

Other information indicates that the crime clocks may actually be ticking at a much faster rate. This information is based on a different approach to gathering data known as *victimization studies.*

In a victimization study, a representative sample of people are asked whether they or members of their families have been the victims of a crime or crimes during the previous year. These studies have consistently reported a much higher rate of crime than official records. For example, a study by the National Opinion Research Center (NORC) surveyed 10,000 households as part of a study requested by the President's Commission on Law Enforcement and Administration of Justice. When compared with *UCR* rates, the NORC study revealed almost four times as many rapes, one-and-a-half times as many robberies, slightly more than twice as many aggravated assaults, more than three times as many burglaries, and more than twice as many larcenies.

A similar study of residents and business people in 13 large cities, published by

11:A   Crime and Crime Rates 1960–1985

Crime	1960		1970		1980		1985	
	Reported Crime	Crime Rate	Reported Crime	Crime Rate	Reported Crime	Crime Rate	Reported Crime	Crime Rate
Violent Crimes	288,460	160.9	738,820	363.5	1,308,900	580.8	1,327,440	556.0
Murder and Nonnegligent Manslaughter	9,110	5.1	16,000	7.9	23,040	10.2	18,976	7.9
Forcible Rape	17,190	9.6	37,990	18.7	82,090	36.4	87,340	36.6
Robbery	107,840	60.1	349,860	172.1	548,810	243.5	497,874	208.5
Aggravated Assault	154,320	86.1	334,970	164.8	654,960	290.6	723,246	302.9
Property Crimes	3,095,700	1,726.3	7,359,200	3,621.0	11,986,500	5,319.1	11,102,600	4,605.5
Burglary	912,000	508.6	2,205,000	1,084.9	3,795,200	1,668.2	3,073,348	1,287.3
Larceny-Theft	1,855,400	1,034.7	4,225,800	2,079.3	7,112,700	3,156.3	6,926,380	2,901.2
Motor-Vehicle Theft	328,200	183.0	984,400	456.8	1,114,700	494.6	1,102,862	462.0
Total Crime Index	3,384,200	1,887.2	8,098,000	3,984.5	13,295,900	5,889.9	12,400,000	5,206.5

Source: Federal Bureau of Investigation, Uniform Crime Reports

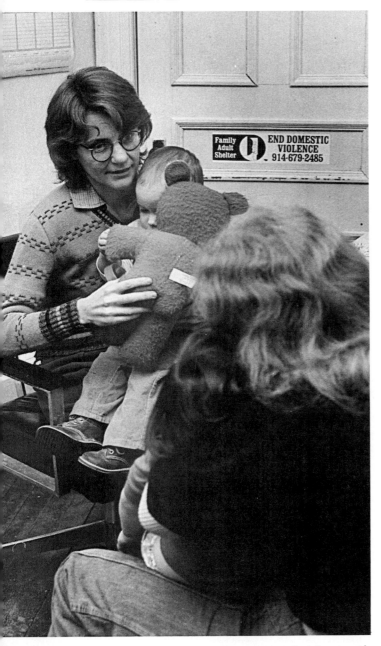

Battered women's shelters provide counseling, shelter, and care for victims of abuse.

the National Crime Panel, a federal agency, showed that the crime rate was at least twice as high as the *UCR* would indicate.

The reasons people gave the NORC researchers for not reporting crime were:

• The victim didn't like, trust, or believe in the effectiveness of the police (55 percent).

• The offender was a relative, lover, or friend; and the victim did not want to bring charges against him or her (34 percent).

• The victim did not know how to enlist police aid (9 percent).

• The victim feared reprisal (2 percent).

Rape is the most under-reported violent crime. Most rape victims wish to avoid ugly publicity, painful questioning, and allegations that they encouraged the assault.

Types of crime. Crime assumes many diverse forms. In this section, we will examine four major types of crime — juvenile delinquency, organized crime, white-collar crime, and victimless crime. (These categories do not include all crime, and sometimes they overlap.)

Juvenile delinquency. Crimes attributed to juveniles (usually people under 18 years of age) have been increasing twice as fast as crimes attributed to adults. In 1985, 30 percent of those arrested for serious crimes were juveniles ranging in age from 17 down to 10. Though juveniles are much less likely than their elders to be arrested for murder, the homicide rate among the young has also risen. About one out of every 10 people arrested for murder in the United States is a juvenile.

Cases involving youthful offenders are handled by a separate system of juvenile courts and correctional facilities. This separate system was created as a result of a social movement in the late 19th and early 20th centuries, whose leaders social scientists have recently labeled *child savers.* Child saving rested on the assumption that all offenders could be rehabilitated with early guidance and attention. This view was reflected in the statement attributed to Father Flanagan of Nebraska's Boys Town that "there is no such thing as a bad boy." Thus, the object of juvenile courts is to return offenders to their families and homes as soon as possible. Punishment is usually quite lenient by adult standards.

In recent years, juvenile court judges have been alarmed by the insensitivity of many youthful offenders. These judges frequently find these youths show no sense of guilt or remorse for their behavior. A Washington, DC, Superior Court judge, for example, commented: "I asked a boy the other day why he had committed a robbery, and he said, 'Because I wanted to.' I asked him if he was sorry, and he just glared at me." Many juvenile delinquents belong to violent gangs that sometimes terrorize city neighborhoods. Gangs commit roughly 25 percent of all juvenile crime. The life of a juvenile gang leader is described in the following article adapted from *Time* magazine:

His small, round badge of courage is on his back: the puckered scar left by a bullet wound. He

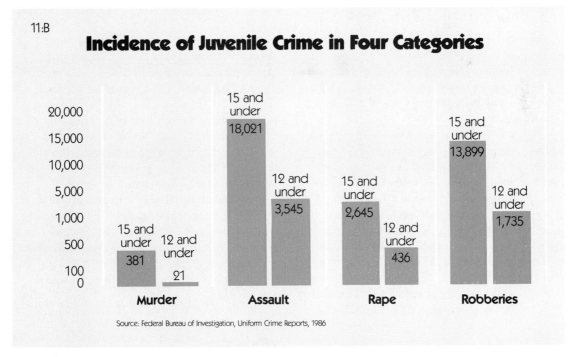

11:B

Incidence of Juvenile Crime in Four Categories

Source: Federal Bureau of Investigation, Uniform Crime Reports, 1986

The Guardian Angels, *a citizen protection group, on a New York City street.*

is proud of the scar, and prouder still that he can shrug it off as an accepted part of his life-style. "Almost everybody's been shot," smiles the 19-year-old black youth known as "Bartender," a leader of one of the street gangs that flourish in the Los Angeles area.

Bartender's real name is Lyle Joseph Thomas on police records. He has been arrested 11 times on charges that include assault on a police officer, simple assault, strong-armed robbery, and possession of a carbine. But, thanks to the vagaries of juvenile justice, he has never served time in jail.

With both of his parents working, Bartender grew up on his own in suburban Compton, gradually drifting into trouble. "They hate me," he says of his mother and father. "They take turns getting on me." A high school graduate, Bartender makes $121 a week as a porter at Kaiser Foundation Hospital. But his real life belongs to the Piru, the street gang of about 150 members who hang around Compton's Leuders Park taking drugs, playing basketball, and planning robberies and burglaries. But mainly the Piru plots, attacks, and defends itself against its hated enemies, the local chapter of the Crips, which is perhaps the most vicious and largest street gang in the area.

The rivalry between the two gangs started with fistfights four years ago in the high school cafeteria. Then someone brought his mother's gun to school, and the killing started. . . . Police estimate that about 10 members of the Piru and the Crips have been killed to date. "People get high and just don't care sometimes," Bartender explains. "Somebody says let's go do something, and everybody is game for it because they don't want to look like they're scared. But after a while, you can't be."

Asked what he thinks of the juvenile justice system, Bartender laughs and says, "I wish I were still a juvenile."

⚜ Should Bartender have been tried as an adult for the crimes he committed as a juvenile? Explain your answer.

Organized crime. Providing illegal goods and services to people who want them is the business of big-time criminals who are as well organized as any large corporation. Their rackets include prostitution, gambling, narcotics, loan-sharking, pornography, and cigarette bootlegging.

Organized crime is one of the biggest industries in the U.S. Although exact figures are not known, law enforcement agencies estimate that "the mob" makes about 26 billion dollars a year in untaxed profits from illegal operations. By comparison General Motors Corporation, the largest industrial corporation in the U.S., reported net profits (after taxation) of 2.9 billion dollars in 1986.

Organized crime is dominated by a national organization known as the *Mafia,* or *Cosa Nostra.* According to the FBI, the Mafia is remarkably small with no more than 1,700 members, all bound by vows of loyalty and secrecy. In addition, criminologists (sociologists who study crime) estimate that at least 50,000 other criminals can be considered confederates of the Mafia. The organization itself is divided into 24 "families," the smallest of which has only 20 members. A "commission" of about a dozen of the most powerful bosses supervises the Mafia's national organization. The most influential leaders usually come from New York, because they control the most people and rackets.

The mob uses its huge profits to buy control of many legitimate businesses.

One example, cited by *NBC Nightly News* involved the Badger State Cheese Company of Forestville, Wisconsin. According to NBC, the cheese company was bought by the Gambino Mafia family of New York, which stripped the company of its assets and bankrupted it intentionally eight months later. As a result of the bankruptcy, 55 people were put out of work, dairy farmers were left with a half-million dollars in unpaid milk bills, and banks were left with $200,000 in defaulted loans. The Justice Department estimates that organized criminals may own as many as 10,000 legitimate businesses in the U.S. in such industries as trucking, construction, and private garbage collection.

Organized crime flourishes mainly because so many "respectable" people are willing to pay for the goods and services provided by its rackets, even if they are illegal. Another reason is that some public officials are "bought" by the mob, allowing it to operate relatively unhindered. Evidence of this corruption is sometimes supplied by mob figures who become FBI informers. One of them, Vincent Teresa, described a well-known Mafia leader in a book titled *Vinnie Teresa's Mafia:*

"Luchese . . . was one of the most popular crime bosses. He was very big in the garment industry, and his crime family was well respected throughout the mob world for its smooth operations in gambling, narcotics, loan-sharking, and labor and construction racketeering. But he was best known as the mob's corrupter — the man who had friends in all branches and at all levels of government — the man the

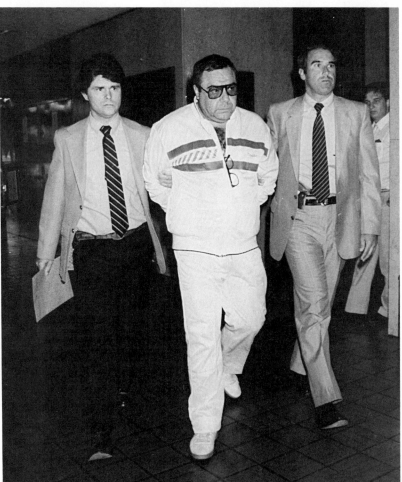

A Wall Street investment broker after being sentenced to two years in prison and fined $362,000 for fraud, perjury, and tax evasion. Left, member of Gambino Mafia family led from court after indictment on racketeering charges in New York.

Mafia depended on to make its wishes known to legislators and judges."

White-collar crime. While public fear of crime centers on street muggers and burglars who threaten our lives and property, the cost of their crimes is dwarfed by the illegal activities of highly respectable people in business, government, and the professions. During the mid 1980's scholars and various law enforcement and other government agencies estimated that street crimes, such as auto theft, robbery, burglary, and larceny, resulted in $4 billion in lost property. In a sharp contrast, the annual cost to victims of *white-collar crime* — dishonesty by business people, public officials, corporate officials, doctors, and lawyers, among others — was estimated to be as much as $200 billion. In addition, an estimated 30 percent of business failures each year are attributed to employee dishonesty.

Some of the most common white-collar crimes are tax evasion, bribery, false advertising, embezzlement (stealing from employers), and, as the following example shows, consumer fraud. In the 1960's, people who bought a product made by the Dr. Madis Laboratories in Hackensack, New Jersey, thought they had purchased a medication that would induce vomiting in a child who had swallowed poison. Unknown to them, however, the laboratories had found that they could substitute a chemical called *ephedrine* for two other essential ingredients. The substitution was 30 times cheaper and increased the product's profitability enormously. It had only one disadvantage: It did not induce vomiting.

Oddly, most Americans judge white-collar criminals much differently than they do other criminals. In a small town, the president of a bank made loans to many business friends who did not bother to pay back the money. At the time the crime was discovered, the bank was short 1.4 million dollars of its money. When the bank president was arrested, leading citizens drew up a petition on his behalf. The petition said that the town "is a finer place to live in because of his progressive and unselfish leadership."

Because people tend to be sympathetic toward "respectable" citizens who break the law, their crimes are punished lightly, if at all. Usually the offenders are let off with relatively small fines that are paid by their companies. Yet a stick-up man who is caught after taking $100 from his victim may get a sentence of from one to 25 years in jail. On the whole, our society is remarkably tolerant of white-collar crime, while it demands stiff penalties for ordinary criminals.

Victimless crime. More than one third of the arrests made each year in the United States are for crimes that have no victims. These include gambling, prostitution, unlawful drug *use*, homosexual activities, and drunken behavior in public. If no one (except, perhaps, the offender) suffers from them, why does our society regard them as crimes? The answer lies in our cultural values. The dominant groups in American society regard these activities as morally wrong. The police themselves often feel that it is futile to try to enforce laws against victimless crimes and sometimes ignore them. Ironically, these laws

In spite of an increase in legalized gambling in the United States, illegal gambling continues to flourish. Some criminologists believe all laws against gambling should be repealed.

help promote organized crime. As already noted, the mob makes its money by supplying the illegal goods and services that many people want and are willing to pay for.

🔊 Some people believe that laws against victimless crimes should be repealed. If this were done, they say, the police and courts could concentrate on more serious crimes.

Do you agree or disagree? Why?

Who are the criminals? At first glance, FBI statistics seem to give us a fairly clear picture of the typical criminal. They indicate that:

• Twenty-one year-olds account for a higher percentage of arrests for serious crimes than persons of any other age.

• Males are arrested far more frequently than females.

• Crime rates are higher in big cities than in small towns or rural areas.

• A disproportionate number of blacks are arrested for serious crimes.

Based on this information, the typical American criminal would appear to be a young male who lives in a city. These statistics also would indicate that blacks, who represent 12 percent of the U.S. population, are arrested for more than their statistical share of crime.

Many sociologists doubt, however, that this is an accurate picture of the typical criminal. They point out that FBI statistics do not include many white-collar crimes such as income-tax evasion, bribery, price-fixing, and embezzlement. If these crimes were included, the typical criminal would certainly become whiter and older.

FBI statistics also ignore all those criminals whose crimes are undetected and unreported. When asked by researchers in one study whether they had ever broken a law for which the punishment was a fine or a jail sentence, more than nine out of ten people answered that they had. Does this mean that there are no distinctions between habitual criminals and usually law-abiding citizens? Of course not. However, the following analysis of the social characteristics of arrested criminals drawn from *Uniform Crime Reports* must be studied with these qualifying factors in mind. In addition, arrest statistics do not give a completely accurate picture of who commits crime, because no one is arrested for many crimes, not all suspects are proven guilty, and some suspects are arrested many times in one year.

Sex. Males are arrested about five times as often as females. Arrests of females outnumber those of males in only two categories — prostitution and juvenile runaway cases. Sociologists believe that there are two reasons why the great majority of those arrested are males. First, our society encourages aggressiveness in males and passivity in females. Second, law enforcement agents tend to deal more leniently with female suspects.

In recent years, however, crime among females seems to be accelerating. From 1960 to 1985, arrests of females for serious crimes rose three times as fast as arrests of males. Between 1981 and 1985, arrests of teenage girls for serious crimes rose one percent versus a nine percent

drop for boys. Most females arrested are charged with larceny-theft.

In Chicago, police once caught a gang of six teenage girls who had terrorized elderly people for months. One of their victims was a 68-year-old man who was brutally beaten. "I was amazed," said police lieutenant Lawrence Forberg. "They were indignant toward their victims. . . . This is the first time I've encountered young girls this tough."

Age. As already noted, about one third of all arrests for serious crimes are of youths who are not yet 18. And more than 55 percent of arrests for serious crimes are of persons under 25. The most likely age for violent crime arrest is 21. The 25-and-under age group accounts for 50 percent of all violent crime arrests.

Race and ethnicity. Statistics indicate that crime rates vary among racial and ethnic groups. Judging from *arrest* records, Asian Americans and Jews have below-average crime rates; while blacks, Puerto Ricans, Mexican Americans, and Native Americans have above-average crime rates. In 1985, 27 percent of all those arrested were black. However, many sociologists do not take these statistics at their face value. One reason for them, they say, may be prejudice. Some law enforcement agents tend to see members of some minority groups as potential criminals. As a result, more of them may be arrested. Another reason may be that a great many minority group members are poor and live in slums, which have always bred crime and violence. In the past, poor immigrant groups from Europe living in city slums also had high crime rates.

Among middle-class blacks and Puerto Ricans today, the crime rate is as low as it is for middle-class people from any other ethnic group.

Social class. Most people who are arrested for assault, robbery, and burglary come from the lower social and economic groups. This is especially true among juvenile offenders. Arrest statistics show that the great majority of juvenile delinquents are poor males. Does this mean that middle-class juveniles generally do not commit crimes? Sociological surveys have found that young members of the middle class probably commit more crimes, including thefts and assaults, than arrest records show. But middle-class delinquents are much less likely to get arrested than their poorer counterparts. Why is this so? In making arrests, sociologists say, the police are strongly influenced by the race, appearance, and attitude of juvenile offenders.

One sociologist, William Chambliss, carefully observed two teenage gangs in the same town. One gang was middle class, the other was lower class. Both were white. The middle-class gang, whom Chambliss called the "Saints," was constantly involved in truancy, drinking, wild driving, petty theft, and acts of vandalism. Yet not one Saint was ever arrested during the two years that Chambliss observed them. To the community and the local police, they were basically "good" boys who were just "sowing their wild oats." The lower-class gang, whom Chambliss called the "Roughnecks," was equally as mischievous as the Saints. The town, however, looked on these boys as "delin-

A 16-year-old gang leader sheds a tear for his mother upon being booked for purse-snatching.

quents" who were "headed for trouble." The main reason for this double standard, Chambliss said, was that the Saints appeared "apologetic and penitent" when accused of wrongdoing. But in the same situation, the Roughnecks showed "hostility and disdain." Several Roughnecks were arrested a number of times, and two were sentenced to six months in reform schools.

Repeaters. A large proportion of criminals are repeaters. Seven out of 10 adults in the nation's prisons have already been in jail at least once before. This is equally true of juvenile offenders. A study of 10,000 young people in Philadelphia showed that 627 of them became habitual offenders. These 627 were responsible for more than half of all offenses committed by the entire group during a period of eight years.

The challenge of crime in a free society.

"The existence of crime, the talk about crime, the reports of crime, and the fear of crime have eroded the basic quality of life for many Americans." This statement was made in 1967 by the President's Commission on Law Enforcement.

Today, crime's grip on America seems even greater than it was then. "The land of the free and the home of the brave" feels threatened, not by foreign armies, but by criminals who prowl the streets and invade homes, offices, schools, hospitals, and even churches. The fear of crime may be measured by statistics. One poll revealed that nearly seven women out of ten are afraid to go out of their homes at night. Another indicated that more than half the families in America keep guns for their personal protection. The fear of crime is reflected in streets that are deserted after dark; in shop windows that are covered by heavy iron grilles; in apartments whose doors are locked, chained, and bolted.

Americans are taking extraordinary measures to protect themselves against criminals. "We're getting a lot of nice upper-class couples who are buying pistols," said the manager of a gun and sporting goods store in Franklin Park, Illinois. About 40 percent of the store's customers are female and include young working women as well as elderly widows. Women are also arming themselves with tear-gas fountain pens and cans of oven cleaner that contain lye.

More and more Americans are equip-

Fear of crime has turned many American homes into armed fortresses.

ping their homes with electronic burglar alarms that cost from $300 to several thousand dollars. A typical system fits miniature radio transmitters to all the doors and windows of a house. When tripped, they blow sirens, flash on floodlights, and trigger calls to an office which then relays them to the police. Seven percent of American homes are now equipped with burglar alarms.

Protecting society from crime has become a big business. American citizens have spent about $51 billion in a year for private anticrime measures such as alarms, iron window bars, private security guards, and video cameras.

Some Americans are forming groups for self-protection. In a few neighborhoods, residents armed with clubs are patrolling the streets at night. In one Chicago neighborhood, an organization composed of 22 blacks, half of them Vietnam veterans, has sworn to eradicate crime in their area by any means. One of them said: "Folks dealing in dope get their doors kicked in and their junk messed up. When we find someone doing wrong, we wear him out."

As long as government agencies are unable to provide adequate protection against crime, it is understandable that people seek protection in locks, guns, alarms, and guards. But as Americans turn their homes and offices into fortresses, what becomes of the "land of the free"?

≈§ Would you say that citizen fear of violent crime in your neighborhood is high, moderate, or slight? What evidence can you give to support your answer?

What Causes Criminal Behavior?

Sociologists who study crime have developed a number of theories by which they seek to explain the causes of criminal behavior. In this section, we will explore four broadly based explanations for crime — none of which explains all crime.

Societal characteristics. While no sociologist would ignore the influences of a society on the criminal behavior of its population, some place more emphasis on the effect of these forces than others. Four social characteristics that have been linked with high crime rates are:

Political freedom. The more freedom a society has, the more likely it is to have crime. Repressive societies, whether Communist or right-wing dictatorships, are likely to have much less crime than we do, but they also have much less individual liberty. In such countries, punishment for crime is very severe.

Racial and ethnic diversity. The presence of many racial and ethnic minorities in a country is usually linked with a high crime rate. Members of minority groups often feel "left out" by the dominant group. In anger or despair, some turn to crime. Japan, a nation that has few ethnic minorities, has a relatively low crime rate. It is the only industrial society where crime is actually declining.

Unemployment. A high rate of unemployment is often linked with crime. Teenagers are affected most in the U.S. In 1984 about 50 percent of black teenagers who were looking for work in this country were unable to find it. Many sociologists say that a person without a job or hope for the future is more likely to turn to crime than someone who has a stake in society. Sociologist Norval Morris places the blame even more squarely on society's shoulders: "It is trite but true that the main causes of crime are social and economic."

A "young" population. Changes in a population also affect crime. The "baby boom" that took place in the United States after World War II, for example, greatly increased the number of young people. In 1950 there were 24 million Americans between the ages of 14 and 24. By 1985 there were about 46 million in this age group. Young people, as we have seen, commit a high proportion of such crimes as burglary, larceny, and auto theft. In 1985, 51.2 percent of those arrested in this country were under 25.

Can you think of other social forces that might contribute to crime? Name as many as you can. What probable impact will the "baby bust" described in Chapter 10 have on crime rates?

The classical school's view. A time-honored cliché in our society is that "crime doesn't pay." Many criminologists, however, no longer accept this. The rewards of a criminal "career," they maintain, are far greater than the risks of punishment. It is only natural, therefore, that many people pursue a life of crime. This view was first expressed in the 18th century by two writers, Cesare Beccaria and Jeremy Bentham. They claimed that people are rational and prefer to do things that give them pleasure rather than pain. If the cost (or pain) of punishment outweighed the profit (or pleasure) of crime, people would not break the law. The way to decrease crime is to increase the certainty and the severity of punishment. This theory is called the *classical view of crime.*

Social scientist James Q. Wilson and others who support this view today cite the following evidence: In 1985 the FBI reported that arrests were made in about 47 percent of reported violent crimes and in 18 percent of reported property crimes. Of adults arrested, 80 percent were prosecuted. Sixty-eight percent were found guilty as charged. Eight percent were found guilty of a lesser offense. And 24

percent were either acquitted or the charges against them dismissed. Disposal of charges against juveniles is much harder to check because procedures vary widely. However, the FBI reports that about nine out of ten juveniles arrested are either released without formal charges or are referred directly to juvenile authorities.

Clarence M. Kelley, a former director of the FBI, said: "Criminals feel that the odds are largely in their favor. . . . Crime statistics plainly tell us that a high percentage of the criminals beat the risk. They are able, for a variety of reasons, to make a profit out of their crimes."

When criminals are sent to prison, social scientists disagree about the best way to prevent them from committing more crimes. In the cartoon below, which figure represents the classical view?

Copyright © 1988 Colorado Springs Sun

Merton's theory of goals and opportunities. Sociologist Robert Merton believes that the seeds of crime lie in the emphasis that our society places on upward mobility while at the same time denying many people the opportunity to achieve that mobility through socially accepted ways. Most people, Merton says, are imbued by our society with the desire to become wealthy or, at least, to reach middle-class status. As one young mugger with a drug habit put it: "Wow, I'd like to be richer than the Rockefellers! I'd have a Cadillac and a chauffeur. I would go the whole route and get a Rolls-Royce too. I would have a diamond ring for each day of the week. I would change clothes three times a day, and I'd have a whole lotta homes. . . ."

From Merton's point of view, first published in 1938, this young man has acquired the goals that our society promotes with little chance of achieving them outside a life of crime.

Merton notes that this conflict between society's goals and opportunities for achieving them is particularly prevalent among minority group members who are often severely handicapped by poor education and discrimination. Minority youths often feel frustrated by their inability to get jobs that will enable them to attain "the good life." Unable to "make it" by socially acceptable means, many of them turn to crime. They believe that it is the only possible way for them to achieve "success."

A prominent black writer, Claude Brown, author of *Manchild in the Promised Land,* supports Merton's theory of crime.

In an article for a national newspaper: Brown wrote:

"To place a poor man in an affluent society, indoctrinate him through all the various mass-communication media of modern technology and Madison Avenue ingenuity to aspire to an abundance of luxuries and comforts (the American Dream) he'll never be able to afford, and then bid him not to steal, is the epitome of absurdity. Nevertheless, this is what the American Establishment imposes upon the minorities who populate — or, more precisely, overpopulate — the Harlems of America. . . ."

Merton's theory, of which we examined only one part, deals with *why* people become criminals. The next theory we will discuss deals with *how* criminals are made.

Cultural transmission theory. During the 1920's, sociologists Clifford Shaw and Henry McKay studied high-crime neighborhoods in Chicago. They found that although the racial and ethnic character of these neighborhoods had changed many times, the crime rate remained consistently high. Shaw and McKay's explanation was that newcomers to these neighborhoods learned criminal ways from those who already lived there. They called this process *cultural transmission.*

Another sociologist, Edwin Sutherland (1883-1950), tried to explain how both criminal and law-abiding behavior are transmitted through a culture (or subculture). According to Sutherland, everyone is exposed to different definitions of right and wrong behavior. A young person, for example, may find his parents endorse one kind of behavior and his friends another. Sutherland believed that a person who spends a great deal of time in intense contact with people who endorse criminal behavior is more likely to become a criminal than a person who often associates with law-abiding citizens. Sutherland believed that white-collar crime, as much as other forms of crime, can be learned through this process. In his book, *White Collar Crime*, Sutherland quoted a used-car salesman who seemed to demonstrate his theory:

When I graduated from college I had plenty of ideals in honesty, fair play, and cooperation which I had acquired at home, in school, and from literature. My first job after graduation was selling typewriters. During the first day I learned that these machines were not sold at a uniform price but that a person who haggled and waited could get a machine at about half the list price. I felt that this was unfair to the customer who paid the list price. The other salesmen laughed at me and could not understand my silly attitude. They told me to forget the things I had learned in school, and that you couldn't earn a pile of money by being strictly honest. When I replied that money wasn't everything they mocked me: "Oh! No? Well, it helps." I had ideals and I resigned.

It was quite a time before I could find another job. During this time I occasionally met some of my classmates and they related experiences similar to mine. They said they would starve if they were rigidly honest. All of them had girls and were looking forward to marriage and a comfortable standard of living, and they said they did not see how they could afford to be rigidly honest. My own feelings became less determined than they had been when I quit my first job.

Then I got an opportunity in the used-car business. I learned that this business had more tricks for fleecing customers than either of those I had tried previously. Cars with cracked cylinders, with half the teeth missing from the flywheel, with everything wrong, were sold as "guaranteed." When the customer returned and demanded his guarantee, he had to sue to get it and very few went to that trouble and expense. . . . If hot [stolen] cars could be taken in and sold safely, the boss did not hesitate. When I learned these things I did not quit as I had previously. I sometimes felt disgusted and wanted to quit, but I argued that I did not have much chance to find a legitimate firm. I knew that the game was rotten but it had to be played — the law of the jungle and that sort of thing. I knew that I was dishonest and to that extent felt that I was more honest than my fellows. The thing that struck me as strange was that all these people were proud of their ability to fleece customers. They boasted of their crookedness and were admired by their friends and enemies in proportion to their ability to get away with a crooked deal; it was called shrewdness. Another thing was that these people were unanimous in their denunciation of gangsters, robbers, burglars, and petty thieves. They never regarded themselves as in the same class and were bitterly indignant if accused of dishonesty; it was just good business.

Once in a while, as the years have passed, I have thought of myself as I was in college — idealistic, honest, and thoughtful of others — and have been momentarily ashamed of myself. Before long such memories became less and less frequent and it became difficult to distinguish me from my fellows. If you had accused me of dishonesty, I would have denied the charge, but with slightly less vehemence than my fellow businessmen, for after all I had learned a different code of behavior.

◆§ Do you think Sutherland's theory adequately explains this man's behavior? If so, how? If not, can you think of other explanations?

Cultural anthropologist Walter Miller applied Sutherland's insights about criminal behavior to juvenile gangs in high-crime neighborhoods which he studied during the 1950's. Miller identified several values or "focal concerns" of poor urban culture which he believed were learned and adopted by the juvenile gangs. Among them were:

1. *Toughness.* An emphasis on physical strength.

2. *Smartness.* The ability to "con" others and not be "conned" oneself.

3. *Excitement.* Getting one's "kicks" to relieve the drabness of ghetto existence.

4. *Autonomy.* A resentment of any controls. It is often expressed in the sentence, "Nobody's gonna push *me* around."

5. *Fate.* A feeling that many forces are beyond one's control, and that "luck" plays a large part in life.

Do you believe these values might lead to criminal behavior? If so, how?

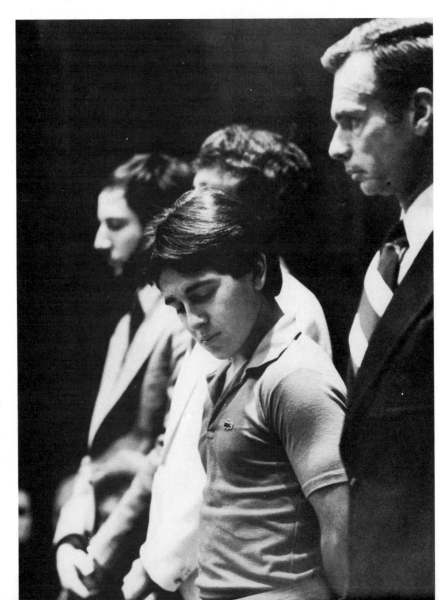

Convicted murderer Ronnie Zamora, 15, claimed in his defense that television was to blame for his criminal actions.

What Can Be Done About Crime?

Changing the social environment. Anthony V. Bouza is Commander of the New York Police Department in the Bronx, a borough of New York City. An interviewer for WNET-TV talked with Chief Bouza on a program called "The Police Tapes." This excerpt from the interview supports the theory that the main causes of crime lie in the social environment:

. . . We have a subculture in our society, and it resides in the ghetto. And we are conditioning that subculture, and their [the residents'] reaction is very predictable. B.F. Skinner would have no difficulty identifying what is happening there. We are conditioning people to fail. We are conditioning people to become alcoholics. We are conditioning them to be violent. And we give them no other mechanisms with which to cope.

There is nothing inevitable about it. It is a process that is taking place because of forces that are conditioning this response, just as forces are conditioning my response to educate my children effectively — make sure they get a good education.

I pay my mortgage, pay my taxes. I resolve my disputes with my wife or my colleagues through communications. In the ghetto I'd be stabbing and punching and kicking and scratching and doing everything else that everybody else is doing — simply because I'm a human being, and I'm conditionable. . . .

The levels of rage and frustration have created an emotional gorge that people are permanently endowed with in the ghetto. So it may take quite a while for me to get you angry enough to be violent; if you were walking around with an emotional gorge up to here, it would take only another fraction of an inch to get you to respond.

And that's really what is happening. The frustrations that I'm talking about: the heat, the misery, the lack of rest, the whole miserable condition of poverty. And Aristotle did say 2,500 years ago that poverty is the parent of revolution and crime. It is still true. And when you're going around with those levels of frustration and permanent anger, and you don't even know what you want, the first available target becomes the focus of the violence.

America attacks the problems that it sees. It doesn't see these problems. They're now under the rug. The fact is that we have ignored them. They are being more ignored now than they ever have been. They're [ghetto residents] poorer than they ever have been. There hasn't been a significant redistribution of income in this nation for 30 years. The bureaucracy and the government are failing, and fundamentally, the federal government has simply got to look at what is happening in the city ghetto and address it. And one of the reasons it hasn't done so is that no one is filming it, no one is writing about it, no one is doing stories about it. It is just invisible, and if you go out into the streets of the Bronx, you will see a lot of black and Hispanic energetic young men and women all dressed up, no place to go, nothing to do, no jobs, no point in living, and seeking any form of escape that they can find, whether that form is drugs or alcohol or whatever. . . .

To the degree that I succeed in keeping the ghetto cool, to the degree that I can be effective — to that degree, fundamentally, am I deflecting America's attention from discovering this cancer? And the longer the discovery is deferred — as in Vietnam — the greater the moral dilemma, the greater the moral problem when it is ultimately discovered. So maybe I would be better off failing. Maybe I'd be better off not working quite so hard. Maybe I'd be better off not being as effective as I presume myself to be.

Do you agree with Chief Bouza that poverty is the parent of crime? If so, which of the following would you endorse?

Better housing?

An end to racial and ethnic discrimination?

Guaranteed employment for anyone willing to work?

Guaranteed minimum income?

Widespread job training?

Something else?

Increasing the certainty of punishment. Others believe that the way to deter crime is to increase the certainty of punishment. They point to statistics that show that few habitual criminals serve time in prison for many of the crimes they commit. One study showed that an adult burglar has only one chance in 412 of going to jail for any single job. Among juveniles, there was one chance in 659 burglaries.

A number of other studies have shown that when a high proportion of people charged with a certain crime were imprisoned, the incidence of that crime tended to be low. Conversely, when the rate of imprisonment was low, the crime occurred more often. In the United States, for example, drunken driving is common. In Norway, it is rare. The difference, according to some criminologists, is that Norwegian courts always impose a prison sentence for driving under the influence of alcohol.

Violent juvenile crimes would also be reduced if stiffer penalties were handed out, say some sociologists. This view is shared by many law enforcement agents.

In a Miami courtroom, a defendant is sentenced for drunk and disorderly conduct. Some sociologists say that the only way to curb such offenses is to change the social environment.

"The laws have to be changed," said one New York City detective. "The idea [of juvenile courts] was to protect kids who had minor skirmishes with the law from getting a record. This kind of treatment was not made for 14- and 15-year-old kids who are killers."

Some officials believe the solution is to enact stiffer penalties for juvenile crimes. New York City courts began handing out five-to-ten year sentences to juveniles for mugging elderly people. Arrests for this crime dropped 40 percent. Another law permitted 13, 14- and 15-year-olds charged with serious crimes to be tried in adult courts. In New Orleans juvenile laws were enacted to send violent repeaters to jail. In two years murders by juveniles dropped from 29 to 5. "If you take a career criminal off the streets," said a district attorney, "his peers get the message. They do not want to follow him."

Many law enforcement agents also want to see stiffer penalties for white-collar crimes. Bigger fines and more frequent prison sentences would, they say, do much to deter "respectable" criminals. A top law officer said: "People should insist on the same strict enforcement of the law for business and government officials who break the law that they demand for those without status. They ought to be as outraged when bilked by corporation fraud or government corruption as they are when assaulted or robbed by a stranger. . . ."

Other authorities emphasize the need to reform the system of sentencing criminals. Judges, they say, differ greatly in their views of various crimes. In 1975, for example, 50 judges were given the facts

about 20 actual cases and asked what penalty they would impose in each. In one case, the defendant had been found guilty of being a drug-pusher. One judge said he would put him on probation. Another said he would sentence him to five years in prison. A second case involved a union official who was convicted of extortion. One judge said he should serve three years. Another judge said he should get 20 years plus a fine of $65,000. Some judges try to avoid the problem of how long to send a criminal to jail by giving him an "indeterminate" sentence. This leaves it up to a parole board to decide when the criminal may go free.

Some critics of the criminal justice system say that it would be improved by "flat-time" prison sentences. This means that each crime would have a specific penalty. Let's say, for example, that the penalty for armed robbery was set at eight years in prison. Judges would then give all defendants convicted of armed robbery the same sentence — eight years. Flat-time sentences would be mandatory — judges would *have to* impose them. No one convicted of a crime would be allowed to go unpunished.

Sociologist Marvin Wolfgang believes that society should concentrate on identifying and convicting criminals who have committed three or more offenses. Some criminologists say that repeaters are responsible for two thirds of all violent crimes in the United States. Wolfgang recommends that they should be "incapacitated" — imprisoned for long terms so that they cannot harm society for the duration of their sentences.

Does punishment really deter criminal behavior? Many sociologists believe that it has little effect. They point out, for example, that during the 18th century, picking pockets was a crime punishable by death. Apparently, few pickpockets were deterred by the threat of such severe punishment. In fact, they often worked their trade at public executions, picking the pockets of spectators. In a 1959 study, sociologist Thorsten Sellin found that murder occurred just as often in states that imposed the death penalty as in those that did not. He found no significant change in homicide rates after a state had either abolished or restored the death penalty.

⌇ Do you believe that increasing the certainty of punishment will deter criminals? Do you think there are other ways to reduce crime?

Founded in 1853, San Quentin is California's oldest and largest prison. Located on San Francisco Bay, it has been the scene of numerous riots.

Rehabilitation. Is the main purpose of prisons to punish criminals? Or is it to rehabilitate them? University of Michigan law professor Francis Allen, who studied recent legislation, says that public attitudes shifted in the late 1970's in favor of punishment. This attitude prevailed in the 1980's. Yet many Americans believe that if prisons teach inmates new attitudes and skills, inmates will become law-abiding citizens when they are released.

The rehabilitation record of U.S. prisons is not good. As already noted, about 70 percent of all prisoners are repeaters. Some sociologists say that, far from reforming inmates, prisons are actually "schools of crime." It is there that first-time offenders learn the tricks and attitudes of hardened criminals.

Prison work programs rarely prepare inmates for useful jobs on the outside.

Combatting Police Burnout

"If you're a cop, you're going to burn out. It's that simple," says Ed Donovan an expert on police stress. "The public's expectation of a cop requires that he be all people - police officer, doctor, lawyer, judge, juror, psychiatrist, social worker, ambulance driver, plumber, veterinarian, locksmith, and every other occupation. It's an impossible demand."

America's 500,000 police officers do have demanding jobs. They make a combined total of about 12 million arrests each year. For a policeman, any incident can suddenly lead to unexpected dangers. And, yet, while the public focuses its attention upon the criminals and their victims, very little attention is devoted to helping police officers cope with the unusual stresses of their jobs.

This high stress often leads to burnout. Experts define *burnout* as the loss of physical and mental energy that occurs when people lose their enthusiasm for work. Dr. Jack Seitzinger, director of the Greater St. Louis Police Academy, estimates that as many as 20 percent of a department's officers suffer from such job-related stress.

Although many officers begin their careers with an idealistic hope of reforming society, they quickly discover that their jobs involve a series of unending frustrations. "If you're manning a speed station," one officer complains, "you're not there when your wife is having a baby. If you're delivering a baby in an emergency, they wonder why you're not there to catch the speeders whizzing past them."

Such unrelenting frustration can cause severe depression and fatigue — two major symptoms of burnout. An officer who is tense usually does not turn to his or her colleagues for support. One researcher explains why: "There is a social norm among many police officers that says, 'Thou shalt not have unexplained emotional reactions.' So they spend the bulk of their lives denying to themselves and to others that they have them."

Burnout can lead to a number of costly problems. It can affect an officer's judgment and impair his or her reflexes in critical situations. Experts believe that stress may be responsible for auto collisions and other job-related accidents. But the most significant cost is the loss in effectiveness of many excellent officers. "Many of the people who develop psychological problems are highly trained, highly skilled people in which the department has invested thousands of dollars," noted Dr. Martin Reiser of the Los Angeles Police Department. "They have knowledge and experience that's irreplaceable."

Dr. Reiser and others have begun pioneering programs to help officers combat burnout. Their programs usually begin with a behavioral profile of each officer. Specially trained supervisors use these profiles to spot stress-related problems.

Officers who have developed signs of burnout are asked to join a counseling program which may include family members. In Boston specially trained officers who have experienced burnout themselves help officers facing similar feelings. Program like these can play an important role in helping police officers learn how to cope with the difficult pressures of their jobs.

Thinking Critically

1. What part do conflicting roles play in the frustration experienced by police officers?

2. Why are self-help groups an effective way to help burned out police officers?

Above, a family visit at a Swedish prison.

11:D

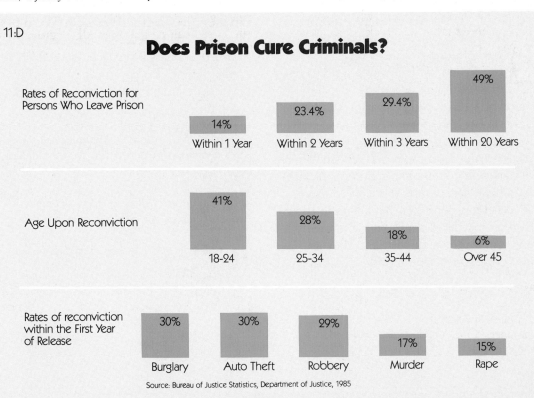

Does Prison Cure Criminals?

Rates of Reconviction for Persons Who Leave Prison

14%	23.4%	29.4%	49%
Within 1 Year	Within 2 Years	Within 3 Years	Within 20 Years

Age Upon Reconviction

41%	28%	18%	6%
18-24	25-34	35-44	Over 45

Rates of reconviction within the First Year of Release

30%	30%	29%	17%	15%
Burglary	Auto Theft	Robbery	Murder	Rape

Source: Bureau of Justice Statistics, Department of Justice, 1985

Most inmates work at dull, unskilled jobs, such as making license plates. One reason is that both unions and businessmen are opposed to prison work that might compete with private industry. Another is that so little money is actually spent on rehabilitation efforts. It costs from $15,000 to $40,000 a year to maintain a criminal in prison. This is more than it takes to send a student to most colleges for one year. However, 95 cents of every dollar spent on prisoners goes toward feeding, clothing, housing, and guarding them. Only five cents goes toward rehabilitation.

Most evidence indicates that long imprisonment does not improve the mental attitudes of inmates. The loss of all freedom, personal privacy, and normal sexual activity imposes terrible psychological strains on prisoners. Dehumanizing conditions cause many inmates to crack, or become embittered. According to many sociologists, prisons don't rehabilitate people at all. On the contrary, they breed hatred of society and turn inmates into hardened criminals.

In Sweden, where people tend to regard most criminals as *victims* of society, many prisons look like vacation resorts. They house fewer than 100 inmates and have no walls or guard towers. Prisoners have private rooms with TV sets and share the use of an outdoor swimming pool, athletic field, and a miniature golf course. What's more, prisoners have keys to their own rooms. They may come or go freely, and entertain female visitors. They are also entitled to a one-month vacation.

The Swedes believe that work and study are the best ways of rehabilitating prisoners. Inmates are taught useful trades and are paid the same wages as workers on the outside. If they prefer, they may go to school. Some attend classes within the prison, but others are allowed to travel into towns where there are more advanced courses. They go on bicycles, unescorted by any guards.

Prison terms are short. Most are for four months. When prisoners are released, they are helped to find jobs and places to live.

There is no evidence from crime rate statistics to indicate that the Swedish system works any better, or any worse, than strict prison systems elsewhere. But the Swedes believe that their system is much more humane than other systems and worth the effort. As one prison official said: "It certainly does no harm, and it might just do some good. Therefore, we are obliged to try it."

Greater citizen involvement. The following article from *U.S. News and World Report* tells of a variety of citizen efforts to combat crime. Do you think any of the projects described would be useful in your community?

In hundreds of cities, large and small, hundreds of thousands of citizens — fed up with high and ever-rising crime rates — have organized to do such things as these:

• Encourage victims to report all crimes — and testify against the criminals who committed them.

• Help the police by patrolling their own neighborhoods.

• Serve as auxiliary police or sheriffs' reserves.

- *Keep watch on neighbors' homes.*
- *Spur reporting of suspicious activities in their neighborhoods.*
- *Teach people how to strengthen the security of their homes and mark their property for identification if stolen.*
- *Educate youngsters to obey the laws and respect police.*
- *Keep watch on courts to spot and seek action against judges who are "soft on crime."*
- *Demand stronger anticrime laws.*

Such aid from citizens is welcomed and encouraged by law enforcement officials who are overwhelmed by the mounting numbers of criminals and dismayed by a national crime total that has tripled in the last 15 years.

The federal government has begun to get involved in the growing citizens' movement against crime. The Federal Bureau of Investigation, for the first time, is promoting citizen participation with experimental programs in four cities. The Law Enforcement Assistance Administration (LEAA) has helped develop a national Neighborhood Watch program that has citizens cooperating with 2,000 police or sheriffs' departments.

But most of the initiative has come from private citizens themselves.

"Citizens are mad," says Sergeant Lee Kirkwood, head of the crime-prevention section of the Los Angeles police. "They see crime rising. They are tired of it. They say, 'Hey, I want to do something about it.' All we have to do is show them the way."

"The size and variety of citizens' groups that are becoming involved in crime control is astounding," says Milton G. Rector, president of the National Council on Crime and Delinquency, a nonprofit, privately financed organization which has councils in 20 states.

Citizens' efforts are beginning to show dramatic results in some places. Orinda, California, reports a 48 percent decrease in burglaries after two-and-one-half years of work by neighbor-hood groups. In Camden, New Jersey, where 2,100 people joined a volunteer patrol program called Towne Watch, nonviolent crimes have dropped 41 percent in two years. In Onawa, Iowa, a community of 3,000 population where citizens have been patrolling streets on foot and in cars at night for eight months, a patrol leader reports that "petty theft has almost come to a standstill."

In many communities, however, results are slow to show up in statistics, and it is a problem to maintain enthusiasm among citizens. Several once-promising efforts have died out because of discouragement or weariness of participants. Apathy is a constant problem. But many community leaders report a recent upsurge in citizen enthusiasm. "Until this last year, apathy caused every program we started to be unsuccessful," says Francis Hawkins, chairman of the Tulsa, Oklahoma, Metropolitan Citizens Crime Commission. "Now we are seeing a change. The environment is more receptive. It's gotten to where you don't just read about crime or burglaries in the newspaper. You hear it from your neighbor next door who tells you it happened to him."

Because of renewed interest, the Tulsa commission is reviving Crime Check, a program calling for residents to watch for suspicious activity in their neighborhood. It is also trying to stir up public support for such things as revision of the bail system that returns many suspects quickly to the streets, sterner sentences for crime "repeaters," and revival of the death penalty.

"Citizen participation is the key," Mr. Hawkins insists. "We're not going to be able to control crime until the citizen gets off his backside and gets busy."

◄§ How much do you think such citizen efforts can limit violent crime? Property crime? White-collar crime? Organized crime?

application

How might the following agents of socialization influence whether or not a person becomes a criminal?
   Family?
   Television?

summary

Are reports of crime in the United States exaggerated by the news media? The most reliable statistics on crime are published each year by the FBI. And they indicate clearly that crime has become epidemic in our society. According to the FBI, the number of serious crimes increased from about 3.4 million in 1960 to more than 12 million in 1985. The problem may be much greater than even these figures indicate. FBI statistics cover only those crimes that are known to the police. Studies show, however, that more than half the serious crimes in this country are *not* reported to the police. Many victims either do not trust the police, or do not wish to bring charges against the offenders.

Crime is the violation of any law. It is sometimes sorted into these four kinds:

1. **Juvenile delinquency.** In most states, crimes committed by people under 18 years of age. About one third of all serious crimes in 1985 were committed by juveniles.

2. **Organized crime.** The business of supplying illegal goods and services to people who want them. This business includes prostitution, gambling, and narcotics. It is dominated by a confederation of criminals known as the Mafia.

3. **White-collar crime.** Unlawful acts committed by "respectable" businesspeople, government officials, and professionals. Some of the most common white-collar crimes are fraud, cheating on income taxes, bribery, and embezzlement (stealing from employers).

4. **Victimless crime.** Violations of laws that are intended to regulate morality. Victimless crimes include illegal drug *use*, gambling, prostitution, adultery, and public drunkenness.

Studies of arrests records indicate that the great majority of criminals are male, and most are young. More than 55 percent of all arrests for serious crimes in 1985 were of persons under 25. Blacks, Puerto Ricans, and Native Americans have above-average arrests rates. Many sociologists believe this may be due to two reasons. First, many minority group members are poor and live in slums, which have always bred crime. Second, many law enforcement agents are prejudiced against some minority groups and arrest their members more often than others. Most people who are arrested for crimes such as assault, burglary, and robbery are poor, regardless of ethnic background. Some sociologists say that certain characteristics in our society — political freedom, racial and ethnic diversity, high unemployment, a young population — foster crime.

Sociologists have many views about the causes of crime. Generally they attribute crime to social conditions, including high unemployment, discrimination, and a large number of young in the population. Sociologist Robert Merton's theory of **goals and opportunities** blames crime on the fact that our society emphasizes material success while it denies many people the opportunities to achieve it by legitimate means.

Another theory about the causes of crime is that of **cultural transmission.** Proponents of this theory say that, the more a person associates with criminals, the more likely this person is to become one.

Some students of crime have another point of view, called the **classical school**. They believe that people engage in criminal behavior because it is highly profitable, and the risk of being punished is small. The way to reduce crime, these authorities believe, is to increase the certainty of punishment. They favor strict enforcement of the law and mandatory prison sentences for all those convicted of crimes.

Does punishment really deter criminal behavior? Other sociologists doubt it. They point out, for example, that murder occurs just as often in states that impose the death penalty as in those that do not. And many sociologists are highly critical of our prison system. They say that, far from reforming inmates, prisons are schools of crime. It is there that first-time offenders learn the tricks and attitudes of hardened criminals.

more questions and activities

1. Explain two methods for determining how much crime there is in a community.

2. In dollars and cents, which type of crime discussed in this chapter takes its greatest toll on our society? Give some examples of different crimes in this category.

3. List three major theories about the causes of crime discussed in this chapter and explain which one you consider the most valid. Give reasons to back up your choice.

4. Obtain the latest copy of the FBI's *Uniform Crime Reports.* Use it to find the latest statistics for the categories listed in Chart 11:A of your textbook. Write them on a piece of paper or the chalkboard. Has the number of these crimes increased or decreased? Has the rate increased or decreased?

5. For one week keep a log of crimes reported in a daily newspaper. For each crime, list what you consider to be the best way to have prevented it. You may list one of the solutions discussed in this chapter or others based on social research but not considered here.

6. Monitor as many television crime shows as you can in one week. List the crimes that are portrayed. Then compare them with what you have learned about the kinds of crime in the U.S. Do the shows give an accurate or a distorted picture of crime in our society? Give examples to support your answer.

7. From a local prosecutor, find out the penalties in your community (or state) for the following offenses: littering, premeditated murder, selling cocaine, forging a check for $5,000, armed robbery, selling contaminated food, driving under the influence of drugs or alcohol, bank robbery, shoplifting, child abuse. Which of these offenses would you classify as folkways? As mores? As taboos?

8. Research and report on group processes such as competition, cooperation, and conflict as they function in the operation of organized crime.

9. Invite to your class a speaker from a group of former prisoners, such as the Fortune Society. Ask this person to discuss the social characteristics of the population of the prison or jail where he or she stayed. What type of resocialization took place when the person entered prison? What norms and values appeared to be important to the prisoners? To the guards? Does the speaker feel that people outside prisons stereotype ex-convicts? If so, how?

10. Debate: Separate systems of criminal justice and corrections should always operate for the handling of juvenile offenders.

suggested readings

Bennett, Georgette. *Crimewarps, The Future of Crime in America.* (Anchor Press/Double-day, 1987.) A thought-provoking discussion of how changes in America's population, economy, and government will affect different types of crime.

Brownmiller, Susan. *Against Our Will.* (Simon and Schuster, 1975; Bantam [paperback], 1976.) A feminist analyzes the problem of rape in our society and why it has been neglected so long.

Eitzen, D. Stanley and Doug A. Timmer. *Criminology: Crime and Criminal Justice.* (John Wiley and Sons, 1985). An overview of the causes of crime and of our criminal justice system.

Erdman, Paul. *The Billion Dollar Sure Thing.* (Scribners, 1973.) The exciting novel of international money markets and financial speculation proves the sociological maxim—that if people define a situation as real, they will act as though it is. Unfortunately, the speculation was illegal as well as lucrative, and the author wrote this novel in jail.

Hunt, Morton. *The Mugging.* (Atheneum, 1972.) An actual case history of a mugging serves as a springboard for an analysis of the causes of crime and the working of the criminal justice system.

Kwartler, Richard, ed. *Behind Bars: Prisons in America.* (Vintage, 1977.) An excellent collection of articles drawn primarily from *Corrections Magazine*. Chapter 6, entitled "Is Rehabilitation Dead?," is especially recommended.

Puzo, Mario. *The Godfather.* (Putman, 1969; Fawcett [paperback], 1977.) A highly readable account of a fictional Mafia family, its values, life-style, and personal relationships.

Silberman, Charles E. *Criminal Violence, Criminal Justice.* (Random House, 1978.) An extensive and provocative analysis of crime and justice in the United States.

Sorrentino, Joseph M. *The Concrete Cradle.* (Wollstonecraft, 1975.) A former gang leader, who became an attorney and a juvenile court judge, explores the causes and possible cures of juvenile crime.

Sullivan, John and Joseph Victor, eds. *Criminal Justice.* (Dushkin, 1987.) A collection of over 50 readings from a variety of popular sources. Topics covered include juvenile justice, police, and the judicial system.

Many Americans lead productive careers well into old age.

chapter 12

aging

Joseph Bartlett had led a long and useful life. And he had many good memories. He could remember when the Indian Territory was opened to white settlers and when there had been an oil boom. But at 81, Bartlett was alone and on welfare. His wife and son had died 10 years before, and his friends were dead too. In the dusty Oklahoma town where he had lived since he left farming to become a barber, there were no social services or medical facilities. Because he had been self-employed, he had no Social Security benefits. And even though he was in pain and had no transportation, Bartlett would not ask for help. "I will make do myself," he vowed.

Bartlett's sad situation is only one of many cited by Dr. Robert N. Butler, head of the National Institute on Aging, in his book, *Why Survive? Being Old in America.* Says Butler:

"The tragedy of old age is not the fact that each of us must grow old and die, but that the process of doing so has been made unnecessarily, and at times excruciatingly painful, humiliating, debilitating, and isolating through insensitivity, ignorance, and poverty."

In this chapter, we will look at some of the problems that plague many of the aged in our society — poverty, poor health, and loneliness. We'll trace some of the causes of the problems of the aged, and we'll suggest some ways that they might be better treated in our society.

The Problem

Economic difficulties. The following interview with a retired man, adapted from *The Boston Globe*, reveals much about the life of old poor people:

The money doesn't go far anymore. I don't buy much meat . . . maybe a little Spam or luncheon meat. That's about it, though. The canned stuff goes further. And it's easier on the buck too.

I get a pension. Not much of a one, though, 'cause I only worked about 12 years at the place. The rest of the time I worked a lot of other jobs. . . . The pension and the Social Security is all I have. And it's tough, I'll tell ya.

I got a book in my kitchen where I keep track of everything I spend. The worst thing a fella in my situation can run into is no dough on the 20th of the month. But what would I do then? Beg? Steal? That's why I have that book.

Eileen gave me the TV and, boy, is that thing a lifesaver. I watch all the baseball on it, the news . . . and the bowling shows. I like the bowling shows. Without that TV, things would be really tough.

Last thing in the world I'd want to do is to be a bother to anyone. And besides, you gotta remember one thing. When you're old and you complain, everybody thinks you're getting soft. Just because you're old, you know.

Many elderly Americans like this man live in or near poverty. Based on 1987 government standards, about 3.5 million elderly Americans had incomes below the minimum needed to buy essential food, shelter, clothing, and medical care. (This minimum is called the *poverty line*. In 1987 it was estimated at $5,787 for a single person and $7,397 for a couple.)

An equal number of the elderly live very close to the minimum. In short, almost six million of the nation's 29 million old people are either poor or near-poor by official standards. Most authorities believe that the government's poverty line figures are much too low to meet the minimum standards of one person or a couple today.

Those who study the problems of the aged place much of the responsibility for their dire economic circumstances on our social policies. In many ways, limited income makes growing old much more painful and difficult than it ought to be. Poverty haunts a larger share of the nation's elderly than of the general population. But there is a hopeful sign: Poverty among the aged is declining faster than that among the rest of the population. This is largely due to sizable increases in Social Security payments and to extended working years. Chart 12:A shows the sources of income for people 65 and older.

One of the main problems lies in the way that our society defines old age. When do people become "old"? Most of us know people in their seventies who are more vigorous and mentally keen than others who are much younger. In 1935 when the Social Security Act was passed, however, 65 was set as the age when people could begin to receive benefits. Gradually, 65 became the age at which people were judged "old." Until recently it was the age at which businesses usually required employees to retire. But for many, old age was still years away. In a 1978 report, the National Council on Aging noted the error of labeling all people over

65 as equally "old." In its *Fact Book on Aging,* it said:

"The many stages of human life are dynamic, not static. There is evolution and change not only between but within life stages. Old age is for many people a phase of life lasting 20 years or more — longer than childhood and adolescence combined. The needs, capacities, and strengths of an older person are fluid, changing, and evolving throughout those last decades of life. Yet, the great difference between the younger aged and the older aged is not typically recognized. The income, transportation, housing, health care, and employment needs of a 65-year-old are vastly different from those of an 85-year-old."

For many years, becoming 65 meant "instant poverty" for about half the population. Suddenly, deprived of a means of making a living, they had to cope with life on a fraction of their former incomes. However, in 1978, Congress passed legislation making it possible for most people to work beyond the age of 65. The law ended mandatory retirement ages for most federal workers and required private industry to allow most employees to work until they are 70, if they choose to. In years to come, this law could go a long way toward easing some of the economic problems that the elderly face.

The main causes of poverty among the aged are:

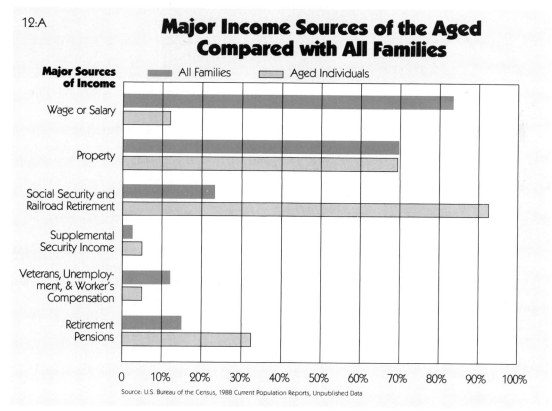

12:A

Major Income Sources of the Aged Compared with All Families

Major Sources of Income — All Families — Aged Individuals

Wage or Salary

Property

Social Security and Railroad Retirement

Supplemental Security Income

Veterans, Unemployment, & Worker's Compensation

Retirement Pensions

0 10% 20% 30% 40% 50% 60% 70% 80% 90% 100%

Source: U.S. Bureau of the Census, 1988 Current Population Reports, Unpublished Data

Job discrimination in one's work life may result in low Social Security payments in old age.

1. *Loss of work.* In 1987 only about 15 percent of those over 65 were still employed. Most were men. As already noted, mandatory retirement rules have been responsible for the loss of most jobs among the elderly. The chances of anyone over 65 finding another job were very slim. Furthermore, many of the jobs open to the elderly are part-time, unskilled, and low-paying. For blacks and members of other minority groups who have had trouble getting jobs throughout their lives, the prospects are even more dismal. In 1984 32 percent of elderly blacks had incomes below the poverty line.

2. *Low Social Security payments.* Social Security is the most important source of income for America's elderly. For nearly one half of the aged, it is the *only* source of income. Although Social Security payments keep millions of people above the official poverty line, at best they provide only a subsistence standard of living. For a large number of retired workers who held unskilled, low-income jobs and widows who receive reduced pensions, Social Security payments are well below the poverty line. More than 11 percent of Social Security recipients also receive public assistance in the form of Supplemental

Security Income (SSI) or food stamps.

3. *Lack of pensions.* Most American workers do not receive any retirement pensions other than Social Security. Although many large companies have private pension plans, employees of small businesses are rarely covered. Pensions depend on length of service and are often minimal.

4. *Inflation.* Rising living costs constantly eat away at the savings and fixed incomes of the elderly. Today, a "nest egg" of $20,000 will buy only half of what it bought in 1948. Apart from home ownership, the majority of people 65 and older have less than $1,000 each in assets. A long illness could easily wipe out their modest savings. Yearly medical costs for the elderly were estimated at more than $3,000 per person in 1987, almost twice the amount needed for people under 65. And Medicare, a federal program of health insurance, only pays about one third of older people's medical expenses.

5. *Fraud.* Elderly Americans are often the victims of dishonest businesses. Rackets involving home repairs, phony investment schemes, and worthless real estate rob many old people of their savings. Dishonest doctors, lawyers, and other professionals also prey on the aged.

Make up a budget that you think would be adequate for a couple in their seventies in your community. Include the cost of food, shelter, clothing, medical expenses. How does your total compare with the government's proverty standard of $7,397? How might you cut this budget if you had to?

Poor health. Apart from an adequate income, the most valuable asset that old people can have is good health. Its importance is illustrated by the following quotation from the book, *Yesterday's Children,* by Patricia Worth Simmons:

I think that the biggest problem that has been with either one of us has been sickness. Ordinarily people after 60, if they had the wherewithal, why that's the time that they travel, see the world, enjoy themselves, and do the many things they've worked for all their lives. Well, that's what we rather figured we'd do. We did do quite a little traveling, till my husband got sick. He hasn't been very well now for the last seven years, and I have a heart ailment that kind of keeps us from doing so many things we'd like to.

My husband has been in the hospital now over eight months. He's getting pretty well worn out with it all. . . . It isn't just one thing. He's had one thing after another.

Poor health has especially severe consequences for the elderly. Often it means:

• The loss of a job with little hope for getting another one.

• Medical expenses that drain their savings with no opportunity to replenish them.

• Withdrawal from social contact.

• Inability to enjoy travel and recreation for which they may have saved.

• Moving out of their homes to those of relatives or to nursing homes.

The extent of health problems. More than four out of five people who are 65 and older suffer from at least one chronic (long-term) illness like arthritis or a heart condition. Chronic illnesses limit the activities of about one third of the elderly, but only about 15 percent are so disabled that they cannot take care of themselves. Surprisingly, the elderly do not get as many acute (short-term) illnesses, like the flu, as younger people. Chart 12:B details the low rate of short-term illness among the aged.

The elderly require more visits to doctors, more frequent hospital admissions, and longer stays in hospitals than younger people. Though they comprise 10 percent of the population, they account for nearly one third of the nation's health expenditures. They are also among the least able to afford major medical expenses.

Doctors who have studied the prob-

lems of the aged believe that many times stress plays a more important role in their illnesses than the aging process itself. And much of the stress that they suffer is the result of poverty and loss of social status.

Treating the old. Unfortunately for the elderly, the medical profession is not geared toward meeting their needs. Most old people, as we have seen, suffer from chronic illnesses. The medical profession, however, focuses on the treatment of acute illnesses. Dr. George Maddox, director of the Duke University Center for the Aging in Durham, North Carolina, states the problem this way:

"We have contrived a system of medicine that does magnificent things for terrible problems, but doesn't deal with chronic illness. . . . We have no cleverness to deal with the medical problems of late life."

As a result, the elderly often receive inadequate or improper treatment. Most general hospitals, for example, have only limited facilities for treating chronic illnesses. Old people are frequently dismissed before they are fully recuperated and able to care for themselves. They must either depend on relatives or enter nursing homes where the quality of treatment may be quite poor. Even Medicare, which was specially designed for the aged, is oriented toward short-term illnesses and accidents.

Doctors who are unfamiliar with the illnesses of the elderly may make incorrect diagnoses. For example, a very sick old man was brought to a hospital in New York. His eyelids drooped, and his hands shook. He wore three sweaters to keep

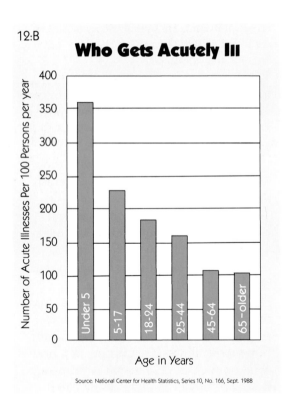

12:B

Who Gets Acutely Ill

Number of Acute Illnesses Per 100 Persons per year

Age in Years

Source: National Center for Health Statistics, Series 10, No. 166, Sept. 1988

warm. When doctors questioned him, he could only mumble. The doctors diagnosed his condition as "a possible stroke complicated by senility." (*Senility* is the loss of physical and mental faculties associated with advanced old age.) His case, they concluded, was hopeless.

Later the man was brought to a hospital that specializes in the illnesses of old age. The doctors there were struck by the fact that he wore three sweaters to keep warm. They suspected that he was suffering from a thyroid deficiency that reduces body heat. A blood test showed that they were right. With daily doses of thyroid hormones, the patient's "senility" cleared up quickly, and he was able to go home.

However, few doctors have the training needed to treat the elderly. In 1976 only two of 125 medical schools gave courses on geriatrics, the elderly. Since then the field has grown. About 50 percent of the country's medical schools have geriatric programs. Yet only about 700 of the half-million practicing doctors consider themselves trained in the field. What accounts for the low number of doctors with such training? Dr. Robert N. Butler attributes it to the following reasons:

1. Doctors find it more exciting to treat acute illnesses that can be cured quickly and dramatically. The treatment of chronic illnesses is often considered both boring and frustrating.

2. Many doctors feel that it is pointless to spend much time treating the elderly. The old, after all, aren't going to be around much longer. The young, however, have many years ahead of them. These doctors try to "brush off" old pa-

tients, but aren't successful. Dr. Butler describes one such case:

"Sam Morris lived to be 102 years old. Near the end of his life he was having pain in his left leg and went to see his doctor. The doctor declared, 'Sam, for Pete's sake, what do you expect at 102?' Sam retorted, 'Look, my right leg is also 102 but it doesn't hurt a bit. How do you explain that?'"

3. Some doctors regard older patients as nuisances. The elderly often need home visits, care after regular hours, and transportation to and from doctors' offices. Many doctors also dislike all the paperwork involved in collecting Medicare and Medicaid payments. (*Medicaid* is a federal and state public assistance program that helps pay the medical bills of the poor, including the elderly.) These doctors may limit the number of patients under Medicare or Medicaid whom they will treat.

⌇ Do you think we should alter our system of medical care to place more emphasis on the care of the elderly? Why, or why not?

Nursing homes. About one million Americans — most of them very aged, white widows — live in nursing homes. They have no other alternative. They can no longer care for themselves. Half have no families to help them. In other cases, families are unable or unwilling to care for them.

For the elderly, entering a nursing home generally is not an easy or a pleasant experience. It usually means the loss of their independence and, often, their

Many elderly people today remain active and creative into late years. They might bicycle to tennis, teach, make violins. The ninety-year-old woman (left) is a photographer.

dignity. Their lives will be tightly regulated by the impersonal rules of the home. Many are depressed by the feeling that a nursing home is simply a place to wait for death.

What kind of care do old people get in nursing homes? During the 1970's, a number of investigations revealed shocking conditions in a large proportion of them. In Chicago, for example, a group of private citizens and newspaper reporters decided to investigate several nursing homes for the elderly. Posing as nurses' aides and janitors, they got jobs in these homes and observed them firsthand. Afterward, they told members of the U.S. Senate Committee on Aging what they had seen. The testimony of one investigator, William Rectenwald, follows in part:

. . . We saw garbage scraped from one tray to another to make meager food supplies go around. We were told to administer drugs and medication within hours after we obtained employment using phony job references that were never checked.

We saw elderly patients struck and kicked because they dared to complain or cried out for mercy.

In one case, an investigator seeking work as a janitor was hired as a nursing-home administrator by an absentee owner who was trying to get the health department off his back.

We saw filth and vermin so overwhelming that in one of the city's largest homes the night staff has surrendered large areas of the building to rats.

I worked in four of these homes and posed as a mentally retarded patient in a fifth. Time after time, I saw the so-called golden years become a grim death sentence in places where nobody cares.

I watched a 91-year-old man, his legs weakened by age, beg for gentle care as two aides attempted to give him a bath. Their response was all too typical of the poorly paid employees of these warehouses for the dying — they slapped him across the face, and he fell into the tub.

Of course, not all of the nation's 23,000 nursing homes are this bad. A few give excellent care, and others provide care that ranges from adequate to good. But all too often, the picture that has emerged from nursing home investigations is one of widespread neglect and mistreatment.

What accounts for the ugly conditions that have been found in so many nursing homes? The chief reason, investigators say, is that most homes are privately owned businesses that are operated solely for profit. If the cost of caring for patients is kept low, a nursing home will produce a high profit for its owners.

Some investigators believe that abuses can be halted by the enforcement of laws requiring nursing homes to maintain decent facilities and services. They also believe that the number of old people in nursing homes should be substantially reduced by setting up community programs that provide health care and housekeeping services to the elderly in their own homes.

Oddly enough, nursing homes were considered a reform for even worse conditions in mental institutions. In 1950, 37 percent of the institutionalized elderly were in mental hospitals. By 1987 less than eight percent were in mental hospitals—because of the trend toward placing those people regarded as "senile" in nursing homes rather than mental institutions.

The right to die. In earlier times, people usually died in their own homes, with their loved ones nearby. Today, 80 percent of all deaths take place in hospitals. In many cases, death is put off as long as possible by machines and drugs developed by medical science. Elderly patients who are hopelessly ill and frequently in great pain sometimes wish they could be spared treatment by these methods. Many would rather die than be kept alive for a few more days or weeks. Dr. Denton A. Cooley, a renowned Houston heart surgeon, has said:

The patients get the treatment all right. They get even more acutely ill. They puke. They bleed. They collect new pains that we gave them. . . .

As a dutiful medical warrior, I am expected to inject poisons into dying people's veins in the name of "chemotherapy," of "sound medical practice." I'm careful to avoid spilling any on my hands, because it burns. I send people downstairs to be bombarded — listen to the language — by isotopes. That's "radiotherapy". . . .

They are denied their right to die in peace, in dignity, at home. With treatment, they often live less comfortably, even miserably, certainly at more expense. But maybe they live a little longer. Maybe not. In some cases, demonstrably not.

Some people believe that patients who are incurably ill should have the right to die peacefully, without life-extending treatment, if they wish it. Others believe that "where there is life, there is hope," and patients should not be allowed to die by having treatment withdrawn, regardless of their wishes. Dr. Alfred Jaretzki of the Columbia University College of Physicians and Surgeons said:

We have all been embarrassed to have individuals who looked as though they had only a few days to live . . . literally pack up their bags and go home and live useful lives for a year or two, or sometimes much longer. . . . This is not just an occasional situation. Doctors cannot help but be influenced by even those two or three that we see in our offices as the years go on, happy, grateful, effective, useful in their families or in their retirement.

What norms and values come into conflict over the question of the right to die? Who do you think should make such a difficult decision? Does your state have any laws regarding this decision?

Loneliness

Widows. One woman whose adult life centered on being a wife and mother told a social worker how she felt after her husband died: "The funeral was over and suddenly I was all alone. No one to shop for. No one to talk to. The loneliness was so awful I thought I'd go out of my mind."

Says another widow: "I don't think anyone who hasn't experienced it can understand the void that is left after losing a companion of so many years. All the little things that come up and you think, 'Oh, I must share that.' And there isn't anyone to share it with."

Of the 28 million people in the United States who were 65 and older in 1984, more than 8 million were widows. As already noted, women in this country outlive men an average of

The Heartache of Alzheimer's Disease

It's 6 A.M. when Jackie walks into Cliff's bedroom. She gently checks to see if he has showered and brushed his teeth before helping him to get dressed for the day. "Want to put your T-shirt on? Hon, are you ready?" asks Jackie.

Cliff is a 58-year-old mechanical engineer who worked on the nose cone for the Atlas rocket. Today he cannot even add up simple figures. When asked what he wants for his birthday, Cliff says, "I wish I could have my brain back." He suffers from an incurable brain disorder known as Alzheimer's Disease, or AD.

Between 2.5 and 3 million Americans suffer from AD, not counting the millions of relatives and friends who share in the pain. One in every five Americans over age 80 has AD, but it is not solely an "old-person's" disease. It can strike in the 40's. It shows no favoritism — AD can hit people of all ethnic and socio-economic backgrounds.

AD is a two-fold disease. First, the mind gradually dies — knowledge of simple tasks disappears, cherished memories vanish, even the names of loved ones fade away. Then, after a decline of 6 to 20 years, the body dies. In total, the disease claims more than 120,000 lives each year.

The financial and personal burdens of living with AD can be devastating. A year of nursing home care costs up to $20,000. Even those with medical coverage might be turned away because AD patients are "too much trouble." Keeping AD victims at home means special gates on stairways and signs labeling such things as "bathroom," "kitchen," or "hot water."

To find a cure for AD involves unlocking the secrets of the brain. Research has shown that people with AD have certain chemical and vitamin deficiencies, which may be the source of the problem. Scientists have also discovered tangled nerve endings in the brain tissues of AD victims. Whatever the cause, AD accounts for over 50 percent of all senility.

Doctors and scientists have labeled AD "the disease of the century." As the tremendous bulge in the American population — the baby boom — ages, more people will become afflicted with AD. Research grants by the federal government and the National Institute for Aging have climbed well above the $70 million mark.

Within just the past few years, scientists have turned up valuable clues about memory loss. Drugs that offset the destruction of brain cells seem to slow down the disease in its early stages. Meanwhile, doctors continue their work to uncover the causes of AD. For victims and their relatives, the current solution is to keep the Alzheimer's tragedy in the public mind, so that there is no letdown in research.

Thinking Critically

1. What are the implications of Alzheimer's disease for the family? How does it alter relationships?

2. Alzheimer's has been called the "disease of the century." Do you agree?

seven years. Because they usually marry men who are older than themselves, they frequently are destined to spend the last years of their lives alone.

Adjusting to widowhood is difficult for young women, but for the elderly, it is much more so. Many older women — especially white, middle-class women — have been socialized to believe that they have no lives outside of their families, yet they feel unwanted in the homes of their children. They are forced into a life of independence for which they are ill-prepared. Their greatest need is to find new roles for themselves, yet they are considered "too old" to enter the job market. And for black women who may have worked in menial jobs all their lives, the situation is even worse. Black widows have the lowest income of any category of the elderly.

Widowers. For men who have lost their wives, the emotional problems of making a new life may be even more difficult. Inexperienced at preparing meals, most suffer from poor diets. Smoking, drinking, and lack of exercise result in serious illnesses for many of them. Their capacity for survival is very poor. The death rate for widowers between 45 and 64 is twice as high as that of married men in this age group.

Many elderly widowers live alone in single rooms in cheap, often rundown hotels. They are called *SRO's* — *single room occupants.* Most have no families or friends, and are quite poor. Many are disabled by illness. The following story, adapted from *The National Observer,* describes the plight of one of them:

Ray considers himself healthy despite a hip injury that keeps him from standing or walking except briefly. Somehow, Ray lives on a disability check of only $70 a month, $60 of which goes for rent. He says he pays $4 for $44 worth of food stamps. That leaves him $6 a month "to blow."

"I'm not an old man," says Ray. "I'm only 56, but as far as this industrial world is concerned, I'm old. I'd rather be working, but because of my hip I can't even go out and watch a parade."

A dozen or more paint-by-the-numbers canvases lie around Ray's room. They are his major occupation, and he works on several at a time. "You gotta have something to do," Ray explains. "You can't sit around here all day or you'll go crazy. I don't have a TV, and there's nothing on the radio but a bunch of arguments."

Ray has lived all his life in St. Louis, the last six years in his present room. "I was married," he says, "but my wife died. In fact, two of my wives died. I decided I'd better quit getting married."

Ray doesn't mix with the other SRO's in his hotel. "I don't like for people to ask me where I'm going or where I've been," he says. "If somebody asks me where I'm going I say, 'What do you care? You're not going with me.'"

Why It's Hard To Be Old

More older people. In 1900 three million Americans, or one in 25, were aged 65 and older. In 1987 there were 29 million Americans in this group, or one in 10. Aged Americans are the fastest growing group in the population. The great rise in the number of old people and in their proportion to the young is due to several forces. Among them are:

1. Modern medicine has increased the average life expectancy from 47 years in 1900 to 74.7 in 1988.

2. The group of people now reaching and passing 65 is largely due to high birthrates in the late 19th and early 20th centuries. This group was also swelled by pre-World-War-I immigrants.

3. Since the 1920's, the birthrate in the United States has declined, increasing the proportion of elderly to young.

4. Immigration declined after World War I, further slowing the growth in the number of young people.

Demographers predict there will be two letups in the steady rise in numbers of the aged. These will occur when the small groups of Depression and World War II babies turn 65. But between 2010 and 2020, when the "baby boom" generation turns 65, the elderly population is expected to increase to 43 million, or 15 percent of the total. By 2030 the aged should reach 20 percent of the total and remain steady. This projection assumes that the birthrate will remain low and that no major breakthroughs will be made in the treatment of heart disease, cancer, and other major killers. Cures for one or more of these diseases would raise the number and proportion of old people significantly.

Ageism. In Japan, old people traditionally have been highly respected. The Japanese consider it a natural duty to care for elderly parents. Three fourths of all people who are 65 or older live with their children. The elderly remain highly productive, helping with housework, gardening, and, at times, the family business. The government awards them medals for attaining certain ages. And they traditionally receive the seat of honor, the deepest bows, the best clothes, and the first dip in the family tub. Throughout the Orient, to neglect one's parents or to leave them in the care of strangers has been considered a disgrace to the family name. (In recent years, however, as Japanese society has become more industrialized and the Japanese elderly have lost much of their land, they have also lost some of their power and prestige.)

In contrast, the elderly are frequently derided in the United States. How often have you heard old people described as "old fogeys" or "geezers"? How often have you heard that they are "out to pasture" or "finished"? These common descriptions reflect a widespread prejudice against the elderly in our society. Dr. Butler has coined a new word for this prejudice — *ageism*. In *Why Survive?*, he defines it as follows:

"Ageism can be seen as a systematic stereotyping of and discrimination against people because they are old, just as racism and sexism accomplish this with skin color and gender."

What accounts for the prevalence of ageism in the United States? Many sociologists attribute it to the high rank we place on a number of values. Among them are:

Youth. Americans idolize youth and hate to get old. The first signs of aging — baldness, gray hair, and wrinkles — often produce panic. Men begin to wear toupees, women dye their hair. When cosmetics can no longer hide wrinkles, some people have face-lifts. "You look much younger than your age" is a compliment that flatters almost everyone who is worried about advancing years. A society that idolizes youth tends to shun or discard the elderly, for they are constant remind-ers that all of us must someday grow old and die.

Independence. The ability to "stand on one's own two feet" is a quality that Americans value highly. We look down on those who cannot take care of themselves, considering them as "parasites" and "moochers." This attitude affects the young and old alike. Many old people feel that it is degrading to accept any help from their children, or fear that it would mean losing their independence. Some value their independence so much that they would rather die than lose it. About 20 percent of all known suicides are committed by people 65 and over.

The work ethic. From earliest times, Americans have been taught that hard work is a virtue and idleness is a vice. Benjamin Franklin expressed the idea

How do these photographs contradict common myths and stereotypes about the aged?

when he wrote in *Poor Richard's Almanac,* "The idle man is the Devil's hireling." In a society that still emphasizes the nobility of hard work, retired people may feel they are of little value to others or to themselves.

Myths and stereotypes. How do you picture old people? Do you see them as mentally and physically feeble, set in their ways, and useless to society? Unfortunately, many people have this image of the elderly. Authorities on aging say that it is a *stereotype* — an exaggerated or oversimplified picture of all old people. Let's look at some of the myths about old people and compare these myths with the truth:

Myth: *All old people become senile.*

Truth: Mental confusion and forgetfulness are *not* necessarily part of old age. Many musicians and artists, among others, have been vigorous and creative in their eighties.

Myth: *All old people are sick.*

Truth: About four out of five elderly people do suffer from chronic illnesses, but only 15 percent are disabled by them. The great majority are able to get along without help. The elderly don't have a monopoly on chronic illnesses. Many young people suffer from them also.

Myth: *Old people are set in their ways and don't like change.*

Truth: The ability to change has little to do with one's age. According to Dr. Butler: "Most, if not all, people change and remain open to change throughout the course of life, right up to its termination. . . . The notion that older people become less responsive to change is not supported by scientific studies."

Myth: *Old people are withdrawn from life and useless to society.*

Truth: Many old people continue to make useful contributions to families and communities, and many are actively employed. In 1984 more than three million people over 65 worked full-time. Many more would work if jobs were available to them. Old people resent the idea that they are useless. One of them told a writer: "I get sick and tired of all this talk about senior citizens and the golden age group. I am not a senior citizen. I am Mrs. G. Cooper, and I will be Mrs. G. Cooper until I die. I do my own work. I take care of my husband, and we are not on charity. I don't want to be placed on the shelf just because I am over 65 years of age, and I do not intend to be. I would like to punch the nose of the next person who refers to me as a senior citizen."

Myth: *Old people have no capacity for sex.*

Truth. A good sex life in youth and middle age is likely to continue into old age. Until recently, our culture scoffed at the idea of sex in old age. As a result, many old people tend to feel guilty about their desires.

What other examples of ageism can you describe?

Changes in the aged population. Not only do the needs and problems of people over 65 vary from person to person, they vary from generation to generation. One noticeable generational difference in older

Americans is their education. In 1965, 23 percent of those 65 and older had completed high school. In 1984 this percentage had reached 47. It was projected that by 1990 one-half of those over 65 would be high school graduates.

As noted in Chapter 7, income and social status tend to increase with education in the U.S. As the aged population becomes better educated and as retirement deadlines advance, more and more old people may be able to contribute to their own support. As equal opportunity laws affect more and more members of racial minorities and women, these individuals may reach old age with more savings, higher income, and higher Social Security payments. Although demographers predict that the ratio of aged men to women will widen to 66 men to 100 women by 1990, it is likely that single women and widows will be better able to support themselves.

What Can Be Done?

Retirement communities. More than a half-million elderly Americans live in "retirement towns" that generally exclude anyone under the age of 50. These communities are relatively new. One of the first, Sun City, Arizona, opened in 1960. It now has a population of 46,000. Retirement towns and villagess are located primarily in Florida and the Southwest where the weather is warm.

Residents of these age-segregated communities like them for a variety of reasons. "I was wild for companionship before I came here," said a 63-year-old resident of Seal Beach Leisure World in California. "Now all I have to do is stand on the patio and yell, 'Coffee!' and six people come running." Like other retirement towns, Seal Beach offers residents free classes in arts and crafts, bridge, and dancing, to name a few. The residents at Seal Beach formed an orchestra and choral group, and put on their own shows. Altogether, they have about 200 clubs, ranging from pinochle players to a group that discusses U.S. foreign policy.

Retirement communities offer residents a number of conveniences. They provide free bus service to shopping centers and entertainment. Many have their own swimming pools and golf courses. Cottages are designed for the safety and comfort of the elderly. Bathrooms have grab bars in tubs and showers, and all electric outlets are high enough to be used without stooping. Some retirement communities have their own medical centers. Seal Beach, for example, has a clinic with doctors and nurses on duty 24 hours a day. Retirement communities also have their own security guards to protect residents from intruders.

For people who are joiners and like to keep busy with friends their own age, retirement towns are ideal. "Heck fire," said one resident, "it's like being on vacation constantly."

But only about one retired person out of 10 can afford to live in retirement communities. And some elderly people are repelled by the idea of being isolated from the young.

Critics of retirement communities

call them "elephant graveyards" where old people wait until they die. "The retirement community," said sociologist Robert Fulton of the University of Minnesota, "is another strategy to cope with death. It segregates and isolates those most likely to die, allowing us to avoid facing the fact of death almost entirely." Other sociologists believe that, for people who prefer to live in them, retirement communities are a useful alternative.

≈§ Do you think you might like to live in a retirement community someday? Why, or why not?

Political action. Older citizens have long been active voters. But not until the 1960's did they begin to act as a pressure group that would make them visible as a power block. The founding of the American Association of Retired Persons (AARP) in 1958 and the National Coun-

In retirement communities, age segregation is voluntary. Some authorities see these usually affluent communities as comfortable havens for the aged, while others view age segregation as unhealthy.

cil of Senior Citizens (NCSC) in 1971 signaled state legislators and members of Congress that the aged meant business.

Lawmakers began to receive a high volume of mail telling how difficult it was to live on a fixed income. The AARP moved to set up a network of lobbyists on Capitol Hill and in each state legislature. From the start, the NCSC allied itself with labor unions.

One of the first signs that the aged were a force to deal with came in 1965 when Congress passed Medicare legislation. This issue put the aged and their allies toe-to-toe against another very powerful lobby — the American Medical Association. And the aged won. Later, in 1967, Congress passed the Age Discrimination and Employment Act which protected people 40 through 64 from discrimination in hiring.

Not until 1970 did a visible leader of this growing social movement emerge. That year in Philadelphia, 65-year-old Margaret E. Kuhn was forced to retire from her job. From then on Kuhn put her considerable energies into forming a more militant group of her peers. Rather than hide her wrinkles, she let them show. "I do not regard wrinkles as hazards but as badges of distinction," she said.

Humorously at first, then seriously, Kuhn and her allies called themselves the *Gray Panthers*. Like the militant civil-rights group, the Black Panthers, they were not satisfied to write letters. They picketed the White House when cuts were proposed in the federal food stamp program. They picketed businesses that discriminated against the aged in their

hiring. And they joined forces with consumer-rights advocate — Ralph Nader.

Although considerably smaller than the three-million-member NCSC and the 11-million-member AARP, the Gray Panthers became the most visible champion of the aged. "Our outrage is properly directed against agencies that purport to serve our needs: nursing homes without nurses, Medicare without a dollar for prevention of illness, retirement homes with admission fees of $10,000 minimum and no say about how our life's savings will be spent," Kuhn said.

In the 1970's, Washington continued to respond to the demands of the aged. The Civil Rights Commission went to work on a report on the effects of ageism; and the Department of Health, Education, and Welfare was assigned to write guidelines to correct them. President Jimmy Carter put an adviser on aging on his staff.

Perhaps the most significant achievement of the aged in the 1970's was the passage in 1978 of legislation to ban or delay forced retirement for most Americans. The bill had attracted little interest until 77-year-old Representative Claude Pepper of Florida started to push for it. Lively and talented, Pepper was a good advertisement for the aged who wanted to keep on working. Said one of the bill's opponents, a lobbyist for the U.S. Chamber of Commerce: "It's such an emotional issue. It's very difficult for any Congressman to vote against the elderly."

And so it was. The bill passed with little dissent. "Old people have come of age as a political force," wrote *The New*

York Times reporter Steven V. Roberts.

Although the problems of the aged were still huge, many people recognized a common interest in solving them. "After all," said Kreal Gilgoff of the NCSC, "we're all going to get old."

≤§ What pressure groups in the United States might have interests that oppose or conflict with those of the aged? Name some and explain your answers.

A longer work life. As noted earlier, Congress in 1978 passed legislation that either delayed or ended forced retirement for most older Americans. Statistics would seem to indicate that this change may go a long way toward easing the problems of the aging experience. Even before the law was passed, there was at least one wage earner in 57 percent of the families headed by someone 65 or older. These families had incomes twice as high as other elderly

families in which no one worked.

Fertil, Incorporated, is a seedling nursery in South Norwalk, Connecticut. Its experience in hiring older workers shows that many people can work well past the age of 65. Fertil's workers — men and women in their sixties, seventies, and eighties — usually put in a six-hour day, but they are allowed to work more or less, if they choose. The company's owner, Hoyt Catlin, is 87. He says he turned to the aged because the young people he once hired were absent too often. He finds his present work force is eager, experienced, and comes to work regularly.

Sociologist Amitai Etzioni has suggested that the aged should be treated according to their achieved statuses of income, physical and mental abilities, and health rather than their ascribed status of old age. One result would be that people could work as long as they are able to do so. Etzioni also suggests allowing

Treating the aged according to their achieved status would allow many capable people to remain productive well past the traditional retirement age of 65.

people to retire as early as 59 if they need to. By widening the retirement-age range, he says, we could ease the shock of leaving work abruptly. Retirees might work part-time or as consultants rather than be forced to make a choice between full-time employment and idleness.

If we treat the aged according to their achieved status, they can receive as much or as little public assistance as they need. In Etzioni's opinion, no one should receive help from the government simply because he or she is old.

✑ Do you agree that financially independent individuals should not receive special assistance simply because they are old? Explain your answer.

application

Apply the seven steps of a social movement described in Chapter 10 to the development of the aged as a political force.

summary

Studies of this nation's 29.8 million people aged 65 and older reveal that a large proportion of them suffer from poverty, ill health, and loneliness. According to U.S. government figures for 1987, the minimum income needed to buy essential food, shelter, clothing, and medical care was $5,787 for a single person and $7,397 for a couple. This minimum is called the **poverty line.** An estimated 3.5 million of the elderly had incomes below the poverty line, and 2.3 million elderly are estimated to have incomes bordering on it.

Social policy may be blamed for many of the problems that beset the elderly, say most authorities. Poverty, they say, has been inescapable for millions of Americans who reached the age of 65. Until 1978 most were forced to retire at this age and live on a fraction of their former incomes. Social Security payments provide only a subsistence standard of living at best, and many retired workers and widows are well below the poverty line. Although private pension plans have been increasing, the majority of American workers are still not covered by them. In recent years, the limited incomes of the elderly have been eroded by sharply rising living costs.

The economic problems of many of the elderly are worsened by heavy medical expenses. Four out of five people who are 65 and over suffer from one or more **chronic** (long-term) **illnesses.** Their medical costs are usually about twice the amount for those under 65. And Medicare, a federal program of health insurance, pays only 43 percent of older people's medical expenses because it focuses on **acute** (short-term) **illnesses.** The medical treatment received by the elderly is often inadequate or improper.

Well-publicized investigations of nursing homes for the elderly have found shocking conditions in many of them. Filth, poor food, and cruel treatment are commonplace. Investigators blame these conditions on the fact that most nursing homes are run for profit. Owners often cut essential services in order to earn high profits.

More and more, the aged are left to cope with life on their own. For elderly widows and widowers, the problem of loneliness is especially acute. Many are ill-prepared to live alone and soon give in to despair. Older people generally need to find satisfying new roles in their retirement years, but our society provides them with little or nothing to do. This discrimination against people on the basis of their age is sometimes called **ageism**.

As the problems of the elderly have increased in recent times, so have their numbers. In 1900 three million Americans were 65 and older. This represented one out of every 25. In 1987 there were 29.8 million aged Americans, more than one in ten. This is partly due to advances in medical science that have extended the average life expectancy from 47 years in 1900 to 74.7 by 1988. The high birthrate of the late 19th and early 20th centuries, combined with immigration prior to World War I, created a huge population which is now elderly. Demographers expect the aged population to increase until about 2030, when one out of five Americans will be 65 or older.

Does old age have to be a time of uselessness, declining health, and loneliness? In Oriental societies, the elderly usually are highly respected and live with their children, who consider it a natural duty to care for them. But in our society, people tend to segregate themselves according to age. In the United States, many older people enjoy living in retirement communities that exclude those under a certain age. These communities offer residents companionship, social activities, and a variety of conveniences. However, most retired people cannot afford them, and some reject the idea of living in age-segregated communities.

To combat the discrimination that so many older Americans experience and to fight some of their problems, some of the aged have turned to political action ranging all the way from letter-writing and voting to picketing. The results of this action have been significant. Medicare legislation and the end of forced retirement for most people are two of an impressive number of their victories. But the problems of poverty, poor health, poor health care, and loneliness remain for many of the aged.

more questions and activities

1. List the three major problems of the aged in our society and tell which is most likely to improve.

2. List four reasons for the great rise in the number of old people in our society and the increase in this group's size in proportion to the young.

3. Explain what is meant by *ageism* and give an example.

4. Find out the size of the aged population in your community. What evidence, if any, can you find of its growing political influence?

5. Using a tape recorder, interview old people in your community about the problems of growing old. You might also ask them what benefits they find.

6. Using the statistical abstract of the United States, prepare a chart or graph showing the growth, since 1900, in the number of people over 65.

7. Find out if your local hospital has a geriatrics unit for older patients. If not, find out where the nearest such facility is located. Interview a doctor or social worker there about the special problems and challenges of treating the aged.

8. Read the *National Geographic* article about the Abkhasians of the Soviet Union listed in the bibliography. Does this article suggest patterns of behavior that might be adopted by U.S. culture? If so, which ones? If not, why?

9. Evaluate retirement communities as an alternative for the elderly. What effects might this kind of voluntary segregation have on their residents? On the younger population?

10. Research the effect of the changes in retirement provisions mandated by Congress in 1978. Do you think these laws are fair to elderly workers? To younger workers?

suggested readings

Butler, Robert N. *Why Survive? Being Old in America.* (Harper and Row, 1975.) An award-winning examination of the problems of the aged in America.

Cox, Harold, ed. *Aging.* (Dushkin, 1987.) An excellent collection of readings on the problems of the aged in America.

Hemingway, Ernest. *The Old Man and the Sea.* (Scribner, 1961.) Santiago, an old Cuban fisherman, shares his feelings about life with a young boy during a three-day hunt for a big fish in this novel.

Hobman, David, ed. *The Impact of Aging.* (St. Martin's, 1981.) A comprehensive collection of articles on the needs of the aged in modern societies.

Langone, John. *Vital Signs.* (Little, Brown, 1974.) A series of dramatic interviews in which people discuss how they feel about their impending death.

Leaf, Alexander. "Every Day Is a Gift When You Are over 100." (*National Geographic*, January 1973.) The Abkhasians of Soviet Georgia are reputedly among the world's oldest people. This superbly illustrated article examines their unique way of life.

Mendelson, Mary. *Tender Loving Greed.* (Knopf, 1974.) A vivid description of the problems in America's nursing homes.

National Council on Aging. *Fact Book on Aging: Profile of America's Older Population.* (National Council on Aging, 1980.) A profile of the health, employment, and housing of America's older population.

Percy, Charles H., and Charles Mangel. *Growing Old in the Country of the Young.* (McGraw-Hill, 1974.) A good introduction to the problems which confront America's elderly population.

Sarton, May. *As We Are Now.* (Norton, 1973.) Seventy-six-year-old Caroline Spencer writes a diary of her life at Twin Elms Nursing Home. An intelligent and sometimes witty novel.

A condemned road in Times Beach, Missouri.

chapter 13

environment

"CAUTION, HAZARDOUS WASTE SITE, DIOXIN CONTAMINATION: STAY IN YOUR CAR, MINIMIZE TRAVEL, KEEP WINDOWS CLOSED."

This grim warning greets all visitors who approach the small town of Times Beach, Missouri. Only people with special business are allowed to travel past the guarded checkpoints which block all roads into the town. Today, Times Beach is a ghost town where abandoned homes and stores line empty streets.

The 2,500 people who once lived in Times Beach remember it as a good place to live and raise a family. The community's troubles began in the early 1970's when Times Beach hired a waste hauler to spray oil on unpaved streets to help control the dust. Delighted children loved to ride their bicycles on the slick oil surface.

Some children slipped on the oil and everyone tracked it into their homes. Unknown to the people of Times Beach, the oilman's truck also contained wastes from a chemical factory. The oil spread on the town's streets contained dioxin—one of the most toxic, or poisonous, chemicals known to science.

The dangerous chemical slowly began to have a deadly impact on Times Beach. Townspeople first noticed large numbers of dead birds. Many of their pets gave birth to stillborn kittens and puppies. Still unaware of the disaster, Times Beach residents noticed that a surprising number of women had tragic miscarriages. A number of other residents were struck with serious illnesses. When investigators from the Environmental Protection Agency conducted tests on the town's contaminated streets, they found dioxin levels 100 times the amount considered harmful for humans.

This news stunned the town. As reports of the disaster spread, some people from the surrounding area refused to do business in Times Beach. In 1983, the Environmental Protection Agency announced a plan to buy out the entire town. "This was a nice place once," one long-time resident sadly explained. "Now we have to bury it."

The Times Beach disaster is part of a difficult and complex environmental problem. American industries produce 300 million tons of toxic wastes each year. Sci-entists have identified at least 10,000 hazardous-waste sites scattered across the entire nation. These toxic-wastes pose a serious threat to our land, air, and water.

Although a pressing concern, toxic chemicals are not the nation's only serious environmental problem. In this chapter, we will also examine the problems caused by air and water pollution, nuclear wastes, and soil erosion. The solutions to these problems are both costly and controversial. In the final section of this chapter we will discuss what scientists and concerned communities are doing to help clean up the environment.

Motorists are warned.

The Problem

In his book, *The Closing Circle,* Barry Commoner describes the nature and importance of our environment:

The environment makes up a huge, enormously complex, living machine that forms a thin dynamic layer on the earth's surface. Every human activity depends on the integrity and proper functioning of this machine. Without the photosynthetic activity of green plants, there would be no oxygen for our engines, smelters, and furnaces, let alone support for plant and animal life. Without the action of the plants, animals, and microorganisms that live in them, we could have no pure water in our lakes and rivers. Without the biological processes that have gone on in the soil for thousands of years, we would have neither food crops, oil, nor coal. This machine is our biological capital, the basic apparatus on which our total productivity depends. If we destroy it, our most advanced technology will become useless and any economic and political system that depends on it will founder. The environmental crisis is a signal of this approaching catastrophe.

Commoner's essential point is that each part of our environment is linked to, and dependent upon, all others. If we damage or destroy any one of them, many others will be threatened. Let us see how pollution endangers our environment and the life it sustains.

Air pollution. In the fall of 1952, London was enjoying clear, cool weather. Many people were taking brisk walks in the sun. In December, however, a heavy mass of clouds settled over the city, and the air became stagnant. Wind meters registered zero. Smoke and fumes from factories, homes, and cars were trapped below the heavy clouds and turned into a thick, yellowish layer of "smog." The poisonous mixture built up and became so dense that people couldn't see in front of them. Drivers were unable to use cars. Pedestrians had to grope along the edges of buildings to find their way. For five days the smog penetrated homes and offices, causing many people to cough and gasp for breath. Finally winds came along that gradually cleared the air, but not before more than 4,000 Londoners had died.

What happened in London is, of course, an extreme case of air pollution brought about by unusual weather conditions. Yet all heavily industrialized, densely populated areas suffer from air pollution in varying degrees. Los Angeles, for example, has a severe problem because it is situated in a valley and the air above it frequently does not circulate. Exhaust fumes from cars and factories become trapped near the ground, creating a smog that stings the eyes. The air of some other cities in the United States is even more polluted than that of Los Angeles, though smog does not develop as readily.

Each year, the United States pours more than 200 million tons of poisonous gases and dust particles into the air. Our country is probably the world's leading air polluter. More than one third of the pollutants come from the exhausts of cars and other motor vehicles. Carbon monoxide, a highly poisonous gas, is the main component of these exhausts. Power plants and factories that burn low-grade coal produce

Heating Up Earth's Climate

Weather Report, Nuclear Autumn, 2030: In the Southwest and West, temperatures continue to soar above 100 degrees. Dangerous levels of ultraviolet radiation persist, as people are warned to stay inside. Water rations remain in effect in California. In the Midwest, swirling dust storms make visibility near zero. Much of the East Coast lies under water as the third hurricane of the season pounds the shores with 25-foot waves. In Alaska, weather remains mild as farmers enjoy a record orange crop.

This may sound like science fiction, but it's based on carefully collected data. It's a scenario for the future if humans continue to pollute the planet's atmosphere. The threat stems from a double whammy: destruction of the ozone layer and the "greenhouse effect."

The ozone layer is a thin blanket of gas that shields earth from the sun's ultraviolet rays. In recent years, synthetic chemicals, known as cholorofluorocarbons (CFC) have begun to bombard — and destroy — the ozone layer. CFCs are used in everything from refrigerator coolants to the materials in plastic cups and mattresses.

When CFCs break down, they rise into the atmostphere and knock out the ozone through a complex chemical reaction. As the ozone decreases, the threat to humans increases. Skin cancer, eye injury, weakening of the immune system, damage to the food chain — these are but a few of the dangers of ultraviolet radiation.

The "greenhouse effect" results in large part from the release of carbon dioxide (CO_2). CO_2 lets in the warm rays of the sun, but keeps heat form escaping — like a greenhouse. The more CO_2, the warmer the earth. In the 20th-century industrial world, humans have produced CO_2 at an unequaled rate by burning fossil fuels such as coal and oil.

Scientists fear the CFCs and CO_2 will drastically change weather patterns. Warmer temperatures will shift winds and storms around the world. Deserts will replace once fertile land. Sea lands will rise as the oceans heat and expand.

Solutions to these problems require global cooperation. It means huge reductions in the use of CFCs and fossil fuels. In 1987, representatives from concerned nations signed an agreement in Montreal, Canada, to cut the production of CFCs by 50 percent by 1990. However, no action has yet been taken to slow the greenhouse effect.

Some scientists warn that if the world does not act soon, it will enter a "nuclear autumn" — a global hothouse of high temperatures and ultraviolet radiation. Are they right? Nobody knows for sure. Meanwhile, the environmental clock ticks.

Thinking Critically

1. How might changing climate patterns affect global society? What new worldwide problems could result?

2. How can the global community stop deadly pollution of the atmosphere?

many poisons, particularly sulfur oxides. When mixed with other chemicals in the air, sulfur oxides turn into sulfuric acid. Other major polluters are home furnaces and waste incinerators.

What harm can air pollution do? It undoubtedly contributes to many illnesses, including lung cancer, bronchitis, and heart disease. According to studies reported in *National Wildlife* magazine, about 21,000 deaths each year are related to pollution from power plants, and another 4,000 deaths are related to automobile emissions. Air pollution blights or kills many other living things. In California, for example, it has killed more than a million trees and caused heavy damage to crops. Polluted air also erodes buildings and statues made of stone, rots house paints, and soils clothes.

Recently it was discovered that fluorocarbon gases used in aerosol spray cans were breaking down the ozone layer that surrounds earth. The ozone layer screens out many of the sun's harmful rays, protecting humans, animals, and plants. The EPA banned the sale of most spray cans containing fluorocarbons after 1979.

∽ Is there a problem with air pollution in your community? If so, try to identify the major polluters.

Water pollution. Like most of us, the million residents of the Ohio River Valley took their drinking water for granted. Then suddenly in January 1988, they found themselves facing a disastrous oil spill which threatened their water supply. A gigantic storage tank at Ashland Oil Company's Floreffe, Pennsylvania, facility near Pittsburgh burst open, spilling 860,000 gallons of diesel fuel into the Monongahela River.

Cleanup crews quickly discovered that their booms and vacuums designed to skim the fuel from the water's surface could not contain the Monongahela's turbulent currents. Instead, the fast-flowing waters broke up the oil slick, enabling it to disperse through the river's depths. Within 24 hours, the oil flowed 23 miles downstream to Pittsburgh's Golden Triangle where it entered the Ohio River.

Closing the river intakes left nearby Robinson Township and North Fayette dry. The pollution also forced more than 70 West Virginia and Ohio towns to impose conservation measures, closing schools and businesses. Luckily, the spill occurred in winter when fish are inactive and many birds fly south. Otherwise, the oil could have destroyed the river's delicate ecosystem.

Oil slicks are not the only threat to our nation's water supplies. The widespread pollution of our rivers, lakes, and oceans takes many forms. Let us take a look at some of the most important problems.

1. *Sewage.* Between 20 and 30 percent of our sewage is dumped raw into available bodies of water. The bacteria in raw sewage makes the water unfit for drinking, swimming, and many industrial uses. Fish in sewage-polluted waters cannot be eaten because they may infect humans with disease. (Many people have become ill with hepatitis as a result of eating contaminated shellfish.) The number and variety of fish also declines.

2. *Artificial fertilizers.* The widespread

Water pollution is not only
dangerous to humans and animals
who swim in such water, it
also endangers drinking
water and the food chain.

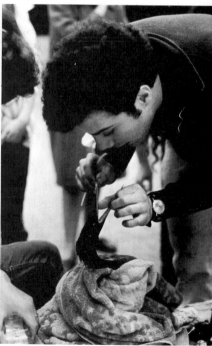

use of nitrate and phosphate fertilizers in farming has had very harmful effects on our water resources. Rain washes large amounts of these fertilizers into rivers and lakes. There they cause huge masses of algae (low-grade plant life) to grow very quickly. When the algae die, much of the oxygen in the water is used up to decompose them. At one time, decaying algae formed a layer of muck 20 to 125 feet deep on the bottom of Lake Erie.

3. *Acid rain.* A phenomena known as acid rain provides a dramatic example of a complex and costly threat to the nation's lakes and rivers. Coal-burning power plants, metal smelters, and other factories in the midwest release tons of sulfer dioxide and nitrogen oxide into the air. These airborne chemicals mix with water vapor and form tiny acid droplets. These droplets eventually fall to Earth as acidic rain and snow.

Recent studies have provided evidence that this precipitation raises the acid levels of fresh-water lakes and streams. The acidity kills fish and threatens plant and animal life. A government report found that 9,000 lakes and 60,000 miles of streams have been affected. As many as 75 percent of the lakes in Rhode Island and New Hampshire and 60 percent of those in Maine and Massachusetts face serious damage unless the problem is controlled.

Experts estimate that acid rain causes about 8 billion dollars in damage each year. It stunts spruce trees in North Carolina and Vermont and has killed bass in New York's once pure Adirondack lakes. The problems caused by acid rain are not limited to wildlife and trees. Acidic pollution weakens the steel in bridges, damages public buildings such as the Washington Monument, and has even caused corrosion of B-52 bombers. One study found that the damage done to homes and other buildings cost each resident of Chicago about $45 a year.

Acid rain has become a source of controversy between the United States and Canada. Canadian officials believe that American industries are responsible for 50 percent of Canada's acid rain. Scientists and political leaders in both countries are trying to find a solution which will control chemical emissions and thus protect the environment.

4. *Overuse of Aquifers.* The United States is blessed with a vast system of underground water. This water is stored in water-bearing rock and underground layers called *aquifers.* For example, the *Ogallala Aquifer* stretches from West Texas to northern Nebraska. This gigantic aquifer contains the world's largest underground reserve of fresh water.

America's aquifers supply half of the nation's drinking water and one-fourth of its irrigation water. Within recent years, ground-water withdrawals have exceeded natural recharge by about 21 billion gallons a day. As a result, water tables are falling and even the Ogallala Aquifer may be depleted in 40 years. The loss of this water would pose a serious threat to agriculture in many western states.

∽§ Is your community water supply clean? If not, try to identify the major polluters.

Land degradation. Recently a Texas farmer recalled the dust storms of the 1930's:

"When those winds hit us, we and our misery were suddenly covered with dust. Here in the Texas Panhandle, we were hit harder than most anywhere else. If the wind blew one way, here came the dark dust from Oklahoma. Another way, and it was the gray dust from Kansas. Still another, the brown dust from Colorado and New Mexico. Little farms were buried, and the towns were blackened."

From the Texas Panhandle north to the Dakotas, great clouds of dust blotted out the sun. On many days, it was necessary to drive with headlights on and to wear protective face masks. The dust seeped through the cracks in windows and the doors of farmhouses despite frantic efforts to stuff them with rags. Everything inside was covered with it. Outside the dust piled up in drifts, burying water holes and killing livestock. Many farmers had to abandon the stricken land; they drove to California to look for work as fruit pickers.

The farmers were not without blame for the disasters that struck them. For years they had ignored the advice of conservationists and had carelessly plowed large areas of thin topsoil. They rarely replanted these areas with grass to hold down and replenish the topsoil. When a long drought came in the early 1930's, the thin crust of topsoil turned to dust, and winds blew it for hundreds of miles. Large portions of Kansas, Texas, Oklahoma, Colorado, and New Mexico became known as the "Dust Bowl" and almost became a desert.

Ironically, after 50 years of research at a cost of 15 billion dollars, soil erosion continues to be the nation's most serious land problem. It takes hundreds of years for nature to produce one inch of topsoil. Yet in some areas topsoil is being lost to wind and water erosion at the rate of several inches a year. According to the Department of Agriculture the nation is losing almost 3 billion tons of soil from its farms each year.

Our land is being despoiled in many ways — by strip-mining, massive road-building, the destruction of forests, and the spread of suburbs into rural areas. Wildlife disappears, the ability of the soil to retain water is diminished, and erosion takes place. Finally the land becomes barren and useless.

The Garbage Crisis. In March 1987, a huge barge left Long Island, New York loaded with 3,100 tons of garbage. The barge headed for North Carolina where its foul-smelling cargo would be transformed into methane fuel. North Carolina, however, refused to accept the garbage. The national press promptly labelled the ship the "garbage barge."

During the next few months, four other states and three countries also refused to accept the trash. After a 6,000 mile voyage, the garbage barge finally returned to New York harbor. Following a long dispute, the rotting garbage was incinerated in Brooklyn and ended up as 400 tons of ash buried in Long Island.

The garbage barge provides a vivid symbol of a growing environmental problem. Americans have the dubious distinction of being the world's leading producer of

The garbage barge in search of a port.

trash. We throw away 400,000 tons of garbage each day. The huge mounds of discarded junk are growing rapidly. Experts predict that by the end of this century, each of us will generate six pounds of garbage a day—twice as much as in 1960.

The problem of waste disposal has deep roots in our history. Archaeologists have uncovered mounds of garbage near the homes of our early settlers. Few Americans paid any attention to the problem because of our vast lands.

Before the early 1960's, most towns burned trash in open dumps or unsophisticated incinerators. The clear-air laws ended this practice. The nation's towns and cities then turned to "sanitary landfills" to hold their waste.

The new landfills proved to be anything but sanitary. Poisonous liquids from household sprays, old oil cans, and rotting food pose a real danger to the surrounding ground-water. Staten Island's 150 foot-high Fresh Kills landfill leaks 4 million gallons of toxic ooze into nearby streams each day. Landfills in Michigan have caused at least 139 cases of ground-water contamination.

Many government officials have tried to solve their waste disposal problem by proposing to build safer landfills. Their plans invariably produce a storm of protest. Citizens' groups, fearful of having a dump located near their homes, have fiercely resisted the construction of new landfills. In New Jersey, angry residents knocked down an official who wanted to locate a waste-transfer station in their area.

While the public battles over what to do with its garbage, the old dumps are rapidly filling up. Half of our existing landfills will have reached their capacity by the mid-1990's. In 1987, there were half as many landfills as there were in 1979. As the problem continued to worsen, the price of waste-disposal began to skyrocket.

How is land used or misused in your community? Are there any problems with erosion? How does your community handle its waste disposal? Are there any programs to recycle waste?

Chemicals. Usually we think of pollution as a highly visible enemy. We see it in smog, dirty rivers and beaches, and ugly dumping grounds. Recently, however, scientists have discovered that thousands of invisible toxic chemicals are deadly hazards to human health. These chemicals are used in pesticides, plastics, fertilizers, detergents, and many other products.

As we have seen, American industries produce 300 million tons of toxic waste each year. Over 10 percent of this waste is buried in thousands of hazardous waste sites located across the country. The Environmental Protection Agency has warned that these dumpsites are "a ticking time bomb primed to go off."

Chemical factories can also pose a serious threat to public health. In December 1984 a cloud of poisonous gas escaped from a pesticide plant in Bhopal, India. Within days, the poison killed over 2,500 people and left thousands blinded and injured. Nine months later a gas leak from a factory in Institute, West Virginia caused over 100 area residents to require hospital treatment.

The tragedies in India and West Virginia have focused public attention upon the dangers of chemical pollution. Solutions will not come easily or quickly. Each year about 1,000 new chemicals are put on the market in the United States. Until Congress passed stringent testing requirements in 1976, these chemicals were not always thoroughly tested before being sold. Sometimes it takes years to discover the harmful effects of a chemical. A chemical compound known as *PCB's* was used for four decades in electri-

cal transformers, fluorescent light fixtures, and various other products. In the 1960's, traces of this compound were found in human tissues, in fish, and in many lakes and streams. It showed up in penguin eggs in Antarctica and in animals captured in Greenland. How was it possible for PCB's to spread to remote places of the world and contaminate so many living things? For years, products containing PCB's accumulated in junkyards. This compound can be destroyed only by burning at extremely high temperatures. In the junkyards, PCB's were washed out by rainfall or evaporated when burned at moderate temperatures. Eventually they were carried hundreds of miles into the air and then returned to the earth in rain or snow.

From laboratory tests, scientists suspect that PCB's can cause reproductive disorders, skin lesions, liver trouble, and metabolism problems in human beings. In laboratory tests with animals, PCB's have caused cancer and mental retardation. The production and use of most PCB's were banned by Congress starting January 1, 1978. However, the effects of this chemical compound will be felt for a long time. Contamination by PCB's has caused the shutdown of commercial fishing in the Hudson River and limited it in some of the Great Lakes.

🔊 Can you name any other chemicals that have created environmental hazards? If so, how did this happen?

Energy and raw materials. The winter of 1973-1974 brought a shortage that surprised many Americans. They had always assumed that the supply of gasoline for their cars was practically unlimited. All anyone had to do was drive into a service station and say, "Fill it up." Gas would soon be gushing into the tank. By the end of 1973, however, strange things were happening. All over the country, service stations were displaying "no gas" signs. When a station did have gas, cars would line up for blocks to get some of the precious fluid. Motorists drove anxiously, with one eye on their gasoline gauges and the other on the lookout for a rare sight of a service station that had gas to sell.

The immediate cause of the gasoline shortage was an embargo on the sale of oil to the United States by oil-producing nations. Eventually the embargo was lifted, but Americans would never again be able to buy gasoline as cheaply as they had in the past. For the first time, many Americans learned that their country's oil resources were dwindling and that the U.S.

was becoming increasingly dependent on foreign oil imports.

The oil embargo and the subsequent dramatic rise in oil prices produced significant changes in the way Americans use energy. During the past decade conservation measures helped to make America more energy-efficient. New more fuel-efficient cars have replaced the old gas guzzlers. At the same time, industry has implemented a number of successful conservation programs. As a result of these efforts, one expert recently described conservation as "one of the remarkable success stories of the last decade."

The rise in oil prices during the 1970's stimulated interest in renewable sources of energy such as wind and solar power. During the 1980's, such sources began to make a significant contribution to the nation's energy supply. By the middle of the decade, windmills, hydroelectric dams, and the sun generated almost 10

The public's delayed perception of the problem of dwindling oil supplies is an example of cultural lag.

percent of the nation's electricity.

Despite these gains, America still continues to face formidable energy problems. Of all modern industrial nations, the United States uses the most energy. With only six percent of the world's population, it consumes one third of the world's fossil fuel resources.

Though technology will help us meet our energy needs for some time, it will probably be at a high cost to the environment. Energy can be provided by building more nuclear power plants; but these produce dangerous, long-lasting radioactive wastes. So far, we have not found a foolproof way of disposing of them. There may be billions of gallons of oil beneath our coastal waters, but offshore drilling sometimes causes spills that contaminate the oceans. There are huge deposits of coal in our western states, but these lie near the surface and would have to be strip-mined. This would result in the destruction of large land areas and the pollution of waters with sulfur from the exposed coal.

Besides fossil fuels, many other natural resources are becoming depleted throughout the world. Among them are tin, copper, aluminum, zinc, and lead. Presently the United States consumes about one third of the world's total production of raw materials. This raises some serious questions for Americans:

• How long can the United States continue to consume a disproportionate share of the world's resources when developing nations require more and more?

• What will happen to our standard of living as these resources become scarcer and more expensive?

Some Causes of Pollution

Historic forces. What accounts for the massive pollution of our environment and the rapid depletion of our energy resources? Many sociologists believe that a number of historic forces have contributed to these conditions:

1. *The Industrial Revolution.* In 1787 the Scottish poet Robert Burns saw an iron foundry that was pouring smoke and flames into the sky. He was moved to write the following lines:

> *We came not here to view your works,*
> *In hopes to be more wise,*
> *But only, lest we go to Hell,*
> *It may be no surprise.*

With this touch of humor, Burns expressed his disdain for the developing Industrial Revolution. But not all people shared his view. Many saw an exciting new world shaping up, a world of machinery and engines, of fast travel and communications, and of cities teeming with life. The English novelist, William Thackeray, said, "We who lived before railways and survive out of the ancient world are like Father Noah and his family out of the Ark."

Only a few people like Burns foresaw the dangerous consequences that the Industrial Revolution would have for our environment. The tendency of industry to cluster around sources of fuel and raw materials has created severe problems. The wastes discharged by one or two factories in an area may be easily absorbed and dis-

Industry, agriculture, and urbanization
have frequently damaged our environment.
Above, the Novelty Iron Works in New
York City about 1840; right, clearing
a frontier farm in the late 18th century;
below, automobiles parked on a
Massachusetts beach in the 1920's, and
suburban Daly City, California, today.

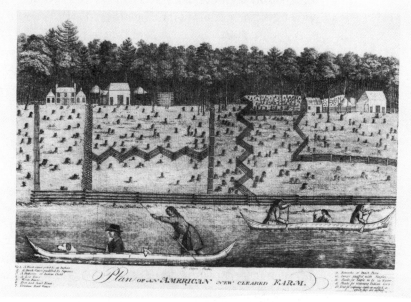

Plan of an AMERICAN NEW CLEARED FARM.

solved by the environment. But the wastes of 10 or 20 factories concentrated in the same area overtax the environment's ability to absorb them, resulting in heavy pollution.

2. *The gasoline engine.* The development of the gasoline engine stimulated the enormous growth of motor vehicles in this century. There are now more than 100 million cars in the United States alone. They comprise nearly half of the world's total. In urban areas, they account for 60 percent of the pollutants in the air.

3. *The population explosion.* The rapid rise in the number of people since about 1800 created great pressures to produce more food. This often led to the destruction of forests, and to farming practices that exhausted or eroded the soil. In recent times, the heavy use of chemical fertilizers has contributed substantially to water pollution. The population explosion also spurred industrial production, with adverse effects on the environment.

4. *Urbanization.* Cities are practically barren of plants and trees that help sustain life by producing oxygen. Urban centers consume large amounts of fuel and produce a wide variety of wastes. The growth of cities in modern times has reduced the life-supporting capacity of our environment.

Attitudes, values, and beliefs. Science and technology have undoubtedly improved living conditions for millions of people in industrial societies and created a great variety and abundance of goods. But have they created an earthly paradise? An exhibition devoted to the environment might show the following signs of "progress" in our time:

• the land littered with automobile junkyards and billions of throw-away cans and bottles;

• the skies darkened by smoke and fumes, and rivers clogged with filth;

• once-green landscapes blackened and torn by strip-mining operations.

In industrial societies, most people still believe that progress means the ever-increasing use of technology to produce more and more abundance for "the good life." Yet in recent years many people have suggested that technology is a two-edged weapon, creating material wealth at a tremendous cost to our natural environment. Some look back nostalgically on earlier times when people grew their own food and lived in closer harmony with nature. And some have actually moved to rural areas to try their hand at simple farming. Environmentalists often contrast our way of living with that of the early Native Americans who respected nature and conserved their environment. Anthropologist Dorothy Lee, for example, quotes a member of the Wintun tribe:

"The white people never cared for the land or deer or bear. When we Indians kill meat, we eat it all up. When we dig roots, we make little holes. When we build houses, we make little holes. . . . We shake down acorns and pine nuts. We don't chop down trees. We use only dead wood. But the white people plow up the ground, pull up the trees, kill everything. . . . How can the spirit of the earth like the white man? . . . Everywhere the white man has touched it, it is sore."

What Can Be Done?

The big clean-up. Once the environment has become polluted, is it possible to clean it up? It not only can be done, but it has been done in hundreds of communities throughout the United States. Towns, cities, and states have cooperated to rejuvenate beaches and parks, to reduce air pollution, and to halt the flow of wastes into rivers and lakes. Campaigns to bring life back to rivers have been especially successful. In many instances, fish have returned to waterways once considered dead. The following story is about one of these rivers:

Not many years ago, the 187-mile Willamette River in Oregon was little more than an open sewer. Wastes dumped into it by industry and towns had made it so dirty that one area resident recalled, "You could almost walk on it." There were no fish in the river, and swimming in it was a distinct health hazard. Today people can fish or swim along the entire length of the Willamette.

Cleaning up the river proved difficult and slow. The campaign began when voters created a State Sanitary Authority to reclaim the polluted river. The Authority ordered towns along the Willamette to construct primary and secondary sewage-treatment plants. In *primary plants* sewage is screened to remove large solid wastes; in *secondary* the sewage is disinfected. The Authority also ordered pulp and paper mills to reduce discharges into the river.

The campaign to clean up the Willamette River cost over 200 million dollars and required many years of work. The greatest triumph for many Oregonians was the return of fish to the Willamette. Today the river teems with salmon.

Other states are taking actions to protect their environment. In 1986, California voters passed a bill which prohibits the release of toxic wastes into water supplies. That year, voters in New Jersey and New York voted to finance the cleanup of hazardous waste sites.

Congress has also passed laws to help fight pollution. A new Superfund bill passed in 1986 committed 9 billion dollars to clean up many of the most dangerous toxic dumps. The Clean Water Act of 1987 included tough regulations to improve water quality. And, finally, a new soil erosion program would enable farmers to replant highly erodible land with soil-saving vegetation.

While the states and federal government have passed new laws, American industry has begun to use new technologies to help dispose of toxic wastes. For example, a small company in Texas has developed microbes that eat PCB's and other toxic chemicals. As noted by the executive vice-president of the National Wildlife Federation, "The success stories should remind Americans that environmental progress is still possible despite the formidable problems we face, and despite the pressure on our diminishing resources."

Saving energy. Modern industrial nations are in a race against time. Their economies are powered primarily by oil and gas, and these fuels are rapidly running out. The development of alternative sources of

Sophisticated sewage treatment plants such as the one above have been helpful in salvaging polluted water.
Below, East Rutherford, New Jersey, workers pile up a 50,000-pound mountain of aluminum cans for recycling.

energy, such as atomic fusion, solar heat, and synthetic fuels, may take decades. Conservation, most experts agree, will help buy that time.

As fuel costs continue to rise, most consumers *have* to save energy. Practically every major industrial firm in the country has some sort of conservation program under way. Most involve simple "house-keeping" adjustments. General Motors, for example, now uses cooler water to wash auto parts and disconnects the lights in cafeteria vending machines. These and other economies saved the equivalent of more than five million barrels of oil between 1972 and 1977, enough to heat 150,000 homes for a year.

More and more Americans are becoming energy-conscious, lowering their thermostats at home, installing insulation, and buying cars that are economical on their use of gas. According to *Newsweek* magazine, perhaps the most energy-thrifty town in America is Davis, California, which is about 70 miles northeast of San Francisco. Although winter temperatures there often dip into the thirties, some residents rarely have to use their gas furnaces. Like Linda and Mark Pearlman, they use solar-heating systems. In the Pearlmans' home, three water-filled tanks rise

from the floor of their living room to the ceiling. The floor itself is made of tiled concrete. On cold winter days, shutters in the ceiling are opened to let the tanks and the floor absorb the sun's heat. Once the heat is stored up, it continues to radiate through the house during the night. The system also pays dividends during the summer. Then the ceiling shutters are kept closed and the tanks absorb heat from inside the house. At night the windows are opened, and the heat is ventilated outside. Even when outside temperatures reach 100 degrees, the house is comfortably cool — without air conditioning.

The use of solar energy isn't the only way that people in Davis conserve fuel and electricity. The city's 46,500 residents own more bicycles (24,000) than cars, and there are bicycle lanes on some major streets. Some roads are made narrow to reduce traffic speeds and heat buildup

13:A

Where Savings Could Be Made

If all homes had six inches of insulation:	600,000
If every home was caulked and weather-stripped properly:	580,000
If thermostats were lowered an average of six degrees F.:	570,000
If clothing were washed in cold or warm water:	100,000
If home appliances were 20% more efficient:	500,000
If the average load per commuter car increased by one person:	700,000
If all electric motors were 1% more efficient:	1 million
If autos averaged 20.8 miles per gallon now:	500,000

Savings = 50,000 barrels of oil equivalent per day

in the summer. Builders are required to install six inches of insulation in the attic of every new house. One builder estimated that a new home with solar heating and heavy insulation will save 80 to 90 percent of normal energy use.

Chart 13:A indicates how much fuel Americans could save each day by various conservation measures.

᪨ What other ways can you think of to save energy? Under what conditions would you find using a bicycle instead of a car attractive?

Nuclear energy. Was it the dawn of a brilliant new age of limitless power? Or was it something to be dreaded, a technological monster that might cause untold calamities? Near Idaho Falls, Idaho, 16 atomic scientists had come to observe an experiment. Could a nuclear reactor provide energy to generate electricity? The scientists kept their eyes glued on four 200-watt bulbs. After a few anxious minutes, the lights began to glow. Most of the scientists cheered. One of them wrote on a concrete wall: "Electricity was first generated here from atomic energy on December 20, 1951." But another scientist was not so happy about the achievement. On the same wall, he drew a head of the devil exhaling steam.

During the next 35 years the benefits of nuclear power seemed to outweigh the risks. By 1986, America's 101 commercial reactors generated 17 percent of the nation's electricity. However, these same reactors also produced an annual total of over 1,300 metric tons of radioactive waste. This ever increasing stockpile of nuclear wastes has to be safely stored for a 1,000 years before it becomes harmless.

The storage of nuclear waste poses a serious environmental problem. The possibility of a disaster occurring at a nuclear reactor site poses an even greater danger. This threat became a reality in 1979 when a near-disaster at the Three Mile Island nuclear reactor in Pennsylvania allowed some radioactive material to escape into the air. Seven years later a serious accident occurred at the Chernobyl nuclear-power plant inside the Soviet Union. The disaster released a radioactive cloud which spread across Europe. The following article from *U.S. News and World Report* shows how the readioactive fallout from Chernobyl has already begun to affect life in northern Scandinavia.

To Paul and Mai Klemetsson, there was nothing very significant in a radio news bulletin about a nuclear accident in the Soviet Union. "It went in one ear and out the other," recalls Paul. "It seemed so far away."

They know better now. Nearly a year after the Chernobyl nuclear-power-plant disaster of April, 1986, the Klemetssons are living through a nightmare that threatens their own livelihood and the entire reindeer-herding economy of northern Scandinavia. Chernobyl's impact continues to reverberate around the world. In few places, however, is fallout from the accident more poignant or sobering than in this isolated rural area 1,300 miles north of the now sealed Soviet reactor.

To all outward appearances, life goes on here much as it always has. A bright winter sun glistens on snowy fields and frozen lakes.

Healthy-looking reindeer roam the pine forests that blanket much of the countryside. . . . But the unseen reality is far different. Reindeer that spend the winter in local forests are badly contaminated by radiation. Worse, lichens that are the animals' staple winter food have soaked up so much radiation that they may not be safe for grazing for some 30 years.

Long-range effects of fallout from Chernobyl are still disputed, but the pattern of damage here is highly evident. The explosion on April 26 released cesium 137 and other poisonous substances into the air. These radioactive materials drifted northwest until May 1, when rains brought them back to earth in the parts of Sweden and Norway devoted to reindeer herding. . . .

The middle-aged Klemetssons—part of Scandinavia's 70,000 Lapp minority—are struggling against what they call the "invisible enemy." In good times, a herd of 1,000 reindeer provides the basis of a thriving lifestyle. But those times may be gone for decades. Last September, each kilogram or 2.2 pounds of meat from slaughtered reindeer registered 5,000 to 6,000 Becquerels — a measurement of radiation contamination in food. By last November, the level was as high as 40,000 Becquerels per kilo, or more than 100 times as much as Swedish authorities consider safe for human consumption.

The situation could prove catastrophic for the Sami, as Lapps prefer to be called. Cheerful, stocky people with a strong sense of community ties, the Sami have survived centuries of isolation in a harsh environment. The reindeer is the core of their culture and the mainspring of their far-north economy. The animals provide most of the people's basic needs: Meat for food, antlers for knife handles and glue, and skin for tents, coats and shoes. Today, many Sami live in towns, and snow scooters and plastic lassos have taken the place of ropes and sleighs. But the reindeer is still the central focus of a 2,000-year-old tradition.

"We are shaken," says Nikolaus Stenberg, head of Sweden's largest Sami group. "Our whole way of life is built upon nature. Reindeer are the basis of our culture. If the reindeer industry disappears because of contamination, our culture will go, too."

This dire possibility has been deferred at least momentarily by a decision by Sweden and Norway to buy all contaminated reindeer meat at 1985 prices. The meat is destroyed or fed to minks being raised for fur and thus outside the human food chain. With 85 percent of all slaughtered reindeer exceeding permissible contamination levels, this purchase plan will cost Sweden more than $20 million a year. . . .

Despite the economic reprieve, many Sami are bitter about what has happened. "It's something that's around you, but you can't deal with it," says Olof Sikku, a youth organizer. Adds Sigvard Johnsson, a 60-year-old herder, "What's the purpose, when our reindeer are just going to the garbage dump?"

In many ways, the Sami lifestyle already was being undermined by the logging of forests, the construction of hydroelectric-power dams that destroyed grazing lands and the development of mass tourism in a once deserted region. But the impact of Chernobyl is different, both in kind and in its threat to the entire reindeer culture. To the Klemetssons and a great many others, a way of life suddenly seems threatened with extinction.

application

In what ways might the concept of
cultural lag discussed in Chapter 10 help
explain many environmental problems?

summary

As the modern world becomes more complex, the balance of life
between humans and their environment has grown more precarious. All
too often the "miracles" of science have been accompanied by unforseen
dangers. Take for example the chemical dioxin. When it became available
in the late 1950's, farmers used it as a weedkiller. Unfortunately, its manufacturers were not always careful about disposing of leftover chemicals. In
the town of Times Beach, Missouri, a waste hauler mixed dioxin in the oil
he poured on unpaved streets. As time went by, the toxic effects of concentrated dioxin were recognized. Meanwhile, dioxin was seeping into the
soil of Times Beach. Birds died. Dogs and cats were often stillborn. Eventually, the effects began to be seen in humans. By 1983, the contaminated
town had to be abandoned.

Practically all living things exist within a thin layer of air, water, and
soil on the earth's surface. Each form of life that it sustains is linked to,
and dependent upon, all others. We cannot damage or destroy any one of
them, environmentalists say, without threatening the entire chain. Pollution of the environment endangers life on our planet in the following
ways:

Air pollution. All heavily industrialized, densely populated areas suffer from air pollution in varying degrees. Cars, industry, and homes pour
into the air enormous quantities of poisonous fumes and dust particles that
cannot be absorbed or dissolved. When trapped near the surface by layers
of clouds, they form a highly visible "smog." Air pollution contributes to
many human illnesses, including lung cancer, bronchitis, and heart disease. It can also damage or destroy trees and crops.

Water pollution. Many forms of life are endangered by the widespread contamination of our rivers, lakes, and oceans. Raw sewage and industrial wastes dumped into these waters kill fish or make them unfit to
eat. The supply of drinking water is diminished. Chemical fertilizers that
are washed into rivers and lakes cause a reaction that is deadly to all forms

of water life. Chemicals released from factories into the air mixed with water vapor and fell to the earth as acid rain. It polluted lakes, rivers, and streams, killing fish and threatening the life of other animals and plants. It weakens the steel in bridges and damages buildings and aircraft. Some environmentalists warn that the continued pollution of rivers and lakes may result in a serious "water famine" by the year 2000. And, thus, they say, plans to "farm" the oceans for food will come to nothing.

Land degradation. Large areas of land in the United States are threatened by erosion because of careless farming techniques, the destruction of forests, strip-mining, and massive road-building. Land is also polluted by the dumping of more than 3.5 billion tons of solid wastes each year. This refuse includes 200 million tons of garbage and trash collections.

The pollution of our environment is due to several developments: the gasoline engine, urbanization, accelerating industrial production, and population increases. These forces have also caused a rapid dwindling of the world's natural resources, including the fuels that power industrial societies. Modern industrial nations are already in the grip of an "energy crisis" as supplies of oil and natural gas become more and more scarce. Experts agree that conservation is needed until technology can develop new alternatives.

more questions and activities

1. Describe the conflict in values sometimes present in attempts to clean up the environment. Give an example.

2. What norms in American culture contribute to environmental problems? Do you believe that these norms can be changed through socialization?

3. Describe four historic forces that have led to pollution and depletion of natural resources in the world today.

4. In light of the four historical forces behind many of our environmental problems, discuss forces that would be necessary for change. Is there any evidence that these changes are already occurring?

5. Invite speakers to your class from a local environmental group and from some institution that promotes industrial development, such as the chamber of commerce, the local power company, or a local industry. On what issues do they agree? On what issues do they disagree?

6. Invite a speaker to your class from the U.S. Department of Agriculture's soil conservation service. Interview this person about the problems of soil erosion and land degradation in your area and ask what is being done to solve these problems.

7. Make a bulletin board display or a collage of symbols of American culture associated with the destruction of our environment.

8. Research and report on the science and technology associated with solar energy. To what extent has solar technology been used in your area?

9. Apply the seven steps in the life cycle of a social movement as described in Chapter 10 to the development of the environmental lobby today.

10. On March 28, 1979, the cooling system malfunctioned at the Three Mile Island nuclear power plant near Harrisburg, Pennsylvania. For six days, the nation watched to see if there would be a disastrous explosion at the plant. Although some radiation escaped, a major catastrophe was averted. Nuclear power advocates pointed out that the incident cost no lives and that the situation was brought under control. Nuclear power critics said that it was simply luck that prevented a major disaster and that the accident proved the potential peril of nuclear power plants. You may want to research news reports from that period for more details. Do you think this accident should influence future nuclear power plant development? If not, why? If so, how?

suggested readings

Brown, Michael H. *Laying Waste: The Poisoning of America by Toxic Chemicals* (Pantheon Books, 1980.) A powerful description of the costs and consequences of chemical pollution.

Commoner, Barry. *The Closing Circle: Nature, Man, and Technology.* (Bantam, 1974.) An important analysis of the environmental crisis by a prominent ecologist.

Fuller, John G. *The Poison That Fell from the Sky.* (Random House, 1977.) The incredible story of how an explosion in a chemical factory released a deadly poisonous cloud which turned the Italian community of Seveso into an uninhabitable ghost town.

Goldstein, Eleanor C., ed. *Environment.* (Social Issues Resources Series, Inc., 1987.) A collection of readings on a number of environmental issues.

Nader, Ralph, Ronald Brownstein, and John Richard, eds. *Who's Poisoning America?* (Sierra Club Books, 1981.) A collection of articles on the polluters and victims of toxic chemicals.

National Wildlife. "The 19th Environmental Quality Index." (*National Wildlife*, February-March 1987.) One of an annual series of reports which evaluates the environmental quality of life in the United States. Each year's reports includes excellent charts and graphs.

Rienow, Robert, and Leona Train Rienow. *Moment in the Sun.* (Ballantine, 1969.) A readable account of the forces which have damaged our environment.

Walton, Bryce. *Harpoon Gunner.* (Crowell, 1968.) In this novel, the 16-year-old son of a harpoon gunner goes on a modern whaling expedition. His ambition to follow in his father's footsteps diminishes as his awe of the nearly extinct blue whale increases.

The New York City skyline from the suburbs.

chapter 14

cities and suburbs

Patrick Turner grew up in New York City, and he probably would still live there if he hadn't lost his job as a city planner. But in 1975, when Turner was 27, his job was discontinued because New York was forced to cut its budget.

After six months of looking for another job, Turner found one in a suburb 20 miles north of New York, and his new employer insisted he move there. So Lowrie Turner, Pat's wife, quit her city job and took another directing a program for the suburban poor and disadvantaged. The couple moved to a three-bedroom apartment in suburban Tarrytown.

The Turners were not sure they would like living there; they associated the suburban county they moved to with the rich, and they hated to leave their friends. Recalls Mrs. Turner: "I remember when we first moved here, Pat would use any old excuse to go to the city. He'd want to take his laundry to the city; or if he wanted a pastrami sandwich, we'd get into the car and drive to Katz's delicatessen on East Houston Street."

But gradually the Turners cut their ties to the city and made a life in Tarrytown. "I've always believed that, if you want to feel a part of a community, you have to begin to plant roots there," says Lowrie Turner. The Turners had their first child in 1978, and now they travel less and less into the city. They still miss certain things about the city — exotic foods, disco dancing, and late-night movies —

but they plan to stay in Tarrytown. They think it's a better place to raise a family.

And so Pat and Lowrie Turner became a part of one of the greatest migrations in U.S. history — the move from the cities to the *suburbs* (smaller communities that cluster around most cities). In the past 40 years, millions of Americans have fled the shrinking job markets, crime, and congestion of big cities to search for a better life in the suburbs. The 1980 census revealed that the U.S. has become a predominantly suburban society. At that time, 44.5 percent of the population lived in the suburbs; about 30 percent lived in central cities; and the rest lived in small towns and rural areas.

This chapter examines the deterioration in parts of many of the nation's large cities. It examines several patterns by which good neighborhoods have become slums. We'll see how the suburbs have drained the cities of many of their valuable resources. But we'll also see how many urban problems have become suburban problems too. Some of the solutions to urban problems are programs to lure upper- and middle-class people back to the city to work, to shop, to play, and to live. We'll pose the question of whether suburbs have the right to zone out the poor. And finally, we'll take note of some cities that have succeeded economically where others failed and examine some reasons why.

After his presidency Jimmy Carter worked to restore buildings in New York.

The Problem

The ghetto. In October 1977, President Jimmy Carter paid a visit to the worst slum in New York and possibly the worst in the United States — the South Bronx. After observing some of the misery of this area, which covers four square miles, the President said: "It was a very sobering trip for me to see the devastation that has taken place in the South Bronx. . . . Maybe we can still turn it around."

The South Bronx that Carter saw has often been compared to cities that were heavily bombed in World War II. On block after block, there are vacant lots covered with the rubble of apartment houses that were abandoned, vandalized, burned, and finally demolished because they were in danger of collapsing. On top of the rubble are heaps of garbage. Rats scurry through them, and packs of wild dogs search for food. Many other apartment houses are burned-out ruins. Their doors and windows are shattered, and many are covered with sheets of metal. Not all of these buildings are completely abandoned. Some are inhabited by dope addicts, and the area's 30 street gangs often make their headquarters in them.

Who lives in the South Bronx? The 1980 census showed about 453,000 people in the area. This represented a drop of over 300 thousand people since 1970. Whites comprised a majority of those leaving the South Bronx. The population today is about equally split between blacks and Puerto Ricans.

Living conditions deteriorated in the South Bronx at a staggering rate during the 1970's and 1980's. From 1973 to 1977, 300 business and industrial firms left the area, taking with them 10,000 jobs. By the 1980's an estimated 30 percent of the eligible workers were jobless. And one out of three residents was on welfare. Income per person was less than half of the national average and declining.

Housing got worse and worse. Some 43,000 apartments were lost between 1970 and 1975 as a result of fire or abandonment. Over the next two years, there were 7,000 more fires in the area. Of those apartments remaining — many of which were publicly assisted or publicly financed — more than three quarters were in violation of the city's building code.

For many residents and businesses in the South Bronx life was extremely dangerous. During the late 1970's and early 1980's the South Bronx experienced a high rate of violent crime, which caused many people to leave. Although the crime rate has declined in recent years, the fear of crime still influences daily life.

The South Bronx is an extreme example of an urban ghetto. However, most of the nation's older industrial cities have areas with similar problems.

Despite gains made by many minority group members in recent years, in 1980, 60 percent of the nation's blacks and 50 percent of its Hispanic minorities still lived in the most depressed ghettos of central cities. Most of them were badly handicapped by lingering discrimination, poor education, and a lack of job skills. The unemployment rate among black

Faces of the homeless. Above, a homeless
man and restaurant patron. Left, a homeless
family in a shelter. Below, homeless man prepares his blankets for life on the street.

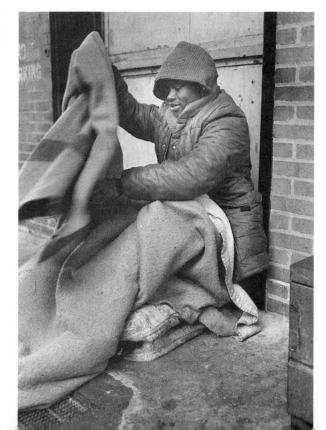

males in slum areas (30 percent) was three times as high as for white males, and was highest among black male teenagers (40 percent).

Many ghetto dwellers feel trapped by their enduring poverty, and have given in to feelings of despair and, at times, rage. The pessimism that grips people in urban ghettos was expressed by a black man in Gary, Indiana:

Outside of this district, they build better and they have better. But you come down here and you see the same thing year after year. People struggling, people wanting, people needing, and nobody to give anyone help. You just sink and you can't get out of it. I guess it's the low adequacy of the housing, the low morale of the whole place. It's one big nothing. I mean, you can live here for millions and millions of years and you will see the same place, same time, and same situation. It's just like time stops here.

The concentration of poor blacks and Hispanics in central cities and the flight of middle-class whites to the suburbs has produced a new pattern of racial segregation in the United States. Our metropolitan areas have become racially divided as whites live increasingly in the outlying suburbs, while the central cities are inhabited increasingly by blacks and Hispanics.

The decline of an urban neighborhood. The South Bronx was not always a fear-ridden, impoverished slum. Earlier in the century, it was a bustling neighborhood that represented a step upward economically from the crowded slums of downtown New York. Its residents then were chiefly working-class European immigrants and their children. Before World War II, the neighborhood began to change, and afterward the process was accelerated. What happened in the South Bronx is not unique. A similar pattern of change has taken place in many central-city neighborhoods throughout the United States. In a 1957 study of Chicago's deteriorating neighborhoods, Beverly and Otis Duncan identified a four-step pattern of neighborhood change:

1. Minority group members moved into a white working-class or middle-class neighborhood. The newcomers were often of the same social class and were seeking to escape from the slums.

2. Because of racial prejudice, the older residents tended to overlook the fact that the new arrivals were employed and upwardly mobile. They interpreted the presence of minorities as a sign that the neighborhood was about to deteriorate. (Since 1957 it has been documented that real estate agents frequently encourage this impression.) The older residents began to move out, often to suburbs where housing was more plentiful. Vacancies were filled by other upwardly mobile minority group members.

3. Soon the number of vacancies exceeded the number of upwardly mobile minority group members who wished to move in. Landlords rented to people with inadequate incomes and families too large for the space they rented. (In such situations, banks and savings institutions frequently decide the neighborhood is a high-risk area. They refuse to give mortgages and home-repair loans on property in the area. This policy has been labeled *red-lining.*)

4. Many of the houses were already old and deteriorating. They now offered little protection against vandalism, which added to the landlord's maintenance costs. Caught between higher costs and lower income, the landlord stopped making needed repairs. Buildings deteriorated further. The better-off tenants moved out, and soon the first junkies moved in. They supported their habits by stealing from their neighbors. Meanwhile the neighborhood became more and more crowded. The police were unable to cope with rising crime. Sanitation services failed to keep up with the mounting piles of garbage. Hazardous fire conditions developed.

By this time the landlord decided that the rundown property was more trouble than it was worth and abandoned it completely. The tenants were now without heat, water, gas, and electricity. Most moved out. Only a few squatters remained, mostly junkies. Soon teams of looters ripped out pipes and wiring, which could be sold for salvage. Fires, either accidental or deliberate, gutted the entire building. Pockets of abandoned buildings doomed block after block. The residents of occupied buildings knew that they would soon be overwhelmed by crime, fires, rats, and uncollected garbage. They moved out too. Finally, bulldozers arrived and leveled the abandoned, burned-out ruins.

◄§ How might a reduction in racial prejudice arrest this cycle?

Traffic Jams. Long waits in traffic pose a significant daily problem for many urban and suburban communities. The following

article from *U. S. News and World Report* describes the causes and extent of our traffic problems.

Traffic! It's maddening, harrowing, blood-boiling, even murder-provoking — and it's the single most unpleasant and unavoidable fact of daily life for most Americans. In the national pursuit of happiness, it's traffic that determines how fast we get there. And the sad truth, is that the process of "getting there" is getting worse, much worse.

No doubt, past planning failures helped produce "the problem." But could anyone have foreseen the prosperity that filled suburban garages to overflowing with all the autos of the new two-income families? Or could anyone have dealt rationally with a national propensity for equating mobility with freedom? Unhappily, few believe any of the proposed cures such as new roads or slower suburban growth will work.

Traffic tie-ups, of course, are not new. There were probably chariot jams in Roman times, and there were more cars on downtown Houston streets in the pre-freeway era back in 1940 than there are today. But now traffic congestion is pandemic, affecting hundreds of metropolitan areas and afflicting tens of millions of people.

Compounding the difficulties for planners is the unforeseen growth of traffic within the ever expanding suburban belts. For example, between the once tranquil Chicago suburbs of Rolling Meadows and Arlington Heights, 80,000 vehicles a day pass through a single intersection — enough cars to stretch bumper to bumper to Cincinnati, or most of the way to St. Louis. Farther out in exurbia, "many drivers are locked in rush-hour traffic while surrounded by bucolic vistas of cornfields, farmhouses and grazing cattle," says Kenneth Orski, a national traffic consultant. Indeed, "rush hour" has become meaningless. Traffic on the North Central Expressway in Dallas at noon is the same as in the morning and evening.

Even more discouraging is the road ahead. Their vision of the 21st century is a Dante-like nightmare . . . by the year 2010, average rush hour speeds in Los Angeles may crawl to as low as 7 mph.

Traffic engineers cannot calculate the costs of such a snail-paced future. They have all they can do to keep up with estimating the mounting costs of today's traffic. Commuters, they say, spend an estimated $150 billion a year to travel to work and back — in vehicles worth an aggregate trillion dollars or so. Time lost in traffic jams last year in the Los Angeles basin alone amounted to 84,000 hours each day. The money required to deal with the air pollution created by the traffic is difficult to calculate.

Is this any way to live? How did we get ourselves into this mess? Transportation consultant Alan Pisarski sees the convergence of three postwar booms — in jobs, autos and suburban growth. As a result, there are now 110 million commuters in the United States, compared with 59 million in 1950.

Households have grown even faster than jobs, as family units have become smaller. That has fueled a quantum jump in automobile ownership. Most households now have two vehicles — and 13 percent have three or more. In 1986, according to a Hertz Corporation survey, Americans drove 1.78 trillion miles. Commuters averaged 6,000 miles, with 95 percent of the travel at least part way by car or truck. Compounding the problem is the fact that most commuters prefer to drive alone. Despite all the urgent pleas for carpooling, particularly during the oil crises of the '70s, three out of four commuting autos have no passengers other than the driver.

But what really set off today's traffic explosion was the largely unforseen flight of jobs to the suburbs. Two thirds of all jobs created from 1960 to 1980 were in the suburbs, and the trend has accelerated in this decade. Today, 57 percent of all metropolitan jobs are outside the central business district.

The end result: "Cities have turned inside out," notes urban geographer Peter Muller of the University of Miami. Urban cores have been supplanted by a phenomenon in search of a name that will stick: "Megacenters," "suburban downtowns," "hypurbia," even "polynucleated metropolises." Whatever it is, "we are seeing the urban expression of the end of the industrial era," says Muller.

The new era has even more emphatically become the era of personal mobility. Adds Muller: "The auto has won the battle, and the evidence is staring us in the face."

⇜ According to the article, what is the main cause of the "traffic explosion" in American cities? What are some other causes cited in the article? Has the area in which you live undergone a traffic explosion? What do you think can be done to solve the traffic problem?

Do you think the predictions of congestion for the future are accurate?

The troubled suburbs. For millions of Americans after World War II, the suburbs became a promised land where they

A neighborhood party in a typical suburban cul-de-sac. To many people in the 1940's, 50's, and 60's, the suburbs were symbolic of the American Dream.

hoped to find "the good life." There they would exchange the city's congestion, pollution, crime, drugs, and racial tensions for grass, trees, friendly neighbors, and good schools. As homeowners, they would be free of landlords who periodically raised their rents. Even better, taxes would be low.

At first, most seemed to find what they were looking for. In a 1970 Time-Harris poll, two out of three suburbanites maintained that, if it weren't for their jobs, they would never set foot in the city again. As more and more people moved to the suburbs, however, it became increasingly difficult to distinguish between these communities and the cities that everyone wanted to leave behind. High-rise office and apartment buildings began to spring up; and traffic, noise, and pollution be-

came commonplace. New schools and sewage systems were needed, so taxes rose every year. Suburbanites sometimes came home at night to find that their homes had been burglarized. Some discovered, to their sorrow, that their kids were experimenting with drugs. In short, as the suburbs became more populated and urbanized, they began to have the same problems as the cities, and perhaps a few others besides.

Typical of many suburbs today is Hoffman Estates, Illinois, a middle-class community about 30 miles northwest of Chicago. The following description of the community is adapted from *U.S. News and World Report:*

When it was first developed in the late 1950's, one resident recalled, "You could look for miles and see nothing but farmland." At that time, a new, single-family house sold for about $20,000. Before long, however, vacant land became more scarce. Builders had to pay $20,000 for an acre of land they once could buy for $1,000. It was no longer possible to put up moderately priced, single-family homes. Instead, the builders began constructing apartment houses or attached town houses. The population of Hoffman Estates rose to 32,500, and the dream of "spacious living" faded. During commuting hours, cars are lined up bumper-to-bumper on streets leading into the Northwest Tollway, the six-lane road that is the town's major link with metropolitan Chicago. Only a few years ago, one woman recalled, Hoffman Estates was so quiet it was almost "eerie." Today she declines to use her car in the late afternoon because "it's no use trying to fight that traffic." The tollway itself becomes more crowded every year, its traffic swollen by commuters from many other growing suburbs. On Friday nights, a commuter driving home from downtown Chicago can spend an hour covering the first 10 miles in competition with thousands of other suburbanites.

Many of the town's earlier residents feel resentful toward the newcomers who have moved into the apartment houses. One homeowner said: "We've heard some people describe the apartment complexes as a tumor engulfing the whole area. The people are OK, but these apartments crowd the schools and raise taxes." At a time when many older communities are closing schools because of the declining birthrate, Hoffman Estates is still building new ones to prevent crowding in existing facilities. Education costs already account for 60 percent of the taxes paid by homeowners.

How do the apartment and town-house dwellers feel about life in Hoffman Estates? Many believe that they are being slighted by the town's officials and excluded from some of the community's activities and organizations. Some complain that it is difficult to form personal relationships under the circumstances. One apartment renter said: "It's growing so fast, people come and go so fast, you don't get involved in a lasting relationship. Nobody wants to help you, even in the stores. Did we expect too much?"

Many teenagers in the community also feel estranged. Bryan Styer, the town's director of youth services, said that teenagers are apathetic because they have fewer things to do than in Chicago and they lack transportation to visit friends. According to Styer, they are being exposed to drugs at a very early age. There have been instances, he said, of seventh- and eighth-graders who have become drug users.

One popular myth about the suburbs is that they are all affluent places, inhabited by people who have tennis courts and swimming pools in their backyards. In 1977, however, a government census study showed that 6.8 percent of suburban families had incomes below the poverty line of $6,191 for a family of four. And in some suburban areas, 21.6 percent of all families were considered poor.

For many middle-class people, the suburbs represented a haven from the wave of crime that seemed to be engulfing the cities. Yet in 1985, the FBI reported that crime in the suburbs was increasing at a much faster rate than in central cities.

◦§ What other city problems have become suburban problems? Can you name any problems that suburbs have that cities don't have? Explain your answers.

Imagine that it is the end of the 20th century, and the United States has run out of oil. (You may want to re-read Isaac Asimov's scenario in Chapter 10.) Write a description of life in the suburbs under these conditions.

How It Happened

Urban flight. In the early 1920's, Henry Ford, the industrialist who began the mass production of automobiles, made a bold prediction. "The cities are finished," he proclaimed. Ford believed that cars would give people greater mobility, making it unnecessary and undesirable to live and work within cities. Today his prediction has very nearly come true. The growth of the suburbs in recent decades was spurred by a number of other factors:

• Massive road-building programs, subsidized by the federal government, made commuting by car convenient in many areas.

• The postwar "baby boom" created a great demand for housing. Land for new housing was already scarce in the cities, but was plentiful in the outlying areas.

• The postwar economic boom made it possible for millions of Americans to buy homes for the first time. They were aided by federal agencies that made mortgage loans available at low interest rates.

As the middle class flourished in the suburbs, stores, restaurants, and other businesses developed there also. New suburban shopping malls proved more attractive and convenient than shopping in the central cities. These malls were often enclosed and air-conditioned, with piped-in music, colored fountains, and sculpture. Some had as many as 150 to 200 shops, plus restaurants, movie theaters, lounges, and nurseries to care for young children. All, of course, had huge parking lots to accommodate cars.

Large corporations joined the exodus to the suburbs, attracted by cheap land, lower taxes, and more modern facilities. Many suburbanites found that they no longer had to travel into the cities at all. Almost everything they needed, including jobs, could be found within a few minutes' driving distance from their homes. A large number of suburbs became self-sufficient communities, no longer dependent on the cities that had spawned them. For the cities, the effects were disastrous. Deprived of much of their economy and tax base, they tended more and more to become "reservations of the poor."

What happened to Detroit is typical of the fate of many American cities in recent decades. This description is adapted from an article in *U.S. News and World Report:*

A once-vital urban center, Detroit lost 20 percent of its population between 1950 and 1970. The population of its suburbs increased 28 percent during the same period. Business and industry followed in the wake of the middle class. Ten airlines shifted their reservations and sales offices to outlying communities. While 100 restaurants closed within the central city, 57 others moved to the suburbs. General Motors, Bendix Corporation, the Budd Company, and many other big business organizations built new factories and offices in suburban areas. An executive of the Chamber of Commerce in one fast-growing suburb said, "Although many of our residents still work in Detroit, we easily have enough jobs within our boundaries to support our own population."

While retail sales slipped in Detroit, they increased spectacularly in the suburbs. Reflecting the feelings of many suburbanites, a resident of Troy said, "The only time we shop downtown is at Christmas, to see the lights."

Some suburbanites, however, feel that Detroit is more than a place to work or shop, and is worth saving. One of them said: "Spiritually, without downtown, something would die. Detroit has cultural and recreational facilities the suburbs don't have — the zoo, Cobo Arena, Tiger Stadium, the Detroit Institute of Arts, the main library."

But a new sports complex, the Silver Dome in suburban Pontiac, has already lured away two of Detroit's major sports teams, the Lions (football) and the Pistons (basketball). And as lack of funds has forced Detroit to charge admission fees to some of its cultural attractions, the suburbs may very well establish their own.

The exodus of the white middle class to the suburbs has been joined in recent years by a growing number of middle-class blacks. They are moving for much the same reasons — to get away from the cities' problems. Alfred D. Smith, a black urbanologist who works in Boston, told *The New York Times* reporter Paul Delaney why he and his wife decided to live in the middle-class suburb of Newton: "For us the choice was easy. We wanted to provide our children with the best education we could, and they were not getting it in the city."

Mrs. Wesley Crossons, a black housewife who moved from New York City to a Long Island suburb, said: "We just got tired of the city. Here it is quiet and peaceful, and I have a feeling of safety."

The movement of blacks to the suburbs has been slowed, however, because of discrimination in housing. Some middle-class blacks who moved to the suburbs have been targets of firebombs and other harassment. And some blacks fear a loss of identity if they leave urban neighborhoods. In 1977 only six percent of the suburban population was composed of black people, as compared with 11.5 percent for the entire population.

Commuting by automobile from suburb to city has become the norm for many Americans.

Migrations into the city. Even before the white middle class fled the cities, most of the new arrivals were poor; many were members of minority groups. The greatest number of newcomers were blacks from the rural South.

In 1900 almost nine out of ten blacks lived in the South, and fewer than one out of four were urban residents. The migration of rural blacks to Northern and Eastern cities began during World War I when many were attracted by high-paying jobs in defense industries. The movement slowed during the Great Depression of the 1930's, but gained momentum during World War II. Once again blacks from the rural South were lured to cities by jobs in defense plants. As the defense industry spread across the country, blacks also moved westward, especially to California. In 1980 about half of all black people in the United States lived outside the South, and 82 percent of them lived in metropolitan areas. Of the total black population of 26.5 million, 27 percent were concentrated in 12 central cities. This represented a drop from 1970 when one third of the nation's blacks lived in these cities. During this period the number of blacks moving from urban areas to the suburbs increased from 88 thousand a year to 220 thousand a year in the early 1980's. Chart 14:A shows how these changes have affected the black population of 12 cities.

Other groups of poor people who have moved to the cities include:

• A substantial number of Puerto Ricans and other Hispanics in the New York-New Jersey area.

• Whites from Appalachia in Chicago, Detroit, and other North Central cities.

14:A   Black Population of 12 Cities

City	Percentage of Blacks				Black Population
	1910	1950	1970	1980	1980
New York, NY	2	10	21	25	1,768,000
Chicago, IL	2	14	33	40	1,202,000
Detroit, MI	—	16	44	63	757,890
Philadelphia, PA	6	18	34	38	649,440
Washington, DC	29	35	71	70	446,600
Los Angeles, CA	—	9	18	17	510,000
Baltimore, MD	15	24	46	55	432,850
Houston, TX	30	21	26	27.6	440,220
Cleveland, OH	—	16	38	44	252,560
New Orleans, LA	26	32	45	55	306,900
Atlanta, GA	—	—	51.3	66.6	283,050
St. Louis, MO	—	—	40.9	45.6	206,368

U.S. Bureau of the Census

• Mexican Americans in the Southwest who were formerly farm laborers and are now seeking urban employment.

• An estimated three to five million illegal immigrants, most of them from Mexico.

Because of their lack of training for skilled, technical jobs, many members of these groups face chronic unemployment. Pierre de Vise, a professor of urban sciences at the University of Illinois, has said that this is the basic problem of the cities today. "The cities," he said, "are becoming dumping grounds for minority people, poor people, and people who are not in the labor force but are dependent on welfare. Historically, poor people were drawn to the city because their labor was needed. That need no longer exists."

Antiurban bias. Are cities stimulating and exciting places where people may enjoy life fully? Or are they by their nature evil and corrupting? Philosophers have debated these questions almost ever since there have been cities.

The ancient Greek philosopher Aristotle spoke for most of his compatriots when he said: "Men come together in the city to live. They remain there in order to live the good life." City boosters maintain that even today the big city is the best place for large groups of artists, musicians, scientists, intellectuals, publishers, journalists, entertainers, and a host of others whose work supports the good life of which Aristotle spoke. Where else, they ask, can one find so many fine arts institutions such as opera, theater, and museums? Where else is there such ethnic and racial diversity? And where else is one free of the prying of one's neighbors?

On the other hand, Rousseau, an 18th-century French philosopher, detested cities. Cities, he said, are "the sink of the human race." He believed that when people lived close to nature, like the Native Americans, they were noble and pure. But when people lived in cities, they became self-indulgent and morally corrupt. The answer to the ills of society, Rousseau suggested, was a return to nature.

In the United States, many people have shared Rousseau's view of cities. Thomas Jefferson, for example, believed that cities were "pestilential to the morals, the health, and the liberties of man" and that honest government would endure as long as our society remained agricultural, and its people were self-reliant farmers. "The mobs of great cities," Jefferson said, "add just so much support of pure government as sores do to the strength of the human body."

A distrust of cities has long been prevalent in American life and persists today. It is often expressed — in its mildest form — by people who say that cities are nice places to visit, but they wouldn't want to live in them. Americans have been less proud of their cities than Europeans and often neglect to beautify them. The decay of our cities today is due, at least in part, to this traditional antiurban bias.

≈§ Who do you think was right about cities, Aristotle or Rousseau? You might want to have a classroom debate on this subject with one side favoring city life and the other side favoring rural, small town, or suburban life.

What Can Be Done?

Urban homesteaders. After President Carter commented on the "devastation" he had seen on his visit to the South Bronx, he ended on a hopeful note. "I'm encouraged in some ways," he said, "by the strong efforts of tenant groups to rebuild. I'm impressed by the spirit of hope and determination by the people to save what they have."

President Carter was referring to the renovation of an abandoned five-story tenement, Venice Hall, by a group of neighborhood residents called the People's Development Corporation (PDC). The PDC is one of many neighborhood groups in New York City that have started to renovate abandoned apartment houses. Only one member of the group, Carlos Ramos, was a skilled craftsman. The other members, according to Ramos, "couldn't handle a hammer or saw or anything." The story of the PDC's first project, adapted from *Saturday Review*, follows:

The PDC was organized in December 1974 by Ramon Rueda, a young Spanish-speaking American who grew up in the slums of the South Bronx. "I had no problem with drugs or street fighting," he says, "because my ma and grandma kept us tight. But all the friends I grew up with are lost now, a half a dozen of them, to drugs or heavy drinking." Rueda's only preparation for leading a neighborhood self-help project was a course in urban housing at New York University. He soon attracted about 40 volunteers, more than half Spanish-speaking, and most of the rest black. The abandoned building they chose to renovate was one of the worst in the neighborhood. It was a

completely gutted, rotting shell, more than 70 years old. Rubble, rats, and dead dogs were everywhere. The basement was filled with mud up to the knees, piles of garbage, and fleas. Why did the PDC choose such a rundown building to work on? One member said, "We wanted a place where anything we did would be an improvement."

The PDC bought the building from the city, which had claimed it for default of taxes, for one dollar. The members' first job was to clean out the mountains of junk from the tenement. Then, in February 1975, they went to City Hall for a construction loan. The Housing Development Authority (HDA) turned them down at first. It said that the renovation plans were too ambitious and would be too expensive. (The plans included a roof garden, a big music room, and other "frills.") Once the plans were scaled down, the HDA approved a loan of $311,000. There was one condition — the renovation had to be completed within a year. The PDC got other help. A state agency gave it a $220,000 grant under a job-training program. It was also helped during the summer by Youth Services workers — high school dropouts paid by the city.

Each PDC member who would get an apartment in the building had to pledge at least 10 hours of "sweat time" each week for which they would receive no pay at all. The biggest problem was the members' almost complete lack of construction skills. The PDC could not afford to hire union craftsmen to do any of the actual labor. Instead, it hired them from time to time to teach the PDC members how to do each job. One of these teachers said: "You show somebody here how to do something, turn away and look back, and he's doing it right. Nobody has to be hounded or even watched. There's that kind of spirit."

When the project was completed, it contained 28 bright, clean apartments, and a large recreation-meeting room with a basketball and handball court behind it. There is also a solar heating unit on the roof that will provide about 85 per-

New residents of Venice Hall, shown below left before its restoration, contributed at least 10 hours of "sweat time" each week.

cent of the building's hot water. And an adjacent lot, that once was piled high with garbage, has been cleaned up and made into a small park.

With their newly acquired skills, members of the PDC began work on renovating five other abandoned buildings in the neighborhood. This time the money was advanced by three major New York banks that seemed eager to participate. Said one member of the PDC: "All around this area you see people sleeping in doorways, drinking all day, cleaning a car for three dollars when they can get it. Their fathers taught them nothing, and they don't know nothing. We want to change all that. We want to create a village of 10,000 people surviving on their own — people for maybe 40 blocks living good, the way everybody else lives good in this country."

The renovation of six apartment houses in the South Bronx is, of course, a drop in the bucket, but it symbolizes the neighborhood's determination to reverse the tide of decay. And it is a start that inspires other "homesteaders" to do the same. An official of a city housing agency said: "Twenty-six building renovations have started in the last year, and another 50 or so are in the planning stage. People see it happening and say, 'If they can do it, so can we.' "

Urban restoration by groups like the PDC will need a lot of help if they are to make a significant dent in ghetto areas.

In the 1970's, there were other restoration projects of housing in old, rundown sections of Baltimore, Philadelphia, Washington, and Milwaukee. Many of the restorers were middle- and upper-class homeowners who thought city property was a good investment.

⋳ Do you think that urban homesteading and other restoration projects are good solutions to the problems of urban decay?

Urban restoration. During the early 1800's, textile manufacturing helped to make Lowell, Massachusetts an important industrial center. A century later, its old mills stood empty, abandoned reminders of a proud past and a discouraging future. Most middle-class residents fled the city, preferring to live in the suburbs and shop in the new malls.

Lowell's rebirth began when a local congressman helped convince Congress that the city's old downtown could be restored. In 1978, Congress appropriated $40 million from the National Historical Parks Program to transform the downtown into a 137-acre preservation district.

A Visitors' Center, quilt museum, and apartments for the elderly now occupy a restored carpet mill. Visitors admire the city's newly cleaned canals while they shop in a variety of small stores. Wang Laboratories and other high-tech firms gave the project a further boost when they decided to make Lowell their home base. A modern new hotel which had previously been planned for the suburbs decided instead to relocate in Lowell.

The restoration project in Lowell is not an isolated example. During the 1980's, 1,800 cities and towns renovated 17,000 historic buildings. "Almost every city . . . has done something," says sociologist Louis Mazotti. "It's not a fad, . . . the 1980s have been the decade of cities' revival."

A number of forces have contributed to the revitalization of our urban heritage. The economic prosperity of the mid-1980s provided capital to finance ambitious restoration projects. At the same time, Ameri-

The Heartland's Season of Despair

In 1985, a deafening cheer went up from the crowd as the 14-hour benefit concert began in Champaign, Illinois. Almost 80,000 people had come to listen to some of the nation's top country, folk, and rock musicians. A wide array of talent — Willie Nelson, Loretta Lynn, Arlo Guthrie, John Cougar Mellencamp, and others — had come for the same purpose. They wanted to raise money for American farmers.

The concert known as Farm Aid was aimed at easing heartache in the nation's heartland. Here, among the rolling hills and prairies of the Great Plains, farmers had fallen upon some of the hardest times since the Great Depression. In the late 1970's, many farmers had banked on the future and mortgaged their farms to buy costly land. Then bumper crops drove down the price of commodities. At the same time, land prices fell.

Farmers were clearly in trouble. When bad weather hit in the early 1980's, their plight worsened. Burdened with heavy mortgage payments, farmers watched in despair as crop yields plunged. The foreclosures began, and, by the late 1980's, the problems of farmers had won national attention.

All across the heartland, a story of woe was told. Members of the clergy reported a rise in divorce, alcohol abuse and even suicide. Awesome financial burdens forced some farm families to swallow their pride and accept food stamps. Others filed for bankruptcy. Whatever action they took, the net result was emotional and economic depression.

With grim determination, farmers hunkered down to hang onto their land as long as possible. In 1986, they lashed out at the federal government when the Farmers Home Administration (FHA) ended a two-year moratorium, or delay, on foreclosure of its loans to farmers. Farmers also blasted Congress for bills to stabilize farm prices. "Too little, too late," said many.

Today signs of agricultural hardship dot the prairies. Businesses in many small towns have shut down. Farm-related industries have also been hit. The makers of large farm equipment have slowed production as the sale of tractors, combines, and other machinery has fallen off. Industries involved with grain storage or farm shipment also feel the pinch.

As weather across the Midwest improves, farmers have begun to piece together their lives. Debt-ridden growers see stark times for the rest of the 1980's and early 1990's. Payments for crops must often be endorsed by creditors such as banks or the FHA to make sure the debts are met. A third-generation farmer in Iowa captured the feelings of many when he said, "The question I have is what about my sons, what is their future?"

Thinking Critically

1. How did an agricultural crisis produce sociological crises among American farm families?

2. Would layoffs in industry produce similar consequences? Explain.

cans developed a new attitude toward their cities. As we have seen, Americans have historically distrusted urban living. However, a new generation of jet-age travellers discovered the beauty of old buildings and streets while touring Europe. Many returned home with a renewed interest in restoring historic buildings and neighborhoods in their communities.

The federal government also played a key role in making urban revivals possible. In 1966, Congress established the National Register of Historic Places. This act provided preservation grants to the states. Recent changes in the tax laws enable developers to receive tax credits when they renovate historic buildings.

The changing attitudes toward cities and the new laws have combined to produce a number of impressive success stories. The tourist boom prior to World War II helped turn South Miami Beach into a major vacation center. Hundreds of small hotels lined the ocean front and nearby streets. The district began to decline, however, when tourists headed to the new postwar Caribbean resorts. In an effort to restore the old hotels, the Miami Design Preservation League successfully got the area listed on the National Register of Historic Places. At least 40 of the hotels have been restored. As a result, the area has already begun to attract tourists and many other projects are underway.

Restoration projects have also helped to revitalize many small towns. Located about 75 miles west of Houston, the small town of Brenham, Texas contained a number of handsome buildings constructed between 1870 and 1925. But hard times and

years of neglect had slowly robbed them of their original beauty. Convinced that Brenham could be revived, determined townspeople successfully won state recognition for their pre-1935 buildings. During the 1980's, a $7 million face-lift restored the iron columns and brick facades to their original beauty. Pleased merchants have recorded increased sales and local pride is back. A Brenham attorney proudly points out that, "People are telling us now, 'We can see your love.'"

Have there been successful restoration projects in your community? Are there any areas or buildings that could be restored?

Revising suburban zoning. Many people believe that the suburbs could ease many of the cities' problems by changing their zoning regulations. Typically, these regulations prohibit the construction of inexpensive homes on small lots and of all multiple-unit housing, such as apartment buildings. Suburbs that bar inexpensive housing simply make it impossible for low-income families to live in them.

An indirect effect has been that these regulations exclude all but the most affluent racial minority group members. Critics of such zoning regulations claim that those who suffer most from them are the urban poor. As more and more businesses have left the cities for the suburbs, the number of jobs for city-dwellers has declined. Low-income workers cannot even afford the cost of transportation to suburban jobs. So the poor are trapped within central cities amid mounting unemployment. If they were permitted to move to the suburbs, some say, they could support themselves and the city would have fewer unproductive citizens.

But many suburbanites contend that zoning regulations are necessary to maintain their way of life. If they permitted low-cost housing, they say, they would soon have the same problems that drove them out of the cities. Low-cost housing is often occupied by families with many children. This means new schools must be built, and more taxes must be raised. The burden of taxes falls mainly on affluent homeowners. Low-cost housing, suburbanites claim, invariably produces more crime, welfare, and pollution. These too result in higher taxes, as well as destroy the suburb's "quality of life." Finally, they say, the presence of inexpensive housing reduces the resale value of their own homes.

In recent years, a number of organizations have gone to court to challenge the legality of suburban zoning regulations that exclude the poor. In an unusual case, black citizens of Mount Laurel, New Jersey, won a major victory.

Until the 1940's, Mount Laurel was a farming community of about 2,000 people, many of whom were black. Blacks had lived there for more than a century, and some of them had fought in black regiments during the Civil War. After World War II, new highways were built that encouraged suburban development in the area. By 1970 Mount Laurel had gained about 9,000 new residents, almost all of whom were middle class and white. It had also gained many new businesses, which clustered near the highways.

In an effort to check runaway growth, the town council enacted zoning laws that required all new homes to be substantial single-family dwellings built on plots no smaller than a half acre. Such homes would cost about $70,000 each and would require a family income of at least $30,000 a year to maintain.

Meanwhile, what was happening to the old-time black residents of Mount Laurel? Many of them were tenant farmers. They lived on land that was needed for the new highway construction and the commercial developments that followed. As the land was sold and the houses were torn down, the blacks had to find other places to live. The new zoning laws made it impossible for them to buy homes in Mount Laurel. Some moved into a still-rural section of the town where the housing was particularly run-down. Others had to move out. A number settled in a crowded ghetto of nearby Camden, New Jersey.

In 1971 Mount Laurel blacks took their case to court. They charged that the town used zoning laws to prevent low-cost housing and, in effect, was driving them out. They further charged Mount Laurel with failure to seek federal funds for public housing. The Mount Laurel blacks were joined in their suit by the city of Camden. Its attorneys charged that Camden did not have enough housing or services to accommodate the influx of poor blacks from Mount Laurel. Attorneys for Mount Laurel did not deny that its zoning laws were restrictive, but claimed that they were enacted for the "general welfare" of the town and were legitimate.

Restoration in three communities. Above, Union Park in Boston, Massachusetts. Below, Brenham, Texas, and Miami Beach, Florida.

The trial judge ruled that Mount Laurel had been practicing "economic discrimination." He said that the town had an obligation to accommodate a fair share of the region's poor people. Later the New Jersey Supreme Court upheld the decision of the trial judge. It called Mount Laurel's zoning laws "selfish and parochial." The decision virtually struck down all zoning regulations in New Jersey that were intended to exclude the poor.

◦§ Do you believe that suburbs should be allowed to keep out poor people? Explain your answer.

Newly booming cities. Are all of America's cities suffering from financial miseries and decay? While many are reeling from the impact of middle-class flight, a few, like Charlotte, North Carolina, are enjoying extraordinary growth and prosperity.

Charlotte can't be called a boom town exactly, but during the last 10 years almost 1,500 new firms located there, bringing with them $1.3 billion in investments and more than 28,000 new jobs.

The jobs are mostly good — like making terminals and floppy disks for computers or working in one of the 140 branches of the city's 14 banks. Charlotte has been a banking city for 150 years and is the center of the banking industry in the southeast. No one bank, however, has as many jobs as Duke Power, the area's largest employer with 8,000 workers.

This diversity of employment keeps Charlotte's economy fairly stable (unlike cities such as Detroit and Houston who depended largely on a single industry, cars and oil respectively).

Charlotte lies between Greenville, South Carolina, and Durham, North Carolina. While much of this area has struggled to overcome dependence on textiles, tobacco, and furniture, Charlotte has sailed into the eighties with assurance.

Although 30 and 40-story buildings punctuate its skyline, Charlotte has maintained an attractive low-key pace. People are still friendly, even folksy. Race relations in this once- segregated city are good enough to permit a black mayor. Property values have remained relatively stable in residential areas, and the public schools are integrated. Still, there has been flight to the suburbs. One of Charlotte's challenges is to pull back some of this growth.

Like many cities around the country, Charlotte is reclaiming an old part of its core city that had become rundown. The Fourth Ward is a thriving inner-city neighborhood. Condominiums and low-income housing have successfully mixed in with Victorian architecture. Development in the neighborhood has been financed by local banks who put up $25 million for home loans below the usual mortgage rate.

In another effort to reign in the sprawl, developers have surrounded a man-made lake with apartments and a shopping mall in the university area.

◦§ Do you think it is the diversity of employment or the type of available jobs that contribute most to Charlotte's success? Can you think of other ways a city might attract residents?

application

How do the processes of racial and
ethnic acceptance and rejection described
in Chapter 8 relate to the development
of American cities and suburbs?

---

summary

Since 1950, millions of people have fled America's big cities to live
in outlying suburbs. This movement comprises one of the greatest mass
migrations in the nation's history. The 1980 census revealed that the
United States had become a predominantly suburban society. At the time,
44.5 percent of the population lived in **suburbs** — smaller communities
that cluster around central cities. About 30 percent lived within central
cities; the rest, in rural areas.

Why have so many people deserted America's big cities? Most were
seeking to escape the problems that have engulfed the cities in recent decades — congestion, crime, drugs, racial tensions, and pollution, among
others. In the suburbs they saw the promise of a better life. There they
would find grass and trees, roomy backyards, friendly neighbors, good
schools, and crime-free streets.

The growth of the suburbs after World War II was spurred by a
number of factors:

• Massive road-building programs, subsidized by the federal government, made commuting by car convenient in many outlying areas. These
roads frequently destroyed vital parts of the cities.

• The postwar "baby boom" created a great demand for housing.
Land for new housing was already scarce in the cities but was plentiful
outside them.

• The postwar economic boom made it possible for millions of
Americans to buy homes for the first time.

Those who fled to the suburbs were mainly members of the white
middle and working classes. As they left, the cities were increasingly populated by poor people, many of whom were members of minority groups.
Despite gains made by many members of minority groups in recent years,
60 percent of the nation's blacks and 50 percent of its Hispanic people
still lived in the most depressed ghettos of the central cities in the 1980's.
Many were badly handicapped by lingering discrimination, poor

education, and a lack of job skills. The unemployment rate among black males in slum areas was 30 percent, three times as high as for white males. It was highest among black male teenagers — 40 percent. Many ghetto-dwellers felt trapped by their enduring poverty, and had given in to feelings of despair and, at times, rage. Attempts to replace old city housing with new apartment buildings through urban renewal usually made city neighborhoods less attractive to older residents.

The concentration of poor blacks and Hispanics in central cities and the flight of middle-class whites to the suburbs, critics say, produced a new pattern of racial segregation in the United States. Our metropolitan areas became racially divided as whites lived increasingly in the outlying suburbs, while blacks and Hispanics lived increasingly in the central cities.

The exodus of white middle-class residents and businesses to the suburbs has been the single most important reason for the decline of America's older cities. Financially, it has sharply reduced the cities' sources of tax revenues. At the same time, the influx of poor minority groups who need more services than the middle class put a further strain on the cities' finances. New York City, a city which contains great wealth, almost went bankrupt in 1975 as a result of these and other problems.

As members of the middle and working classes moved to the suburbs, stores, restaurants, and other businesses followed. High-rise office buildings and industrial facilities sprang up. Many suburbanites found that they no longer had to travel into the cities. Almost everything they needed, including jobs, could be found within a few minutes' driving distance from their own homes. But as the suburbs became more populated and urbanized, they began to have the same problems as the older cities. Traffic, noise, congestion, pollution, and crime increased steadily. In many parts of suburbia, the dream of "the good life" faded.

During the 1980's, many major cities in the United States were striving to lure back the middle and working classes. The main thrust of these efforts was to revive decayed downtown centers with bold, and often spectacular, new buildings. The high-rise hotels, offices, and apartment complexes of the 1980's frequently assumed dazzling new shapes.

Some critics of these developments say that they will do little to solve the problems of urban ghettos. They see more hope for the ghettos in the efforts of neighborhood groups to buy and restore abandoned housing, with the assistance of government agencies and private banking institutions eager to stem the tide of decay.

more questions and activities

1. Give four reasons for the financial troubles of the cities.

2. Describe the antiurban bias in our society and some of its origins.

3. Describe the impact on both cities and suburbs of suburban zoning regulations that exclude the poor.

4. Write or draw your description of an ideal community in which to live. Be able to defend your solutions.

5. Plan an exchange visit with another class in a community different in size from your own. In what ways do the social patterns of that community influence the school? Does your exchange lend any insight into your own community and school, and how they reflect each other?

6. Analyze the five major institutions listed in Chapter 1 as they function in your community. How might each of these institutions vary from city to suburb to rural area?

7. "So long as suburban land was cheap, and the South booming, we could afford to cede our downtown areas to dependent populations, and abandon their stagnant economies to the underclass. But now that the scent for an urban revival is in the air, cities increasingly look like those reservations we ceded so solemnly to the Indians — until we noticed they had uranium underneath."

The preceding quote, taken from an article titled "The Urban Crisis Leaves Town," in *Harper's* magazine, December 1978, states a concern that has sometimes been expressed about downtown revivals and renovations: that they leave no place for the poor to go. Do you think this is a legitimate concern? If not, why? If so, what might be done to protect the poor?

8. Examine the photographs throughout the chapter. In your opinion, which photographs show desirable patterns of urban and suburban development? Explain your answers.

9. The homeless people of America have become a major urban problem in the 1980's. Research the topic, and attempt to come up with a possible cause.

suggested readings

Abrahamson, Mark. *Urban Sociology.* (Prentice Hall, 1980.) A textbook overview of sociological research of the growth and problems of cities.

Birmingham, Stephen. *The Golden Dream.* (Harper and Row, 1978.) A highly readable report on the problems and successes of America's suburban communities.

Caro, Robert. *The Power Broker: Robert Moses and the Fall of New York.* (Knopf, 1974; Vintage [paperback], 1975.) A lengthy, but fascinating, account of how one man influenced a multitude of institutions and actually changed the landscape of New York City.

Herbers, John. *The New Heartland.* (Times Books, 1986.) A highly readable description of the movement to low density communities which are neither urban or suburban. The author describes how this flight beyond the suburbs is changing America.

Klebanow, Diana, Franklin L. Jonas, and Ira M. Leonard. *Urban Legacy: The Story of America's Cities.* (Mentor, 1977.) An excellent history of the use, growth, and problems of America's cities. Chapters 9 and 10 on "Black Urbanites in a Changing City" and "Dilemmas of Urban Policy" are particularly useful.

Kowinski, William Severini. *The Malling of America.* (William Morrow and Co., 1985.) An examination of the growth and impact of shopping malls.

Macdonald, Michael C.D. *America's Cities: A Report of the Myth of Urban Renaissance.* (Simon and Schuster, 1984) A critical look at the reports that America's cities are solving their problems.

Sandburg, Carl. *The Complete Poems of Carl Sandburg.* (Harcourt Brace Jovanovich, 1969.) The "Chicago Poems" of this famous American poet lend insight and detail to the neighborhoods and characters of one of our nation's largest cities.

Shi'ite terrorists in Beirut, Lebanon.

chapter 15

terrorism

The one hundred and fifteen passengers flying on Flight 840 from Rome to Athens had thus far experienced a routine trip. With their landing only twenty minutes away, many of the tourists tried to spot ancient ruins tucked in the rugged mountain valleys beneath them. Others looked forward to meeting old friends and relatives.

Suddenly, a loud explosion and a flash of light jolted the plane. The next 20 minutes were filled with terror and fear for the passengers and seven crew members. Frightened passengers quickly grabbed oxygen masks which automatically dropped from overhead compartments. Flying debris and a swirling wind swept across the cabin. "The plane shook," remembered one passenger. "I thought I was dying."

The Captain immediately requested permission to make an emergency landing. He then urged his passengers to remain calm. After a few tense minutes that must have seemed like hours, the plane landed safely in Athens. The relieved passengers and crew burst into cheers.

Tragically, everyone did not escape safely. In the first moments of shock, most of the passengers and crew did not realize that a bomb had blasted a nine-foot by four-foot hole in the plane's fuselage. Four Americans, one of them an eight-month old baby, had been blown out the hole and had fallen to their deaths 15,000 feet below. Had the bomb exploded 10 minutes earlier when the plane was at its cruising altitude of 29,000 feet, the loss of pressure could have destroyed the entire plane.

Police officials promptly launched a

mass investigation to determine who was responsible for this crime. Their search soon led them to suspect a Lebanese woman who travelled under the name May Elias Mansur. On April 2, 1986, Mansur flew from Cairo to Athens. The same plane then travelled to Rome and returned to Athens. Officials speculated that Mansur carried a small plastic bomb which metal-detecting machines failed to spot. Once on board, she may have hidden the wallet-sized bomb in a life preserver under her seat.

Mansur flew to Beirut shortly after the damaged plane landed in Athens. A few days later, a woman claiming to be Mansur denied having any role in the crime. Meanwhile, a little-known group called the Arab Revolutionary Cells claimed responsibility for the bombing. The group promised in a handwritten statement that there would be more attacks against American targets "across the world."

The explosion on Flight 840 and the threat of more violence provided chilling proof that existing security measures could not prevent other attacks on commercial airlines. The deaths of four passengers and other acts of violence in Europe and the Middle East convinced thousands of Americans to change their travel plans. During the summer of 1986, many Americans avoided these regions of the world.

The attack on Flight 840 was a serious example of terrorism. *Terrorism* may be defined as the threat or use of violence by an individual or group to achieve political aims. Experts agree that terrorists use violence to shock or intimidate both the im-

mediate victims and those who oppose their political goals. The attack on Flight 840 was thus part of a broader effort by Arab terrorists to change American policies in the Middle East.

Sociologists make a distinction between two different types of terrorism. The attack on flight 840 was an example of international terrorism because it involved citizens or territories of at least two nations. Over 8,000 major incidents of international terrorism have taken place since 1968. American citizens were the intended victims in over half of these terrorist acts. In 1985, there were slightly more than 3,000 terrorist acts, about 500 less than occurred in 1984. These included 1,527 bombings, 990 facility attacks, such as attacks on military facilities or embassies. There were 374 assassinations and 109 kidnappings. Hijackings comprised a mere .3 percent, only 10 occurring in 1985.

Terrorism that involves the citizens of only one country is called local terrorism. Serious acts of terrorism have declined in the United States since the 1970's. During the 1980's, acts of local terrorism occurred most frequently in Latin America. The most violent and active of these terrorist groups operated in El Salvador, Colombia, Peru, and Chile.

The cost of defending against international and local terrorism is high. Airlines are already spending over $220 million a year on security. For example, new scanners that can detect plastic weapons cost up to $70,000 each. American businesses spend over $20 billion a year to protect their foreign plants and executives. In 1986, the United States government developed plans to spend over $4 billion to strengthen its embassies around the world.

Each new act of terrorism has sharpened public awareness of how serious the problem has become. For example, a recent survey revealed that the public ranked a terrorist act as the most serious of 103 different violent crimes. In this chapter, we will see that the problem of terrorism is a very old one. We'll also examine how modern technology has greatly multiplied the powers of terrorists. After we study some of the causes of terrorism, we'll discuss the question, What makes a terrorist? As we shall see, terrorism is a particularly difficult problem in a society where individual freedom is highly valued and where some solutions pose dangers to that freedom.

Terrorists look out from door of hijacked TWA jet, after firing shots to frighten away news photographers. Three crew members were aboard aircraft.

The Problem

History of terrorism. Though terrorism is far more dangerous today than ever before, it is not a new development. Groups have used systematic violence to intimidate others many times in the past. In ancient Judea (now Israel), for example, a small band of ardent Jewish patriots known as the "Zealots" was dedicated to overthrowing Roman rule. They regarded Jewish moderates, who sought to live at peace with the Romans, as their chief enemies. The favorite weapon of the Zealots was a short sword that they carried under their coats. On holidays, when many people gathered in Jerusalem, they would mingle among the crowds and murder leaders of the moderate parties.

In the 12th century, a secret order of Muslim fanatics known as the "Assassins" killed many of their enemies while under the influence of the drug hashish. The word *assassin,* in fact, comes from the Arabic word *hashish.* Based in Persia and Syria, the Assassins murdered both Christian crusaders in the Holy Land and Turkish overlords. The weapon they used was always the dagger. For them, the murder of an enemy was a sacred act. Many of them sought martyrdom as a reward.

In modern times, terrorism as a political weapon was revived in the last century. It was especially prevalent in Russia where young, often idealistic, revolutionaries struggled against the repressive rule of the czars. In 1879 a small terrorist group known as the "People's Will" pledged itself to assassinate Czar Alexander II as the only way to end autocracy (one-man rule) in Russia. Two spectacular attempts to kill the czar with blasts of dynamite failed. One dynamite charge, placed on a railroad track, blew up the wrong train. The czar's train had already passed over it safely. Another charge was set off in the basement of the czar's palace in St. Petersburg (now Leningrad). Although many palace guards were killed or injured by the blast, the czar himself was not hurt. "Why do they hunt me like a beast?" Alexander asked.

The People's Will achieved its objective on March 1, 1881. That day the czar was returning to his palace in a carriage. A terrorist hurled a bomb at it that killed a guard and wounded several other people. Again, however, the czar was not injured. Stepping out of his carriage to inquire about the wounded, Alexander thanked God for his own narrow escape. The terrorist, who had been captured, looked at him and said, "It may still be too early to thank God." A moment later, a second terrorist hurled a bomb that shattered the czar's body. He died within hours.

The People's Will and other revolutionary groups claimed that violence was the only recourse they had to change Russian society. The despotic rule of the czars did not permit reforms by peaceful, democratic methods. When U.S. President James A. Garfield was assassinated in 1881 by a deranged office-seeker, the People's Will condemned the deed:

"In a land where the citizens are free to express their ideas, and where the will of the people does not merely make the law but appoints the person who is to carry the law into effect . . . political assassination is morally wrong."

Terrorism in Russia inspired a wave of anarchist violence in other countries. *Anarchists* are people, sometimes peaceful, sometimes violent, who oppose any form of government authority. Anarchists took the lives of four heads of state in Europe between 1894 and 1900. U.S. President William McKinley was shot and killed in 1901 by an anarchist. Racist and chauvinist groups like the Ku Klux Klan frequently use terror as a weapon. In recent times, many terrorist movements have sprung from the aspirations of colonial people to achieve independence. And terrorist methods have sometimes been used to suppress would-be revolutionaries.

◄§ Do you think that the assassination of political leaders is ever justifiable? Explain your answer.

The assassination of Czar Alexander II as portrayed by an engraver.

The problem today. During the last 20 years nearly 700 terrorist groups have claimed credit for at least one terrorist act. Many groups are composed of ordinary criminals who rationalize their activities with political slogans.

Other terrorist groups, like the Palestine Liberation Organization (PLO), have specific political objectives. Founded in 1964, the PLO is dedicated to the destruction of Israel and the establishment of an independent Arab state. Still other terrorists, like the Irish Republican Army (IRA), are primarily regional independence movements. Because of the conflict between the IRA and the Protestant authorities in Northern Ireland, as described in this article from *Junior Scholastic*, many young people in Northern Ireland have never known a time of peace.

Kevin Doherty just turned 16. He lives in a Catholic ghetto on the west side of the River Foyle. Since 1969, his neighborhood, the Bogside, has seen some of the worst fighting between the two groups and between Catholics and British soldiers.

A bulldozer roars in front of the housing project where Kevin lives. He watches a forklift tearing down one of the buildings and wonders out loud if his will be the next. He says that this is where many of the attacks on the police take place.

"They throw the petrol (gasoline) bombs from up there," Kevin says, pointing to the roof. "You have to look up when you go by." Blocks of cement and other objects get hurled down as well, often by teenagers. At a time when most kids in the U.S. are learning to throw baseballs or footballs, kids in the Bog-

side are becoming crack shots with stones. The police and British soldiers are their most frequent targets.

British soldiers were sent to Northern Ireland in 1969, after the police could no longer control riots between Catholics and Protestants. At first, Catholic housewives welcomed the troops with smiles and tea. Catholics looked on the troops as protection against the mostly Protestant police force. But gradually the troops lost popularity. In 1972, British soldiers shot 13 unarmed Catholic protesters during an illegal march in Derry.

Kevin is too young to remember the start of the troubles here. But the years of violence have hit his family hard. One older brother is in prison. Another lost his eye to a plastic bullet. Still another joined a terrorist group. "It's calm here now," Kevin says. "But it will start up again. You never really know when the boys will come out."

"The boys," as they are often called in Catholic communities, are the Provisional IRA (Irish Republican Army). They have been responsible for most of the violence against Protestants and British soldiers in Northern Ireland.

Even though Catholics make up 39 percent of Northern Ireland's population, they were long denied equal voting rights. Nearly all members of Northern Ireland's civil service and police force are Protestants. And until recently, Catholics were excluded from any jobs.

Resentment over these conditions led to Catholic civil rights marches in 1968-69. The marchers demanded equal opportunities in jobs and housing. The marches triggered the present troubles in Northern Ireland. Protes-

The Media and Terrorism

On June 14, 1985 two Shi'ite Moslems hijacked a TWA flight traveling from Athens to Rome. During the next three days the terrorists forced the captain and his terrified passengers to criss-cross the Mediterranean Sea as they flew back and forth between Beirut and Algiers. The terrorists brutally killed a U.S. Navy diver before finally forcing the pilot to land in Beirut. They then held 37 passengers and three crew members as hostages.

During the next 17 days, President Ronald Reagan and his advisors conducted negotiations with terrorist leaders, which finally led to the hostages' release. While these negotiations took place, American television networks broadcast frequent coverage of the unfolding drama. On several occasions, the terrorists permitted a hostage spokesman to make statements and answer questions at televised news conferences. As the TV cameras rolled, Allyn Conwell, a spokesman for the hostages, condemned Israel and repeated the terrorists demand for the release of Arab prisoners held there.

This widely watched press conference helped trigger a national debate about what television's proper role should be during a hostage crisis. Network spokespeople argued that TV coverage helped the hostages by easing their isolation and letting their families know that they were alive and well. Broadcasters also pointed out that television provided the terrorists with an outlet for announcing their demands.

Others strongly disagreed. They complained that the media allowed themselves to be used by the terrorists. TV's extensive coverage actually prolonged the crisis by giving the terrorists free publicity and encouraging the belief that their demands would ultimately be met. Other critics emphasized that successful negotiations should be conducted quietly. They claimed a media-produced crisis atmosphere limits the President's options by creating public pressure for him to take immediate actions.

Following the TWA hijacking crisis, a government Task Force on Combatting Terrorism issued a report containing recommendations for the coverage of future hostage crises. Although the report did not endorse a "press blackout," it did urge the media to serve as their own watchdog and develop self-limiting guidelines. For example, the Task Force recommended that the media avoid broadcasting reports of planned military responses or interviews with terrorists and their hostages.

These recommendations made many journalists uncomfortable. "We can't say absolutely no interviews on TV or no terrorists quoted in newspapers," says Fred Francis, chief NBC-TV correspondent at the Defense Department. "Once you make those decisions, how much more will you decide the American people shouldn't know?"

Thinking Critically

1. What are the pros and cons of media coverage of a hostage crisis?

2. If you were on the Task Force what recommendations would you make?

tants, *fearful of losing their privileged position, attacked the marchers. This led to terrorism by the IRA, and counterterrorism by Protestant terrorist groups. . . . In recent years, more Protestants than Catholics have been killed in Northern Ireland. (The opposite was true in the late 1960's and early '70's.) . . . They fear that if British soldiers leave, the IRA might take control.*

A few Protestants took part in the first Catholic civil rights marches in 1968-69. But now even moderate Protestants feel frustrated. . . . They argue that recent reforms have given Catholics equal voting rights and better housing. Yet the violence continues, on both sides. Whether Protestant or Catholic, they share a common land. Says one Protestant girl, "I feel a lot closer to Catholics in Northern Ireland than Protestants in England."

In spite of the troubles, most people who live in Londonderry prefer to stay. For all the bomb blasts and bullets, both Catholics and Protestants still cling fiercely to this city.

How do terrorists today compare with those of the 19th century? Walter Laqueur, a noted historian and a leading authority on terrorism, said:

"Today's terrorism has become indiscriminate — far more brutal than in the past. Terrorists leave a bomb in a supermarket and couldn't care less who gets killed. . . . Human life has become cheaper in our time, partly as a result of the mass killing of the first and second World Wars."

The victims of terrorism today are often men, women, and children who have no role in government at all. They may be tourists on an airliner, commuters on a train, people at work, or students in a classroom. They are often held as hostages and threatened with death unless the terrorists' demands are met by government authorities. As Laqueur indicated, many of today's terrorists have few scruples against slaying civilians. On May 15, 1974, for example, three Palestinian guerrillas invaded a school in the Israeli village of Maalot and held 85 teenagers as hostages. The guerrillas demanded the release of 10 terrorists serving life sentences in Israeli jails on charges of murder and sabotage. "You had better hurry," the guerrillas warned, "or at six o'clock you are going to get 85 dead bodies."

The Israeli cabinet met in an emergency session to consider the Palestinians' demands. It had been the policy of the Israeli government not to negotiate with terrorists at all. It believed that any concessions made to terrorists would only encourage more blackmail. But now, because the hostages were so young, the government decided to yield. It agreed to free the 10 prisoners named by the guerrillas.

But as the terrorists' deadline approached, they made a further demand. They had been promised air transportation for themselves and the freed prisoners to Damascus, Syria. Now they insisted on taking half of their young hostages with them on the flight. This demand was completely unacceptable to the Israelis, but they pleaded for more time to discuss it. The Palestinians refused. Minutes before the terrorists' deadline expired, Israeli sharpshooters opened fire on them while other soldiers stormed the building. One of the guerrillas was killed immediately, but the two others fired their automatic weapons point-blank at the hostages. When the gunfire ended, 16 students were dead and scores were wounded. Five of the wounded died afterward in hospitals.

The terrorist's self-image. Terrorists who commit such acts usually think of themselves as idealists. Society is sick, they say, and cannot be cured by reforms or half measures; oppression can only be removed by violence. Any action that benefits the terrorist cause is justified, they say, even if innocents must sometimes die. Eventually, when the cause succeeds, terror will no longer be necessary and violence will be only an unpleasant memory. Terrorists of a wide variety of political beliefs explain their actions in this way. Recently, for example, a leader of the PLO stated the case for violence as follows:

You must distinguish between the kind of violence used to exploit people and that used in self-defense — legitimate violence. The bullets that I shoot are not the bullets used to exploit or subdue. They are just the opposite. They will remove exploitation inflicted upon me.

It is true that innocent people might suffer, might be killed. Why do we do it? Do you think Palestinians love to kill? Of course not. I am committed to killing to save my people, who have been humiliated more than 30 years by Israel. It may take 50 or 100 years of struggle, but even so it is the only solution. The end will come with the establishment of a progressive socialist society throughout the world.

The terrorists' belief that "the end justifies the means" is bolstered by their conviction that they comprise an elite, or superior, group. Ordinary people, they say, have neither the intelligence nor the courage required to make bold changes in society. Only rare and special people — themselves — are equipped to take the extreme measures that are necessary to remove oppression. In the 19th century, a fanatic revolutionary named Sergei Nechayev wrote a statement of his beliefs that many modern terrorists might subscribe to:

The terrorist must break every tie with . . . all laws, conventions, and generally accepted conditions of life in this society. He is mercilessly hostile to society. He continues to live in the society only so that he may eventually destroy it.

He despises public opinion. He despises all the pretensions of conventional morality. Everything that glorifies revolution is moral to him. Everything that interferes with it is immoral and unjust.

He who feels pity for anything in this society is not a revolutionary.

International possibilities. Why should a Lebanese terrorist explode a bomb on an American airliner? Why would the group claiming responsibility threaten to attack other American "targets?" Why should the Libyan dictator, Colonel Muammar Khadaffi, supply weapons to IRA terrorists in Northern Ireland? Why should the IRA train Basque nationalists from Spain in secret camps in Ireland? The answer to these questions comes from Dr. George Habash, leader of the Popular Front for the Liberations of Palestine (PFLP), the most extreme group in the PLO. Speaking before an international revolutionary congress held in North Korea in 1970, Habash said:

"At this time of people's revolution against the worldwide imperialistic system, there can be neither geographic nor political borders, nor any moral prohibitions against the terrorist enterprises of the people's camp."

Habash was saying, in effect, that terrorist groups throughout the world and governments sympathetic to them should cooperate with each other because they have common ideological goals. And, in fact, terrorists from many nations have been collaborating with each other to a remarkable degree. Experts on terrorism agree that a united, international terrorist organization does not exist at this time.

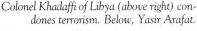

Colonel Khadaffi of Libya (above right) condones terrorism. Below, Yasir Arafat.

But they do not discount the possibility that close collaboration among terrorist groups may lead to one.

In his book, *Terrorism from Robespierre to Arafat,* Albert Parry tells how Habash planned one of the most complex terrorist operations of recent times. This account is adapted from the book:

In 1971 Dr. Habash's agents set up a secret office in Tokyo to recruit Japanese volunteers for training in Lebanon to aid Palestinian guerrillas. The recruits came chiefly from the ranks of the Japanese Red Army. Despite its name, the "army" is actually a very small group whose members often hire themselves out for terrorist missions in other countries. In May 1972, three of these terrorists were recruited by the PFLP for a murderous mission that would eventually take them to Israel's main airport near Tel Aviv. From

Japan, they were first flown to Lebanon, where they were given a commando course at a guerrilla base. From there, they journeyed to Frankfurt, Germany, and Rome, Italy. In Frankfurt, they picked up false passports. In Rome, they received Czech automatic weapons and grenades, which they packed into their luggage. They had no problem boarding an airliner for the last leg of their journey from Rome to Tel Aviv. Their luggage was not even examined. Arriving at Tel Aviv, they entered the passenger terminal. It was crowded with tourists from all over the world. In a moment, the three terrorists took out their weapons and began firing indiscriminately at the people inside. Before Israeli guards gunned down two of the Japanese and captured the third, 28 men and women were killed and 67 wounded. Most of the victims were religious pilgrims from Puerto Rico and other countries who had come to visit the Holy Land's shrines.

At his trial, the captured Japanese assassin, Kozo Akamoto, insisted that he was normal, yet expressed no remorse at all for his deed. He told the Israeli court that he and his accomplices had undertaken the mission because Japanese terrorists needed to gain the world's attention.

"This cooperation with the PFLP," he declared, "was a springboard for us to propel ourselves onto the world stage. This attack was proposed by them, the PFLP, and it afforded us unity of action. They approved of it. I am a soldier and I approved of it, so I joined the operation."

As for his victims, Akamoto made only this mystical statement: "When I was a child, I was told that a man becomes a star after his death. Those people we killed are now stars in the firmament. The world revolution will continue, and there will be more stars. When I think that their stars and our stars will one day shine in the same heaven, I am very happy."

Although Akamoto expressed a wish to join the firmament of stars soon, he will have a long wait. He was sentenced to life imprisonment.

Experts on terrorism fear other dangers from terrorist groups. Among them are the following:

1. *The possibility of an aggressor nation employing terrorists to destroy an enemy.* Suppose, for example, that a nation had designs on the territory of its neighbor but considered a military invasion too risky. It might be tempted to employ a terrorist organization to enter the "enemy" country and disrupt it with sabotage and assassinations. The cost to the aggressor nation would be small; it could deny any connection with the terrorists; and the results could be as effective as any military operation.

2. *The possibility of terrorists using nuclear weapons to blackmail nations.* With nuclear weapons, terrorists could threaten the destruction of large cities. Some physicists, such as Theodore B. Taylor, believe that it would be comparatively easy for a group of terrorists to steal nuclear materials and build a crude, but deadly, fission bomb. The bomb could be made, Taylor wrote, "using materials and equipment that could be purchased at a hardware store and from commercial suppliers of scientific equipment for student laboratories."

Taylor issued his warning in 1977, after reading a term paper by a Princeton University student, John A. Phillips. The paper described how a nuclear bomb could be constructed at a cost of $2,000. Phillips said that all his information came from books available in the school library and from public government reports.

Other scientists say that Taylor underestimates the difficulties of stealing nuclear materials and the risks of constructing a nuclear bomb. A more likely possibility, they say, is that terrorists might seize a nuclear power plant or a nuclear weapons storage facility, and threaten a catastrophe unless their demands are met.

3. *The possibility that terrorists might use chemical or biological weapons to blackmail nations.* Unlike nuclear devices, these weapons are small, easy to steal, and easy to conceal and carry anywhere.

◄§ Analyze news accounts of a terrorist attack not described in this chapter. What part, if any, did the news media play in the terrorists' plans? Were innocent people harmed? Was there any international assistance for the terrorists?

Dimensions of Terrorism

Advanced technology. The dramatic increase in terrorism in recent years has been stimulated by a number of factors, including modern technology. Advanced technology enables small terrorist groups to operate with greater facility and to wield greater powers of destruction than ever before. This became evident in 1968 when the first hijackings of jetliners for terrorist purposes took place. The technique of political hijacking was developed by Habash of the PFLP. Habash's most spectacular venture in hijacking occurred on September 6, 1970. That day, members of the PFLP seized *three* airliners — one Pan American, one TWA, and one

Swissair — enroute from European airports to New York. Two of the planes were forced down in Jordan, the other in Cairo, Egypt. After the passengers and crews were removed, all three planes were blown up.

What did Habash hope to accomplish? Primarily he wished to gain publicity for himself and his movement. In this respect, he was highly successful. Millions of people became aware of Habash and the PFLP as they followed the news of the hijackings on TV, on the radio, and in the press. At the same time, the triple hijacking conveyed a clear message. Unless his goal — the destruction of Israel — was achieved, *no one* was safe from terrorist attacks. Because of the ease with which airliners could be seized and controlled, hijacking became a favorite weapon of terrorists in the early 1970's. Since then, greater security precautions have led to a decline in the number of hijackings.

Modern technology has also provided terrorists with a variety of highly destructive, portable weapons. Among them are plastic bombs, letter bombs, booby-trapped "books" and "candy boxes," and even ground-to-air missiles capable of shooting down a 747 jetliner. On September 5, 1973, police in Rome, Italy, arrested five Palestinians on suspicion of plotting to shoot down an Israeli El Al airliner. The police found in their possession two Soviet SA-7 rockets complete with infrared homing devices and lightweight shoulder launchers.

Terrorists have been assisted too by the expansion of electronic communications throughout the world. Terrorist threats and ultimatums can be delivered swiftly, and negotiations can be carried out from distant havens. Even more important, newspapers, radio, and television assure terrorists of widespread publicity for their causes.

Lack of international controls. Two reasons that terrorist groups flourish today are that many governments are sympathetic to them, and that others fear to offend them. In January 1977, for example, French intelligence agents arrested Abu Daoud, a Palestinian terrorist who was strongly suspected of masterminding the kidnapping that led to the slaying of 11 Israeli athletes at the 1972 Munich Olympic games. The French acted on a tip from West German police that Daoud was in Paris to attend the funeral of a friend.

Both West Germany and Israel wanted to try Daoud for the Munich slayings, and requested the French government to extradite him. Four days after Daoud's arrest, a French court denied the requests and freed Daoud. He was allowed to fly to Algeria, whose government supports the Palestinian terrorist movement. Daoud's release was severely criticized in many countries. It was widely believed that France had given in to pressure exerted by Arab nations and, perhaps, the threats of terrorist groups.

Efforts to arrive at international agreements aimed at curbing terrorism have generally been ineffective. Some nations will not sign them, and usually the agreements contain so many loopholes that the punishment of terrorists is made very difficult. As a result, terrorists fre-

A democratic society may have difficulty balancing social control with individual rights.

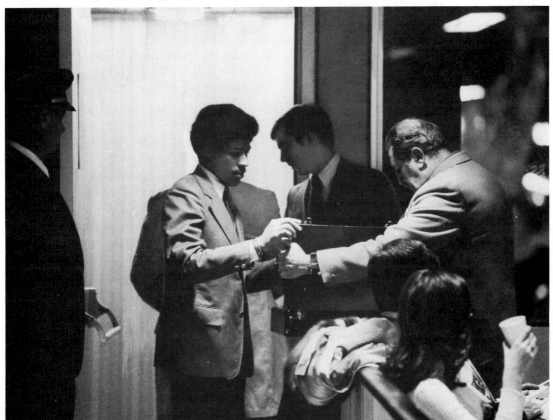

quently get away with the most heinous crimes. According to a recent study, a terrorist involved in a kidnapping has an 80 percent chance of escaping capture, and an almost even chance that all or some of his demands will be granted. Of the approximately 115 terrorist hijackings between 1968 and the end of 1975, less than a dozen ended in the death or imprisonment of the terrorists. For the small proportion of terrorists who were caught and tried, the average sentence was less than 18 months.

Terrorists sometimes receive weapons, training, money, fake passports, and asylum from many countries. Most frequently involved are the Soviet Union and eastern European nations it controls. Others include various Arab nations, Cuba, North Korea, and China. The Soviet Union does not approve of such groups as the Baader-Meinhof gang in West Germany or the Red Brigade in Italy. Occasionally it even denounces them as "Robin Hood adventurers." Not surprisingly, these groups are opposed to Soviet-style communism. However, the Soviet Union gives substantial support to terrorist groups in the Middle East and Africa that it considers engaged in "wars of national liberation." At the Patrice Lumumba Friendship University in Moscow, specially chosen students from Africa, Latin America, and Asia are given courses in terror techniques, including sabotage and assassination. In the early 1970's, some of these students rebelled and demanded — successfully — to be returned home. An African student explained his reasons to Albert Parry:

Originally I went to Lumumba University to become a physician. But instead of medical studies, I was surprised to find myself being trained in making explosives and how to plant them at various strategic points of my homeland. That was why I, together with others in similar situations, mounted demonstrations in Moscow to be returned home at once as peaceful citizens, not terrorists. We won. But others did remain to continue and complete such training.

This does not mean, however, that all terrorism is committed by people with left-wing political ideas. Right-wing terrorists, often members of the military, have long been active in Latin America.

In 1973, for example, a military junta seized control of the government of democratically elected Marxist President Salvadore Allende in Chile. Allende reportedly killed himself upon learning that the coup was successful. His widow later charged that the United States was responsible for the takeover. Although the charges were not proven, they were echoed by some government officials in the U.S.

In the years that followed the fall of Allende's government, thousands of his supporters were arrested and questioned by the Chilean secret police, the DINA. Many were severely tortured, and some 1,500 people had disappeared before President Augusto Pinochet announced in 1977 that he was disbanding the DINA.

The head of the DINA was among those charged with the 1976 killing of Orlando Letelier, a Chilean leader in exile in the United States. Letelier and an aide died when a bomb exploded in their car as they drove along a Washington, DC, street.

The social backgrounds of terrorists.

Terrorists come from a wide variety of social backgrounds. Those involved in nationalist movements, such as the Irish Republican Army or the Front for the Liberation of Quebec, come mainly from the working class.

West European, Latin American, and Japanese terrorists, whose goals are the destruction of "the bourgeois Establishment," generally come from the middle and upper classes.

Charles A. Russell and Captain Bowman H. Miller, counterintelligence experts of the U.S. Air Force, studied more than 350 terrorists from 18 urban groups. They found that:

• More than two out of three terrorists came from the middle or upper classes.

• Most terrorists have been single men aged 22 to 24, although the leaders tend to be older. Most have had some college education, if not a college degree.

• With some exceptions, women terrorists occupy supportive, rather than leadership, roles.

Typical of most urban, middle-class terrorists were the Tupamaros of Uruguay. Organized in the 1960's, they took their name from an Incan Indian chief, Tupac-Amaru. In the 18th century, Tupac-Amaru led an unsuccessful revolt against the Spanish conquerors of Peru and was brutally executed. Among the Spanish, his name was a synonym for "troublemaker." Almost two centuries later, it became a badge of honor for Uruguayan terrorists.

At the time the Tupamaros became

Katherine Boudin, member of the Weather Underground, after being charged with 33 criminal counts for her part in an armored car robbery that left two police officers and a guard dead.

active, Uruguay was quite unusual among South American nations. A small country of three million people, it had a long tradition of humane, democratic government. About 1955, however, its economy began to falter and hard times set in. Unemployment and inflation caused widespread unrest.

At the height of their movement, the Tupamaros had about 1,000 members who were concentrated in the capital city of Montevideo. They were inspired by the success of Fidel Castro's revolution in Cuba, and were also trained by Cubans.

Until 1970 the Tupamaros shed little blood and expressed considerable remorse when they did kill. For the most part, the Tupamaros robbed banks and gambling casinos, or kidnapped people for ransom. Some of the proceeds from these robberies and kidnappings were shared with the poor.

But violence became much more commonplace after July 1970. At that time, the Tupamaros kidnapped Daniel Mitrione, an American who had been a police chief in Richmond, Indiana. He had been sent to Montevideo by the United States Agency for International Development. Officially, Mitrione was supposed to help the Uruguayan police in traffic control and communications. The Tupamaros charged that he was an undercover CIA agent sent to train the police in counterinsurgency techniques, including torture. The Tupamaros demanded the release of 150 political prisoners as ransom for Mitrione. When the government refused to comply, Mitrione was executed by the Tupamaros.

From then on, the number of kidnappings and killings carried out by the terrorists increased sharply. One of their kidnap victims was Geoffrey Jackson, the British ambassador to Uruguay. They kept him in a dungeon for 245 days before releasing him. In a book called *People's Prison* about his experience, Jackson wrote:

"Most of my captors were students, and many were quite abnormal. Ferocity, far more than precise ideology, was the single and common component of their assorted personalities."

In April 1972, the government declared a state of "internal war" against the Tupamaros. Democratic freedoms were suspended as the police and the army ruthlessly hunted and destroyed Tupamaro bases. The Tupamaros fought back, but they were crushed by the end of the year. Soon after, Uruguay became a right-wing military dictatorship, just the opposite of what the Tupamaros had wanted. Most of the surviving Tupamaros fled to other South American countries and to Europe. Many, however, ceased to be political activists. Gerald McKnight, a British journalist, interviewed one of them, called "Romeo," in Buenos Aires. Romeo's story, adapted from McKnight's book, *The Terrorist Mind,* follows:

He was tall, thin, nervous, and dressed completely in black. He smoked cigarettes incessantly, even though he suffered from asthma. His father was an accountant. Romeo qualified as a bachelor of law, but never practiced the profession. Before becoming a revolutionary, he was an actor who played bit parts. Romeo said that his interest in the Tupamaros began on December 22, 1966. That day he saw the police fire on a group of unarmed left-wing students. One of the students was killed. Romeo, who was then 23 and a Marxist, said: "I didn't know him, but his death appalled me. When I got down to thinking about what it meant, what was happening to my country, I knew I had to do something about it."

Romeo did not join the Tupamaros right away. He still had many scruples against violence, and he had to consider all the risks of joining a terrorist group. Two years of travel in Latin American countries, talking to students and revolutionaries, dispelled his doubts.

"When I came back, I showed openly that I was in full sympathy with the movement. I supported every one of its aims — to free the workers and the country from tyranny and corrupt rule. I think there were some 70,000 like me at the time, all sympathetic, all wanting to do something about it. The leaders could pick whomever they wanted."

One day Romeo found a letter under his door. It was from the Tupamaros. It designated three meeting places, and the hours he was to be at each one. It also gave him a password. Twice Romeo was not approached by anyone. He surmised that the Tupamaros were being careful, checking to see whether anyone had followed him. The third time, he was approached by a group of young men. "They came up and spoke to me, and I gave them the password. Then we went off together."

Romeo was assigned to a group of six or seven revolutionaries and given his first duties. He was simply to keep his eyes and ears open and to pass along any information that might be useful.

"My work was strictly intelligence," Romeo said. "I think I was very good, very objective. But as to the actions — the raids on banks, the kidnappings, and bombings — I knew nothing about them until after they had happened."

When the group was sure that Romeo could be trusted, it told him to begin planning his own terrorist operations. Before he could carry any of them out, however, he was arrested.

"One of the top men who had been held by the police for days gave my name, or else it was found in his pocket. Anyway, he was later proved to be a traitor."

At first the police questioned Romeo without any roughness. But after three days, they demanded a full confession.

"Admit you are a Tupamaro," they said, "and it will all be over." They put a piece of paper on the desk in front of me and handed me a pen. "Sign it," they said. "Sign it and get it over with. You'll do it in the end anyway."

Fearing for his family's safety, Romeo denied that he was a Tupamaro and refused to sign the confession. It was then that the torture started.

"First they used the picana — an electric prod they press into your naked body wherever it hurts the most. It feels as if your whole inside is being torn out by red-hot irons. I've never known such agony. Somehow, I stood it. I didn't talk. I didn't sign anything. And still I insisted that I was not a Tupamaro."

Romeo was subjected to many other tortures. On one occasion, he was taken to the roof of the prison and held over the ledge.

"At that moment I was sure I was going to die. But the one consolation I had was that I had not talked."

After a year in jail, Romeo was released "for lack of evidence." He fled to Buenos Aires, where he still lives. Does he feel as strongly now about the need for terrorism?

"My outlook has changed," he said. "I no longer believe in the guerrilla movement. There is too much violence. I don't believe any more that it gets results."

⌁ Which of the social characteristics of a modern terrorist does Romeo appear to have? Explain your answers.

What Can Be Done?

"Get tough" measures. What can nations do to protect themselves against terrorists? Because effective international agreements to curb terrorism are lacking, nations have had to deal with the problem individually. In recent years, some countries have taken a hard-line approach and are fighting fire with fire. Israel led the way in July 1976 with a daring rescue of 104 hostages from a hijacked French jetliner at Entebbe, Uganda. The hijacking was carried out by the PFLP. In April 1986, President Reagan ordered American bombers to attack military and intelligence targets in Libya. The raid was designed to punish Colonel Muammar Khadaffi for his support of terrorist groups around the world. An overwhelming majority of the American public supported the President's decision.

Some experts advocate other "get tough" measures to combat terrorism. They are in favor of:

• more certain punishment and stiffer penalties for terrorists;

• greater security precautions to protect vital power, transportation, and communications facilities;

• the increased use of intelligence operations to warn of approaching attacks.

Robert S. Strother and Eugene H. Methvin, editors of *Reader's Digest,* favor increased intelligence by means of "spies, networks of paid informers, wiretaps, bugs, computerized dossier systems — the whole spectrum of clandestine warfare. . . ."

Other people warn of the dangers of

Italian political leader Aldo Moro while a prisoner of the Red Brigades.

overreacting to terrorism. They fear that an emphasis on security and intelligence-gathering may, in the end, turn out to be as bad as terrorism itself. Once a democratic nation sanctions such measures as wiretapping and paid informers, they say, it is well on the way to losing the very freedoms it wishes to protect. As an example, they point to Uruguay, a democratic nation that, as we have seen, suspended many guarantees of freedom when it began to wage "internal war" on the Tupamaros. Eventually its government became a military dictatorship. This problem troubles conservatives as well as liberals. James Burnham, an editor of the conservative *National Review,* wrote in 1974:

"Effective antiterror action requires methods normally considered incompatible with democratic principles and civil

rights, and — if the terrorism is both serious and long-continued — apparently also
requires a certain amount of counterter-
ror. . . . Sensible people understand that
a constitutional republic must occasionally
resort to undemocratic and normally illegal means to meet an emergency. . . .
But sensible people also realize that the
use of normally illegal undercover and terrorist methods is always a danger to the integrity of the republic and a fatal danger
when the methods become routine and
pervasive."

Democracies, of course, are especially
vulnerable to terrorism. Terrorists take
advantage of all the freedoms and legal
protections they enjoy in these societies to
carry out their activities. The dilemma
faced by democratic nations is this:

• If they react too strongly against
terrorism, they violate their most basic
principles and may open the door to a
military dictatorship.

• If they tolerate terrorism, or do not
deal with it effectively, they are in danger
of increasingly severe disruptions and loss
of life.

≈§ What precautions do you think the
United States should take against the possibility that terrorists from other nations
are operating within its borders? Against
the possibility that terrorists will use nuclear, biological, or chemical weapons?
Would any of these precautions endanger
constitutional freedom of the press, free
speech, the right of assembly, or the pro-
vision against unwarranted searches?
Explain your answers.

Negotiations.

In the past, most nations
yielded to some or all of the demands of terrorists rather than let innocent hostages
be killed. In recent years, however, an increasing number of nations have adopted
a tough policy of "no negotiations, no
concessions." Essentially these nations
believe that making concessions to terrorists encourages further blackmail. This
attitude was expressed by former President
Richard M. Nixon in March 1973, after
two U.S. diplomats, George Curtis Moore
and Cleo A. Noel, Jr., were killed by
Palestinian terrorists in Sudan. The ransom demanded by the terrorists — the
release of a number of Arab and West
German assassins — had been refused by
the United States and other governments.
President Nixon said:

"All of us would have liked to have
saved the lives of these two brave men.
But they and we knew that in the event
we paid international blackmail, it would
have saved their lives, but it would have
endangered the lives of hundreds of others
all over the world. Because once the terrorist has a demand . . . that is satisfied,
he is then encouraged to try it again."

Whether or not a policy of toughness
deters terrorism, there is no doubt that it
often has tragic consequences. Israel's
refusal to negotiate with the Palestinian
terrorists who captured a number of its
athletes at the 1972 Olympic games ultimately led to their deaths. Similarly, the
refusal of the Italian government to
negotiate with the Red Brigade terrorists
who, in March 1978, kidnapped Aldo
Moro, the country's leading statesman,
eventually led to his death.

Some experts on terrorism, such as Brian Jenkins of the Rand Corporation, doubt that a "no negotiations" posture deters terrorists. Jenkins maintains that the primary objective of terrorists is not to wring concessions, but to gain publicity for their cause. Jenkins believes that the best way to combat terrorism is not a hard-line attitude during a crisis, but determined action afterward to capture and convict the terrorists.

Because of the terrible risks involved when hostages are taken, Walter Laqueur, for example, says that under certain circumstances, concessions may be advisable:

For example, President Reagan and his closest advisors believed they could make concessions to Iran in exchange for Iranian help in gaining the release of Americans held hostage in Beirut, Lebanon. The deal called for the sale of United States arms to Iran. However, the secret deal backfired when it became exposed. Many Americans believed that the government had no business making concessions with terrorists or to those who support terrorists.

In the aftermath of the scandal, the United States government reaffirmed its policy of not negotiating with international terrorists, no matter what the cause.

However, in the United States, law enforcement agencies have chosen to negotiate with domestic terrorists in hostage situations and to avoid the use of force whenever possible.

Their views were expressed in a special report submitted to the federal government, which said: "Society should aim to outwit the terrorist rather than to outfight him."

U.S. lawmen have developed a set of rules for dealing with terrorists. Among these rules are the following:

1. *Know the enemy.* This means learning everything possible about the terrorists, including the nature of their grievances and how desperate they are.

2. *Play for time.* This means talking to the terrorists for hours or days, if necessary, yet never saying anything that may sound threatening. Time is the law officers' ally. After a while, the terrorists have a chance to think about the possible consequences of their actions, and the will to slaughter hostages may fade.

3. *Negotiate — but not too much.* Make minor concessions, encouraging the terrorists to believe that their grievances may be satisfied without anyone having to die. Even when a demand cannot be met, keep talking. Talk costs nothing and may save lives.

4. *Keep cool.* One shot fired by a law officer could end in a disaster. Patience pays off. Sooner or later the terrorists may become exhausted and wish to surrender.

What do you think is the best way for a democratic nation to combat terrorism? Do you think a "no negotiations" position is ever justified? If so, under what circumstances?

Do you think law enforcement officials should negotiate with terrorists? If so, how? Do you think they should make false promises to induce terrorists to surrender? Explain your answers.

15:A

A World of Terror

Japanese Red Army:
Western Europe, Lebanon

Aryan Nations:
United States

IRA:
Ireland

Basque Separatists:
France and Spain

Red Brigades:
Italy

Abu Nidal Group:
Syria

Palestine Liberation Organization:
Lebanon and Iraq (includes PFLP)

Tuparamos:
Uruguay

application

How do the concepts of internal and external social control as discussed in Chapter 1 contribute to our understanding of terrorists? Can you think of positive and negative sanctions that would curb terrorism? Name some of both.

summary

Since the late 1960's many nations throughout the world have been plagued by an alarming increase of terrorist activities. **Terrorism** is the systematic use of violence, or the threat of violence, by a group to achieve its aims. Basically it is intended to intimidate all those who are not in sympathy with the group's goals. From 1968 to 1986, there were 8,000 separate incidents of terrorism. In 1985 alone, there were 3,010 incidents. They included 1,527 bombings and 990 facility attacks. There were 374 assassinations, 109 kidnappings, and 10 hijackings. The great majority of them occurred outside the United States.

One authority on terrorism estimated in 1977 that there were then 140 terrorist organizations active throughout the world. Some, like Italy's Red Brigades, have only vague political ideologies; they simply believe that the societies they live in are evil and deserve to be destroyed. Others, like the Palestine Liberation Organization, have specific political objectives. The PLO, in 1987, was still dedicated to the destruction of Israel and the establishment of an independent Arab state of Palestine. Still other terrorists, like the Irish Republican Army, regard themselves primarily as regional independence movements. Sometimes right-wing governments have used terrorism to curb revolutionaries. Finally, some terrorist groups are composed of ordinary criminals who rationalize their activities in political slogans.

While the victims of political terrorism in the past were generally government leaders, today's victims are often men, women, and children who have no role in government at all. They may be tourists on an airliner, commuters on a train, people at work, or students in a school. They are often held as hostages and threatened with death unless the terrorists' demands are met by government authorities. In other cases, terrorists set off explosives in public places to pressure officials to meet their demands.

Terrorists who commit such acts usually think of themselves as idealists. Society is sick, they say, and cannot be cured by reforms or half measures. Oppression can only be removed by violence. Any action that benefits the terrorist cause is justified.

The growth of terrorism in recent years has been spurred by a number of factors, including modern technology. Advanced technology enables small terrorist groups to operate with greater facility and to wield greater powers of destruction than ever before. The ease with which jetliners could be seized and controlled led to a rash of hijackings in the early 1970's. The expansion of electronic communications throughout the world also assisted terrorists. Their threats could be swiftly delivered, and negotiations carried out from distant havens. Even more important to the terrorists is the fact that newspapers, radio, and television assure them of widespread publicity for their causes.

Terrorists come from a wide variety of social backgrounds. Those involved in regional independence movements, such as the IRA, tend to be from the working class. Terrorists who aim to destroy "the bourgeois Establishment" tend to come from the middle and upper classes. This is particularly true of urban guerrillas.

Efforts to curb terrorism through international agreements have been largely ineffective. Many nations are sympathetic to terrorist movements and help them, while others are afraid to offend them. As a result, terrorists frequently get away with the most heinous crimes. According to a recent study, a terrorist involved in a kidnapping has an 80 percent chance of escaping capture, and an almost even chance that all or some of her or his demands will be met. For the small proportion of terrorists who are caught and tried, the average sentence has been less than 18 months.

What can democratic societies do to protect themselves against terrorists? Some experts urge greater security precautions and the increased use of intelligence operations, including spies, networks of paid informers, and wiretapping. Other people warn that an emphasis on security and intelligence-gathering may turn out to be as bad as terrorism itself. They say that once a democratic nation sanctions such measures as wiretapping and illegal searches, it is well on the way to losing the very freedoms it wishes to protect. As an example, they point to Uruguay, a democratic country that suspended many guarantees of freedom when it began to wage war on internal terrorists. Eventually its democratic traditions eroded, and Uruguay became a military dictatorship.

more questions and activities

1. Define *terrorism* and describe its extent as a world problem today.

2. List examples of three possible dangers to world peace posed by terrorism.

3. What three social characteristics seemed to predominate in the 18 urban guerrilla groups studied by Air Force counterintelligence?

4. What measures of social control to prevent terrorism do you believe are acceptable in a democratic society?

5. How might sociologist Emile Durkheim analyze suicide missions by terrorist attackers?

6. Read the book *Carlos: Portrait of a Terrorist* listed in the bibliography, and report on leadership patterns among groups discussed in the book.

7. Reexamine the definition of collective behavior in Chapter 9. In what ways is terrorism similar to some forms of collective behavior? In what ways is it different?

8. Two terrorists have taken control of a Los Angeles to New York flight with 150 passengers aboard. They are now over Colorado and have three hours' fuel. They demand: nationwide coverage for their political goals, free passage to a nation sympathetic to their cause, one million dollars, the release of two of their group who were previously imprisoned for threatening the life of a U.S. Senator, and a promise that they will not be prosecuted.

You are on the ground in charge of negotiations. Which, if any, of these items would you negotiate? Which would you be willing to deliver if the terrorists released their hostages unharmed? Explain the reasons for your answers.

suggested readings

Laqueur, Walter. *Terrorism.* (Little, Brown, 1977.) Laqueur compares and contrasts the causes, methods, and goals of terrorism in the 19th and 20th centuries.

Lineberry, William P., ed. *The Struggle Against Terrorism.* (Wilson, 1977.) An excellent collection of readings which examine the extent of terrorism and various means to combat it.

Liston, Robert A. *Terrorism.* (Nelson, 1977.) An easy-to-read introduction to the problem of terrorism.

Melman, Yossi. *The Master Terrorist.* (Adama Books, 1986.) A disturbing account of the life and terrorist activities of Abu Nidal, one of the world's most wanted and dangerous terrorists.

Parry, Albert. *Terrorism: Past, Present, Future.* (Vanguard, 1976.) An authoritative history of terrorism.

Peck, Ira. *Raid at Entebbe.* (Scholastic, 1977.) A highly readable account of the hijacking of an Air France plane whose Israeli passengers were taken to Uganda and rescued by Israeli commandos.

Smith, Colin. *Carlos: Protrait of a Terrorist.* (Holt, Rinehart and Winston, 1976.) A revealing look into the recruitment, training, and activities of a terrorist leader.

U.S. News and World Report. "Hostage to Terror." (*U.S. News and World Report,* February 9, 1987.) A description and analysis of the terrorist groups operating in Beirut.

glossary

The numbers in parentheses indicate the chapter in which the term is defined.

achieved status. A social position that a person acquires primarily through his or her own efforts. (1)

acting crowds. Crowds in action—rioting or engaging in other extreme forms of behavior. (9)

acid rain. Type of pollution created when airborne chemicals mix with water vapor to form tiny acid droplets. (13)

acute illness. Short-term illness for which there may be a specific, short-term treatment. (12)

ageism. Stereotyping and discrimination against people because of their age. (12)

altruistic suicide. A pattern of suicide that occurs among people who see group norms and goals as all-important and their own lives as insignificant. (2)

amalgamation. The biological merging of ethnic and racial groups within a society. (8)

anomic suicide. A pattern of suicide that occurs during times of crisis or rapid change when traditional norms break down and people are left with a sense of aimlessness. (2)

apartheid. A system of racial segregation enforced in South Africa. (8)

aquifer. Underground layers of water-bearing rocks. (13)

argot. A vocabulary peculiar to members of a subculture. (3)

ascribed status. A social position that is assigned to people at birth or at later stages in their lives. (1)

assimilation. The process by which minority groups give up their own cultures and adopt the dominant culture of a society. (8) Also, changing details of a rumor to fit one's personal prejudices. (9)

authoritarian personality. A personality attributed to one who is intolerant, highly conformist, submissive to superiors, bullying to inferiors, and likely to be prejudiced toward other racial and ethnic groups. (8)

baby boom. Name given to the generation born during the high birthrate years between 1946 and 1964. (6)

behaviorist. A school of psychology based on the theory that all human behavior is learned and can be controlled through the presence or absence of rewards. (4)

birth dearth. Name given to the sharp drop in the birth rate since 1964. (6)

burnout. Loss of physical and mental energy that occurs when people lose their enthusiasm for work. (11)

caste system. A closed system of social stratification in which a person's status is inherited and permanent. (7)

casual crowd. A spontaneous gathering of people who have little involvement with what they are watching or each other. (9)

chronic illness. Long-term illness especially common among older people. (12)

city. A relatively large, densely populated, permanent settlement of a variety of kinds of people. (In the U.S., the Bureau of the Census defines a city as any settlement of more than 2,500 people. Many other countries define a city as 20,000 or more people.) (14)

collective behavior. Spontaneous, brief,

unstructured behavior on the part of large numbers of people. (9)

collectivism. A political theory emphasizing centrally controlled group activity rather than individual initiative. (4)

competition. A social process in which two or more individuals or groups seek to outdo each other to achieve a reward. (5)

conflict. A social process in which two or more individuals or groups seek to coerce, harm, or destroy each other. (5)

conjugal family. A family pattern where relatives establish separate households near each other in order to see each other regularly. (6)

control group. In an experiment, a group that is not exposed to the independent variables, giving the researcher a basis of comparison with a group that is. (2)

conventional crowd. People gathered for a specific purpose who behave according to established norms. (9)

cooperation. A social process in which two or more individuals or groups work together to achieve a common goal. (5)

craze. A fad or fashion that becomes an obsession. (9)

crime. A violation of a law. (11)

criminologist. A sociologist who studies the causes, extent, and treatment of crime. (11)

crowd. A temporary gathering of people who are aware of, and sometimes influenced by, each other's presence. (9)

cultural diffusion. The spreading of culture traits from one group or society to another. (10)

cultural integration. The extent to which the elements of culture mesh together harmoniously within a society. (3)

cultural lag. The time gap between the introduction of new technology and the cultural adjustments the technology requires. (10)

cultural pluralism. The existence within a society of ethnic groups that retain their cultural identities without suffering discrimination. (8)

cultural relativity. The practice of looking at another culture's customs within the context of the entire culture and evaluating them on the basis of the functions they perform. (3)

culture. The way of life of a group including its knowledge, customs, values, beliefs, and material creations. (3)

culture shock. The emotional stress that frequently occurs when people of one culture encounter another culture whose values and customs are markedly different from their own. (3)

demography. The scientific study of the size, composition, distribution, and changes in human population. (10)

dependent variable. The subject of a scientific investigation that is affected by the independent variables. (2)

discrimination. The unequal or unfair treatment of members of minority groups. (8)

divorce. A legally sanctioned end to a marriage. (6)

dominant group. The group within a society that has more power, privilege, and status than any other group. (8)

ego. According to Sigmund Freud, the part of the self that acts as a mediator between the drives of the id and the demands of the superego. (4)

egoistic suicide. A pattern of suicide that occurs among people who lack the support of strong group ties. (2)

endogamy. The practice of marrying a member of one's own social group. (6)

ethnic group. A group of people who are linked by cultural ties such as language, national origin, or religion, and who share a sense of common identity. (8)

ethnocentrism. The tendency to consider other cultures, customs, and values inferior to one's own. (3)

ethnomethodology. A method for studying society's unwritten rules of social behavior. (1)

experiment. A study of groups carried out in an environment controlled by the researcher. (2)

expressive crowd. A gathering of people who express feelings and behave in ways they would not consider doing elsewhere. (9)

expressive movement. A social movement that seeks to change the inner spiritual lives of its members and provides them with ways of expressing their emotions. (10)

expulsion. The forcible removal of a minority group from a society. (8)

extended family. A family unit consisting of a nuclear family plus one or more relatives all living together. (6)

fad. A trivial variation in behavior that lasts a short time. (9)

family. Usually two or more adults living together and cooperating in the care and rearing of their children. (6)

fashions. Currently accepted styles of dress and appearance. (9)

folkways. Norms that are a matter of custom or tradition. Their violation causes expressions of disapproval but no legal punishment. (1)

gender. The learned characteristics associated with masculinity or femininity. (4)

genocide. The deliberate extermination of an entire ethnic or racial group. (8)

ghetto. During the Middle Ages, a section of the city surrounded by a wall behind which Jews were forced to live. In modern times it has come to mean any section of a city to which members of an ethnic or racial minority are confined, and which is characterized by deteriorating living conditions. (8)

greenhouse effect. Rise in the average temperature caused by the release of carbon dioxide into the atmosphere. (13)

group. Two or more people who interact with each other and engage in a common activity. (1)

Hawthorne effect. In an experiment, behavior that is influenced by the conduct of the experimenter rather than by the independent variables. (2)

high technology. The application of electronics to industry, communication, medicine, and other aspects of life. (10)

horizontal mobility. A move from one occupation to another within the same social class. (7)

hypothesis. A tentative relation between two variables which a researcher seeks to prove or disprove in his or her study. (2)

id. Freud's term for the inborn collection of sexual and aggressive urges as well as all bodily pleasure. (4)

ideology. A set of beliefs that justifies the interests and goals of those who hold it. (10)

incest. Sexual relations with one's immediate family. (6)

independent variable. Factors which explain changes in the dependent variable. (2)

in-group. A group with which a person identifies and feels that he or she belongs. (5)

instinct. A behavior pattern that is biologically inherited and common to all members of a given species. (4)

institution. A distinctive and stable pattern of norms, values, statuses, and roles that develop around a basic need of a society. (1)

institutional discrimination. Unequal treatment that is built into the entire structure of a society. (8)

intergenerational mobility. A change of social status of family members from one generation to the next. (7)

juvenile delinquency. Crime committed by persons usually less than 18 years of age. (11)

language. A system of verbal and, in many cases, written symbols that enables people to preserve and communicate meanings and experiences. (3)

laws. Formally written rules of conduct that are enforced by governments. (1)

leveling. Shortening a rumor to easily remembered details. (9)

looking-glass self. According to Charles Cooley, the image of the self that is provided by the reaction of others to one's behavior. (4)

maintenance leader. A leader whose chief function is to maintain the harmony and morale of a group. (5)

marriage. A formal and socially approved union between members of opposite sexes. (6)

marriage gradient. The tendency of men to marry women who are slightly below them in social status. (6)

mass hysteria. Irrational behavior on the

part of large numbers of people, usually caused by an unfounded belief. (9)

metropolitan area. (Also called a Standard Metropolitan Statistical Area by the Bureau of the Census.) A county or group of counties which contains at least one city of 50,000 inhabitants or more or "twin cities" with a combined population of at least 50,000. (14)

minority group. A group of people who are singled out for unequal treatment within a society and who consider themselves victims of discrimination. (8)

monogamy. The marriage of one man with one woman. (6)

mores. Norms which are usually considered morally significant and whose violation is considered a serious matter. (1)

negative sanction. A punishment that is imposed by a group or a society for behavior that violates its norms. (1)

norms. Rules or standards of behavior that have been developed by a group and which its members are expected to follow. (1)

nuclear autumn. A global hothouse created by high temperatures and ultraviolet radiation. (13)

nuclear family. A family unit consisting of a married couple and their dependent children. (6)

open-class system. A social class structure that permits and encourages people to move upward or downward. (7)

organized crime. A network of criminals, dominated by 24 Mafia families, that provides a wide range of legal and illegal goods and services. (11)

out-group. A group with which a person does not identify and does not feel that he or she belongs. (5)

ozone layer. A thin blanket of gas that shields the earth from the sun's ultraviolet rays. (13)

panic. The frightened, disordered behavior of a crowd whose members feel threatened and entrapped. (9)

participant observation. A research

method in which the investigator takes part in the daily activities of the group that he or she is studying. (2)

peer group. A group of friends or associates of about the same age and social position. (4)

personality. The patterns of behavior, values, and attitudes that are characteristic of an individual. (4)

polyandry. A form of polygamy in which a woman is married to more than one man at the same time. (6)

polygamy. Marriage to more than one mate at the same time. (6)

polygyny. A form of marriage in which a man is married to more than one woman at the same time. (6)

population. In a survey, the entire group that a researcher wants to learn about. (2)

positive sanction. A reward that is given by a group or a society for behavior that conforms to its norms. (1)

power. The ability to control or influence the actions of others. (7)

prejudice. A strong and irrational like or dislike for members of another racial or ethnic group. (8)

prestige. The degree of respect accorded to a person because of his or her social status. (7)

primary group. A group characterized by close, personal, and informal relationships. (5)

primary plants. Facilities which screen sewage to remove large solid wastes. (13)

propaganda. Ideas or information designed to influence public opinion by appealing primarily to emotions and prejudices. (9)

psychoanalysis. The process, pioneered by Freud in which patients try to gain insight into their present emotional state by relaxing and attempting to recall events from earlier in their lives. (4)

public opinion. What a large group of people who share a common interest think about a particular issue. (90)

racial group. A group of people who share inherited physical characteristics such as skin color, facial features, or hair texture. (8)

random sampling. In a survey, a method of

choosing a sample of the population being studied that gives every member an equal chance of being selected. (2)

reference group. A group that serves as a standard for evaluating one's own achievement, behavior, and values. (5)

reform movement. A social movement that seeks to change some parts of the social order but does not wish to uproot it entirely. (10)

resistance movement. A social movement that seeks to prevent change, or to abolish change that has already taken place. (5)

resocialization. A process that involves a radical change in role behavior and values that is inconsistent with one's previous upbringing or experience. In its most intense and extreme form, resocialization aimed at revising a person's political attitudes is popularly called brainwashing. (4)

revolutionary movement. A social movement that seeks to overthrow the existing social order and replace it with an entirely new one. (10)

ritual. An established form of procedure, particularly in religious ceremonies. (3)

role. The pattern of behavior expected of a person in a given social status. (1)

role conflict. A dilemma that arises when there are opposing demands with a role or between two roles played by the same person. (1)

role confusion. The inability to attain a clear sense of personal identity because of feelings of mistrust, doubt, guilt, and inferiority. (4)

role relationship. A stable pattern of interaction between two or more people in the roles they play. (1)

rumor. An unverified story that circulates from one person to another and is accepted as true. (9)

sample. A representative number of people selected from the population being studied. (2)

Sapir-Whorf hypothesis. The theory that language does not simply reflect culture, it also shapes one's thoughts and directs one's interpretation of the world. (3)

scapegoating. Blaming members of a minority group for one's troubles. (8)

science. The logical systematic methods by which reliable knowledge is obtained. (10)

scientific method. A set of procedures designed to increase the probability that research will lead to valid and accurate conclusions. (2)

secondary group. A group characterized by impersonal, relatively formal relationships. (5)

secondary plants. Facilities which disinfect sewage. (13)

secondary research. Research which uses previously collected data. (2)

segregation. The physical and social separation of a minority group from the dominant group within a society. (8)

self. An individual's awareness of a distinct personal identity: self-concept. (4)

sex role. The learned patterns of behavior expected of each sex in a society. (4)

single-parent family. A family headed by one adult and containing one or more dependent children. (6)

social change. Alterations in patterns of social behavior and institutions. (10)

social characteristics. Aspects of a person or group's social background that influence the way they act. (1)

social class. A group of people within a society who have similar amounts of property, power, and prestige. (7)

social control. The processes by which a group maintains conformity to its rules. (1)

social interaction. A form of human behavior that occurs whenever two or more people act toward or respond to one another. (1)

social mobility. The movement of people up and down the stratification system. (7)

social movement. A large number of people who have joined together to bring about, or resist, social change. (10)

social pattern. A recurring form of human behavior that can be described and predicted. (1)

social processes. The regularly recurring patterns of interaction that occur in human groups. (5)

social ranking. The evaluation—high or low—of a status according to criteria that a group's members consider important. (1)

social stratification. The pattern of social classes that results from the unequal distribution of power, property, and prestige in a society. (7)

socialization. The process by which human beings learn the physical, mental, and social skills they need to become individuals and to function in society. (4)

society. All of the people who live within a certain geographic area, share a common way of life, and have a feeling of solidarity that binds them together as a social unit. (1)

sociological imagination. The ability to see the link between our personal experiences and the wider society. (10)

sociology. The scientific study of the patterns of human group life. (1)

status. The position that a person occupies within a group. (1)

status symbol. A material object or a privilege associated with a social position that indicates its rank. (1)

stereotype. A mental image of members of a group that exaggerates or oversimplifies their characteristics. (8)

stratified random sampling. In a survey, a method of choosing a sample that reflects the proportions of different groups in the population being studied. (2)

subculture. A group whose life-style and values differ somewhat from those of the dominant culture within a society. (3)

superego. According to Sigmund Freud, the part of the self that internalizes society's view of right and wrong and acts as one's conscience. (4)

superordinate goal. A goal that is attractive to two or more groups but cannot be achieved without a joint effort. (5)

survey. A method of obtaining information about a large population usually through interviews and questionnaires. (2)

symbol. Anything that represents something other than itself. Symbols include words, objects, gestures, colors, and designs. (3)

taboos. Powerful social beliefs that certain norms are unthinkable to violate. (1)

task leader. A leader whose chief function is to organize and direct the activities of a group. (5)

technology. The practical application of scientific knowledge. (10)

telecommunicating. Working at home using a computer terminal linked to an office. (10)

terrorism. Systematic use of violence, or threat of violence, by a group to achieve its aims. (15)

test group. In an experiment, a group of subjects who are exposed to the independent variable under conditions controlled by the researcher. (2)

theory. A logical explanation of how some facts are apparently related to other facts. (2)

urban. Localities in which economic activities are predominantly nonagricultural. See also *city*. (14)

value. A conception of desirable behavior that influences the behavior of group members. (1)

vertical mobility. The upward or downward movement of people within the stratification system. (7)

victimless crime. Activities which the dominant groups in our society regard as immoral and which are against the law, although there may be no victims. (11)

wedding. The public announcement that a man and woman intend to live together and raise any children they may have in a socially approved manner. The announcement is usually accompanied by a ceremony and an exchange of gifts. (6)

white-collar crime. Dishonesty by people in business, government, and the professions. These people are usually protected by their "respectability." (11)

zoning. Laws by which cities regulate the kinds of construction and activities that will be allowed in a geographical area. (14)

index

Scholastic Sociology Photo and Illustration Credits